Hani A. Faris is Adjunct Professor in the Department of Political Science at the University of British Columbia. He has written extensively on Arab nationalism, the Middle East in world politics, Zionism, Lebanese politics, the history of the Palestinian issue and Third World development.

The Failure of the Two-State Solution

The Prospects of One State in the Israel-Palestine Conflict

EDITED BY

HANI A. FARIS

This study is published in collaboration with Trans Arab Research Institute (TARI), an independent American think tank registered in the State of Massachusetts, USA, and the Center for Arab Unity Studies (CAUS) headquartered in Beirut, Lebanon, which is involved in research and publishing on the subject of Arab unity and related issues.

Published in 2013 by I.B.Tauris & Co. Ltd
6 Salem Road, London W2 4BU
175 Fifth Avenue, New York NY 10010
www.ibtauris.com

Distributed in the United States and Canada
Exclusively by Palgrave Macmillan
175 Fifth Avenue, New York NY 10010

ISBN: 978 1 78076 094 0

A full CIP record for this book is available from the British Library
A full CIP record for this book is available from the Library of Congress

Library of Congress catalog card: available

Designed and typeset by 4word Ltd, Bristol
Printed and bound by CPI Group (UK) Ltd, Croydon, CR0 4YY

Contents

Contributors

Hani A. Faris is Adjunct Professor in the Department of Political Science at the University of British Columbia in Vancouver, Canada. He has served on the faculty of Kuwait University, the American University (Washington, DC), Harvard University, McGill University and Simon Fraser University. Dr Faris has authored *Sectarian Conflict in the Modern History of Lebanon* (1980), *Beyond the Lebanese Civil War* (1982) and *US Policy in the Middle East* (1984), co-authored *The Arab Position on the Israeli Invasion of Lebanon* (1983) and edited *Arab Nationalism and the Future of the Arab World* (1987). He has written on such topics as Arab nationalism, the Middle East in world politics, Zionism, Lebanese politics, the history of the Palestinian issue and Third World development. Dr Faris has served as Assistant Director General of the Palestine Research Center (1967–8), Academic Vice Dean for Graduate Studies at Kuwait University (1978–81), President of the Association of Arab-American University Graduates (1984–5), advisor to the Canadian Institute for International Peace and Security (1989–91), member of the Board of Editors of Arab Studies Quarterly (1987–90), member of the Board of Editors of Contemporary Arab Affairs (2008–present) and President of the Board of Directors of Trans Arab Research Institute (2007–present).

Salman H. Abu Sitta is a researcher on Palestine, founder and President of Palestine Land Society (London), and author of *From Refugees to Citizens at Home* (2001), *The Atlas of Palestine 1948* (2005) and *The Return Journey* (2007). He is also a member of the Palestine National Council and general coordinator of the Right of Return Congress.

Ali Abunimah is a Palestinian political activist and co-founder of the leading on-line analytical forum on Israel–Palestine, *Electronic Intifada*. He is the author of many related studies and essays, and the book *One Country: A Bold*

Proposal to End the Israeli–Palestinian Impasse (2006); he co-authored *The Palestinian Right of Return* (2001).

Susan M. Akram is Clinical Professor of Law, Boston University. She specialises in immigration law, refugee law, and domestic and international refugee advocacy. She is the author of numerous articles on the Palestinian right of return.

Naseer H. Aruri is Chancellor Professor (Emeritus) of Political Science, University of Massachusetts-Dartmouth. He has published nine books, including *Jordan: A Study in Political Development* (1972), *The Obstruction of Peace: The US, Israel and the Palestinians* (1995) and *The Dishonest Broker* (2003), and co-authored with Samih Farsoun, *Palestine and the Palestinians: A Social and Political History* (2006). He co-edited (with Muhammad Shuraydi) *Revising Culture, Reinventing Peace: The Influence of Edward W. Said* (2001). He edited *Occupation: Israel Over Palestine* (1983). He is a founding member of the Arab Organisation for Human Rights (Cairo and Geneva) and former member of the boards of Amnesty International USA and Human Rights Watch/Middle East. He is a former President of the Arab American University Graduates and Trans Arab Research Institute (TARI).

George E. Bisharat is Professor of Law at Hastings College of the Law in San Francisco. He teaches in the areas of criminal procedure and practice, law and anthropology, Islamic law and law in the Middle East. He is the author of *Palestinian Lawyers and Israeli Rule: Law and Disorder in the West Bank* (1989) and many journal articles on law and politics in the Middle East, with particular focus on Palestine. His commentaries have appeared in the *New York Times*, *Wall Street Journal*, *USA Today*, the *Los Angeles Times* and many other newspapers in the USA and abroad.

Marc H. Ellis is retired University Professor and Director of the Center for Jewish Studies at Baylor University. Currently he is Senior Visiting Lecturer in Peace and Conflict Studies at the University for Peace in San Jose, Costa Rica. He is the author and editor of more than 20 books including *Toward a Jewish Theology of Liberation* (1987), now in its third edition, and most recently *Encountering the Jewish Future* (2011).

Leila Farsakh is Professor of Political Science at the University of Massachusetts-Boston. She is author of *Palestinian Labor Migration to Israel: Labor, Land and Occupation* (2005) and of *Commemorating the Naksa, Evoking the Nakba* (2008, EJMES special edited volume). She has written numerous articles on the political economy of the Arab–Israeli conflict and is a Senior Fellow at the Center for Development Studies at Birzeit University.

As'ad Ghanem is a lecturer at the School of Political Science, University of Haifa. He has been the initiator and designer of several policy schemes and empowerment programmes for Palestinians in Israel. He has authored *Palestinians in Israel – Indigenous group politics in the Jewish state* (2008, in Arabic), *Palestinian Politics after Arafat: a Failed National Movement* (2009), *Ethnic Politics in Israel – The Margins and the Ashkinasi Centre* (2010), and with Dan Bavely, *Bi-Nationalism – Towards a Lasting Peace between Palestinians and Israelis* (forthcoming, 2013).

Nadia Hijab is Director of Al-Shabaka, The Palestinian Policy Network, and Senior Fellow at the Institute for Palestine Studies. She is a consultant on human rights, gender and development to the UN and other international organisations. She is also author of *Womanpower* (1989) and *Citizens Apart* (1990).

Ghada Karmi is Honorary Research Fellow, Institute of Arab and Islamic Studies, Exeter University, Visiting Professor at London Metropolitan University, and author of *Jerusalem Today* (1996), *The Palestinian Exodus* (1999), *In Search of Fatima* (2002) and *Married to Another Man* (2007).

Joel Kovel is Distinguished Professor of Social Studies at Bard College. He is the author of *Overcoming Zionism* (2007) and founded the Committee for Open Discussion of Zionism. His most recent work is *Overcoming Impunity* (2009).

Smadar Lavie is a scholar-in-residence at the Beatrice Bain Resesarch Center on gender at U. C. Berkeley. She is the author of *The Poetics of Military Occupation* (1990) on resistance theatre of the Mzeina Bedouin of the South Sinai, Egypt. The book won the 1990 Honorable Mention of the Victor Turner Award for ethnographic writing. She co-edited *Creativity/Anthropology* (1993) and *Displacement, Diaspora and Geographies of Identity* (1996). Lavie was awarded the 2009 Gloria Anzaldua Prize from the American Studies Association for her paper, 'Staying Put: Crossing the Palestine/Israel Border with Gloria Anzaldúa', published in *Anthropology and Humanism Quarterly*. Lavie specializes in the anthropology of Egypt, Israel, and Palestine, with emphasis on issues of race, gender, and religion, and has served in several feminist and anti-racist social movements and NGOs.

Saree Makdisi is Professor of English and Comparative Literature at UCLA. He has published extensively on the culture of modernity in Europe and its afterlife in the contemporary Arab world. He is the author of *Romantic Imperialism* (Cambridge University Press, 1998), *William Blake and the Impossible History of the 1790s* (University of Chicago Press, 2003) and *Palestine Inside Out: An Everyday Occupation* (WW Norton, 2008, revised and updated, 2010). He is also co-editor of *The Arabian Nights in Historical Context* (Oxford University Press, 2008). He has published extensively on the question of Palestine in leading journals as well as in major newspapers around the world.

Norton Mezvinsky is a Distinguished University Professor of History (emeritus) of Connecticut State University and the president of the International Council for Middle East Studies (ICMES), a Washington, D.C. think tank. He is the author of numerous books and articles, including J*ewish Fundamentalism in Israel* (1999 and 2003), which he co-authored with Israel Shahak, and is an editor of and contributor to *Anti-Zionism: Analytical Reflections* (1989).

Nancy Murray is founder and president of the Gaza Mental Health Foundation, Inc. She is on the advisory board of the US Campaign to End the Israeli Occupation, and a member of various activist groups, including the Boston Coalition for Palestinian Rights. She has campaigned and written on civil liberties, civil rights and human rights issues, and serves on the editorial committee of the journal *Race & Class*. Among her publications are *Palestinians: Life under Occupation* (1991) and numerous articles on the Israeli–Palestinian conflict, most recently 'Dynamics of resistance: the apartheid analogy' (2008).

Ilan Pappé is Professor of History at the University of Exeter, Director of the university's European Centre for Palestine Studies and Co-director of the Exeter Centre for Ethno-Political Studies. He is author of *Making of The Arab-Israeli Conflict 1947–51* (1994), *The Israel/Palestine Question* (1999), *The History of Modern Palestine* (2003), *The Ethnic Cleansing of Palestine* (2006) and many other titles on Israeli/Palestinian history and politics.

Gabriel Piterberg is Professor of History at the University of California, Los Angeles (UCLA). He teaches and writes on the history of the Ottoman Empire, and on settler colonialism, Zionism and Israel/Palestine. He is the author of *An Ottoman Tragedy* (2003) and *The Returns of Zionism* (2008). His article 'The literature of settler societies: Albert Camus, S. Yizhar and Amos Oz' has appeared in *Settler Colonial Studies* (September 2011). He writes for *New Left Review* and *London Review of Books*.

Virginia Tilley is Professor of Political Science and Director of graduate studies in Governance at the University of the South Pacific. She is author of *The One-State Solution: A Breakthrough for Peace in the Israeli–Palestinian Deadlock* (2005), editor of *Beyond Occupation: Apartheid, Colonialism, and International Law in the Occupied Palestinian Territories* (2012), and numerous chapters and articles on the Israeli–Palestinian conflict. Her areas of research interest include the politics of ethnic, racial and national identity, with a special emphasis on the Israeli–Palestinian conflict; the politics of indigenous and tribal peoples, especially in Latin America; and the impact of state-led economic development strategies on ethnic and racial relations and conflict.

Husam Said Zomlot is Visiting Fellow at Harvard's Center for Middle Eastern Studies. He served as a PLO representative to the UK (2003–8). His previous experience includes the United Nations, the London School of Economics, the Oxford Research Group and the Palestine Economic Policy Research Institute. His most recent work appeared in the volume *State Formation in Palestine: Viability and Governance During a Social Transformation* (2005). In January 2007, he helped establish the Palestine Strategy Study Group. A document by the group entitled 'Regaining the initiative: Palestinian strategic options to end Israeli occupation' was launched in Ramallah on 27 August 2008, generating an ongoing national and international debate.

Abbreviations and Acronyms

AAM	anti-apartheid movement
AIPAC	American Israel Public Affairs Committee
ANC	African National Congress
BDS	Boycott, Divestment and Sanctions
CAIR	Council on American Islamic Relations
CAT Eyes	Community Anti-Terrorism Training Initiative
CBS	Central Bureau of Statistics
CJP	Combined Jewish Philanthropies
DFLP	Democratic Front for the Liberation of Palestine
DIME	Dense Inert Metal Explosives
DoP	Declaration of Principles
HILA	Hebrew acronym for 'Parents for the 'Hood'
ICJ	International Court of Justice
IDF	Israeli Defense Forces
ILA	Israel Land Administration
JNF	Jewish National Fund
MOPIC	Ministry of Planning and International Cooperation
NIF	New Israel Fund
NGO	non-governmental organisation
NPT	Non-Proliferation Treaty
OIP	Oslo Interim Period
OPT	Occupied Palestinian Territory
OSM	One State Movement
OSS	one-state solution
OT	occupied territories
PA	Palestinian Authority
PCIJ	Permanent Court of International Justice
PFLP	Popular Front for the Liberation of Palestine

PLO	Palestine Liberation Organisation
PNC	Palestinian National Council
SHATIL	Sherutei Tmikha v'Ye'utz l'Irgunim (Support and Consulting Services for NGOs)
SOAS	School of Oriental and African Studies
SSI	Security Solutions International
TARI	Trans Arab Research Institute
UNCCP	United Nations Conciliation Commission for Palestine
UNGA	UN General Assembly
UNHCR	United Nations High Commissioner for Refugees
UN OCHA	United Nations Office for the Coordination of Humanitarian Affairs
UNRWA	United Nations Relief and Works Agency
UNSC	United Nations Security Council
UNSCO	United Nations Special Coordinator's Office
UNSCOP	United Nations Special Committee on Palestine
WBGS	West Bank and Gaza Strip
WZO	World Zionist Organization

Acknowledgements

This volume took about two years to plan and develop. It was inspired by the workings of a conference on the one-state idea held in Boston, Massachusetts, in November 2009. Following the event, a scheme for the book was drawn in consultation with colleagues who specialised in the Israeli/Palestinian conflict, and a number of the programme participants were invited to write on specific topics. Virginia Tilley, who had not been at the conference, was asked to write a chapter on the logics and strategy or 'deeper politics' of Jewish settlements in the Israeli-occupied West Bank in recognition of her expertise in this field.

The idea of the conference surfaced in the winter of 2008 when the Board of Trans Arab Research Institute (TARI), an independent American think-tank, at the suggestion of Professor Naseer Aruri, decided to organise a conference to deal with the concept of the one-state for Israel/Palestine. The Board entrusted me with the position of Conference Chairperson. The William Joiner Center for the Study of War and Social Consequences at the University of Massachusetts-Boston agreed to co-sponsor and host the conference. The Center's Director, Professor Kevin Bowen, ensured that his institution's and Center's facilities were made available to the organisers, and made valued contributions to the development of the Conference Statement. Dr Khair El-Din Haseeb, Director General of the Beirut-based Center for Arab Unity Studies, gave unwavering support and encouragement to the project in all of its phases, and precious advice.

From the outset, the plans for this activity were highly ambitious in terms of the tasks set for the conferees and the logistics needed to shoulder a function of this type and calibre. These plans called for the participation of leading specialists on the subject who were called upon to address an international audience. Evidently, a large number of highly qualified and experienced people was needed to translate the vision for this event to reality. Of these, the contributions of Professor Elaine Hagopian, Nazik Kazimi, Professor Leila Farsakh and Erica Mena made a qualitative difference. A special word of appreciation is due to

Maher Abiad who truly is 'The Tech Guru' he says he is for his design of the conference website, and the conference information and registration systems.

To those in the media who reported on the workings of the conference, their efforts were indeed helpful in disseminating information to and educating the public on a subject of critical importance to world security and peace. Among these, I wish to mention Nabih Hakim, Louay Al-Jondi and Michael Haider of Arabic Hour; Wadah Khanfar, General Manager, and Mohammad Dalbah, News Producer, of Al-Jazeera; Warren David, General Manager of Arab Detroit; Mansoor Sabbagh of Global Voices for Justice; John Grebe of WABC Radio News, Greater Boston; Al-Quds Al-'Arabi (London); As-Safeer (Beirut); Al-Hayat (Beirut) and Hadeeth An-Nas (Nazareth). Among academic journals, *Contemporary Arab Affairs* (London) and *Al-Mustaqbal Al-'Arabi* (Beirut) were unreservedly supportive and played a major role by each dedicating an issue to the publication of selected papers from the conference.

Two other groups were critical to the success of this project. First, my colleagues in the Board of Trans Arab Research Institute (TARI) who assisted me in every way and gave of their time and thought. To Professor Naseer Aruri, Professor Seif Da'na, Professor Mujid Kazimi, Professor Munir Akash and Professor Saree Makdisi, I owe an immeasurable debt. Second, the authors of the 20 chapters in this volume, who determined its content, deserve any and all forthcoming praise for this volume's intellectual contributions.

To the publisher, I owe a great deal of gratitude. After taking the decision to publish this work, I.B.Tauris went all out in providing counsel and support. A great deal of time and effort was expended in reviewing and editing the manuscript. No fewer than three people read the text thoroughly and provided extensive comments and suggestions. I am impressed and appreciative of the time and effort the I.B.Tauris team, under the direction of Iradj Bagherzade, Chairman and Publisher of I.B.Tauris, invested in this work.

One final personal note: I would not have been able to dedicate almost two years to this project without the support and encouragement of my family. To my wife Jomana and my brothers Mohamad and Nabih, I am in your debt.

Preface

Israel and the Palestinians, supported by many international efforts, have been involved for a whole generation in a process whose stated aim is to resolve the conflict and achieve peace based on a two-state solution. Yet they are still far from achieving this end. The peace process and its conflict-resolution mechanisms have failed to achieve even minimum results. Their visions differ irreconcilably to date, and the obstacles to a peaceful and just resolution of the conflict that is workable for all parties have multiplied. The impact of the Gaza War (2007–8) has further complicated the pursuit of a solution. While realism demands the Israeli and Palestinian sides, and the international community, recognise their failure in effecting a settlement, it would be unwise to abandon the search for a solution. Such a course would have tragic consequences, both regionally and internationally.

Leading scholars from Palestine, Israel, the USA, Canada and Europe have here provided ideas, perspectives and insights examining paths to a workable and lasting resolution of the current conflict, which also addresses the aspiration for justice so central to the whole problem. This volume thus reflects a serious attempt to describe and set out a path which until recently represented thinking the unthinkable, but which has now entered the discourse on the Israel–Palestine issue. The book clearly comes with a viewpoint and its editor and contributors are, it would be fair to say, advocates of a very earnest consideration of the one-state solution – a one-state solution based on justice, fair play and pragmatic common sense, which recognises the national, cultural and religious aspirations of both Israelis and Palestinians as well as their concerns for security and peace, and the difficulties of reconciling their national narratives. Given the intractability of the problem and the desperate need on all sides to explore resolutions, the book intends to make a contribution to achieve this goal.

CHAPTER 1

Introduction: The Failure of the Two-State Solution and Delimiting the One-State Idea

Hani A. Faris

Situating a Problematic: The Two- and One-State Solutions

The Israeli–Palestinian conflict has been among the longest enduring conflicts in modern history. It has been also, and remains, among the most destructive and dangerous conflicts, threatening not only the stability of the Middle East, but also the peace and security of the world. To illustrate, nuclear alerts on a global scale were declared in the past by the super powers in response to developments in the 1973 October War.[1] Moreover, Israel is known to have a significant cache of nuclear armaments and is reported also to have declared a nuclear alert during the same war after Egyptian forces crossed the Suez Canal,[2] destroyed the Bar-Lev line[3] and moved east toward the Sinai passes. Also, some Middle Eastern countries are believed to have chemical and biological weapons in their arsenal – their use cannot be ruled out in future conflagrations. Much depends on how the conflict evolves and whether the international community succeeds in defusing or resolving the conflict issues. Given the prospects, the incessant search for solutions which has earmarked this conflict is understandable. Within this context, and given the abject failure of the existing conflict resolution, the peace-making process and the old-new idea of a solution based on the establishment of a one-state in Israel/Palestine is worthy of careful and detailed consideration.

Many Palestinians and others believe the international community should recognise that the conditions Israel has created in the occupied territories render the two-state solution impossible. For them there is an urgent need to start exploring in earnest the only option left for a final negotiated settlement offering peace with justice for all concerned: Israeli Jews and Palestinians. The latter consist of Palestinian citizens of Israel, Palestinians in the West Bank and Gaza, 1948 Palestinians and their descendants in the *shatat* (Diaspora). They envision the two communities becoming citizens of a single democratic, secular and multicultural state in all of historic Palestine.

A few words about the one-state are in order. The idea has been the subject of misguided ridicule by a number of Jews and Palestinians alike. It has been described as a 'total illusion' and its advocates as 'inveterate dreamers' and 'time wasters'. The attacks by both sides are principally due to a misunderstanding of what the one-state solution is in both the Israeli and the Palestinian spheres. The following three points illustrate and address some of the existing misconceptions.

First, there is a general tendency among people to think in either/or dualities or bi-polar relationships, rather than in a continuum or a dialectical interaction. The one-state idea is seen as the antithesis of the two-state idea. Since the latter represents today the international consensus on the solution to the Palestinian–Israeli conflict, and both sides to the conflict pay it lip service, many observers discuss the one-state idea as an attempt at undermining the international effort to resolve the conflict. But the one-state idea is not the inverse of the two-state solution. Were Israel to remove Jewish settlers, withdraw to 1967 borders, allow the establishment of a sovereign Palestinian state and address the Palestinian right of return, a predominant sector of the Palestinian population would support such a settlement. Those who would only support such a two-state outcome for the foreseeable future believe a future merger of the two states is feasible. However, facts on the ground tell a different story. For all practical purposes, a viable two-state solution is out of reach and for many a point of no return has been reached. To Palestinians the growth of Jewish settlements in the West Bank is so obvious and invasive, and the number of settlers so large, that many of them firmly believe that Israel intends to annex rather than withdraw from the territories. Alongside the growth of settlements, 'Israel checkmated itself'[4] and shattered the two-state solution by adopting policies such as the expropriation of vast expanses of West Bank territory under different guises, the construction of an elaborate network of Jewish-only bypass roads, modification of the demography and character of Arab East Jerusalem, and control of the water aquifers and other natural resources in the West Bank. Together, these policies have forced the issue of the one-state on to the table again.[5] To one-state advocates the rise of a meaningful two-state system (i.e. two sovereign states along the 1967 borders) is now impossible. They consider the long drawn-out peace process, ongoing for nearly 20 years, as simply furthering the Israeli settlement project, allowing it to continue to annex the land and effect a quiet population transfer. The most the Palestinians could hope for in such circumstances is what they see as a bogus Palestinian entity with a minuscule and truncated structure. If Palestinians view the 'peace process' as a total waste which is not addressing their human rights and national life of their kin under occupation, then they unsurprisingly ask who the dreamer is and who the realist is in assessing the prospect of a viable two-state settlement.[6]

The second point is that all sides – Palestinian, Israeli and international – ultimately invoke the same rationale to explain their opposition to the one-state idea. They all believe that the overwhelming power the Israelis enjoy will prevent the one-state idea from ever being realised. The Israelis are advantaged by the status quo and could, in time, force the Palestinians to yield to their demands on West Bank territory, resources and demography. Solutions are dictated by the powerful and the only one-state solution the Israeli political/military establishment favours is one that yields control to Israel over most of historic Palestine, if not all of it. However, this form of thinking reflects a static view of power relationships and assumes that political and military powers are permanent barriers to fundamental change. This ignores the experience of the late twentieth century in South Africa where a powerful player, always militarily strong, failed to impose its positions on its militarily weaker adversary. All its efforts and the much larger capabilities it marshalled over a relatively long period of time proved of no value. Rather, it was the African National Congress (ANC) that wrested major concessions and forced change on their opponent. Had the ANC tailored its national aspirations to reflect the realities of power relations, the South Africa apartheid system would still be in place and thriving.[7]

Finally, some of the public, politicians and intellectuals on each side to the conflict view the one-state in terms that are injurious to the other side. To those Israelis, it is a realisation of Greater Israel and securing Zionist hegemony. To their Palestinian counterparts, it is a chance to return Palestine to pre-Israeli days with Palestinian Arab dominance. Properly understood and applied, the one-state is the only scheme that presents the Jewish Israeli and Palestinian sides with a win-win situation, co-existence and the hope of lasting peace. A two-state solution, regardless of its terms, will not resolve the conflict on a permanent basis. At best, it is a solution that may address the needs of the residents of the West Bank and the Gaza Strip who represent only about one-third of Palestinian society. Israeli/Palestinian negotiations since Oslo (1993) indicate that Israel will not concede the Palestinian right of return and the Palestinian Authority (PA) may not insist on strict Israeli adherence to this popular Palestinian demand for the right of return if Israel meets its territorial demands in the West Bank and Arab East Jerusalem. The unsettled status of the Palestinians inside Israel and the *shatat* will forever raise questions about Israel's legitimacy and the acceptance it seeks from the region's populations. While Israeli Jews may be confident about their present power advantage, they are understandably concerned about what the future holds for them. Similarly, the Palestinians and Arabs in general deplore what they perceive to be their present weakness but have confidence in the long-term future of their aspirations. In other words, irrespective of what may happen with the two-state solution (i.e. whether it fails or succeeds and whatever its contours might be), the conflict will persist until there is a settlement that attends to all the people of both parties. Meanwhile, for those whose concern is the maintenance of an ethnic/religious entity, it would be wise to recall the words of Albert Einstein:

> I should much rather see reasonable agreement with the Arabs on the basis of living together in peace than the creation of a Jewish state. Apart from practical consideration, my awareness of the essential nature of Judaism resists the idea of a Jewish state with borders, an army, and a measure of temporal power no matter how modest. I am afraid of the inner damage Judaism will sustain – especially from the development of a narrow nationalism within our own ranks, against which we have already had to fight strongly, even without a Jewish state.[8]

Additional to the above misconceptions, the objections to the one-state solution of many Israelis are based on additional considerations that derive from Jewish historical experiences in Western societies and are rooted in Zionist doctrines. Foremost among them is the fear of demographic trends among the two communities. The number of Palestinians is expected to equal and start to exceed the number of Jews in historic Palestine by 2017.[9] Being in the minority is viewed as an existential threat and allows for their persecution or for their dominance over a Palestinian majority. The rise of a binational political entity is another cause of concern, since it spells the end of the Jewish character of the state and threatens to replace it with pluralist arrangements and possibly secular public institutions. Finally, a noticeable number of Israeli Jews would not consider living with Palestinians and often display attitudes of superiority towards them.

One-state advocates must attend to legitimate concerns of Israeli Jews about their future welfare within the framework of a single state if their plans are to have a chance of success. The majority of Israeli Jews will not shift positions unless they are certain their individual and communal security and prosperity would be secured and enhanced. Until then, although short-sighted, they will opt for the status quo and conflict management.

Rebirth of the One-State Idea

Both Arab Palestinians and Israeli Jews have shifted positions over time on keeping historic Palestine united and sharing the country under a single state. The Palestinians, from the start of the conflict that followed the founding of the World Zionist Organization (WZO) in 1897 and until the 1970s, were almost to a man advocates of the one-state. Other than members of the communist parties who heeded Moscow's directives after 1948, hardly any opted for the two-state solution. Meanwhile, the Zionists under the Mandate aspired and worked diligently for a predominantly, if not exclusively, Jewish state in all of historic Palestine.[10] The 1917 Balfour Declaration made such a vision seem feasible and the memorandum the WZO submitted on 3 February 1919, to the Paris Peace Conference, delineated their territorial demands which included part of present-day Lebanon, Syria and Jordan.[11] Later in the Mandate, the Zionist leadership made the tactical decision to publicly support a partition of the country to two states and bide their time for a more opportune moment to achieve a single Jewish state outcome. They basically had no other choice given their demographic minority status and their limited land ownership.[12] The war of 1948 provided them with the opportunity to establish their domain by force of arms in 78 per cent of the land.[13] The remaining 22 per cent were acquired in the June 1967 War. Since then, all of historic Palestine has been under Israeli dominion: directly in the West Bank and de facto in Gaza since 2005.

The Palestinian leadership began seriously to consider a two-state solution after the 1973 October War. It revealed its intention in a staged approach and over time. The process began with the Palestine Liberation Organisation (PLO) announcing its acceptance of the binational state, and floating the idea that Palestinians would set up a national Palestinian authority in any area evacuated by Israel, irrespective of the size of the area.[14] A sarcastic public referred to this scheme as the Jericho state. In time, the PLO officially announced its acceptance of the two-state solution to end the conflict.[15] Finally, it formally accepted, in 1993, UN Resolutions 242 and 338, recognised Israel and revoked its right to armed struggle.[16] Its stated aim was to establish a sovereign Palestinian state in the West Bank and Gaza, and secure the right of return for Palestinian refugees.[17] Meanwhile, the Israeli government position began to shift slowly towards the two-state solution after the 1993 Oslo Accords, except that its position on the issue of boundaries was intentionally left unclear. Finally, the international community, including the Arab countries, followed in the steps of Israeli and Palestinian officials and adopted the two-state solution as the only way to end the conflict and establish peace.[18] Nevertheless, almost two decades have passed since Oslo and all the subsequent negotiations have come to nothing despite all the fanfare and lip service paid to the two-state solution by Israel and the world powers. Palestinians remain stateless and under occupation, their situation desperate, and the likelihood of a total or even near-total withdrawal from the West Bank, including Arab East Jerusalem, is seen as next to impossible.[19]

It is this impasse which drove a range of figures – multi-religious, multi-ethnic and multinational – to revive and promote the one-state idea as the only rational alternative to the failed two-state solution. As early as 1999, the late Edward Said, after becoming totally disillusioned with Oslo and losing faith in the leadership of the PA, shifted course and openly called for a binational Israeli–Palestinian state. He made several constitutional, institutional and political proposals, but his main contribution was to promote 'the idea and practice of [equal] citizenship, not of ethnic or racial community, as the main vehicle for coexistence'.[20] A number of leading Jewish intellectuals also announced their support of the one-state. The case of Tony Judt stood out. In an outspoken statement, Judt asked his audience to think the unthinkable. Israel, he opined, had become an 'anachronism' and 'dysfunctional', it was time 'to convert Israel from a Jewish state to a binational one', and not only was this solution 'increasingly likely, but actually a desirable outcome'. What was needed to affect this outcome is 'a new political class' among both Arabs and Jews.[21] Inevitably, Said lost favour with the official leadership of the PLO and Judt's essay triggered a wave of attacks on him and his ideas.[22] Nevertheless, given the high regard with which these two individuals were held and their large circle of admirers, the idea of the one-state began to arouse wider interest among intellectuals and across religious and ethnic lines.

Since the turn of the last millennium, international conferences on the one-state and the rise of formal groups propagating the idea gathered momentum. Among such conferences, five stand apart in terms of programme, attendance and information value. The first was the Madrid Conference held on 2–6 July 2007, under the title 'Israel–Palestine: One Country, One State'.[23] The themes debated over five days by 22 Palestinian and Jewish scholars, mainly academics, were: 'reimagining the conflict', 'rethinking the geography and the nation', 'Israel and international law', 'future paths' and 'translating ideas into action'. It was suggested in the sessions that the conferees were involved 'in a profoundly political exercise... a program of action',[24] that the most powerful tool for the one-state cause was its morality,[25] that Palestinians would be ill-advised and offering Zionism a victory to engage in negotiations at present[26] as this would advance the Zionist cause, and that the one-state movement should position the Palestinian refugees at the core of its organisation.[27]

Shortly after, a second international conference on the one-state was held in London on 17–18 November 2007, under the title 'Challenging the Boundaries: A Single State in Palestine/Israel'.[28] While much of the programme covered the same grounds as the Madrid Conference, it featured a novel element. Both Palestinian and Israeli grass-roots activists and some non-governmental organisation (NGO) representatives participated as speakers and discussants.[29] Participants in the Madrid and London conferences issued, on the 60th anniversary of the 29 November 1947 UN Partition Resolution, a statement they named 'The One State Declaration', which has since served as the manifesto of the one-state movement.[30] It rejected the historical, legal, political, diplomatic and moral foundations of the two-state paradigm, and offered a rationale based on justice and reconciliation for a permanent one-state solution.

The 28–29 March 2009 Boston conference on 'One State for Palestine/Israel: A Country for all its Citizens' was a qualitative improvement on the Madrid and London conferences in several ways. The programme topics were more varied, the speakers represented more constituencies and the after-effect of the conference was more pronounced.[31] The discussion of strategies, logistics, methods, policies and organisational means required for the implementation of the one-state conferred on the programme practical and realistic dimensions that were not sufficiently addressed by previous conferences. The Boston Conference had much more exposure and international media coverage.[32] Overall, this conference seemed to have struck a chord, attracting a large, diverse and enthusiastic audience that hailed from all over the USA and Canada, with a notable presence from Europe and the Middle East. Registration for the conference had to be stopped several weeks before the event when the number of registrants exceeded the capacity of the conference venue. The two organising institutions concluded that the topic of the one-state was arousing considerable interest on the North American continent.

The fourth international conference, titled 'Israel/Palestine: Mapping Models of Statehood and Paths to Peace', was held on 22–24 June 2009 at York University in Toronto.[33] It differed markedly from previous conferences in a number of ways. Unlike the others, which were primarily the work of already committed academics and activists, this conference was organised by two law schools at two prestigious universities: Osgoode Hall Law School at York University in Toronto, Ontario, and the Faculty of Law at Queen's University in Kingston, Ontario. It was also sponsored by them and the Social Sciences and Humanitarian Research Council of Canada. The four organisers were members of the two law faculties. In addition, the conference was quite different in conception. It was not a one-state conference, but an assessment and debate on the utility of alternative state models for resolving the conflict. The two-state was considered alongside the one-state solution. Also, rather than being an assembly of like-minded participants, the Toronto conference included advocates of the one-state and two-state solutions as well as others. Many Zionist Israelis were present and 'the atmosphere was quite charged and at times heated... people remained quite polarised at the end, maybe even more so than at the beginning'.[34] Finally, the number of speakers with assigned topics was larger than anything seen before, reaching as many as 57. In spite of the differences, the Toronto conference made a major, perhaps lasting, contribution to the one-state paradigm. By providing a prestigious academic forum for the discussion of what Zionist advocates often describe as an anti-Semitic idea,[35] the conference helped break the existing circle of fear often associated with any questioning of conventional Zionist thinking and thereby opened new vistas.

The fifth conference was held on 20–21 June 2008, under the title 'Haifa Conference for the Right of Return and the Secular Democratic State in Palestine'.[36] Undoubtedly, the convening of this conference gave the one-state paradigm a new dimension. The idea had gone beyond the confines of academics and had struck roots in the ranks of the Palestinian community inside Israel. It was seen as part of the recent political awakening process they had been experiencing and offered them a platform to aid their ideas and help unify their ranks. Leaders of the principal parties active among Palestinians in Israel, namely the Democratic Front for Peace and Equality (Hadash), the National Democratic Alliance (Balad) and Abnaa El Balad, addressed the conference. The conference stood out also as a meeting of primarily Palestinian grass-roots activists and youth, supported by a good number of Jewish activists, expressing ideas about their future; this introduced realism to the theoretical debates which the intellectuals of the one-state movement had been engaged in thus far. The conference issued at its concluding session what came to be known as 'The Jaffa Declaration'. Encouraged by the conference success and the enthusiasm it engendered, a sequel to it was held in Haifa again on 28–30 May 2010. In the invitation to the conference, the organisers described themselves as a 'group of activists and individuals from different political movements and parties, human rights organisations, civil society and various sectors of public life'. They announced that one of the principal aims of the second Haifa conference was the establishment of a permanent structure and an international coalition dedicated to the goal of the one-state. Many hoped that the one-state movement inside Israel might turn into a popular Palestinian community organisation, operating in the context of a Palestinian–Jewish coalition and supported by an international body.

Beyond the matter of international conferences, interest for the one-state idea has recently manifested itself in two other ways. First, support for the idea among all Palestinian constituencies, namely Palestinians in Israel, the West Bank, Gaza and the *shatat*, has increased. Polls by the Jerusalem Media and Communication Centre have documented a change in attitude towards the one-state option in both the West Bank and Gaza since the second Palestinian uprising (Intifada) of 2000. In 2001, respondents who favoured the binational state in all of historic Palestine made up 18.3 per cent. They reached 20.6 per cent in June 2009. In April 2010, the Centre's poll indicated their numbers jumped to 34 per cent compared to 43.9 per cent favouring the two-state solution.[37] Significantly the rise in the number of one-state advocates was matched by a rise in the 'optimism' quotient towards the future among respondents which reached 63 per cent in October of 2009. The shift towards the one-state solution appeared to reflect confidence rather than desperation.

A number of scholars and commentators have noted their observations of a change in the attitude of Palestinians. Reporting her observations from the West Bank, Leila Farsakh, a Palestinian scholar, wrote that despite the prevailing depressed mood, 'there is much rumour about the importance of thinking of the one-state solution, yet little coordination between the people talking about it'. She describes the 'grass-roots initiatives' appearing everywhere and how informal groups are being formed in several cities by different, politically oriented activists and university students in the West Bank, Gaza and inside Israel. She concludes that it is 'a matter of time before these islands connect again'.[38] Another well-known Palestinian, Khaled Amayreh, reported from the West Bank that '… a growing number of Palestinians, including intellectuals, academics as well as ordinary citizens are abandoning the goal of Palestinian statehood. Their new strategy is the creation of a democratic, unitary and secular state.'[39] The spread of the one-state idea was also reported as taking place among the Palestinian leadership by no less than the former president Jimmy Carter following a visit to the West Bank and Gaza. He wrote in a *Washington Post* op-ed:

> A more likely alternative to the present debacle is one state, which is obviously the goal of Israeli leaders who insist on colonising the West Bank and East Jerusalem. A majority of the Palestinian leaders with whom we met are seriously considering acceptance of one state, between the Jordan River and the Mediterranean Sea. By renouncing the dream of an independent Palestine, they would become fellow citizens with their Jewish neighbours and then demand equal rights within a democracy. In this nonviolent civil rights struggle, their examples would be Mahatma Gandhi, Martin Luther King Jr. and Nelson Mandela.[40]

Equally noteworthy is the adoption of the one-state strategy by prominent Palestinian figures as evidenced by the proposal of the Palestine Strategy Study Group. Funded by the European Union, the group of 27 Palestinians 'drawn from across the political spectrum' called for a change in strategy to demand a single state: 'This… would regain the strategic initiative for the Palestinians.'[41]

Second, the increasing interest in the one-state idea is manifesting itself also in the rapid manner in which associations for the one-state are proliferating among Palestinians, wherever they live. Many of these associations go by the name 'One State Group'. They are found in Europe, Arab countries and Israel/Palestine. Some have adopted different names. The association in Syria, for example, which is a joint effort by the Palestinian Bader Group in Syria and Natreenkum (Waiting for You) group in Israel, advertises itself rather colourfully as Ajras al–Awdah (Bells of Return).[42] The Association in Geneva, Switzerland, is registered under the name Association for one Democratic State in Palestine/Israel.[43] But in spite of their numbers, these associations lack organisational links or coordination among themselves. Their effect, therefore, is largely localised. It remains to be seen if an international movement that links them together will rise to make them bigger players in the discourse.

Principal Themes

The 20 chapters in this volume are thought-provoking and carefully reasoned. They are written by established scholars, many of them from leading universities. The chapters deal with critical topics and divide into four themes. Chapters 2 to 6 address the basic question of whether the two-state solution, which has formed the basis of the international consensus on the needed outcome for the peace process at least since the Oslo Accords, remains feasible. The analysis provided by Virginia Tilley, Saree Makdisi, Husam Zomlot, Naseer Aruri and Nancy Murray concludes that the existing conditions have rendered the establishment of a viable Palestinian state alongside Israel impossible. Tilley maintains that the Jewish settlements must be viewed as permanent, a situation that imposes a one-state solution. Makdisi claims that Israel has ensured the failure of the two-state solution by adopting drastic policies to 'Judaise' Jerusalem, knowing that Palestinians would not accept a state without East Jerusalem as its capital. Zomlot traces the Palestinian efforts that went into building a state under occupation and describes how the Western powers that sponsored the Oslo Accords chose not to challenge Israeli policies that undermined these efforts. In other words, the only framework on the table for a settlement between the parties was by definition not workable for the Palestinians. Aruri's overall assessment of the present situation is that Israel, with US support, has crippled the two-state solution and sees the existing peace process as a process to shelter Israel from what is considered to be the threats that come with peace. Finally, Murray's chapter evaluates the difficulties for co-existence, cohabitation and future statehood created by what Palestinians view as a deliberate policy of destruction and debilitation directed against their aspirations, and the ways in which the two-state solution faces insurmountable challenges given the current situation.

The second theme considers the guiding beliefs of both Palestinians and Jews in order to identify the fundamental principles that may guide a historic settlement. Four chapters by Gabriel Piterberg, Marc Ellis, Ali Abunimah and Ilan Pappé propose a new Jewish/Arab liberating narrative. This would explore Jewish and Israeli values, credit the Jewish sense of justice, review essential Palestinian rights, and assess the one-state idea within the frame of morality, international conventions and the imperatives of justice. Their analyses caution against the apparent simplicity and logic of political proposals that seek to divide Palestine, people and country, into two permanently separate entities whose interests are irreconcilable to each other and therefore whose perception will always be mutually hostile.

The third theme, looking at the practicalities of the situation, has three chapters. Susan Akram, Salman Abu Sitta and Smadar Lavie deal with the Palestinian right of return, the idea of implementing the right of return for Palestinians and, finally, the essential role the Mizrahim and Mizrahi women will have to play to arrive at an Israeli/Palestinian concord.

The fourth and final theme addresses organisational issues needed for building one country and one state. Seven chapters written by George Bisharat, Norton Mezvinsky, As'ad Ghanem, Nadia Hijab, Leila Farsakh, Joel Kovel and Ghada Karmi discuss the building of movements for the one-state among Palestinians, within Israel, in the Arab world, among world Jewry and internationally. The accounts they provide point to the intricacies and enormous challenges involved in these formidable tasks. Several of the chapters point to how a shift in the position of the official PLO leadership in support of the one-state idea can have immense consequences at all levels and galvanise international support for the idea.

These chapters are a sample of the kind of thinking that explores the failure of the two-state solution and a vision for another, more equitable resolution of the conflict in historic Palestine. Such a vision seeks complete and permanent closure. It should look to resolve the conflict issues rather than simply manage them, and allows both Israelis and Palestinians to realise what seem to be their innermost yearning to live and prosper in an undivided state in historic Palestine if it is shared by both peoples. This volume explores the rationale and the route to such an outcome.

Notes

1. For the reciprocal threats the two super powers exchanged on 24 and 25 October 1973, and the worldwide US mobilisation of its armed forces, see Henry Kissinger, *Years of Upheaval* (Boston, MA: Little Brown, 1982), pp. 575–91.

2. Recently declassified state archive documents hint at Israel readying its nuclear arsenal in the 1973 October War. See Yossi Melman, 'Did Israel ever consider using nuclear weapons?', *Ha'aretz*, 7 October 2010. On Israel's nuclear deterrent strategy, see Warner D. Farr, *The Third Temple's Holy Of Holies: Israel's Nuclear Weapons*, The Counterproliferation Papers, Future Warfare Series No. 2, USAF Counterproliferation Center Air War College, September 1999.

3. A 160 km fortified sand and mud barrier, supported by concrete walls, 8 to 10 metres in height and 8 to 10 metres deep, built by Israel after the war of June 1967 all along the eastern bank of the Suez Canal. It was named after the Israeli chief of staff, Haim Bar-Lev.

4. The phrase was coined by Professor Emeritus Elaine Hagopian in a message to the author dated 2 March 2009.

5. Jerusalem is a case in point. Perhaps more than any other, the future of Jerusalem is a defining issue to both Israelis and Palestinians. Israel's 'de facto' policies no longer allow for a neat redivision of the city into Jewish West and Arab East Jerusalem. Not surprisingly, all the diplomatic solutions under discussion point in one direction. A future Jerusalem acceptable to both Israelis and Palestinians can only be reached as part of a larger political solution, and governing Jerusalem will require, in turn, a measure of coordination that can only come from one binational authority. Since the two-state solution has been rendered obsolete, the two communities are doomed to an unacceptable status quo unless they move toward a binational authority in the country and, by extension, in the city. In other words, Jerusalem requires a one-state solution to the Israel/Palestine conflict if it is to become again a city of peace and the home of multiple faiths. For a detailed exposition of this argument, see the article by Mick Dumper, 'A false dichotomy? The binationalism debate and the future of divided Jerusalem', *International Affairs*, 87(3), May 2011, pp. 671–85.

6. When asked about the two-state solution, the veteran Israeli journalist Amira Hass replied: 'Two states – it's more like 10.' The only difference now between Labour and Likud, she said, was a discussion about 'the size and number of the Bantustans' (see www.vancouverobserver.com/search/node/Amira%20hass). She added that the behaviour of the two-state advocates resembles that of a frog. When thrown into boiling water, it senses the danger and leaps out to safety. When placed in warm water and the heat is raised slowly, it stays calm because it gets used to warmth although it is facing imminent death. Israel has been using this policy with the Palestinians in the West Bank since 1967. It confiscates their lands, freedoms and rights. Soon, they will have no homeland left to build a state on. Like the frog, Hass said, two-state advocates among the Palestinians are unaware of the dangers. Editor's notes from a lecture delivered by Amira Hass at the University of British Columbia in Vancouver, Canada, on 28 September 2011.

7. For an incisive analysis on the parallels between the South African and Israeli systems, see Virginia Tilley, 'Has Palestine passed the tipping point? Sovereignty and settler colonialism in South Africa and Israel–Palestine', Paper delivered at the Centre for Humanities Research and Department of History of the University of the Western Cape in South Africa on 17 February 2009, and distributed in North America by Academics for Justice on the same date.

8. From a speech Einstein delivered on 17 April 1938, at the Commodore Hotel in New York City. Einstein reproduced the speech in Albert Einstein, *Out of My Later Years* (New York: Philosophical Library, 1950), p. 263.

9. There are many ways in which to signify the geographical area to which this book refers. In order to impose a sense of continuity, throughout this book, we have chosen the moniker 'historic Palestine' to encompass present-day Israel, the West Bank and the Gaza strip.

10. As late as 1942, the WZO Biltmore Program declared the whole of Palestine a Jewish 'commonwealth'. Many regard the expression as a euphemism for statehood.

11. For the text of the WZO memo, see www.jewishvirtuallibrary.org/jsource/History/zoparis.html.

12. For an account of the calculations of the Zionist leadership regarding the 1947 UN General Assembly's Partition Resolution, see Walid Khalidi, 'The Hebrew Reconquista of Palestine: from the United Nations Partition Resolution to the First Zionist Congress of 1897', *Journal of Palestine Studies*, 39(1), Autumn 2009, especially pp. 26–7.

13. The Zionist offensive was carried out according to a pre-planned scheme known as Plan Dalet. For the details of the plan, see Walid Khalidi, 'Plan Dalet: master plan for the conquest of Palestine', *Journal of Palestine Studies*, 18(1), Autumn 1988, pp. 4–19.

14. In point 2 of the Ten Point Program approved by the Palestinian National Council on 8 June 1974, the Program stated: '… to establish the independent combatant national

authority for the people over every part of Palestinian territory that is liberated'. For the text of the Program, see www.un.int/palestine/PLO/docone.html.

15. The PLO endorsed the two-state solution in the 15 November 1988 Declaration of Independence by accepting post-1947 UN Resolutions. For the text of the Declaration, see www.albab.com/arab/docs/pal/pal3.htm.

16. See the Yasser Arafat letter of 9 September 1993 to Yitzhak Rabin at http://usembassy-israel.org.il/publish/peace/isplorec.htm.

17. The most lucid argument outlining the case for the establishment of a Palestinian state within the framework of a two-state solution was made by Walid Khalidi in 'Thinking the unthinkable: a sovereign Palestinian state', *Foreign Affairs*, 56(4), July 1978, pp. 695–713. The article reflected and guided the political thinking of the Palestinian leadership. It also had an effect on Palestinian intellectuals.

18. The two-state solution dominates the agenda of the USA and all major Western governments. Countries of the developing world, most of whom are sympathetic to the cause of the Palestinians, adopt the positions of the PLO.

19. Lately, a number of Palestinians who were former architects, advocates and negotiators for the two-state solution changed positions. The latest among them is Ahmad Qurei' (Abu Ala'), the man behind the Oslo Accords and the Chief Palestinian negotiator with the Israelis and Americans over a long period of time. In an article published on 17 March 2012, in the *Al Quds* newspaper, Qurei' declared the two-state solution 'dead', and announced that Palestinian negotiators were easy victims who fell through political deception into a trap and have totally wasted more than a decade pursuing a futile goal. He called on the Palestinians to start an internal national discussion on alternatives, especially the one-state solution, which he described as morally superior and fit to be the foundation for future Palestinian struggle and more capable of 'providing satisfactory answers to many puzzling questions; including questions dealing with the destiny of Palestinians and the answer to a permanent solution'. Ahmad Qurei' (Abu Ala'), '*hal aldawlatayn bayna alfashal wa altafsheel*' [The two-state solution between failure and causing to fail] *Al Quds*, 19 March 2012, www.alquds.com/news/article/view/id/341469.

20. See Edward Said, 'The one-state solution', *New York Times*, 10 January 1999. Said acknowledged in his article that 'enlarging the concept of citizenship' belongs to Azmi Bishara, a former Palestinian member of the Knesset.

21. Tony Judt, 'Israel: the alternative', *New York Review of Books*, 23 October 2003.

22. In the week following the essay's publication, the *New York Review of Books* received more than a thousand letters decrying Judt, and *The New Republic* removed him from its editorial board.

23. The conference was organised by Universidad Nómada and the Fundación Europa de los Ciudadanos.

24. The statement is attributed to Virginia Tilley based on the author's copy of an unpublished record of the sessions drafted by the conference secretariat.

25. Ibid. The statement was made by Steven Freedman.

26. Ibid.

27. Ibid. The idea is attributed to Omar Barghouti.

28. The conference was organised by the London One-State Group and the University of London School of Oriental and African Studies (SOAS) Palestine Society. The conference featured 21 speakers of different nationalities, and several hundred were in attendance. To review the programme, check the conference website at www.onestate.net.

29. For a report on the workings of the conference, see Rumy Hasan, 'Just one state', *Al-Ahram Weekly Online*, 20–26 December 2007.

30. The Declaration was authored by 15 participants and endorsed by another 54. For the text, check http://electronicintifada.net/v2/article9134.shtml.

31. To view the programme, speakers and the Boston Declaration, check the conference website at www.onestateforpalestineisrael.com.

32. The full workings of the conference were carried live by TV and radio. Al Jazeera Arabic TV reported on the conference. The Arabic press reported widely on the conference and the Declaration it issued. Reports were featured in the London-based *Al Quds Al Arabi* (22 June 2009), Beirut-based *As Safeer* (18 June 2009), Nazareth-based *Hadeeth An Nas* (26 June 2009) and *Al Mustaqbal Al Arabi*, No. 365 (July 2009), among others. Additionally, four of the submitted papers were featured in a special issue of the journal *Contemporary Arab Affairs* (London), 2(4) (October–December 2009), and five of the submitted papers were translated into Arabic and published in *Al Mustaqbal Al Arabi*, No. 375 (May 2009).

33. For the conference programme, check its website at www.yorku.ca/ipconf.

34. From an email sent by George Bisharat, a conference participant, to the author, dated 26 June 2009.

35. The organisers were aware that such an accusation might be levelled at them and sought to guard against it by including the following provision in the programme's opening statement: 'Our commitment to ensuring that neither anti-Semitism nor any other form of racism has any place in this forum informs both the conference and all aspects of its planning process.' See the conference website under the item 'Welcome'.

36. For the conference programme, see its website at www.ror1state.org. The workings of the conference are reviewed by Yoav Bar at www.ror1state.org/drupal/?q=en/node/93.

37. Poll No. 70 was conducted between 10 and 15 April 2010, on a random sample of 1,198 respondents in both the West Bank and the Gaza Strip, and had a margin of error of +/– 3 per cent. See www.jmcc.org/documentsandmaps.aspx?id=749.

38. From 'Islands of voices' by Leila Farsakh, published by *Lux Magazine*, University of Massachusetts-Boston, April 2009.

39. See http://weekly.ahram.org.eg/2008/889/re61.htm. For another highly interesting account by Meron Benvenisti, see his 30 April 2009 article in *Ha'aretz* entitled 'The binationalism vogue', at www.haaretz.com/print-edition/opinion/the-binationalism-vogue-1.275085.

40. The op-ed was published on 6 September 2009, and is available at www.washingtonpost.com/wpdyn/content/article/2009/09/04/AR2009090402968.html.

41. The *Guardian* reported on the work of the Group on 4 September 2008 (see www.guardian.co.uk/world/2008/sep/04/israel.palestinians).

42. Check their website at http://ajras.org/en.

43. Check their website at www.odspi.org.

PART I

Is the Two-State Settlement Feasible?

CHAPTER 2

The Deeper Politics of Jewish Settlements

Virginia Tilley

Of all the many obstacles to peace in Israel–Palestine, Jewish settlements in the occupied Palestinian territories are most often cited as the most intractable. All realistic analysis of a stable two-state solution in historic Palestine accepts that the West Bank Jewish settlements shatter the geographic contiguity of a Palestinian state past imaginable viability and conclude that all or most of them must therefore be either withdrawn, 'dismantled' or turned over to Palestinian use. Considering that the establishment of a viable Palestinian state within the context of a two-state solution is in the strategic interest of Israel, it is therefore perplexing to many observers that the settlements continue to expand. Not understanding the reasons for this continued growth, international diplomacy has laboured under the misconception that it might stop.

In fact, withdrawal of the settlements, or even a freeze on their growth, cannot realistically be expected to materialise. The best way to understand why, and why Jewish settlements in the West Bank and East Jerusalem impose a one-state solution in historic Palestine, is by grasping the reasons they must be considered permanent. Some reasons for the settlements' permanence are well known and can be summarised briefly, but the deeper and less obvious reasons, which are the true driving motivations for the settlements, will require discussion at more length.[1] During 2005, the Jewish settlements in the Gaza Strip were evacuated, dismantled and razed, leaving Gaza as one Palestinian canton in terms explained later. Hence the question of settlements now pertains to East Jerusalem and the West Bank.

The Permanence of the Settlements

The first and most obvious reason to consider the West Bank settlements to be immovable and permanent is that their stated purpose is to be permanent. Much has been written about the settlements and many sources on their purposes can be cited today, but the most concise expression remains the 'Master plan for the development of settlement in Judea and Samaria 1979–1983', issued in 1978 by the World Zionist Organization (WZO). Written by WZO head Matityahu Drobles and often called the Drobles Plan, this Master Plan framed all subsequent master plans for Jewish settlement in the West Bank. The WZO Settlement Department remains the principal planning architect of West Bank settlements today (in slightly modified form, after fusing with the Jewish Agency's Settlement Department) and the Jewish Agency and WZO function as 'authorised agencies' of the state of Israel under Israel law. Hence the preface of the Drobles Plan stands as seminal to understanding the strategic purpose and design of the settlements as well as their origins in Israeli state policy:

> Settlement throughout the entire Land of Israel is for security and by right. A strip of settlements at strategic sites enhances both internal and external security alike, as well as making concrete and realizing our right to Eretz-Israel.
>
> … It must be borne in mind that it may be too late tomorrow to do what is not done today. … There are today persons who are young or young in spirit who want to take up the challenge of national goals and who want to settle in J&S [sic]. We should enable them to do so, and sooner is better.[2]

The Drobles Plan detailed the settlement blocs that did not then exist but dominate the landscape today: Rehan, Maarav, Shomron, Kedumim, Karnei Shomron, Ariel, Gush Etzion, Givon, Modi'im and so forth. Their strategic growth was also plainly explained:

> The disposition of the proposed settlement will be implemented according to a settlement policy of blocks of settlements in homogeneous settlement areas which are mutually interrelated – this enabling, in time, the development of common services and means of production. Moreover, in the wake of the expansion and development of the community settlements, some of them may combine, in the course of time, into an urban settlement which would consist of all the settlements in that particular bloc.[3]

Ensuring that the settlements provided Jewish immigrants from Europe and North America with the requisite first-world living standards also required inequitable management of natural resources, particularly water. Such measures cannot be carried out without damaging the social fabric of Palestinian movement and land use that allowed a healthy Palestinian economy.

Thus it is not simply the settlements' physical presence in the West Bank that presents an obstacle to peace. Although illegal under international humanitarian law, their presence could be less ruinous to a future peace settlement if their growth represented some spontaneous process of civilian settlement that linked organically to adjacent Palestinian towns and villages in ways typical of rural development elsewhere. Such a process would tend over time to generate full annexation and a one-state solution; however, full integration of the population under occupation is, for reasons discussed later, precisely what Israel wishes to avoid. Hence the settlements' placement (and infrastructure) has been adjusted to preclude a one-state solution yet make a true two-state solution impossible. How the settlements accomplish this dual goal, crucial to Israel's interests, is the question requiring greater attention because it explains both their permanence and their true implications for any peace agreement, as discussed later.

The second feature suggesting the settlements' permanency, and the most commonly recognised, is their impact on the 1949 Armistice line or 'green line'. The green line demarcates the internationally recognised borders between Israel and the occupied Palestinian territories and therefore the territory considered in international law to be under belligerent occupation by Israel. Hence it marks the borders considered in international diplomacy to demarcate the territory from which Israel must eventually withdraw and in which the Palestinians will eventually form a state.[4] It is precisely this vital border, however, that has been systematically effaced by settlement growth. In the vicinity of Jerusalem, this effacement has been completed by constructing an unbroken array of urban growth so vast as to defeat any notion that the border can be meaningfully restored. Hence few people today who have witnessed the scale of the urban settlements now straddling the green line believe that a two-state solution is possible without significant adjustments to the line itself. This 'reality' was incorporated into international diplomacy when the principle of border adjustments was formally endorsed by President George Bush in 2004 and has not been retracted.[5]

To be politically acceptable to Palestinians, who believe they have maximised land sacrifices by giving up claims to land within Israel, such adjustments are usually discussed as 'swaps' that would be roughly equitable in size.[6] That is, land inside the West Bank that is transferred permanently to Israel will be of approximately the same extent as land on the Israeli side transferred to a state of Palestine. Whether or not swaps are precisely equal, mutual adjustments may seem both fair and feasible at first brush. For example, a shift of the border just a few hundred metres eastward would suffice to move the entire contiguous settlement complex of HaOranim and Lapid (in the northern West Bank) entirely into Israel. A comparable shift westward would place Palestinian Arab villages such as Beit Awwa (in the southern West Bank) entirely into Palestine.

The swap principle becomes more tortuous, however, regarding settlement blocs located more deeply inside the West Bank, such as the major Jewish settlement-city of Ariel (with a population of approximately 25,000), near Nablus. A border adjustment that incorporates Ariel into Israel would require that Israel annex a deep tongue of land plunging deep into the northern West Bank and divide it into northern and central sections. Israel has proposed that a system of tunnels and bridges might help to reduce the impact on Palestinian movement and restore 'travel contiguity'. But the detrimental impact for Palestine may be glimpsed by considering why a comparable measure – for example, a tongue of Palestinian sovereignty extending deep into Israel to embrace the overwhelmingly Arab city of Nazareth in the central Galilee – would not be remotely acceptable to Israel.

The swap principle also fails progressively with closer proximity to Jerusalem. In the strategic 'ring settlements', urban Jewish 'neighbourhoods' become so dense as to compel wildly gerrymandered borders to accommodate remaining Palestinian enclaves. Again, an elaborate tunnel and bridge system, combined with border controls, would be required to get from one neighbourhood to another. But given ongoing Israeli construction of these settlements – and the massive infrastructure of highways and power grids that integrates them into greater Jerusalem and Israel itself – the more likely outcome is annexation of the entire middle 'waist' of the West Bank to Israel. Thus the principle of swaps cannot ignore power inequities, which will combine with geographic realities to make land swaps complicit, fragmenting the Palestinian West Bank.

Obstacles to withdrawal on a scale that would ameliorate such difficulties are well known. One oft-cited factor is security. Israel would arguably be safer if it handed the West Bank over to a Palestinian state, because it would defuse threats associated with the conflict and eliminate the need for a buffer zone against neighbouring Arab attack. Nevertheless, too much Israeli–Jewish public opinion, stoked by continual government arguments that Israel is under constant threat of annihilation, holds that the territory is a vital buffer against such attack. A broad belt of Israeli control around Jerusalem, for example, is non-negotiable to this view, as is Israel's retention of the Jordan Valley. (The security argument persists despite its obvious gaps; for example, which regional land army might attack Israel is entirely unclear, and how the tiny West Bank can act as a buffer to missile strikes, which are today the principal threat to Israel's security, is equally unexplained.) A related geographic question is what is sometimes called 'water security'. No Palestinian government can function effectively without reclaiming control over the dwindling West Bank aquifers, but they are vital to Israel's increasingly strained national water supply and Israel therefore cannot and will not give them up.[7]

Also intractable are the economic and political costs of withdrawal. Economically, the West Bank settlement grid presently has a value thousands of times that of the settlements in the Gaza Strip, where withdrawal cost Israel some US$3 billion in compensation and demolition. Costs of withdrawing from and razing the West Bank settlement grid would therefore exceed any resources that might imaginably be found.

Given Palestinian weakness, some outside power with special political fortitude and capacity could alter these geographic, economic and security equations. Yet such a power is notably absent. US foreign policy remains bound to its pro-Israel commitments, due partly to the leverage exerted by the powerful pro-Israel lobby on the country's domestic Congressional politics and partly to the density of military and intelligence cooperation that shapes the 'special alliance' between Israel and the USA. Many European states are sympathetic to Palestinian rights, but European interests in Israeli trade, technology transfers and other cooperation easily trump these sentiments, and, in any case, individual European member states remain unwilling to challenge US prerogatives on the conflict. Arab states have had no political will sufficient to alter the political calculus either for Europe or North America: thoroughly embedded in their Western alliances via corporate oil agreements as well as vast private and state investments in Western economies, they are also politically vulnerable to domestic pressures and therefore anxious to sustain external Western support. The Arab world also has no leverage with Israel. Even full peace deals, recently offered by Syria and Saudi Arabia, could not induce Israel to give up any land in the Golan Heights, let alone in the Zionist ideological heartland of 'Judea and Samaria'.[8] The so-called 'Arab Spring' of 2011 has not materially changed these power balances – at least at the time of writing.

This much is readily observable. Still, none of this would seem to preclude an Israeli withdrawal from the West Bank settlements if conditions were right. To observers both inside Israel and abroad, the cost–benefit analysis seems both clear and compelling: if the benefit for Israel of withdrawing the settlements is a comprehensive peace, and the alternative is sabotage of the two-state solution which is the only clear way to ensure survival of a Jewish state, then surely some sagacious and foresighted Israeli government will finally muster the political will and leadership to orchestrate a withdrawal. This commonplace wisdom is profoundly mistaken, however, because it misses the deeper politics of the settlements.

The true purposes of the settlements, and how they operate geographically to serve Israeli state strategies, explains why their withdrawal, or even a settlement freeze, cannot be anticipated. These purposes can be grouped into three general categories:

1. how the West Bank settlements express and consolidate a Jewish national pact regarding Jewish statehood;
2. how they serve Israel's strategy for steering Palestinian self-governance in the occupied Palestinian territories; and
3. how they serve Israel's project to annex the West Bank while remaining a Jewish state.

Jewish Statehood and Jewish 'National' Unity

The ideological significance of the West Bank settlements to Jewish statehood is not well understood by most observers. Instead, their ideological importance is too often attributed narrowly to some religious strands of Zionist thought. Religious Zionist views are indeed important. 'Judea and Samaria', as the settler movements and the Israeli government call the West Bank, are the territories in which most compelling narratives of the Jewish Bible (Old Testament) play out. Strong currents of modern Zionist thought therefore celebrate this highland territory as the Jewish homeland in Palestine that was divinely granted by God to the Jewish people. This assumption precludes, as a violation of divine ordinance, any giving this 'sacred landscape' over to a Palestinian state. A small minority of settlers – possibly 10 per cent of the half-million Jewish settlers now residing in the West Bank – have accordingly vowed to defend the settlements at all costs, including armed resistance, on these religious grounds.[9]

Appreciating the tensions raised by these religious sentiments is therefore appropriate, but two logical errors often follow: that the settlements are primarily products of religious zealotry, and that only religious settlers stand in the way of their withdrawal. These assumptions incorrectly reduce the state's burden to that of overcoming a zealous but otherwise marginalised minority, and makes withdrawal seem merely a matter of mustering the necessary political will and assembling a majority parliamentary coalition to implement it. The latter is not as easy as it might sound: if a majority of Israeli Jews consider 'Judea and Samaria' to be irrelevant to Israel's modern life and the West Bank itself expendable for a stable peace, enough would be scandalised by its loss to retract the slim electoral majority that, for example, allowed the government to confront the Gaza Strip settlers. Indeed, given the sway exerted by small parties in Israel's political system, no Israeli government would survive the effort. Nonetheless, it would seem that, under compelling conditions, a 'secular' majority in Israel could orchestrate sufficient electoral power to isolate religious zealots enough to allow a withdrawal adequate to a two-state solution.

This assumption misses the real political significance of the settlements in two ways. First, as noted earlier, the settlements are not religious projects: they are overwhelmingly projects of the Israeli state, which even today remains dominated by Ashkenazi secularists. The founding motivation for the state to build the settlements was cited earlier. Today, every government ministry is heavily involved in planning and funding the settlements, working closely with the Jewish Agency and WZO, which design and manage the settlements directly and via their affiliated agencies and holding companies.[10] Much of the Israeli private economy is also linked into the settlements directly or indirectly, through investment in their construction, services, businesses, industrial zones and agriculture. Hence the common complaint that Israel is being 'held hostage' by religious extremists should be recognised as, at most, a convenient fiction that provides the Israeli government with plausible deniability for its involvement in the settlements. In fact, the settlement project in the West Bank springs from heavy investment by Israel's entire public sector and extensive parts of the (secular) private sector as well.

The concept of being 'held hostage' by religious extremists nonetheless flags the second problem, which is far more debilitating to a settlement withdrawal. Even if support for the settlements were confined to a religious extremist minority, which it is not, the political problem would not be opposition by that minority per se, but what its defection would signify for Israel's claim to be a Jewish state. This risk is not simply a matter of parliamentary politics, which might imaginably be overcome through adroit leadership: it strikes at the heart of the Zionist project. In 1948, Israel was founded on a kind of national pact among secular, liberal, conservative, revisionist, labour and religious-Orthodox Zionist factions. The resulting Declaration of Independence, a non-binding ethical and visionary framework of Jewish statehood, reflects the result: an internally contradictory statement of principles for governing Israel that accommodated the vision of each faction sufficiently to bring it on board. This pact has been uneasy since it was crafted, however, because some of these strains – for example, liberal democrats and ultra-Orthodox – hold contradictory ideas about how Israel must be constituted in order to comprise a true Jewish state. For example, liberal Zionists would deny that Israel was a true Jewish state if it failed to constitute itself as a liberal democracy that allows the collective expression of Jewish liberal values, which, for them, reside at the heart of Jewish identity. Religious Jewish Zionists would deny Israel the mantle of Jewish state if it failed to provide the conditions for Jewish religious life as they understand it, which for some factions requires retaining the highland territories. Defection of either strain from the pact endorsing Israel as a Jewish state would damage the crucial claim of Israel to represent the entire Jewish 'people'.

If some segments of world Jewry openly repudiated any affiliation with Israel, Israel's entire raison d'être – and its associated foreign policy – would lose its principal pillar. Indeed, if Jewish unity about Israel were to suffer serious schisms, they could even implicate the essential Zionist claim that Jews are properly understood to constitute a 'people' or 'nation' in the first place. Israel's most basic claim to legitimacy – that Jews constitute a 'people' or 'nation' that requires and deserves a separate state for its representation and defence – therefore rests on papering over such differences. Accordingly, no Israeli government will consider triggering an existential crisis for Jewish statehood by making any serious effort to withdraw from the Biblical heartland. The political theatre that accompanied Israel's withdrawal from the marginal Gaza Strip settlements in September 2005 would not approach the genuine rift in Zionist discourse that would greet any attempt to withdraw from 'Judea and Samaria'. Hence the settlements materially signal the underlying fragility of the Jewish-national claim and their continued growth represents the state's onus of precluding a dangerous existential threat to Jewish-national unity from within.

The Settlements and Palestinian 'Self-government'

The second type of deeper politics expressed by the settlements is signalled by a seeming conundrum. Reviewing the rate of settlement growth since the 1970s reveals that it has remained impressively consistent in speed and the general schema of Drobles Plan and other early master plans, no matter what was happening in the 'peace process'. Especially significant is that settlement construction proceeded even more quickly after the signing of the Oslo Accords in 1993 and 1995, when both sides were supposed to be consolidating conditions for a stable two-state solution.[11] Since settlement construction remains a state project, as earlier discussion has clarified, this accelerating growth cannot be attributed to private actors (such as religious zealots) or government inattention. Rather, it signals that, when Yitzhak Rabin and other Israeli leaders spoke in the early 1990s of 'courageous decisions' and dramatic and difficult actions to create peace, they did not mean a settlement freeze or even any substantive change in the West Bank settlements' locations or rate of growth – or, certainly, any withdrawal.[12] Rather, Israel's accession to the Oslo Accords signified two policy changes that indeed constituted a blow to some visions of Jewish-national relation to the territory: first, the withdrawal of Jewish settlements from Gaza; and second, a more robust accommodation for autonomous Palestinian governance in the West Bank, at least in those geographic cantons demarcated for Palestinian residence by the settlement blocs.

The first withdrawal from Gaza was a meaningful sacrifice only for a small proportion of the Jewish-Israeli public. The Gaza settlements were relatively small (a total population of between 7,000 and 8,000), their defence was costly and the water sources on which they were strategically positioned were limited and declining in quality. Most importantly, given the problem of Jewish-Zionist unity noted above, southern Gaza is relatively obscure to the Zionist religious/ ideological imaginary, as the territory falls outside the highland territory in which the Biblical narratives play out. Hence withdrawal was controversial in principle – withdrawal of Jews from any land under Israel's control, which might set a precedent – rather than specific to any high social or ideological value placed on the territory itself.

The truly difficult question for larger streams of Zionist thought was the shift to provide for some form of Palestinian political autonomy within territory under Israel's control. No strand of Zionism had ever conceived such an arrangement and in Israeli occupation policy no provision for Palestinian self-governance was ever made. In the Allon Plan, Drobles Plan and settlement master plans, Palestinian Arab society – with its cities, towns, villages and agriculture dating to antiquity – has been described only as 'minorities', a 'population' or 'population centres'.[13] Only when confronted by mass insurrection in the first intifada (1987–90) did Israeli strategists recognise that Jewish settlement could not proceed in the West Bank unless Palestinian political frustrations were pacified sufficiently to preclude open rebellion. This onus compels some form of Palestinian autonomy.

Another dilemma for Israel arose from the civilian character of Jewish settlement. In the first two decades of the occupation, the Jewish Agency and WZO had promoted the West Bank settlements as destinations for Jews who would value the spiritual dimension of 'return' to what was held to be the Jewish national home and a sacred landscape. Jewish settlers motivated by religion did take up this call – many of these came directly from other countries, especially the USA – but by the early 1980s it was clear that settlements were growing more slowly than expected. Most Israeli Jewish civilians were not sufficiently motivated by religious fervour or romantic nationalism to move into areas where their quality of life would suffer a more risky security environment. Hence, in the mid-1980s, the Jewish Agency redesigned settlements to attract a much larger market: secular Israeli–Jewish civilians looking for discounted housing in scenic peaceful settings. This tactical shift required installing a more complete civilian infrastructure: shopping malls, recreation centres, health and education systems (including a university based in Ariel), industrial zones and business centres to provide local employment, and so forth. Private Israeli and foreign investment in the settlements (in housing, office blocks, services, industry, agriculture and tourism) were subsidised by the state to help build this essential infrastructure. The plan was to consolidate the social and economic integration of what would become mostly secular settlements more seamlessly into Israel's national life.

Through most of the 1980s, this strategy worked reasonably well. As late as November 1987, direct Palestinian confrontations with Israeli soldiers had been sporadic and rarely involved guns or serious casualties, and were usually dominated by male youths engaged in stone-throwing that obtained an almost ritualistic or game-like quality. Military rule in these conditions was relatively easy and low-cost; military patrols in the West Bank were composed of middle-aged (if armed) reservists who were noted for strolling Palestinian city streets with relative impunity. In this quiet climate, settlements and Palestinian towns could co-exist reasonably peacefully if uneasily in the same landscape, although settlers typically went armed when they shopped or visited Palestinian towns. As settlement growth accelerated in the mid-1980s, however, Palestinian resentment and tensions grew. The intifada, erupting spontaneously in December 1987 and quickly mobilising most of the civilian population in mass strikes, confronted the occupation forces with opposition on an entirely new scale.[14]

Such mass resistance could not be repressed without destroying the security environment for Jewish civilian settlement. It was this dilemma that inspired the Israeli government to reconsider its relationship to the Palestine Liberation Organisation (PLO) and strike the pact to re-install the PLO leadership into the Occupied Palestinian Territory (OPT), where it could be made responsible for repressing Palestinian violence. Thus the Oslo Accords provided for a 'Palestinian Interim Self-Government Authority' that, albeit with provisions for a popular electoral mandate, was by arrangement dominated by the PLO political elite, led by Yasser Arafat, which had its own reasons to uphold the deal.[15] Israel's decision to withdraw the marginal settlements from the Gaza Strip was made in this same context.

This accommodation shaped the tone of the Oslo negotiations and was widely seen at the time as historic. To all appearances, Israel had finally accepted that Palestinians' self-determination could not endlessly be denied and Palestinians had accepted that a state in part of historic Palestine would suffice. The presumption that both parties had agreed to accept co-existence in a two-state solution shaped all subsequent absorption by the international community with questions that seemed to impede a pragmatic final status agreement: precise borders, control of water, access to Jerusalem, return of refugees and so forth.

In hindsight, however, the true historic significance of Israel's accommodation was quite different: to consign part of the land for Palestinian autonomy zones (possibly called a 'state') in territory over which Israel would retain ultimate control. In this strategic vision, the Jewish settlements were not anachronisms, whose withdrawal would be intrinsic to the final peace agreement, as many observers and certainly the PLO delegation believed. Rather, settlements were the essential instrument of political-geographic engineering, designed to ensure that Palestinian self-government would function permanently on debilitated terms that could never challenge Israel's prerogatives.

The Settlements and Jewish Statehood

Israel's geographic strategy to cantonise and debilitate Palestinian self-rule is not concerned only with the occupied territories, however. The tenacity of the settlement project is only comprehensible in light of its second function, which is to protect Jewish statehood by averting what Zionist discourse calls the 'demographic threat'. Today, international human rights norms require that all states provide citizenship to all people born and resident in their territory and provide equal rights to all citizens of the state. Full ethnic mixture in Israel–Palestine would therefore require that Palestinian Arab residents of the territory be granted civil rights; otherwise, Israel would become an apartheid state. As Palestinians comprise some 50 per cent of the combined population, however, enfranchising the entire population would spell the end of Jewish statehood, because Palestinians would be certain to seek changes in the Basic Law, public law and public policy that now privilege Jewish individuals and cultural life. The Palestinian electorate is also certain to seek the return and enfranchisement of Palestinian refugees, which would quickly tip the demographic balance even more decisively.

Hence the strictures Israel imposes to keep the populations apart do not arise fundamentally from the frontier dilemma – although these steer the precise tactics and geography of closures and separation – but from a basic imperative associated with Jewish statehood itself: that human rights norms and political exigencies of any mixed society in the twenty-first century require either the destruction of democracy (to preclude political voice by ethnic others) or dismantling ethnic domination. Thus Israel's surviving as a 'Jewish *and* democratic state' (the formula in Israel's Basic Law) requires that Palestinians be physically excluded from the polity. The same conundrum confronted the USA and Canada in the nineteenth century and 'White Australia' in the twentieth.

It may seem evident that this imperative should impel Israel to vacate the occupied territories precisely to protect itself from the demographic threat. Yet this logic misses the underlying dilemma, which can be summarised here briefly. Withdrawal is not enough to affect a stable two-state solution: a viable, stable and peaceful Palestinian state also requires open borders to develop its economy and normalise relations with its neighbours. The Palestinian state's main market would be Israel, the economic giant on its doorstep (and in whose territory the Palestinian state may indeed be geographically nested). But if Israel opens the borders to allow essential trade and other human movement, then ethnic mixing would ensue, particularly given old family and business ties of Palestinians with the Palestinian Arab population of Israel, which numbers about 1.3 million people. As noted earlier, in so small a country – especially one divided into gerrymandered cantons in densely populated areas – such mixing would imperil the social and ultimately the political separation that now secures the Jewish majority and its political dominance. Moreover, Israel's former dependency on Palestinian labour would quickly re-emerge. As in South Africa, labour dependency and daily peaceful social mixture would then tend to corrode the logic, psychology and ethos of separation. Therefore, Israel cannot open the borders on terms that accord with normal international practice and a stable two-state solution without unleashing socio-economic forces that would swiftly threaten and dismantle Israel's identity and character as a 'Jewish and democratic' state.

But if Israel does not open the borders, then development in the Palestinian state will be crippled. Since Palestinians are bound to resist crippling limitations resulting from closed borders, as they have in Gaza, Israel cannot give up control over security in West Bank Palestinian areas. Therefore, Israel cannot give the Palestinians a state that enjoys real sovereignty. Since Jewish settlements in the West Bank – with their exclusive ethnic zones and special highway system – presently ensure that the Palestinians cannot form a workable state, the settlement's core function is therefore to preclude a political future that would imperil the Jewish 'character' of Israel itself.

The fatal flaw in this strategy is the Palestinians' refusal to be forever deprived of full civil rights. Israel's solution to this problem, consistent with the imperative of ethnic demography noted above, can be interpreted from the conditions it put forward during the Oslo Accord negotiations.

Contrary to common beliefs, no agreement or accord in the Oslo process specified creation of a Palestinian state or withdrawal of the settlements. Rather, they proposed a sequence of reciprocal measures involving the designation of geographically nested 'areas' from which Israeli security forces would be progressively withdrawn and in which a 'Palestinian Interim Self-Governing Authority' would progressively assume responsibility. Progress from stage to stage was contingent on successfully completing each. That final status talks have not commenced is attributed by Israel to the Palestinian Authority's (PA) failure to suppress 'violence' (i.e. entirely suppress Palestinian resistance to the occupation). This explanation is contradicted, however, by the Israeli state's concomitant accelerated rate of settlement construction, which fosters that resistance. The true purpose of the Oslo framework from Israel's perspective therefore must come under fresh scrutiny in order to grasp how the settlements serve that purpose.

The term 'Palestinian Interim Self-Government Authority' (the full name of the Palestinian Authority as specified in the Oslo II Accord of 1995) provides a useful point of entry for this reassessment. Much of the international community, and certainly the great majority of Palestinians, interpreted 'interim', coupled with 'self-governing', as signifying a capacity- and institution-building process for Palestinian governance that would culminate in full Palestinian independence. In other words, the PA was understood to comprise a Palestinian proto-state charged with preparations for Palestinian sovereignty. The high mood of Palestinian optimism and energy associated with Palestinian state-building in the late 1990s reflected this interpretation.

In hindsight, however, more caution would have been advisable – again by noting the close parallels of Oslo with the Bantustan policy of South Africa.

Under apartheid, black 'self-government' was developed in the 1950s as a culminating juridical status for 'Black Authorities' who were assigned to govern black South Africans in designated areas, removing them from the ambit of civil rights and protections accorded to white citizens. In the late 1960s, international pressure inspired the apartheid regime to redefine black self-governance as a stage toward full 'independence'. By satisfying the white regime's criteria as spelled out in various legislation and constitutional documents, black South African authorities in the Homelands could gain the regime's recognition as 'states'. This status would ultimately deprive black people transferred to the Homelands of their South African citizenship, thus preserving a white majority and white domination in South Africa. As the white regime wished to ensure that black independence would never threaten white control over land, resources and trade, however, its version of 'independence' carefully fell short of granting powers and authority associated with full sovereignty. Self-government in the Black Homelands was instead a facsimile of sovereignty, which permitted a flag, national anthem, police force and even elections, but only within parameters set and monitored by white South Africa. The African National Congress (ANC) and United Democratic Front (the domestic civil movement against apartheid) accordingly rejected the Homelands as a fraud perpetrated on black Africans in order to deprive them of their inalienable rights to equal citizenship in South Africa.

No one negotiating or closely observing the Oslo Accords was alerted to this cautionary South African parallel at the time. Hence the Palestinian delegation did not recognise how closely the 'interim' arrangements for the PA were following the same track established for 'interim' self-rule by black Africans which culminated in the South African Bantustans.[16] For the purposes of this discussion, the similarities between Palestinian and black African self-rule can be grouped into four categories as follows.

Local and Private Authority

Authority of the PA is confined to local and civil affairs: agriculture, banking, education, electricity, fisheries, forests, land registration, the civil registry, the postal service, telecommunications, water and sewage, and so forth. Authority is denied over any matter, such as transportation or national resources that cross borders into territory designated for Jewish settlement, or that have economic or security implications for Israeli affairs. This arrangement closely parallels those for the South African Bantustans, where the authority of Homeland governments was similarly confined to agriculture, education, fisheries, forests, the civil registry and so forth, and was prevented from impacting development or interests in intervening white-owned lands and communities.

Plenary Power

The Oslo Accords provided Israel with plenary power over Palestinian governance in the cantons by placing authority for economic development, security, water and so forth with joint Palestinian–Israeli committees in which Israel holds a veto. South Africa sustained similar influence in the Homelands by requiring that all legislation be approved by a Minister or the President of the Republic.

Demilitarisation

The PA has responsibility for civil policing and security in the sense of the suppression of dissent but not defence. The PA has no authority or capacity to develop any military or security forces that can defend Palestinian territory against Israeli forces or incursions. They are also prohibited from exercising prosecutorial authority over Jewish civilians who commit offences in their territories. The Bantustans were similarly charged and limited.

Liminal Status

Although the PA has some powers of autonomy in the cantons under its authority, the cantons function as enclaves within territory in which Israel is the empirical sovereign, holding ultimate and exclusive control over the population, the land and its resources, and foreign policy. Nonetheless, the Oslo Accords make the PA responsible for security and other key governance issues. Imposing sovereign obligations on an 'Authority' that lacks sovereign powers confuses the international politics involved. It also confounds the application of international law governing belligerent occupation.[17]

In combination, these arrangements return the analysis of the settlements to their purpose. As apartheid South Africa attempted to preserve white supremacy by creating weak black 'states' in the Bantustans, Israel has sought to preserve Jewish statehood by confining Palestinian governance within a fragmented geography. In these enclaves, Palestinian authorities cannot assume any meaningful governance without permission from the state controlling the intervening territory and their external borders. Thus the Jewish settlements function to reify a geography of permanent conquest, in which not only the PA's territorial authority, but also its structural, juridical and political dependency and vulnerability, is permanently consolidated. It is not surprising, therefore, that the settlements are still being built, with state approval and according to state designs, with such vigour.

The Settlements and Israeli Sovereignty

The third essential function of Israeli settlements is implied by the previous discussion: how they implement Israel's subtle strategy regarding its sovereignty in the West Bank. Israel has not formally annexed the West Bank and does not call the territory 'Israel' in its public diplomacy. But in all other ways, Israel behaves as the rightful sovereign and asserts associated rights: for example, maintaining direct or ultimate control over all movement, natural resources (especially water), economic development, public planning, civil infrastructure, security, telecommunications and cyberspace, customs and tax duties, government maps and so forth. The result is empirical annexation: the seamless social, economic, legal and geographic integration of the West Bank settlement blocs into Israel, as noted earlier, such that the old armistice border is thoroughly effaced. In international critiques, this effect is seen as accidental and anachronistic: the settlements pre-empt a final peace agreement simply by creating irreversible 'facts on the ground' relevant to final borders. This interpretation is not contested here. But pending a final settlement in which juridical Israeli sovereignty is ultimately formalised, the settlements serve a vital interim function: to retain the land while insulating Israel from the onus of granting Palestinian citizenship.

The constraints on Israel's full juridical annexation of West Bank land are indeed not only – not even primarily – international opinion, Palestinian resistance and related political obstacles. Rather, juridical annexation would introduce a serious existential threat to Jewish statehood, also noted earlier, which is that full citizenship for all Palestinian residents in the territory under Israel's control would challenge and probably eradicate the Jewish character of Israel. The settlement strategy is therefore a method serving an overriding strategic imperative: Israel must control but postpone annexation of the West Bank until the Palestinians can be accorded citizenship in a Palestinian state and so permanently insulate Israel from their 'demographic threat'.

The settlements ensure this condition precisely by postponing juridical sovereignty while imposing empirical sovereignty. This is done partly by providing that the settlements serve Jews specifically, rather than Israelis, so that their planning and construction can be affected through partnership with the private settler movements such as the Yesha Council.[18] It is also done partly by employing a skilful discursive twist on human rights norms. Ignoring provisions of international humanitarian law that prohibit the transfer of the occupier's population into occupied territory, Israel's leadership has regularly insisted that Jews have an equal and inalienable right to settle in the West Bank, and that to prohibit Jewish settlement there would be discriminatory and thus even inadmissible on human rights grounds. Thus the power of the state, articulated through every government ministry budget as well as the security forces, is brought to plan, fund, supervise and defend 'private' Jewish settlement. Israeli law consolidates this support by applying Israeli civil law to Jewish settlers in the West Bank rather than the military law that applies to Palestinian civilians in the same territory.

The resulting liminality allows Israel to exclude Palestinian civilians in the West Bank and even Palestinian citizens of Israel from West Bank settlements, precisely because the settlements are not 'Israeli' in this context but explicitly 'Jewish'. Once the settlement blocs are annexed to Israel, the full body of civil rights becomes applicable and the settlements could come under challenge for ethnic discrimination. Thus Israel is not yet annexing settlement blocs formally to itself not simply because it lacks the diplomatic leverage to do so, but because the settlements cannot serve as effectively to confine Palestinians into cantons once Israel has done so. The enabling condition for Israeli annexation of the West Bank is indeed that the settlements remain formally outside Israel's sovereign territory until Palestinian 'self-government' in designated autonomy zones is finalised.

Conclusion

The challenge that settlements present to a stable peace in Israel–Palestine is not to mitigate their impact through border swaps, withdrawal or other final status arrangements. The challenge is to appreciate how their true purpose drives their permanence. Notions that the settlements can be withdrawn in the right context, as by providing Israel with appropriate security guarantees, miss that purpose. The settlements have always been associated by their planners with a strategy of permanent annexation, but in several ways they also operate to permit Israel's survival as a Jewish state. Any alteration to their construction thus presents an existential threat to Jewish statehood and is not a measure any Israeli government can consider undertaking. Accordingly, their withdrawal, handing them over to Palestinian sovereignty or any other solution that has been floated for eliminating their fatal impact on a two-state solution must be discarded as politically impossible.

Taking the South African experience as a cautionary tale, however, the Bantustan solution clearly presaged by the settlement grid will not be stable. Here it may be recalled that the Drobles Plan, albeit disingenuously, originally noted the same difficulty and spoke of a mixed ethnic landscape in territory that would have to be shared:

> Over the course of time, with or without peace, we will have to learn to live *with* the minorities and *among them*, while fostering good neighbourly relations – and they with us. It would be best for both peoples (Jewish and Arab) to learn this as early as possible, since when all is said and done the development and flowering of

the area will be to the benefit of *all* the residents of the land. Therefore the proposed settlement blocs are situated as a strip surrounding the (Judea and Samaria) ridge – starting from its western slopes from north to south, and along its eastern slopes from south to north: both *between* the minorities' population and *around* it.[19]

Such co-existence – essentially, a one-state vision – was negated by a fundamental contradiction: the settlement blocs were always defined as ethnically exclusive zones and so could be created and sustained only at the expense of the territorial contiguity of Palestinian cities and villages. Indeed, the settlements' very purpose was to eliminate that contiguity. Yet the contradiction remains that Bantustan geography can be enforced only by military strength and endless conflict. As in South Africa, it may remain for the international community to determine whether historic Palestine faces such a grim future or can shift its paradigm to seek a unified state, which proved to be South Africa's solution.

Notes

1. For an expanded discussion, see Virginia Q. Tilley, *The One-State Solution: A Breakthrough for Peace in the Israeli–Palestinian Deadlock* (Ann Arbor: University of Michigan Press, 2005), especially Chapters 2 and 3.

2. World Zionist Organization Department for Rural Settlement, 'Master plan for the development of settlement in Judea and Samaria 1979–1983' ('Drobles Plan'), reproduced in Tom Mallison and Sally Mallison, *The Palestinian Problem in International Law and World Order*, Appendix 11 (Essex, England: Longman, 1986), p. 446; also UN Doc. S./13582 Annex (22 October 1979).

3. Ibid., p. 447.

4. That 1949 Armistice Line is internationally recognised as the border of Israel was confirmed in the Oslo Accords, which provided that the 'West Bank and Gaza Strip' be considered one territorial unit for purposes of the process. The International Court of Justice confirmed the international status of the 'green line' in *Legality of the Construction of a Wall in the Occupied Palestinian Territories, Advisory Opinion*, ICJ Rep, 2004, at p. 136.

5. 'Transcript of remarks by Bush and Sharon on Israel', *New York Times*, 14 April 2004.

6. See, for example, Khaled Abu Toameh, 'Abbas: land swap principle reached', *Jerusalem Post*, 23 May 2010. Available at www.jpost.com/MiddleEast/Article. aspx?id=176148.

7. On regional water security, see collected studies in Hussein Amery and Aaron T. Wolf, *Water in the Middle East: A Geography of Peace* (Austin: University of Texas Press, 2000).

8. How the Israeli lobby operates in US politics is detailed in Tilley, *The One-State Solution*, Chapter 4. See also John J. Mearsheimer and Stephen M. Walt, *The Israeli Lobby and US Foreign Policy* (Farrar, Straus & Giraux, 2008); Edward Tivnan's historical study *The Lobby: Jewish Political Power and American Foreign Policy* (New York: Simon and Schuster, 1987); Paul Findlay's *They Dare to Speak Out: People and Institutions Confront Israel's Lobby* (Westport, CT: Lawrence Hill, 2003), third edition; Cheryl Rubenberg, *Israel and the American National Interest* (Urbana: University of

Illinois Press, 1986), pp. 329–76; and Michael Massing, 'The Israel lobby', *The Nation*, 10 June 2002.

9. See Meron Benvenisti, *Sacred Landscapes: The Buried History of the Holy Land since 1948* (Berkeley and Los Angeles: University of California Press, 2002). Peace Now and B'tselem, NGOs that have made special projects of tracking settlement growth, have distinguished between ideological settlers, 'quality of life' settlers, and ultra-Orthodox settlers who simply seek segregated housing: see Lara Friedman and Dror Etkes, 'Settlements in focus: quality of life settlers – January 2007'. Available at www.peacenow.org.il/site/en/peace.asp?pi=62&docid=2175.

10. For details on ministerial funding and collaboration with the WZO and settlement movements in building the Rehan Bloc in the northeastern West Bank, see *The One-State Solution*, p. 41; on Israeli State subsidies to West Bank settlements and settlers, see B'tselem, *Land Grab: Israel's Settlement Policy in the West Bank* (2007), Chapter 5, pp. 57–67. Available at www.btselem.org/English/Publications/Summaries/200205_Land_Grab.asp.

11. See summary statistics at the Jewish Virtual Library, 'The Jewish population in the West Bank and the Gaza Strip', which draws from the Israeli Central Bureau of Statistics, the Israeli Yearbook and Almanac and other sources. Available at www.jewishvirtual-library.org/jsource/Peace/settlepop.html.

12. On 'courageous decisions' see Yitzhak Rabin's Speech at the Signing Ceremony of the Peace Treaty between Israel and Jordan, 26 October 1994, and Speech to Tel Aviv Peace Rally, 4 November 1995: 'This is a course that is fraught with difficulties and pain. For Israel, there is no path that is without pain'. Available at www.mideastweb.org/rabin1995.htm.

13. See, for example, Jewish Agency for Israel, Settlement Department, Central District, and World Zionist Organization, Settlement Division, Central District, *Nahal-Eron Project: Five-Year Plan for the Development of the Eron-Reihan Region* (1988).

14. Observations of the security climate in the West Bank in the mid-1980s are personal observations of the author, drawn also from discussions with students at Birzeit University, an-Najah University and Bethlehem University.

15. The electoral mandate was provided in the 1995 Israeli–Palestinian Interim Agreement on the West Bank and the Gaza Strip, Annex II, Article 1(1). The provisions for Palestinian democratic government were later expanded as the Basic Law of Palestine (2003).

16. Specific provisions for the powers of the Palestinian Interim Self-Government Authority were provided in the second Oslo accord, *Israeli–Palestinian Interim Agreement on the West Bank and the Gaza Strip* (1995): see especially Annexes II and III. Information on the Bantustans in this section is drawn primarily from apartheid legislation: especially, the Transkei Constitution Act (#48) of 1963 and the Bantu Homelands Citizenship Act (#21) of 1971.

17. Article 47 of the Fourth Geneva Convention prohibits any change of status in occupied territory concluded through negotiations between the occupying power and local authorities under occupation. For a detailed analysis of how this provision applies to Israeli policy in the OPT, see Human Sciences Research Council, *Occupation, Colonialism, Apartheid: A Reassessment of Israeli Practices in the Occupied Palestinian Territories under International Law* (2009), pp. 71–81. Available at: www.hsrc.ac.za/Document-3202.phtml.

18. The Yesha Council is a private umbrella organisation for West Bank settlement councils that represents about half the settlers in the West Bank. Its mission and political orientation can be viewed on its website: www.myesha.org.il.

19. World Zionist Organization Department for Rural Settlement, 'Master Plan for the Development of Settlement in Judea and Samaria 1979–1983', op. cit., p. 447.

CHAPTER 3

A Racialised Space: The Future of Jerusalem[1]

Saree Makdisi

The Zionist project to remove or 'transfer' Palestinians from Palestine was a feature of the 1947–8 period. But it did not end in 1948; it continues up to the modern day. This chapter will demonstrate that Israeli policies in Jerusalem – which have systematically cut off and isolated Palestinian parts of the city from the West Bank and have imposed draconian measures on the Palestinian residents of the city intended to pressure even those who have not been formally stripped of their residency rights to give up and leave, while at the same time encircling Palestinian Jerusalem with a ring of Jewish settlements, thereby locking it infrastructurally to Israel – have effectively made a two-state solution impossible. On the one hand, even the Palestinian parts of the city are now so cut off from the rest of the occupied territories by Israeli infrastructure that Jerusalem could never serve as the capital of an independent Palestinian state (and without Jerusalem as capital there would be no such state, due to Palestinian attachment to and insistence upon keeping Jerusalem as the political, religious and social centre of a Palestinian state); on the other hand, the ring of colonies around Jerusalem – in which a quarter of a million Jewish settlers now reside – makes it difficult or impossible to sever occupied East Jerusalem from Israel. By making Jerusalem indivisible, in other words, Israel has all but guaranteed that historic Palestine itself is indivisible. The remaining options are either a continued and even more intensive system of the current discrimination against the Palestinians with two states, unequal in terms of power and resources, or the dismantling of the current system and the creation of a single state free from a singular racial or ethnic or religious claim to identity.

Ironically, then, precisely because it serves as the central hub of the Israeli project to displace and disenfranchise Palestinians, no space more profoundly demonstrates than Jerusalem the fact that, if Palestinians are to retain a viable presence in their ancestral land, it could only be within the framework of a single democratic and secular state. For the situation in Jerusalem illustrates abundantly the human cost required by a politics of racial separation and removal: as the space within which Palestinian individuals, families and communities live is socially engineered around them in the service of a logic of separation, their lives become impossible. Their continued survival in a social, cultural and political – if not literally a biological – sense is incompatible with the logic of separation and removal which is central to Zionist planning. If, in other words, manipulating the spaces and populations of Jerusalem as Israel has done since it captured East Jerusalem in 1967 (and with particular emphasis since its claim to have annexed it in 1980) means the destruction of Palestinian Jerusalem, the survival of Palestinian Jerusalem fundamentally requires an end to that manipulation and the racial politics of separation underlying and motivating it. In other words, nowhere more clearly than in Jerusalem is it demonstrable that the fulfilment of Zionist ambitions fundamentally requires the destruction of Palestinian communities and hence the destruction of the Palestinian claim to the land. Maintaining the Palestinian claim to Jerusalem and indeed to all of pre-1967 Israel – to which the Palestinian refugees consider they have an inalienable right to return and where Palestinians presently constitute a fifth of the population, a ratio that continues to grow – thus fundamentally requires the abandonment of the traditional form of Zionism and separate states. To state this positively rather than negatively: irrespective of what happens to the rest of the occupied territories, maintaining the Palestinian claim to, and life in, Jerusalem can only be secured within the context of a single, new, secular and de-racialised polity, one that does not privilege one community over another, and does not remove one kind of person to make room for another. One that is very different to the de facto single state we see today.

What we see in Jerusalem today is, on the contrary – with its basis in two separate states, and yet effectively under the control of only one – a methodically implemented policy of the replacement of one people by another. This logic is put into practice at two levels: the geographical (involving the reorganisation of social space) and the bureaucratic (involving the status and residency rights of individuals and families). This chapter will address both.

To understand Israel's geographical reorganisation of Jerusalem, it is necessary to understand that the city was divided during and after the war in 1948, during which Zionist forces removed hundreds of thousands of Palestinians in order to secure the space in which to create a Jewish state. When the fighting ended, the western part of the city had fallen under Israeli control. The eastern part, along with the rest of the West Bank, had come under Jordanian control. At that time, what was called East Jerusalem amounted to the area of the Old City and a few outlying neighbourhoods, totalling a little over two square miles. After the 1967 War, during which Israel captured East Jerusalem and the West Bank (as well as the Gaza Strip), the Israelis expanded the territorial dimensions of what they called Jerusalem by adding almost 27 square miles of West Bank land to the city's municipal borders.[2] In 1980, they also claimed to annex this additional land to Israel (an act not recognised by other states or the United Nations). In fact, over 90 per cent of the eastern part of what the official Israeli slogan refers to as 'the eternal and undivided capital of the Jewish people' actually consists of land thus added to Jerusalem after 1967.[3] According to international law, this land has exactly the same status as the West Bank: it is militarily occupied territory, not subject to unilateral annexation.[4]

The land that Israel added to Jerusalem was taken from 28 Palestinian villages in the West Bank and was, in most cases, the property of the people of those villages rather than of (Palestinian) Jerusalemites. In some cases, whole villages and their populations were annexed to Jerusalem. In most cases, however – and certainly wherever geographically possible – the Israeli planners drew the new, expanded municipal boundaries of Jerusalem up to the houses of outlying Palestinian towns and villages in such a way that the towns' orchards, olive groves and pastures were placed on one side of the boundary (inside Jerusalem), while the houses and people were placed on the other side (outside Jerusalem). According to Meron Benvenisti, the delineation of the city's municipal borders after 1967 was explicitly designed to incorporate 'a maximum of vacant space with a minimum of Arabs'.[5]

The Israeli attempt to incorporate Arab land without Arabs often produced anomalous results. The town of Nu'man, for example, was annexed to municipal Jerusalem when the borders were redrawn in 1967, but its inhabitants were classified as residents of the West Bank.[6] Over the years, they filed numerous appeals with the Israeli Ministry of the Interior to change their status to residents of Jerusalem, since their town had been absorbed within the expanded municipal borders. The Ministry consistently rejected these appeals. As a result, the residents of the village, who are technically residents of the West Bank, are considered by Israeli law to be 'persons staying illegally in Jerusalem', because that is where their houses were after the Israelis redrew the municipal borders. They have spent over 40 years living under constant threat of expulsion (the penalty they face according to Israeli regulations). They are also cut off from the infrastructure and services of Jerusalem. Access to educational, medical and infrastructural services such as water tie the village to the West Bank – but, because the town itself is 'inside' Jerusalem, all these arrangements are illegal and subject to interdiction.

The initial post-1967 expansion of Jerusalem was a matter of lines drawn on paper. Palestinian residents were able to cross these lines until the beginning of the so-called peace process in the mid-1990s, when Israel first institutionalised the separation of the different segments of the occupied territories from each other (and further subdivided each of the territories internally as well – breaking the West Bank up, as the Oslo Accords of the mid-1990s specified, into Areas A, B and C, and often isolating each Palestinian town or village from the rest of the territory).[7] Henceforth, the Gaza Strip and the West Bank were cut off from each other, from Israel and from East Jerusalem, which had until then been the focal point of Palestinian life. So, before the Oslo Accords, Palestinian farmers from 'outside' Jerusalem could still physically access their land 'inside' Jerusalem. Today, however, the Israelis have constructed 104 miles of the separation wall in and around East Jerusalem, physically cutting it off from the West Bank. What had once been a line on a map is today a formidable *physical* obstacle, cementing the future of the two states as being trapped in a dynamic of being separate and unequal.

According to a UN report published in July 2007, the wall's route in and near Jerusalem runs deep into the West Bank to encompass the large Jewish settlements near the city, while excluding densely populated Palestinian areas that are currently inside the municipal boundary.[8] In addition, the wall runs through the middle of Palestinian communities in municipal Jerusalem, separating neighbours and families from one another. There are today only 12 gates allowing access to Jerusalem through the wall. Of these gates, only four are even theoretically accessible to West Bank residents, who must go through a long process to obtain a permit from the Israelis in order to enter Jerusalem. In point of fact, an entire generation of West Bank Palestinians has never seen Jerusalem and the sites holy to their religions (including the Church of the Holy Sepulchre and the Dome of the Rock).

Israel's denying Palestinians access to their sites of worship is a violation of international law, as is denying them freedom of movement within and between the occupied territories in general. It is important to note that no such regulation on movement applies to Jewish settlers, who come and go quite freely between Israel, Jerusalem and the West Bank. For the few Palestinians who do obtain permits, crossing the wall into Jerusalem can easily take a couple of hours in either direction. 'A Palestinian pedestrian crossing the checkpoint to Jerusalem [at Qalandia] must first follow a passageway bordered by metal fences,' a recent UN report points out:

> Upon entering the checkpoint, five turnstiles or revolving gates have to be crossed by each person before an identification check is made. Only one person can go through these electric gates at a time. From a hidden post, a soldier surveying the area from a television screen can stop the movement of the turnstiles at any time. When the ID check is made, a security scan of any belongings that are being carried is completed.

There is, the report adds, no human contact between Palestinians and Israeli soldiers: 'The soldiers are seated in booths, surrounded by reinforced glass.

Communication between the soldiers and people crossing is carried out primarily by a speaker system or people are addressed in certain cases through the glass.'[9]

Until the advent of the 'peace process' in the mid-1990s, Arab Jerusalem existed as part of a continuum with the Palestinian communities around it, in the way in which urban centres are tied to surrounding towns and the wider countryside everywhere. Not only do tens of thousands of Palestinians with Jerusalem residency papers work in Jerusalem while living in areas that will soon be (or already are) on the other side of the wall; many Jerusalem Palestinians also work in places in the West Bank, particularly Ramallah.

Today, however, Israel's wall has cut off a quarter of Jerusalem's Palestinian population from the city.[10] According to the 2007 UN report, the wall's route 'runs deep into the West Bank to encircle the large [Jewish] settlements of Givat Ze'ev (pop. 11,000) and Ma'ale Adumim (pop. 28,000), which are currently outside the municipal boundary'. The report goes on to note:

> By contrast, densely populated Palestinian areas – Shu'fat Camp, Kafr Aqab, and Samiramees, with a total population of over 30,000, which are currently inside the municipal boundary, are separated from Jerusalem by the Barrier. Other villages to the north and east of the city, with populations of more than 84,000, are also excluded. In addition, the Barrier runs through the middle of Palestinian communities, separating neighbours and families from one another – this happens in Abu Dis, for example.

North of the city, but still inside the redrawn municipal limits, the wall and a bypass road completely encircle the 15,000 Palestinians living in four villages near Bir Nabala. They can only access the outside world through a tunnel.

Moreover, the wall has greatly worsened the economic prospects facing Palestinians in East Jerusalem which used to be the commercial heart of Palestinian life. Many Palestinian businesses in Jerusalem rely for their supplies, or their commercial survival, on open linkages with the West Bank hinterland. But the wall prevents normal movement of people and goods and has forced Palestinians to alter their economic habits completely. Bringing goods to market from the West Bank to East Jerusalem now involves in effect importing them across an international frontier into Israel – even though the actual international frontier is miles to the west of the wall. Crossing the new 'frontier' requires using the 'back-to-back' system and paying various import taxes. Most small shopkeepers can't afford such expenses. Even if they can, many of their customers are no longer able to reach them. According to the 2007 UN report, for example, Palestinians in Abu Dis used to shop for fruits and vegetables in the markets of neighbouring East Jerusalem; they now must go much further to Bethlehem. Similarly, Palestinians in the suburb of al-Ram now have to shop in Ramallah rather than Jerusalem. Almost 300 shops there have been forced to close in recent years. The East Jerusalem unemployment rate is approaching 20 per cent, compared to around 8 per cent in Israel. The damage done by Israel's separation wall has been just as bad, or worse, for Palestinian communities around Jerusalem now cut off by the wall, which used to depend on the patronage of Palestinians from Jerusalem. Over half the shops in the formerly prosperous al-Ram closed after the wall went up.

Meanwhile, hundreds of thousands of Palestinians in the Jerusalem suburbs and beyond, in the rest of the West Bank, depend on medical services offered by the six Palestinian hospitals in East Jerusalem, such as al-Makassed and Augusta Victoria, which have no equivalent in the West Bank. According to the UN, the number of West Bank and Gaza patients able to access medical facilities in East Jerusalem fell by half between 2002 and 2003, and has continued to decline since then. Al-Makassed Hospital reported a 50 per cent drop in emergency room treatments after the wall went up around Jerusalem – from 33,000 in 2002 to 17,000 in 2005. The St John Eye Hospital also reported a dramatic fall in treatments. Augusta Victoria Hospital, too, registered a one-third drop in its patient load once tightened Israeli controls over Palestinian access to East Jerusalem went into effect. Patients who cannot access these hospitals have no alternatives; without access to East Jerusalem, they simply do not receive the medical treatment they need. Furthermore, more than two-thirds of the hospital's staff are West Bank residents; they must now apply for permits from the Israelis in order to get to work, and since the number of permits that Israel issues varies from month to month, key staff are sometimes unable to get to the hospital at all.[11]

At the same time, thousands of Palestinian students living in East Jerusalem attend classes in schools and colleges which now lie on the other side of the wall in Abu Dis. Every morning, these students face an unpleasant choice: they can try to find ways over, under or around the wall separating Abu Dis from Jerusalem; or they can risk the traffic jams, roadblocks and checkpoints studding the long roundabout route that would take them all the way around Jerusalem and halfway to Jericho before snaking its way back to Abu Dis, near to where they live in East Jerusalem. The wall has also complicated the pursuit of normal family life, separating cousins, nephews, uncles, aunts, grandparents and – in one family out of every five living east of the wall – one parent or another from the rest of the family. According to the UN, a quarter of Jerusalem's Palestinians will find themselves on the east side of the wall when it is finally completed.

However, Israel's geographical reorganisation of Jerusalem by such mechanisms as the wall is only one half of the project to 'Judaise' and 'de-Arabise' the city – to 'de-Palestinise' it, as John Dugard, the former Special Rapporteur on Human Rights in the occupied territories, put it.[12] The other half of the project involves bureaucratic procedures structured by the enforced differentiation between Jews and non-Jews, and the replacement of the latter by the former. According to current or former Israeli officials of the municipality of Jerusalem, the distinction between establishing homes for Jews and denying them to non-Jews has been essential to city planning since 1967. 'A cornerstone in the planning of Jerusalem is the demographic question,' noted Israel Kimchi, director of planning policy for the Municipality of Jerusalem, in 1977:

> the city's growth and the preservation of the demographic balance among its ethnic groups was a matter decided by the Government of Israel. That decision, concerning the city's rate of growth, today serves as one of the criteria for the success of the process of Jerusalem's consolidation as the capital of Israel.[13]

Amir Cheshin, former Israeli advisor on Arab affairs to the mayor of Jerusalem, explains:

> The planning and building laws in East Jerusalem rest on a policy that calls for placing obstacles in the way of planning in the Arab sector – this is done more to preserve the demographic balance between Jews and Arabs in the city, which is presently in a ratio of 72 per cent Jews against 28 per cent non-Jews.[14]

As the percentage of Jews to non-Jews (i.e. Palestinians) began sliding away from the desired ratio, Israeli policy-makers struggled to devise ways to reverse the trend, with the 72:28 ratio firmly in mind as a desirable outcome.

Thus, for example, although Palestinians today comprise 28 per cent of Jerusalem's population, they have access to less than 10 per cent of the land within the redefined city limits. Of the territory annexed to Jerusalem in 1967 – all of it Palestinian land – 90 per cent is today off-limits to Palestinian development because the land is either already built on by Jewish settlements or being held in reserve for their future expansion.[15] Even while doing everything possible to encourage and facilitate the Jewish settlement-building in East Jerusalem, the municipality tries to prevent Palestinian construction in the city, routinely denying building and construction permits to Palestinian residents of Jerusalem. Since 1967, over 100,000 housing units have been built for Jewish settlers in East Jerusalem, with active Israeli government sponsorship – all of it in violation of international law (and specifically the Fourth Geneva Convention's prohibition on population transfers). Over the same period, the municipality has granted only 9,000 permits for housing units for Jerusalem Palestinians.

One inevitable result of all the official bureaucratic limitations and controls on Palestinian growth and development in Jerusalem is a turn to what Israel considers to be 'illegal' construction. Thousands of housing units have been built without official permits by Palestinians since 1967. But this is done at considerable risk. Between 2004 and 2008 alone, over 400 Palestinian homes in Jerusalem were demolished by Israeli authorities.[16] There are today around 9,000 Palestinian homes that have been built 'illegally' in Jerusalem, all of them subject to demolition.

But severe curtailment of Palestinian construction is only one of the bureaucratic methods Israel uses to limit the non-Jewish population of the city. Just as Israeli policy has led to the physical fragmentation of the occupied territories through the construction of walls and roads and the maintenance of roadblocks and checkpoints in the West Bank, it has also redefined personal and family identity as well, according to a parallel (and mutually reinforcing) schema. Being classified as belonging to one or another of the external spaces divided up by Israel has a decisive influence on a Palestinian's private and family life, and the nature, privacy and security of their home, even its vulnerability to demolition by the state. For a Palestinian living under Israeli rule, there is a tremendous difference between being classified as a Jerusalem resident and being classified as a West Banker, a Gazan or a citizen of the state (and, similarly, among inhabitants of the West Bank themselves there are, for example, major differences among residents of the so-called seam zone between the 1949 Armistice Line and the barrier, residents of the Jordan Valley and residents of Nablus: each further subdivision of exterior space comes with its own peculiar forms of interior restriction).

Jerusalem residency does not carry the benefits of Israeli citizenship such as those enjoyed to a limited extent by Palestinian citizens of Israel (who, despite their nominal citizenship, live under the pressures of an extraordinary system of racial discrimination as non-Jews in the would-be Jewish state, which explicitly reserves various rights and privileges, including immigration, access to land and certain marriage benefits, exclusively for Jews, whether they are citizens or not). But a Jerusalem identity card allows a Jerusalem Palestinian a degree of freedom of movement unobtainable for a West Banker or Gazan since the advent of the so-called 'peace process'. So for a Palestinian, a Jerusalem identity card offers a kind of middle-ground between the (second-class) citizenship of Palestinian citizens of Israel and the more stark restricted life of West Bankers and Gazans. It is, however, Israel rather than the PA that decides what identity is conferred on which Palestinian, and they make the decision on the basis of criteria that have little connection with the particular or family circumstances of the individual person in question, but rather according to the division and control of external space based on Israel's own political and territorial claims. It is for precisely this reason that Israel continues to control the official population registries of the West Bank and Gaza, as such undermining the PA's supposed autonomy.

In keeping with these forms of regulation of Palestinian life, Israel's quest to maintain a certain proportion of Jews to non-Jews in Jerusalem begins literally *at birth*. For example, a Jewish baby born in Jerusalem (or for that matter in Israel or in Israeli settlements in the occupied territories) is automatically granted a birth certificate and a state identity number, which, like a US Social Security number, is one of the keys to life in Israel. On the other hand, a Palestinian baby born in Jerusalem is not automatically granted the same status as a Jewish baby. If one of the Palestinian infant's parents is a resident of the West Bank rather than Jerusalem, the parents will be given a 'Notification of Live Birth', but neither an official birth certificate (a different document) nor an identity number. The parents can use the Notification of Live Birth to complete a second-ary application for the child's birth certificate, but they will still not be granted an identity number. 'Parents going to the Ministry to obtain a birth certificate and record the child's name in their identity cards are not always aware that the child does not have an identity number,' a joint B'Tselem and HaMoked report points out:

> [Interior] Ministry clerks do not inform them that they must initiate the process of registering the child, but rather issue a birth certificate without an identity number for the child. Only parents who themselves note that the child does not have an identity number submit a request to register the child.[17]

If the Palestinian child's parents notice that the number is missing, they can apply for a number as a tertiary procedure. However, any of these subsequent applications may require evidence that the family resides in Jerusalem and that Jerusalem is their 'centre of life', which no Jewish family is ever asked to substantiate. If not all the required documents are available or in exact accordance with the stringent Israeli standard of proof, not only will the child be denied an identity number, but the entire family could be expelled from Jerusalem.

This raises another issue. In the mid-1990s, thousands of Palestinians from Jerusalem were trapped by a new Israeli regulation designed to strip Jerusalem Palestinians of their Jerusalem residency papers if they were unable to prove that Jerusalem was and had always and continuously been their 'centre of life'.[18] Palestinians from Jerusalem who could not prove that the city had always continuously been their 'centre of life' might permanently forfeit their right to live there. And since only those Palestinians with Jerusalem residency papers could enter Jerusalem – West Bankers are denied access unless they hold permits, which are extraordinarily difficult to obtain, and for Gazans such permits are virtually impossible to obtain – they would not only be barred by the Israelis from living in the city in which they were born: they would be unable to visit Jerusalem ever again. This would apply to a Palestinian who had gone abroad for a few years to study at a foreign university, to a Palestinian who had found a job in the suburban West Bank, to a Palestinian who had married someone from the West Bank or Gaza, or to a Palestinian who had been forced to rent or buy an apartment in the West Bank because they found it impossible to rent, buy or build a home in Jerusalem proper.

Israel's bureaucratic control of Palestinian life was perfectly expressed in a draconian law passed by the Israeli parliament in 2003, prohibiting Palestinian residents of the occupied territories who are married to Israeli citizens or Jerusalem residents from acquiring Israeli citizenship or residency status – and thus barring them from living with their spouses and their children in Israel or Jerusalem.[19] The law covered children as well as spouses: at the age of 14, the children of Jerusalem Palestinians whose birth was – for whatever reason, including the extreme difficulty of registering in East Jerusalem – registered in the West Bank had to apply for special military permits to go on living with their parents in Jerusalem. Reaching the age of majority, the children would have to leave their parents – or the parents would have to leave Jerusalem along with their children. The law did not affect Jewish residents of the occupied territories (i.e. settlers), or immigrant Jewish spouses of Israeli citizens, who were eligible for instant citizenship under the Law of Return, or, in fact, any Jews at all: it was only directed at Palestinian citizens of Israel and residents of Jerusalem and the occupied territories. Up to 24,000 Palestinian families were affected by the new Israeli law, which has threatened marriages and destroyed families by forcing them apart.

Of course, while one branch of the Israeli Ministry of the Interior revokes Jerusalem Palestinians' right to live in the city of their birth and ancestry, another branch of the same ministry grants instant citizenships to Jews from anywhere in the world who can establish a claim to being Jewish (or at least a claim in keeping with the current theological standards, which are debated in Israel from time to time). So, while Palestinians were being forced to leave Jerusalem in the 1990s, their places were being taken by Jewish immigrants, who had never before set eyes on the city, from Moldova and Russia – about a million of whom were granted entry to and citizenship in Israel, simply because they were Jewish.

After various legal challenges, some of the Palestinians whom Israel had stripped of their Jerusalem residency rights in the 1990s had them quietly restored after the new policy was suspended in 2000. However, the policy was, also quietly, reintroduced, and made more effective by the even more vigilant Israeli policing of entry into Jerusalem made possible through the construction of the wall. Between 1967 and 2006, Israel stripped a total of 8,269 Jerusalem Palestinians of their residency. In 2006 alone, Israel stripped 1,363 Jerusalem Palestinians of their right to live in the city: a number six times greater than the previous year.[20] At the time, that was the highest annual number ever, but Israel has renewed with greater vigour its campaign to strip Palestinians of Jerusalem residency since then, affecting a total of 5,583 Palestinians just in the two years from 2007 to 2009 – and the number of victims of this policy continues to rise.[21]

Removing Palestinians is, of course, only one side of the coin of 'Judaising' Jerusalem, of which the other is implanting a new Jewish population in East Jerusalem. A succession of Israeli governments has ordered five major waves of expropriation in and around Jerusalem, taking land from its Palestinian owners and giving it over to exclusively Jewish areas. Today there are dozens of Jewish settlements in the West Bank and East Jerusalem – every one of them (and not merely the 'illegal outposts' that one hears about from time to time) implanted in violation of international law – with a combined total population of almost half a million people. Because they were geographically distributed in order to maximise Israel's territorial claims – in order to make it as difficult as possible to ever withdraw them – they now blanket the entire territory. According to a UN report published in 2007, the population of Jewish settlers in the occupied territories is increasing at a rate three times that of Israel within its pre-1967 borders; it will double to a million in the next decade. This population is undoubtedly the most formidable 'fact on the ground' created by Israeli policy over the last four decades.

What is at stake here, of course, is Israel's desire to consolidate its claim that Jerusalem is, as the official Israeli government slogan has it, 'the eternal and undivided capital of the Jewish people'. The process of consolidating the Jewish claim to Jerusalem excludes the Palestinian claim to the city. It is the framework of the two separate states which established and then has further compounded this problem.

Notes

1. This paper is adapted from the discussion of Jerusalem in the author's book *Palestine Inside Out: An Everyday Occupation* (New York: WW Norton, 2008).

2. See *Foundation for Middle East Peace. Greater Jerusalem: A Special Report* (Washington, DC: Foundation for Middle East Peace, Summer 1997); B'Tselem, *A Policy of Discrimination: Land Expropriation, Planning and Building in East Jerusalem*, May 1995; Jeff Halper, 'The three Jerusalems and their role in the occupation', *Jerusalem Quarterly*, File 15, 2002; and Meron Benvenisti, *City of Stone: The Hidden History of Jerusalem* (Berkeley: University of California Press, 1996).

3. B'Tselem, ibid.; and B'Tselem. *The Quiet Deportation Continues: Revocation of Residency and Denial of Social Rights of East Jerusalem Residents*, September 1998.

4. Figures from B'Tselem. See www.btselem.org/english/Planning_and_Building/East_Jerusalem_Statistics.asp.

5. Benvenisti, op. cit.

6. B'Tselem, *Nu'man, East Jerusalem: Life Under the Threat of Expulsion*, 2003.

7. See Danny Siedmann, *The separation wall and the abuse of security* (Washington, DC: Foundation for Middle East Peace, 8 December 2004); Amira Hass, 'East Jerusalemites will need permits to visit Ramallah', *Ha'aretz*, 25 January 2005; Amira Hass, 'Separating Jerusalem from the West Bank', *Ha'aretz*, 26 January 2005; Amira Hass, 'IDF said changing its checkpoint policy', *Ha'aretz*, 29 March 2005; Amira Hass,

'Palestinians also sleep in the day', *Ha'aretz*, 31 March 2005; and Meron Rappaport, 'Government decision strips Palestinians of their East Jerusalem property', *Ha'aretz*, 20 January 2005.

8. UN Office for the Coordination of Humanitarian Affairs (UN OCHA). *The humanitarian impact of the West Bank wall on Palestinian communities: East Jerusalem*, June 2007.

9. UN OCHA, *Access to Jerusalem – new military order limits West Bank Palestinian access*, February 2006.

10. UN OCHA, June 2007, op. cit.

11. UN OCHA, 2007, ibid.; UN OCHA 2006, op. cit.; and B'Tselem, *Forbidden Families: Family Unification and Child Registration in Jerusalem*, January 2004.

12. John Dugard, *Report of the Special Rapporteur on the Situation of Human Rights in the Palestinian Territories Occupied Since 1967*, UN Human Rights Council, 29 January 2007.

13. B'Tselem, 1995, op. cit.

14. B'Tselem, ibid.

15. UN Office for the Coordination of Humanitarian Affairs, *The planning crisis in East Jerusalem: understanding the phenomenon of 'Illegal' construction*, April 2009.

16. See NGO Report: Suggested Issues for Consideration Regarding Israel's Combined 10th, 11th, 12th and 13th Periodic Report to the UN Committee on the Elimination of Racial Discrimination (Adalah, 15 December 2005); Parallel Report Jointly Submitted to the UN Committee on the Elimination of All Forms of Racial Discrimination, 69th Session, Geneva (Al Haq and other human rights NGOs in Israel/Palestine, July 2006); and Concluding Observations of the [UN] Committee on the Elimination of Racial Discrimination (International Convention on the Elimination of all Forms of Racial Discrimination, March 2007).

17. B'Tselem, 2004, op. cit.; B'Tselem and HaMoked, *The quiet deportation continues: revocation of residency and denial of social rights of East Jerusalem residents*, September 1998; and Amnesty International, *Torn apart: families split by discriminatory policies*, July 2004.

18. Badil Resource Center for Palestinian Residency and Refugee Rights, *Eviction, restitution, and protection of Palestinian rights in Jerusalem*, 1999; *Economist*, 'A capital question', 10 May 2007; and B'Tselem and HaMoked, 1998, op. cit.

19. Also see figures provided by B'Tselem on its website.

20. *Economist*, 2007, op. cit.

21. See updated statistics on B'Tselem website: www.btselem.org/jerusalem/revocation_statistics.

CHAPTER **4**

Building a Palestinian State Under Occupation: Reassessing the Oslo Process

Husam Said Zomlot

Introduction

When final talks broke down at the Camp David summit in the summer of 2000, effectively ending the Oslo peace process, Palestinian president Yasser Arafat returned not to Tunisia but to his Ramallah headquarters, to be confined there by Israeli Prime Minister Ariel Sharon's government until his death in 2004. By then, 'state-building' *despite* occupation had become the PA's *modus vivendi*, and a defining and fixed feature of Palestinian political, economic and social realities. By means of inclusion and/or exclusion, it defined, confined and to a large extent shaped Palestinian experiences and interactions, creating further rifts between the Diaspora and those living inside historic Palestine, between the West Bank and Gaza and 1948 Palestinians, and between Fateh and Hamas. Premised on the Oslo Agreements and reliant on a Western-led extensive and sustained aid programme, it also came to define Palestinian politics in relation to Israel and the international community.

However, while Palestinian 'state-building' in the Oslo context was and still is considered a prerequisite for statehood, its existence and persistence were by no means conditional upon the creation of the state it supposedly served. What was initiated as a transitory 'trust building measure' for a five-year interim period (1994–9) became permanent, with no horizon in sight as far as a final political settlement with Israel was concerned.

One of Oslo's major tenets was that Palestinian statehood should be largely dependent on the ability to establish and sustain 'governmental' institutions that were able to provide social services (health, education, impose law and order, etc.) to the vast majority of the Palestinian population in the West Bank and

Gaza, and provide security for Israel, while the latter retained overall control of territory, security, borders and resources. This approach was packaged by the Oslo Declaration of Principles (DoP) in terms of 'trust building measures'. In other words, the onus was put on Palestinians to prove state worthy (and this remains the case today).

This placed Palestinians in an unmatched, peculiar situation and ran against the basic principle of the state formation concept. State-building – as was the case for post-colonial state formation processes in general and in the Arab world in particular – is not an act designed to attain statehood, but an outcome of it, whereas in the Palestinian case, post-Oslo state-building predicated statehood and with no time limit on the realisation of a state. Despite the initiation of several peace plans (the Road Map, Annapolis and the ongoing efforts of the Obama administration) following the breakdown of the Camp David talks and the eruption of the second intifada in 2000 – which effectively ended the Oslo peace process – the Oslo interim agreements remain, to date, the only texts that govern and dictate Palestinian politics and relations internally, with Israel and with the international community. To Palestinian state-builders, this formula (state-building as a preface to statehood) assumed a negative correlation between Palestinian 'state-building' and Israeli occupation. That is, that the stronger the former, the weaker the latter. To Israel, however, Palestinian 'state-building' under their grip served a very different purpose. It maintained the status quo, placed the Palestinians in a political and legal limbo, removed the demographic 'threat' and relieved Israel from its responsibility under international law to provide for the occupied population.

Moreover, Palestinian state-building did not hinder Israel in its seizures of territory in the form of settlements, walls, bypass roads and the like. According to the PLO Negotiation Affairs Department, almost 500,000 Jewish settlers currently live in the West Bank, including East Jerusalem, up from 240,000 at the start of the Oslo process in 1993,[1] and the route of Israel's separation barrier built inside the occupied territories restricts Palestinians in the West Bank and the Gaza Strip to less than 12 per cent of historic Palestine.[2] Clearly, Palestinian state-building did not slow, let alone stop, Israel's settlement building in the land that is supposed to be the base for the state to come. Nor did the PA lessen Israel's ability to control almost all aspects of Palestinian life, including the internal movement of people and goods, natural resources and border control, not to mention military incursions into 'Palestinian areas' at will.

This situation, untenable for most Palestinians, is exacerbated further by the Fateh/Hamas schism, which is not over major differences with regard to how to resolve the conflict with Israel (both call for a Palestinian state on the 1967 borders and a resolution to the refugee issue), but rather consists of a power struggle over who should control the apparatuses of the 'state' under occupation.

A growing minority among Palestinians publicly demand the dissolution of the PA as they see state-building under existing circumstances to be a burden on their national project and a strategic weakness that only serves state-builders (e.g. The Palestine Strategy Study Group 2008). Yet state-building, as embodied by the PA, is uncontested by the mainstream political factions. This is due to three main factors. First, state-builders are empowered by the international momentum that is currently gathering pace following the US administration's declared intention to broker a final agreement during Obama's first term. Second, at present there is no viable alternative. The PA emerged in the post-Oslo period as the only institutionalised and internationally recognised Palestinian 'entity', in effect substituting the PLO and reducing it to a historic symbol. Finally, and most relevant to the discussion of this chapter, the PA is the main recipient of generous and sustained external aid (the post-Oslo Western-led international aid programme).

Between 1994 and 2000, the PA received US$3.4 billion in external financial aid, an annual average of around US$500 million.[3] However, external assistance not only continued, but also multiplied following the collapse of the Oslo process and the eruption of the second intifada. In 2008 alone, the PA requested US$2.15 billion (US$1.85 billion in international assistance to cover its recurrent expenditures, plus US$300 million in development aid). It received US$1.25 billion between January and August 2008, accounting for one-third of the West Bank and Gaza gross domestic product – an alarming ratio by any standard.[4] At an international donor conference held in Paris on 17 December 2007, the PA sought US$5.6 billion to support its three-year Reform and Development Plan entitled 'Building a Palestinian State'. While figures are still incomplete and largely contested, it was widely reported that the international community's financial pledges exceeded US$7 billion. Tony Blair, who co-chaired the event for the Quartet of Middle East peacemakers, said it was about 'state-building, not just raising the US$5.6 billion the Palestinian Authority was seeking'.[5] Blair's logic, as in the Oslo interim period, was that international financial contributions aim to lay the foundations for the Palestinian state to emerge – a contested logic to say the least.

While rentierism is often associated with oil-producing countries, the PA resembles a rentier state in the sense that it does not solely depend on extracting internal revenues (taxation) and therefore becomes less responsive to the needs of its 'citizens', as the latter have fewer incentives to challenge it.[6] Instead, by developing the distributive capacity of the state (health, education, social services), it gains what Mann coins as 'infrastructural power', the state through its apparatuses develops a redistributive capacity 'to penetrate civil society, and to implement logistically political decisions throughout the realm'.[7]

Despite the pledging of around US$5 billion for 'rebuilding Gaza' at the Sharm Al Sheikh donor conference – held on 2 March 2009 following the destruction that resulted from Israel's attack on Gaza in December 2008 and January 2009 – the reconstruction project and the promised international financial support remained unfulfilled to date. This was primarily due to Israel's refusal to lift the siege on Gaza, but also due to Hamas' refusal to accept that international assistance to Gaza would go through the Ramallah-based PA.

This chapter seeks to place the post-Oslo Western-led aid programme in the context of Palestinian state-building before and after Oslo. In so doing, it will examine the framework of post-Oslo state-building and trace its development since 1969, highlighting the inherent tensions between state-building on the one hand and the notion of resistance and nation-building on the other. Critiquing the post-Oslo international aid programme, it will assess its framework, political and economic assumptions and institutional settings. It will go on to consider the implications of and draw lessons from the prospects of Palestinian/Israeli peace-making and the role of the international community.

Palestinian State-building Since 1969

Blamed for repeated strategic and tactical blunders, the post-1967 Palestine national movement contributed to:

1. the affirmation of a Palestinian national identity;
2. the mobilisation of a mass movement;
3. the consolidation of a recognised and representative Palestinian entity (the PLO);
4. the creation of a common political arena; and
5. the 'initiation of a process of quasi-state-building'.[8]

The latter – 'state-building' – has come to define Palestinian politics more than any other feature of Palestinian nationalism. Insofar as state-like systems and apparatuses for the purpose of centralising and institutionalising power and the provision of services to mass constituencies have been in operation, the Palestine national movement has been engaged in state-building since 1969. While the Palestinian experience has shared in aspects of post-colonial state formation processes witnessed in neighbouring Arab countries,[9] it has been distinct insofar as state-building has taken place in the absence of a state, in exile (1969–93) and under Israel's reconstructed occupation since 1994.

On the one hand, the pre-Oslo 'state in exile' undertaking was a *voluntary* act that served several crucial functions including reinforcing Palestinian identity and entity by providing for the 'citizens' of the state-to-come, 'territorialising Palestinian nationalism', and consolidating the power and legitimacy of the post-1967 political elite.[10] On the other hand, however, post-Oslo state-building has been an *obligatory* exercise dictated by the terms of the Oslo Accord and the interim agreements.

The Oslo Declaration of Principles (DoP), signed between Israel and the PLO on 13 September 1993, was anything but a final agreement. Rather, it was an agreement between the two parties to defer the main political issues such as 'Jerusalem, refugees, settlements, security arrangements, borders, relations and cooperation with other neighbours'.[11] The DoP stipulated a five-year transitional period during which negotiations would determine the implementation of the DoP and arrangements for the transitional period, and the Oslo process adopted an incremental approach whereby this five-year interim period would serve as a bridge towards final status issues. A gradual transfer of authorities and responsibilities to the Palestinians was supposed to take place in an environment of 'trust-building' and economic development, as ordinary Palestinians were made to realise the agreement's 'peace dividends'.[12] Thus, the 'breakthrough' at Oslo was reached by separating the interim settlement from the final settlement[13] – a proposition that the Palestinian delegation at the Madrid peace talks had adamantly refused.[14] The separation between temporary 'state-building' under occupation and a permanent political settlement has remained firm to date.

Hovsepian defines state formation as the 'historical process through which ruling elites seek to construct local identity, insure social cohesion, and gain support from the ruled'.[15] More radical definitions look at state formation in terms of the state's transformational capacities. That is to say, according to Khan, 'states in the developing countries are frequently and necessarily engaged in reconstructing their societies and economies and thereby overseeing far-reaching processes of social transformation'.[16] However, as Mann and Max Weber before him observed: 'the problem is that most definitions contain two different levels of analysis: the institutional and the functional. That is the state can be defined in terms of what it looks like institutionally, or what it does, its functions.'[17] Whereas functional analysis dominated the assessment of the pre-1993 'state' in exile,[18] the study of the post-Oslo state-building has been almost totally confined to institutional analysis. The latter has been informed by methods of analysis including the neoliberal good governance framework (often adopted by the Bretton Woods institutions and multilateral organisations) and the neo-patrimonial framework – the *personalistic* style of governing often associated with African countries.

While the PA shares some elements with the above processes of state formation, none of these processes fully applies to it. The PA's *function* is not to retain 'a monopoly of binding rule-making',[19] but to serve, as explained above, as a *depository* of the state to come. As such, the PA's functional element, unlike the vast experience of state-formation elsewhere, not only predominates its institutional element but defines it. For example, the establishment of a disproportionately strong Palestinian security apparatus after Oslo is a reflection of its function. The US security coordinator for Israel and the PA, General Keith Dayton, whose main task since 2005 has been 'building' PA security services, describes the newly trained Palestinian police force as 'state-builders' – a mind-set that reduces state-building to a question of security, primarily for Israel. By describing the newly trained Palestinian 'state-builders', Dayton's logic here is clear that the state-building lays more emphasis on security, mostly for Israel in anticipation that Israel would concede its denial of Palestinian statehood on security grounds.

What complicates this matter even further are two inherent tensions that exist in parallel and often in contradiction to the PA's function as the depository of the state to come. First, there is the tension between state-building under occupa-tion, as bound by agreements with Israel and external aid on the one hand, and internal pressure for 'resistance' to occupation on the other. After all, the PA sees itself as an extension of Palestinian nationalism. This tension is reflected by the PA's security 'cooperation' with Israel, while its security forces have sporadically engaged in armed confrontations with the Israeli army (1996 in Gaza, 2002–3 in the West Bank). It is also exemplified by the appointment of a PA minister for East Jerusalem Affairs to counter Israel's settlement-building in the city and the resignation of the latter (Hatem Abed Al Qader) on grounds that the PA's ministry of finance is not committed to his task.[20]

Furthermore, in 2004, at the request of the PA, the United Nations General Assembly went to the International Court of Justice, contesting Israel's Wall built deep inside the occupied West Bank. On 9 July 2004, the Court issued a 14:1 ruling that the construction of the Wall and Israel's settlements in occupied territories are 'contrary to international law', and demanded dismantlement and reparation.[21] However, state-building takes precedence over resistance in the current context, and together with international impotence when it comes to enforcing the law, has led to the ruling being shelved to date.

Second, the post-Oslo approach has created a more acute tension between Palestinian state-building and nation-building, coined by Beshara Doumani as 'Palestine versus the Palestinians'.[22] By default, the post-Oslo state-building exercise has excluded non-West Bank and Gaza Palestinians (who represent almost two-thirds of the total population), and attempts to include/co-opt Hamas in 2006 ended in the 2007 Gaza/West Bank split. Whereas pre-1993 state-building was driven by the Palestinian Diaspora, the post-Oslo process has tended to alienate those outside whose voices, rights and needs, including those relating to representation and social services, have been excluded by post-Oslo state-building. The 1.25 million Palestinians who remained on their land after the establishment of the state of Israel in 1948 and who hold Israeli citizenship were even excluded by the pre-1993 state-building endeavour.

In part, collective identities and memories are formed by shared experiences, as Rashid Khalidi observes: 'the quintessential Palestinian experience... takes place at a border, an airport, a checkpoint... what happens to Palestinians at these crossing points brings home to them how much they share in common as a people'.[23] However, the Oslo period institutionalised Palestinian territorial, political and legal fragmentation, and provided a framework for Israel's long practice of segregation, shoring up the creation of at least five different and distinct Palestinian experiences: those living in Gaza, the West Bank, East Jerusalem, Palestinian citizens of Israel and not least the Palestinians of the Diaspora, who are mostly refugees.

This peculiar situation of a state in-the-making that is potentially emerging from occupation, but lacks the attributes of a conventional state and is restricted by a set of semi-permanent interim arrangements with its survival hanging on the continued extraction of external rent, denies applicability to almost all state-formation definitions and assessment methods. When assessing the PA's institutional performance, the outcome is often mixed, as indicated by numerous studies in this area.[24] A team of Palestinian and international scholars, including the author of this chapter, examined the post-Oslo state formation process in a book edited by Mushtaq Khan entitled *State Formation in Palestine* (2004). The contributors asserted that :

> while the supporters and detractors of the PA each want to focus on a partial picture of its successes and failures, the evidence suggests a more complex story of intense contestation, harsh external constraints and some unexpected strengths and weaknesses.[25]

In assessing the PA's institutional performance, the study found traces of four potential state types: Client, Predatory, Fragmented Clientelist and Developmental. The direction (which state type) the PA takes depends, the book claimed, in part on internal developments but chiefly on external factors, including Israel's interpretation and implementation of the two-state solution, and the role and pressure of the international actors.[26]

It is also worth mentioning that four years after it was established in 1998, the PA's institutional capabilities received high scores in a Council on Foreign Relations' Task Force Report. While the Report asserted that 'much more remains to be done', it emphasised that 'the PA has achieved levels of service delivery, revenue mobilisation, financial accountability, and utilisation of international assistance that are at least commensurate with, and in some aspects exceed, those in countries of comparable development and income'.[27] However, the PA's institutional 'success' proved to be of little value at the Camp David talks a year later. Assessing the institutional performance of the post-Oslo state-in-the-making (PA) is beyond both the remit and the point of this chapter. The aim is not to assess state formation per se, but rather to examine the framework and role of the post-Oslo external financing.

State-building both outside and inside Palestine would not have been possible without generous and sustained external financing. Whereas the expensive salaried PLO apparatus in exile was sustained by the financial support of Arab Gulf states during the 1970s and 1980s, the post-Oslo state-building exercise has been funded by a Western-led international aid programme. The role of external financing has been extremely crucial in sustaining Palestinian state-building and thus influencing the process of Palestinian decision-making. Indeed, it is widely believed that the drying of Arab petro-dollar support to the PLO in the early 1990s contributed to the signing of the Oslo Accord. And the PA would have gone bankrupt long ago without heavy external subsidy. This external rent – the Post-Oslo Western-Led International Aid Program – is discussed in the following section.

The Post-Oslo Western-led International Aid Program

The Post-Oslo International Aid Program's chief objectives were: (1) to uphold peace-making during the Oslo Interim Period (OIP 1994–9, extended to 2000) by improving Palestinian economic conditions so as to provide 'economic incentives' for the political process; and (2) to lay the foundations for the Palestinian state to come. It failed on both counts. The Oslo Peace Process collapsed in September 2000 and, by the end of the interim period, Palestinian economic conditions had deteriorated by all standards of measurement as compared to the pre-Oslo period. Ultimately, the ongoing post-Oslo external assistance programme ended up funding the demise of the very state it aimed to establish, and enabled Israel in the process to reconstruct and sustain its occupation of the West Bank and Gaza.

The proponents of the Oslo Peace Process believed that economic dividends would be crucial for its success. Shimon Peres, former Israeli Prime Minister and the main architect of the Oslo Accords, declared in his book, *The New Middle East*, that a 'rare opportunity to create a new Golden Age in the Middle East' had arisen following the breakthrough of the Oslo process.[28] Arafat was equally optimistic, announcing to the cheering crowd upon his return to the Gaza Strip in May 1994 that Gaza would soon become the 'Singapore of the Middle East'. From the outset, donors recognised the need for rapid improvements in the West Bank and Gaza economy, if the peace process was to take root. They believed that improving economic conditions in the West Bank and Gaza during the OIP would help to resolve the political conflict. Citing the Palestinian's 'extremely difficult' living conditions, the former US President, Bill Clinton, said that 'no peace stands a chance of lasting if it does not deliver real results to ordinary people'.[29] The logic was that economic advances and state-building predicate political advances and statehood.

Yet the West Bank and Gaza economy steadily deteriorated during the Oslo Interim Period. By 2000, despite the disbursement of more than US$3.4 billion of donor funds into the Palestinian economy, almost all economic and social indicators in the occupied Palestinian Territory were worse than they had been at the beginning of the Oslo process in 1993. For example, by the end of the OIP, the West Bank and Gaza per capita gross national product had declined in real terms from an average of US$2,890 during the pre-Oslo period (1988–92) to US$1,824 in 2000, representing a contraction of 36 per cent.[30] Instead of either side being able to grasp the 'peace dividend', Israel's policies over this period led to the territorial and socio-economic fragmentation of the occupied Palestinian territories. By the end of the interim period, prospects for a Palestinian state had been eroded.

What Went Wrong?

Knowing the outcome (i.e. Oslo's failure) does not necessarily help us to understand how we got there. Most donors were not involved in the Oslo process for completely cynical reasons. After the event, it was clear that the process had failed and that in many key respects donors lacked the capacity to enforce and implement critical parts of the agreements. A number of sophisticated arguments have emerged that explain this as a lack of political will on the part of the international community when it came to enforcing any agreements on Israel. It has been argued, for instance, that for some donors their involvement was meant to compensate for their lack of political will, or to compete for 'low politics' as opposed to the 'high politics' monopolised by the United States and Israel.[31]

While to a high extent the post-Oslo international aid programme implementation failure can be described as a failure of political will on the part of the international community, this does not fully explain why donors embarked on the process with such enthusiasm, and why many aid practitioners were genuinely surprised and dismayed when it became clear that the outcome was not going to be a happy one. I assume that most donors did not perceive at the outset that they lacked the institutional or political capacity to implement key aspects of the accords, or indeed that the strategies they were following may have been inappropriate for solving the problem. If this was the case, their subsequent involvement would only have been a 'show', or at best an exercise whose futility was obvious to them from the outset, and it is implausible to explain the expenditure of vast amounts of taxpayers' money on this basis. Nor is such a view consistent with the author's experience of working closely with donors (as a staff member of the United Nations Office of the Special Coordinator in the Occupied Territories) during the early stages of the peace process, when genuine commitment to the process on the part of different donor agencies and a belief that it had a realistic chance of success were very obvious.

It was assumed that the two-state solution was in the strategic interest of Israel. Consequently, the international community hoped that enforcement would not be required for such a peace agreement *as far as Israel was concerned*. The critical issues of settlements, of the precise borders (particularly of Jerusalem) and of the right of return for Palestinian refugees remained, but they were seen to be matters of detail by the international community as they developed an understanding that 'we all know what the solution is'.[32] It is also creditable that donors actually believed that they had the political will to enforce the deal because they perceived that any significant opposition would most likely come from the Palestinians, and they believed that such opposition could be overcome by a particular strategy of aid. In these circumstances, the economists' tool of 'revealed preference' may be used as a way of uncovering the priorities of donors, given the political difficulties attending full disclosure and transparency of objectives in these circumstances. Revealed preference shows clearly that donors must have adhered to what can be loosely described as a combination of carrot and stick, each of which had an internal and external component.

The internal carrot was the provision of large amounts of loosely earmarked aid that could be used to mitigate internal Palestinian political opposition; the external carrot was donor support for Israeli strategies of economic integration and the use of Palestinian territories as labour pools for Israeli investors. The internal stick was the provision of significant amounts of donor financial and technical assistance for building up a security apparatus that could deal with internal opposition; the external stick was the implicit threat that there was no other option on the table, so the failure of this strategy would entail 'exiting history' for Palestinians. The political will from the donor perspective was therefore to make available the fiscal resources for this package, together with a united front on the options available to the Palestinians.

The question before us is not whether Oslo was a good deal from the Palestinian perspective, since it clearly had many deficiencies. Rather, the question is whether Palestinian opposition to the peace process can possibly explain its poor implementation and eventual collapse. There was undoubtedly Palestinian opposition, from Hamas, other militant groups, the Palestinian Diaspora and occasional violence within the territories, but, in the main, the donor strategy of carrots and sticks was remarkably successful for achieving Palestinian acquiescence within the territories to the peace process, despite the deficiencies of the deal. If viability is judged in terms of *realpolitik* rather than the desirability or justice of the outcome, the donor strategy was well designed as far as the Palestinian side of the bargain was concerned, and had the necessary political will backing it for it to be effective and credible to the mainstream Palestinian movement as encapsulated by the PLO.

In the event, implementation was not essentially a Palestinian problem but mainly an Israeli one. Not only did Israel fail to vacate existing settlements, but it accelerated the construction of new ones *after* signing the accords. Additionally, instead of using economic integration of Palestinian labour as a carrot to enforce the peace deal, Israel used Oslo to set up what Khan describes as 'asymmetric containment'[33] and Halper (2000) describes as the 'matrix of control'.[34] This occurred not only because of a failure of political will on the part of the international community, but also a failure of locating the political settlement that was being attempted in the political realities of *both* sides, particularly within the dominant party – Israel. Had the international community assessed the political realities more accurately, the requirement of enforcement on Israel would have been clear from the outset. The donor community would then have a choice of either wasting their money by engaging in a futile exercise, creating the political consensus in their home constituencies for enforcing a settlement on Israel, or saving their money and doing nothing. The argument here is that the question of *appropriate* political will and enforcement requirements were not addressed at the beginning of the Oslo Peace Process because donors were working on a flawed set of assumptions about Israel's interests.

The question is whether there was a viable constituency in the Palestinian territories who saw the prospective package of political and economic benefits as good enough to support the Palestinian leadership's agenda of state formation. And in this very limited interpretation of viability, we find that the failure of Oslo cannot be attributed to the absence of a significant Palestinian constituency supporting this agenda, or the presence of a significant Palestinian constituency sabotaging the implementation of the Agreements from the Palestinian side. As we now know, however, Israel used Oslo to reconstruct and consolidate its occupation of the West Bank and Gaza, and to undercut the very principle Oslo was to achieve: the establishment of an independent sovereign Palestinian state. Furthermore, the Oslo process furthered the fragmentation and alienation of the Palestinian people and the erosion of their internationally guaranteed rights – particularly the right of return, which was implicitly compromised in exchange for promises of territorial gains that never materialised.

The Oslo Accords were indeed inadequate and unfair to Palestinians, and the Palestinian leadership had indeed submitted to these conditions out of desperation. If we accept that the Accords reflected Israel's greater power and preferences, and Palestinian weakness and disunity, and if we agree that the international community (particularly the USA) was complacent about the unequal deal that the Palestinians were being forced to accept, then why was Oslo not implemented? A number of explanations have been mooted in a wide range of literature, ranging from the weakness of the Israeli state such that it could not control small groups of wreckers who went and set up new settlements, as propagated by Israel's 'left', to arguments that a two-state solution does not help to solve Israel's problem of how to maintain Zionism (as opposed to a Jewish majority) in Israel.[35] An in-depth discussion of the motivations and calculations behind Israel's actions is beyond the remit of this chapter, though it does not appear credible that thousands of settlers could move into the occupied territories after the signing of the Oslo Accords without the military and political leadership of Israel acquiescing to this.

Thus the process through which these assumptions unravelled is of substantial importance for us to understand, whether we are Palestinians, the donor community or scholars interested in the analysis of the role of aid in state-building. With regard to Israel, it is essential to understand the extent of the failures of planning, understanding and political analysis by international actors, and to incorporate this understanding into any future round of donor involvement in peace-making in the region and, indeed, elsewhere. The arrangements that were made for enforcing any implementation or agreements on Israel were derisory. This could be interpreted in two ways: we could interpret it as evidence that donors lacked political will when it came to dealing with Israel from the very beginning; alternatively, we could interpret it as a lack of preparedness based on inadequate and one-sided analysis, which led many donors to set up toothless coordination and enforcement mechanisms on the assumption that these would not be required as far as Israel was concerned.

The question then is this: if donors assumed that it was in Israel's interest to create a Palestinian state, why did they continue supporting Palestinian state-building when Israel's intentions and policies started to reveal themselves early on in the peace process? This matter is all the more important today given that Israel's lack of interest in a Palestinian state is all the more apparent. There may be several explanations but most donors, as the author can attest during their several encounters with representatives during 1996–9, were still hoping against hope, believing – or at least wanting to believe – that Israeli obstacles were temporary and that a two-state solution was still possible.

Clearly, there is a substantial problem of political will on the part of the international community when it comes to engaging with the possibility that Israel is an obstacle to peace. There are all kinds of historical reasons for this reluctance in the West that are too well known to need spelling out again. The 'lack of political will' on the part of the international community when it comes to enforcing international law, commitments and agreements on Israel involves an omnibus explanation that can be interpreted in different ways. It has been suggested that Israel can do whatever it likes and the Western countries who lead the 'international community' will not take any action against it. If this interpretation is correct, we should despair. It is hoped, however, that this is not a full interpretation for all the countries playing a role in determining international policy. An alternative interpretation is that Israel has been much more successful in creating confusion about its real interests and strategies, and this has allowed most donors to keep burying their heads in the sand. If this is the reality, it is important to spell it out in detail, so that such mistakes will not be repeated again, and that any future financial involvement by the international donor community is informed by a better reading of the political reality in Israel and matched by political will.

Linking the Past to the Present and Lessons Learned

The international community ought to change both the goalposts and the way to reach them. Ending the occupation predicates building a state and this cannot be reached without a better understanding of the political realities in the region and accumulating enough political will to deal with them. While Israel's lack of interest and commitment to the two-state solution might have been unclear during the Oslo period, it is unmistakable today. Since the breakdown of the Oslo Accords in 2000, Israel's successive campaigns have resulted in the destruction of much of the PA security and civil infrastructure, the expanding of settlements, the building of the separation barrier annexing large chunks of occupied land, the relocation of Gaza settlers to the West Bank, the complete severing of East Jerusalem from the West Bank and Gaza, the building of bypass roads and tunnels and roadblocks in the West Bank, etc. In the last 11 years and during the Oslo period, Israel has redrawn the landscape of the occupied territories (OT) to the extent that establishing a Palestinian independent, sovereign and contiguous state, according to numerous observers, is no longer a possibility. The current Israeli government, headed by Benjamin Netanyahu, further diminishes the hopes of building a solid political base in Israel towards the two-state solution as envisioned by the international community. With Yisrael Beiteinu – under the leadership of Avigdor Lieberman – coming third in the last elections on 10 February 2009, the Israeli polity is certainly veering towards the right. Benjamin Netanyahu, who ran an anti-Oslo campaign and won the 1996 elections, today argues for an 'economic peace'.

What is more, Israel's 'security first' approach that characterised the Oslo period is still at large. Under the pretext of security, the strangulation of Palestinian society is ongoing. Still under the same justifications, most humanitarian aid, not to mention building materials and other basic needs, are not allowed into Gaza, and Netanyahu demands the annexation of almost half of the West Bank into Israel in any final status agreement on security grounds. Israel continues to frame the conflict solely within a security perspective.

While Israel's propagation of the 'security first approach' went unchallenged in a region controlled by autocratic Arab regimes, the advent of the Arab Spring deprives Israel of much of its comfort zone. Security is best attained for both Israelis and Palestinians through an equitable political settlement that addresses people's grievances and legitimate aspirations. The latter comes first, as demonstrated by Tahrir Square and other Arab revolutions.

As the experience of Oslo shows, not only was Palestinian society 'taken hostage' under the pretext of Israeli security, but also the international community and its funding programme were. If this lesson is not learned and should the international community continue to follow Israel's security-first approach, it will shoot itself in the same foot once again.

The experiences of international financial assistance during the Oslo period, and the constructed framework, reveals the false assumption that a rapid movement towards a viable two-state solution was in Israel's strategic interest. This allowed the international community to participate without insisting on any meaningful leverage over Israel. In fact, not only was there a vast asymmetry between the two parties, but also more significantly there was a lack of consensus, or even considerable agreement, within the polity of the dominant party about the key features of the 'end game'. That meant that the international community's strategy of 'staying in the margins', leaving the two sides to 'sort it out' and simply making agreements 'work', was doomed to fail.

Political realities in the Palestinian territories have clearly moved on since the collapse of the Oslo process in 2000 and what may have been viable and possible in the 1990s may not be possible today. The explanation that the post-Oslo reconstruction programme failed because the international donor community was unprepared and unclear about Israel's intentions can no longer hold. More importantly, if donors and the international community really engage with the failure of Oslo and ask themselves why the coordination and implementation of these aid strategies did not result in peace, the answer may be more depressing in the short term but more hopeful in the long run.

It may become clear that the two-state solution that has been formulated will not be implemented by Israel in its own interest, or at least that it will not even lead to the creation of a minimal Palestinian state acceptable to the Palestinians. If that is so, the international community has two choices: it can ask itself if it can ever garner the 'political will' to enforce a solution on Israel that the latter does not deem in its interests (i.e. admitting Palestine as a member state of the UN and imposing sanctions on Israel); alternatively, it may come to ask more fundamental questions about the two-state solution, Israel's strategies in a changing region, its role as perceived by the West (particularly the USA) and the options available to the Palestinians. Such an acknowledgement might not entail immediate solutions, but it will open up the international debate about what these solutions may eventually be. The time is right for that debate.

Notes

1. Amnesty International, 'Israel and the occupied territories: the issue of settlements must be addressed according to international law', 8 September 2003. Available from www.amnesty.org/en/library/asset/MDE15/085/2003/en/84b15c82-d695-11ddab95-a13b602c0642/mde150852003en.html.

2. PLO Negotiation Affairs Department, fact sheet, July 2009. Available from www.nadplo.org/main.php?view=mainextra_know.

3. Palestinian Ministry of Planning and International Cooperation (MOPIC), 1998, 1999, 2000, 2001 and 2003, Quarterly monitoring report of donors' assistance, September, Gaza: MOPIC.

4. The World Bank, *Palestinian Economic Prospects, Aid Access and Reform*, Economic Monitoring Report to the Ad Hoc Liaison Committee, 22 September 2008.

5. *The Guardian*, 'Paris donor nations pledge billions for Palestinians', 17 December 2007. Available from www.guardian.co.uk/world/2007/dec/17/france.israel.

6. F. Zakaria, *The Future of Freedom: Illiberal Democracy at Home and Abroad* (New York, NY: WW Norton, 2003).

7. M. Mann, *The Autonomous Power of the State: Its Origins, Mechanisms, and Results*, Archives Européenes de Sociologie, 25 (1984), pp. 185–213.

8. Y. Sayigh, *Armed Struggle and the Search for State: The Palestinian National Movement 1949–1993* (Oxford: Oxford University Press, 1997), p. 671.

9. Ibid. Sayigh asserts that 'despite their unique circumstances of collective disposition and dispersal and their lack of statehood, the Palestinians ultimately revealed patterns of elite formation and politics, corporate organisation, neopatrimonial bureaucratisation, and authoritarian political management and concentration of power that were typical of the experience of state-building in neighbouring Arab countries'.

10. Ibid., p. 674.

11. *Declaration of Principles on Interim Self-Government Arrangements (DOP)*, 1993. Available from www.jmcc.org/peace/agreements.html.

12. G. Dale, 'Facilitating Oslo, how the Oslo Accord's "secret channel" opened, then closed. Track Two', *States and Conflicts*, 6(2) (1997), p. 6; and M. E. Bouillon, *The Peace Business: Money and Power in the Palestine–Israel Conflict* (London: I.B.Tauris, 2004).

13. A. Shlaim, 'The rise and fall of the Oslo Peace process' in L. Fawcett (ed.), *International Relations of the Middle East* (Oxford: Oxford University Press, 2005), p. 7.

14. S. Roy, *Failing Peace: Gaza and the Palestinian–Israeli Conflict* (London: Pluto, 2007), p. 236.

15. N. Hovsepian, *Palestinian State Formation: Education and the Construction of National Identity* (Newcastle: Cambridge Scholars, 2008).

16. M. H. Khan (ed.), *State Formation in Palestine: Viability and Governance During a Social Transformation* (London: Routledge, 2004), p. 3.

17. Mann, op. cit.; M. Weber, *Economy and Society*, Vol. 1 (New York, NY: Bedminster, 1968).

18. For example, Sayigh, op. cit.

19. Mann, op. cit.

20. Al Jazeera News, 2 July 2009. Available from www.aljazeera.net/NR/exeres/CE154F8C-DC2D-4CE9-B176-0C8AFAB0A106.htm (in Arabic).

21. For the full text of the official International Court of Justice ruling, see http://stopthewall.org/internationallaw/639.shtml.

22. B. Doumani, 'Palestine versus the Palestinians? The iron laws and ironies of a people denied', *Journal of Palestine Studies*, 36(4) (2007), pp. 49–64.

23. R. Khalidi, *Palestinian Identity: the Construction of Modern National Consciousness* (New York, NY: Columbia University Press, 1997), p. 1.

24. For example, Council on Foreign Relations, 'Strengthening Palestinian public institutions', Task Force Report, June 1999. Available from www.cfr.org/publication/3185/strengthening_palestinian_public_institutions.html; Khan, op. cit.; Hovsepian, op. cit.; The World Bank and Government of Japan, *Aid Effectiveness in the West Bank and Gaza* (Washington, DC: The World Bank, 2000); The World Bank and the United Nations Special Coordinator's Office (UNSCO) in the occupied territories. *The Promise, the Challenges and the Achievements: Donor Investment in Palestine 1994–1998* (Gaza: UNSCO, 1999). Also, The World Bank and UNSCO, *Aid Coordination and Post-conflict Reconstruction: The West Bank and Gaza Experience* (Washington, DC: The World Bank, 1999).

25. Khan, *State Formation in Palestine*, p. 64.

26. Ibid.

27. Council on Foreign Relations, op. cit.

28. S. Peres, *The New Middle East* (London: Shaftesbury, 1993).

29. Cited in The World Bank, *The Impact of Prolonged Closure on Palestinian Poverty* (Washington, DC: The World Bank, 2003).

30. UNSCO, *Report on the Palestinian Economy*, Gaza: 2006; UNSCO, 2001 and Ibid.

31. A. Le More, *Bad choices: international aid politics and the Israeli–Palestinian peace process, 1994–2004*, doctoral thesis, Oxford University, 2006.

32. K. Nabulsi, 'The peace process and the Palestinians: a road map to Mars', *International Affairs*, 80(2) (2004), p. 221.

33. Khan, op. cit.

34. J. Halper, 'Losing ground? The politics of environment and space', *Middle East Report*, 2000, p. 216, Fall (online). Available from www.merip.org/mer/mer216/mer216/html.

35. M. H. Khan, 'Security first and its implications for a viable Palestinian state', in M. Keating, A. Le More and R. Lowe (eds), *Aid, Diplomacy and Facts on the Ground: The Case of Palestine* (London: The Royal Institute for Strategic Studies, 2005).

CHAPTER 5

Is the Two-State Settlement Still Viable? An Overall Assessment of the Present Situation

Naseer H. Aruri

Diplomatic Paralysis Embedded in the Peace Process:
Politicide and the Failure of the Two-State Solution

The correct question to begin with is whether a two-state settlement has ever been possible and/or viable at any time at all since 1967. This chapter begins by delineating the salient factors which dealt a severe blow to the two-state solution. It will be argued that the long diplomatic paralysis and the impediments to a peaceful solution capable of yielding two independent and contiguous states, living side by side in the Middle East, are embedded in the 'peace process', whose gridlock reveals no shortage of resolve, and in the Zionist idea that pre-1948 Palestine from the River Jordan to the Mediterranean Sea should be a single state under exclusive Israeli sovereignty. It is suggested in this chapter that peace will not be at hand as long as this ailing peace process fails to take into account the essentials of the Palestinian perspective: the 1948 'Nakba' is not recognised for what Palestinians see it as – a form of ethnic cleansing, an enterprise that covets the land without the people.[1] Peace has also remained elusive as long as the 1967 occupation continues to be entrenched as a form of 'politicide'. The late Israeli sociologist, Baruch Kimmerling, who authored a book by that title, defined 'politicide' as activities designed to destroy the political national existence of a whole community of people and thus deny it the possibility of self-determination. This policy, which may also include partial or total ethnic cleansing, seems to have long been Sharon's goal, whether as a commander in raids during the 1950s, in the 1982 invasion of Lebanon or in his policies as prime minister.[2] The late Tanya Rienhart expressed a similar view:

> After 35 years of occupation, it is completely clear that the only two choices the Israeli political system has generated for the Palestinians are apartheid or ethnic cleansing (transfer). Apartheid is the 'enlightened' Labour party's programme (as in the Allon or Oslo plan), while the other pole is advocating slow suffocation of the Palestinians, until the eventual 'transfer' (mass expulsion) can be accomplished.[3]

Both authors, then, viewed the occupation as the single most important obstacle in the way of independence and liberation for the Palestinian people alongside Israel. 'Politicide' is a process that covers a wide range of social, political, military and bureaucratic activities whose goal is to destroy the political and national existence of a whole community of people, and thus deny it the possibility of self-determination. It will be argued that this is what Israel has been persistently doing to the Palestinian people between 1948 and 2010 – destroying the very fabric of the Palestinian nation. The process is still ongoing, having included the invasions of 1967, 1976, 1982, 2002 (killings in Jineen) and 2006, and the recent war on Gaza (2008/9).[4] In a major 49-page report on 'Gaza's Unfinished Business', published on 23 April 2009, the International Crisis Group warned that Gaza could once again reach boiling point. Gaza, it says, 'is an explosion waiting to happen'.[5]

Israel's stated goal in the three-week offensive was the halting of the cross-border rocket attacks from Gaza. The kill ratio seems to rule out the idea that Israel's attacks were retaliatory for the feeble Qassam rockets.

The national aspirations of the Palestinians for full independence have been inhibited, not only by military means, but also by diplomatic, bureaucratic and demographic policies, all of which can be seen as components of politicide. The single most important element of this politicide throughout these past four decades is diplomacy. American diplomacy has endorsed the vision of a two-state solution when it would seem that this option has never been on Israel's real agenda.

The 'peace process' in Palestinian eyes seems instead to have sheltered Israel from the threat of peace. It has enabled Israel to escape its obligations to the Palestinian people under international law. Not only has the USA succeeded in regularising the 1967 occupation, but it has also engaged in diplomatic outsourcing, thus consigning part of the diplomatic façade to the European community, the Russian Federation and the United Nations – and so a new term, the Quartet, is added to the diplomatic vocabulary.

The international community that declared the 1967 occupation illegal seems now to have become an accomplice by ignoring politicide. Since the inception of the 'peace process', Washington has been paradoxically acting as peace-maker, while at the same time serving as Israel's chief weapons supplier, banker and diplomatic backer. How has it been able to play such a role without ever having to give up its title of honest broker? Let us review the historical record.

A Brief Historical Background of Rejectionism

During the past few decades, Israel and the United States have pursued policies that dealt a crippling blow to the two-state solution, instead of helping create an independent Palestinian state. This derailment was accomplished through futile but resolute diplomatic efforts invested by US presidents from Nixon to George W. Bush.

Over three generations have elapsed since the creation of Israel; and peace has remained hopelessly elusive, with the USA continuing to claim the role of sole peace-maker.

Since 1948, the 'Question of Palestine' has been the focus of numerous United Nations resolutions that upheld the right of the Palestinians to return to their land and property, to establish their own independent state alongside Israel, to receive compensation and to gain restitution. Further UN resolutions were adopted after 1967, calling for an end to the occupation, the dismantling of settlements and peaceful co-existence based on two states, Palestine and Israel, living side by side. The entire compendium of these resolutions, which span the past half-century, constitutes a certain legal framework for the Palestine question, one anchored in international law – a jurisprudence of the Palestine question, if you will.

Indeed, a global consensus had prevailed throughout the 1970s and 1980s in support of a diplomatic settlement based on the international legal framework, but all efforts towards an equitable settlement ended in unremitting failure. As far back as the Rogers Plan of 1969, there is a legacy of rejectionism on the part of Israel and at times the self-designated peace-maker too.[6] Israel has managed to reject a number of US proposals even when some of these proposals did not call for full withdrawal from occupied territories and/or Palestinian sovereignty. The first casualty was the Rogers Plan, followed by Israel's frustration of Governor Scranton's mission on behalf of President Nixon (1970), the rejection of President Sadat's land-for-peace and mutual-recognition proposal (1971), the rejection of President Carter's call for a Geneva International Conference in 1977, the Reagan Plan of 1982, the Shultz Plan of 1988, the Baker Plan of 1989, and the successful effort to thwart President Bush Senior's attempt to link loan guarantees to the issue of Jewish settlements in and around Jerusalem (1990).[7]

The PLO and the Arab states had associated themselves, on the other hand, with the basic elements of the global consensus expressed in countless documents, including the 1971 Sadat offer, the Security Council Resolution of 1976 calling for implementation of Resolution 242, the European Council's Venice Declaration (12–13 June 1980), which recognised Palestinian self-determination, the 1981 Fahd Plan, the 1988 PLO recognition of Israel, the 1998 European Union Declaration, all the way up to the Saudi Crown Prince Abdullah plan, adopted by the Arab League in Beirut in March 2002, offering full recognition of Israel in exchange for ending the 1967 occupation.

The theory and practice of the 'peace process', which was based on the assumption that peace in the Middle East can only emanate from Washington, had, in effect, undermined all serious efforts to bring peace to the region. The history of US foreign policy in the region during the past four decades reveals that every single administration since Israel occupied the West Bank and the Gaza Strip had a Middle East plan named after a US President and/or a Secretary of State. That same history reveals that each of these plans negated true Palestinian self-determination. The common denominator of all these US plans was their failure to recognise the original injustice which Palestinians felt had been done to them in 1948. While the USA voted annually since 1948 in favour of UN Resolution 194, which recognises the right of the Palestinian refugees to return to their homes and property, and to compensation and restitution, it nevertheless failed to join international efforts to give any practical application to that resolution. By 1993, even that *pro forma* vote had been withdrawn, as the Oslo process endeavoured formally to nullify the international framework.

The Palestinians were thus denied all forms of international protection. The USA has used its Security Council veto 43 times, either to shelter Israel from international reproach for violating the human and national rights of the Palestinian people, or to deny the Palestinians international protection from ongoing Israeli moves against them. The US-led campaign against multilateralism has been pursued so vociferously and actively that any mention of international law, the right of return for refugees and even United Nations resolutions came to be considered in US, Israeli and some European ally circles as subversive and obstructionist. Between the signing of Oslo in 1993 and 2008, the USA and Israel managed to effectively remove the Palestinians from any meaningful negotiations. In 2004 (14 April) George W. Bush declared settlements as 'facts on the ground', rendering his much-touted vision of a sovereign, contiguous Palestinian state a mere rhetorical exercise.[8]

What Happened to the Two-State Solution?

We will examine three major diplomatic developments which cut across three US presidencies: Clinton, Bush Junior and Obama. They include the Oslo Accords and Camp David (1993–2001), the diplomatic paralysis of much of the first decade of the twenty-first century leading to the 'disengagement' from the 'peace process', the haphazard diplomacy practised by George W. Bush during the last few years of his presidency and last but not least the Annapolis meetings, followed by the crises in US–Israeli relations under Netanyahu and

Obama. We will examine the impact of these machinations on the prospects for a settlement based on a two-state solution.

The Oslo process set back the prospects for Palestinian statehood, and the subsequent rise of repression (called the 'war on terror') made it possible for Bush to grant Sharon what could be termed a 'new Balfour declaration' in April 2004. Ironically that might have left the vision of a single state for two equal communities as the only solution. The PLO leadership acquiesced to Israel's presence in the occupied Palestinian territories, to oppress, to displace and to dispossess, without being held accountable. Vast amounts of land were confiscated and thousands of people were dispossessed after the Oslo signing. In 1993 when Oslo was signed, there were 109,000 settlers in the West Bank, not including East Jerusalem; 20 years later, that number became about 275,000 settlers living in 230 settlements. There are 625 checkpoints representing a 70 per cent increase since 2005. Meanwhile, about a quarter of a million Jews are living in East Jerusalem today. Furthermore, Prime Minister Netanyahu agreed with his foreign minister Avigdor Lieberman in early April 2009 to build 3,000 units between Ma'ale Adumim and Jerusalem, a step which would cut the West Bank in half and render the two-state solution irrelevant. Recently, it was revealed that the Israeli government and the Municipality of Jerusalem plans call for the construction of 50,000 Jewish residential units in Jerusalem with the intent of radically transforming the religious and ethnic composition of the city's population.[9]

Even if the Oslo agreements were to succeed, the maximum gain for the Palestinians that seems possible would have been a fractured collection of some 120 small fragments, non-contiguous enclaves, on about 40–50 per cent of the West Bank (11 per cent of pre-1948 Palestine). Under optimal conditions, something called the state of Palestine might have emerged, but would have been only nominally independent. Genuine independence had already been ruled out by the agreement between Labour and Likud in January 1997, which insisted on but a single sovereignty (Israeli) in the area between the River and the Sea. Over 13 years later, the same consensus describes the new Israeli ruling spectrum – Likud (28), Labour (12), Yisrael Beiteinu (15) and Shas (11). The Palestinians in the occupied territories (OT) would be residents of enclaves separated from each other and from Israel but, functionally, part of a 'greater Israel'. Ehud Barak emphasised it and Sharon and Olmert implemented it with the so-called separation barrier, named by the Palestinians as the 'apartheid wall', and unilateralist policies that constituted one more factor which hastened the demise of the two-state solution.

In July 2000, Clinton and Barak were able to sway the Palestinian Authority (PA) to accede to a premature (as Arafat insisted) trilateral summit presided over by Clinton himself.[10] There were a number of problems with the way that

summit was conducted. First, UN Security Council Resolution 242, which stipu-
lates the exchange of conquered land for peace, was simply ignored by the USA
in the Camp David negotiations. Second, every proposal that was presented by
the American mediators to the Palestinian side already had Israeli clearance. On
practically every issue – especially on Jerusalem and the refugees – the American
team, it seems, simply adopted and argued for the Israeli position. This view is
bluntly corroborated by Aaron David Miller, a senior negotiator on the Clinton
team at Camp David and an Orthodox Jew. Miller publicly revealed that rather
than serve as a true mediator in peace negotiations, successive US administrations (including Clinton's) have acted as 'Israel's attorney'.[11] Writing on the
Washington Post op-ed page, Miller said that Clinton and his team followed
Israel's lead 'without critically examining what that would mean for our own
interests, for those on the Arab side and for the overall success of the negotiations'.[12] The Clinton team's practice of running everything past Israel first:

> stripped our policy of the independence and flexibility required for serious peace-
> making. Far too often… our departure point was not what was needed to reach an
> agreement acceptable to both sides but what would pass with only one – Israel. The
> result was utter failure…[13]

Third, in its 'generous offer' with regard to land, borders and security, Israel
effectively sought to consolidate and legitimise the gains it made in the 1967
War. However, the 'greatest failure' of the summit was over the issue of the
Palestinian refugees. With regard to the right of return, Israel offered to return
only a few thousand refugees over a ten-year period in the context of a family
reunification plan. In return, the Israelis demanded an 'end of the conflict'. This
would of course release them from any and all further claims. It is interesting
that this Israeli policy towards the Palestinian refugees has remained unaltered
from 1948 until the present. Back in June 1948, Israeli Foreign Minister, Moshe
Sharett, told the Knesset that repatriation of the Palestinian refugees was
rejected on the assumption that 'a wave of returning refugees might explode
the state from inside…'.[14] He said: 'They will not return. This is our policy,
they shall not return.'[15]

Over 60 years later, this policy remains untouched. On 20 November 2006,
the former Israeli foreign Minister Tzipi Livni urged the world community,
especially the Arab countries housing refugees, to annul the right of return. She
issued her command in a lecture she was delivering at the International Institute
for Strategic Studies in London. Remarkably, she used the flawed logic that the
right of return, which is enshrined in international law, is not mentioned in the
Road Map, as if the dilapidated plan superseded international law.

As for Jerusalem, the PA was offered 'custodial sovereignty' over the Holy
Places, but sovereignty on the grounds of the Haram Al-Sharif was vested in

Israel. The alleged offer to return 94 per cent of the OT was not only exagger-ated but also completely misleading. The area Israel defines as Jerusalem has 28 Palestinian villages, all of which were occupied in 1967, but do not enter the calculation of OT since they are arbitrarily regarded as part of greater Jerusalem, rendering percentages and ratios meaningless.

The PA refused to accept the so-called 'generous peace offer'. After all, not only was it far below the minimum aspirations and the internationally guaranteed rights of the Palestinian people, but also it contravened existing international law and United Nations resolutions. The occupation would have remained intact but reconfigured or repackaged.

Why Has Peace Been Such a Threat to Israeli Leaders? And What Are the Salient Features of the Post-Oslo Period?

For Israel, the danger of a permanent peace emanates from a perceived 'demographic threat'. Palestinian Arabs living under Israeli control are gradu-ally becoming the majority population between the River Jordan and the Mediterranean for the first time since 1948. In 2011 the number of Palestinians living between the River and the Sea under Israeli control was approximately 5 million, compared to 5.1 million Israelis. Short of giving the Palestinians equal rights in one state, Israel is left with three options: acquiescing in the establish-ment of a separate sovereign Palestinian state; expelling much of the Palestinian population; or keeping them confined in 'apartheid-style' cantons. The latter in essence is Sharon's plan of 1981, endorsed by George W. Bush in April 2004 when he said that the settlement blocs were 'facts on the ground', strongly implying that the occupation was here to stay. Bush had, in effect, recognised a permanent Israeli occupation of the remaining 22 per cent of what Israel did not conquer in 1948. That is certainly contrary to a two-state solution and stands at variance with the idea of a Palestinian state, of which he often claimed to be the author.

As for Sharon's 'disengagement' from Gaza, it involved a mere redeployment (not withdrawal) from an unwanted, overpopulated, poverty-stricken swathe of land, in return for US acquiescence in a long-term interim agreement that would consolidate and make permanent Israel's control over the West Bank. Indeed, Bush did what has become accepted practice over the past few decades. Israel provides the framework, just as it did in 1978 (Camp David), 1993 (Oslo) and 2000 (Camp David), while the USA signs off on the plan. Sharon sold Bush a recycled version of his 1981 plan to keep at least 50 per cent of the West Bank, relegating the Palestinians to three fragmented entities (Jenin and Nablus in the north, Ramallah in the centre and Hebron/Bethlehem in the south).

In conceding final status issues, such as boundaries, refugees, settlements and Jerusalem, Bush seemed either unaware of or oblivious to what his predecessors had offered on the table of negotiations at Camp David I, Camp David II, Taba or the Clinton parameters (7 January 2001 speech in New York). Nor did Bush seem bothered by the fact that the 400-mile separation barrier has already foreclosed on final status issues such as borders. The impediments to a two-state solution have been marked. To Palestinians there may have been a process, but it was not about peace. For them the 'peace-maker/honest broker' had become a messenger, in addition to having been and continuing to be a banker, arms supplier and diplomatic backer.

Mahmoud Abbas, head of the PA, was destined for failure by Sharon and later Olmert. After Hamas was ushered into power by parliamentary elections in January 2006, replacing the corrupt and inefficient Fateh, Abbas, Olmert and Bush colluded to bar Hamas from assuming actual power. When the 21 Arab heads of state convened in Riyadh, Saudi Arabia, to re-launch their peace proposal for two states, which had already been ratified in Beirut in 2002, Condoleezza Rice asked them to 'reach out' to Israel, ignoring the fact that they have been lambasted by their constituents for excessive concessions. Meanwhile, Israel wanted their peace offer amended, particularly on withdrawal, on Jerusalem and the refugees. Olmert told the *Jerusalem Post* on 30 March 2007 that the return of any Palestinian refugee was 'out of the question': 'I'll never accept a solution that is based on their return to Israel, any number.'[16]

Sharon declared the Road Map null and void and, together with Olmert, he turned his attention to putting in place a running 'apartheid-style' system. Professor John Dugard, the former UN Rapporteur for Human Rights, said the situation in the OT was worse than the one that existed in South Africa. The result of all this is that we have witnessed the beginning of a new discourse about a single state based on the equal protection of the law. Here is Dugard's account of 'apartheid' in Israel and in South Africa:

> There are features of the Israeli regime in the occupied territory that were unknown to South Africans. We never had a wall separating black and white. I know it's called the Apartheid Wall, but that's really a misnomer because there was no wall of that kind in South Africa. And as I've said, there were no separate roads. These are novel features of Israel's apartheid regime. Second, the enforcement of the regime is much stricter. We have repeated military incursions into the West Bank, let alone Gaza. Gaza tends to attract most of the attention, but there are regular raids carried out by the Israeli Defense Forces (IDF) into the West Bank and arrests are made and Palestinians are shot and killed. And what is interesting is that in South Africa, political activists were tried by the regular criminal courts of the land in open proceedings. Whereas in Israel, Palestinians are tried by military courts which

have emergency rules and regulations inherited from the British, but they are not proper courts.

I think perhaps the most important distinguishing feature is that there are no positive features about Israel's apartheid. The South African apartheid regime did attempt to pacify the black majority by providing it with material benefits. And so schools were built, universities were built, hospitals and clinics were built by the apartheid regime. Special factories were built in the black areas in order to encourage workers to work in the African areas. So, there was a very positive side, although it was a materialistic side, to the apartheid order. Whereas in the case of Israel's apartheid Israel makes virtually no contribution to the welfare of the Palestinian people. It leaves it all to the donor community.[17]

Dugard's view was corroborated by former President Carter's own documentation of the sad state of human rights affairs in the Palestinian OT. Carter wrote: 'Israeli human rights activists, such as Uri Davis, in late 2001 called Israel the "last colonial power in the world" for openly practicing "torture, detention without trial, confiscation of land for security purposes and collective punishment".'[18]

Carter added:

A year later, when South African Nobel Peace Prize winner Desmond Tutu visited the area, he drew disturbing analogies between Israel's treatment of Palestinians and how blacks were treated under South African apartheid:

'I've been very deeply distressed in my visit to the Holy Land; it reminded me so much of what happened to us black people in South Africa,' he said in a speech in Boston in 2002... 'I have seen the humiliation of the Palestinians at checkpoints and roadblocks, suffering like us when young white police officers prevented us from moving about,' Tutu added.[19]

The USA, Israel and Hamas

The role of the sole peace-maker is probably approaching its end, particularly since January 2006, when Hamas achieved a decisive electoral victory. Israel, with strong behind the scenes support from the USA, thereafter became determined to undo that victory; first by imposing an embargo, then by abducting and assassinating the top Hamas leadership, and eventually by smashing the Hamas infrastructure while attempting to drive a wedge between the movement and that segment of the Palestinian population who had given Hamas their votes. The crux of the US–Israeli strategy was based on the faulty assumption that Hamas was part of a Middle East component of a global terror network.

Abbas, Olmert and Bush colluded to bar Hamas from assuming actual power, thus contributing to the commencement of a war between Fateh and Hamas.[20] Despite the formation of a government of national unity in the Mecca Agreement, neither the USA nor Israel appeared willing during the closing months of Bush's second presidential term to revive a peace process and pursue negotiations in good faith. Israeli journalist, Yossi Verter, confirmed this obstruction in an article in *Ha'aretz* titled 'Assassinating Annapolis'. He said that Annapolis had been 'shrunk, shredded, and emptied of any meaningful core issues'.[21]

Avigdor Lieberman, head of the right-wing party Yisrael Beiteinu, and a former member of the Kach party, now foreign minister in Netanyahu's government, was one of those 'shredders' who insisted that Israel must make any diplomatic move contingent upon implementation of the first stage of the Road Map, which calls on the PA to eliminate the 'terror infrastructure'; that is, give up all resistance to the occupation, an impossible condition to meet. In fact, Lieberman was among the ministers who voted against the Road Map. He was also the one who first brought up the demand that the PA recognise Israel as a Jewish state, which today constitutes official policy of the Netanyahu government. Lieberman made it clear that 'we are no longer bound by the previous government's undertakings for the negotiation of a Palestinian state. The Annapolis accord of 2007 for a two-state solution? Didn't happen on our watch.'[22] Lieberman has even proposed that all existing Arab Israelis who refuse to swear an oath of allegiance to Israel should be stripped of their citizenship rights.

Meanwhile, the current Israeli Prime Minister, Netanyahu, attached new demands as the price of merely starting negotiations. He said that the Palestinians would have to recognise Israel as the state of the Jewish people as a condition for renewing peace talks, a position which could be unacceptable to the Obama administration.[23] Senator Mitchell, who served as Obama's envoy in the Middle East, added that the USA does not accept Netanyahu's position that the renewal of negotiations should be postponed until the Iranian nuclear threat is removed.[24]

Secretary of State, Hillary Clinton, well-known supporter of Israel, was extremely blunt with Netanyahu's government after seeing how Palestinians in the West Bank have reverted back to the age of the donkey and cart, while Israeli settlers enjoy driving on superhighways for Jews only. She has warned Netanyahu to get off 'the sidelines' with respect to Palestinian peace efforts.[25] In House testimony held during April 2009, Clinton said: 'For Israel to get the kind of strong support it is looking for vis-à-vis Iran, it can't stay on the sidelines with respect to the Palestinians and the peace efforts. They go hand in hand.'[26] That was a direct rebuke to comments from Netanyahu aides who told the *Washington Post* that Israel would not move on peace talks until it sees the USA check Iran's nuclear programme and rising regional influence.

According to other sources, the Obama administration has indeed tried to use Iran as a bargaining chip to restart Israeli–Palestinian negotiations on the basis of two states. Jason Koutsokis put it this way:

> Now US officials are openly using Israeli anxiety over Iran's fledging nuclear program as a bargaining chip to force Israel's hand on giving up control of the West Bank Palestinian territory. No less a figure than White House chief-of-staff Rahm Emanuel – whose father fought with the militant Zionist group the Irgun, and whose appointment had provided such reassurance to Israeli officials – was quoted this week laying down the law to Israel. If Israel wants US help to defuse the Iranian threat, Mr. Emanuel was reported to have told Jewish leaders in Washington, then get ready to start evacuating settlements in the West Bank.[27]

Then came the news that Netanyahu's planned first meeting with President Obama in Washington had been called off. Netanyahu had hoped to capitalise on his attendance at the annual American Israel Public Affairs Committee conference in Washington to visit the White House. But presidential administration officials informed Netanyahu's office that the President would not be 'in town'.[28] Obama thus managed to postpone the meeting until 18 May 2009, thereby making it on his terms and breaking with tradition whereby Israeli prime ministers combine the Annual AIPAC Policy Conference with a meeting at the White House. At the White House meeting, Obama succeeded in placing the two-state solution on top of the agenda, leaving Iran as *the effect*, rather than the cause of an Israeli/Palestinian peace. Netanyahu's strategy was based on the principle that Israel would return to the negotiations table if Obama gave him a freer hand vis-à-vis Iran. Netanyahu had set out to convince Obama that depriving Iran of nuclear weapons would pave the road towards peace in Palestine. Instead, Obama argued that it was the other way around.

Tensions between the Obama administration and the Netanyahu government continued to exacerbate during the spring of 2009, with the Israeli foreign minister upping the ante. Lieberman said on 20 April 2009 that Western-backed peace efforts with the Palestinians had reached a 'dead end' and that Israel intended to present new ideas for diplomacy, such as a Palestinian recognition of Israel as a 'Jewish state'. In response, the State Department re-emphasised the American goal of establishing two states. Robert Wood, the spokesman, reiterated the Obama administration position thus:

> We are going to hear comments from various parties about how they assess things... The important objective for us is to get this process back on track so that we can get to this two-state solution that we think is in the best interests of not only the Israelis and the Palestinians, but the United States and the rest of the world.[29]

In response to these remarks, Lieberman said that external bodies must cease pressuring Israel with regard to the peace process: '[Israel] has never gotten involved in the business of others, and I expected the same, that nobody will stand there with a stopwatch in hand,' Lieberman told members of his party.[30]

Obama remained cautiously quiet during the December 2008–January 2009 invasion of Gaza, hiding under the slogan that there is only one president at a time. And yet, he was the one president on 22 January, but he failed to speak out. He appointed former Senator George Mitchell as his special envoy to the Middle East with the mandate of focusing his attention on Middle East peace. He emphasised his commitment to a peaceful settlement thus: 'It will be the policy of my administration to actively and aggressively seek a lasting peace between Israel and the Palestinians, as well as Israel and its Arab neighbours.' But he declined to elaborate, except by saying that:

> [t]he Arab peace initiative... contains constructive elements that could help advance these efforts. Now is the time for Arab states to act on the initiative's promise by supporting the Palestinian government under President [Mahmoud] Abbas and Prime Minister [Salam] Fayyad, taking steps toward normalizing relations with Israel and by standing up to extremism that threatens us all.[31]

He failed to consider, however, that normalisation could only be envisioned in the context of terminating the occupation in accordance with Resolution 242, and the recognition of self-determination for the Palestinian people. A bundle of fragmented Palestinian enclaves existing on the periphery of an expanding Israel which continued to implant settlements on Palestinian land in the West Bank would make the two-state solution totally unfeasible – a point apparently lost on Obama.

Nor can one fully understand the current hopelessness of the two-state settlement without knowing the patterns of geographical (and other) 'Judaisation' of 1948 Palestine, or without understanding the fate of Galilee: Upper Nazareth; Carmiel and the logically ensuing 'mitzpim';[32] the devastation of Wadi 'Ara; and the erasure (almost complete) of the Palestinian existence on the Carmiel and much of the sea coast. All these (and there are more examples) have been paradigms for what began in 1967 under the Israeli Labour party in the West Bank. Furthermore, the combined design of Ma'ale Adumim, Jabal Abu Ghnaim, Gilo and the stealth takeover of the Hebron region have, at least de facto (and de jure is not far behind), changed the definition of Jerusalem.

Obama and the Middle East

Palestinians long believed that George J. Mitchell, Obama's former emissary to the Middle East, brought unique credentials and goodwill. But success for them would have to mean a fundamental reassessment of failed previous approaches, openness to new ideas, and a willingness to give voice and power to those who have been systematically marginalised, demonised and made voiceless. Inevitably where politics fails, violence takes its place, at ever greater and more horrifying levels. But for Palestinians violence is not the cause of this conflict; it is the symptom of a lack of justice and a lack of alternative paths to justice. So Mitchell's task at its core – indeed the task of any American emissary – was to open an alternative path to justice in order to achieve peace.

Today, there are 11 million people in Israel, the West Bank and Gaza Strip together. Approximately half are Israeli Jews and half are Palestinians. They live in conditions of radical inequality that perpetuates and fuels a bloody and violent conflict. There are several million more Palestinians dispossessed and exiled from their land who consider they have faced injustice for over 60 years. The two peoples are interspersed throughout the land, and historically have proven no more separable than blacks and whites in South Africa, or Catholics and Protestants in Ireland. They have fought bitterly to remain in the same small piece of land.

No peace process will succeed unless there is a sharp break from the habits of American administrations acting as Israel's 'attorney', apologist and defender, arms supplier and financier. US domestic politics is a double-edged sword. Irish America helped the Northern Ireland peace process by encouraging the USA to apply pressure on behalf of the weaker side, levelling the playing field for meaningful negotiations. The pro-Israel lobby, by contrast, has blocked peace by weighing the scales even more radically against the Palestinians. Most observers would conclude that no real negotiations could be possible in the face of so much inequality of power and influence. Senator Mitchell would have had to bridge the gap between Israel and Ireland on how solutions were sought and tested out. Not only would Palestinians have expected him to reject demands such as Palestinian recognition of Israel as a Jewish state, thus disenfranchising the Palestinian citizens of Israel, but they would have expected all segments of the Palestinian people to be included in negotiations – meaning West Bankers, Gazans, the refugees, the Diaspora and Israel's Palestinian citizens. Palestinians consider their consent and participation key to producing a lasting peace. They would also expect the right to elect their own leaders instead of being told who their leaders are. Palestinians of all shades of opinion see the boycott of Hamas as a case in point, despite its status as the most powerful and popular party among Palestinians in the 1967 OT. Just as there could be no peace without Sinn Fein and the IRA in Northern Ireland, they say, there can be no peace without Hamas in Palestine.

Broadly speaking, there are two paths to a solution: two fully independent states – Palestine and Israel, based on UN Resolution 242; or a single unitary or binational state guaranteeing equal rights and protections to all who live in it. Under either scenario, Palestinians insist that the rights of Palestinian refugees, as stated in UN Resolution 194, must be fully respected, including the rights of return, restitution and compensation. Palestinian citizens of Israel (whose inferior status is analogous to that of Catholics in Northern Ireland prior to the Belfast Agreement) must be guaranteed full and equal civil, political, economic and cultural rights. The notion that the issue of peace between Palestinians and Israelis should be limited solely to those who live in the West Bank and Gaza Strip is, in the Palestinian view, a misconception that needs to be abandoned.

Palestinians could not accept that the rights of Palestinians inside Israel and in exile (who actually constitute a majority of all Palestinians) should be traded away for an end to the occupation of the West Bank and Gaza Strip. Palestinians should not be forced to choose among their human rights. They are entitled to all of them. In his speech to the Muslim world from Cairo University on 4 June 2009, President Obama made some significant departures from George Bush's policy, which if translated into action could change the untenable and intolerable status quo. For example, on the settlements, Obama said:

> Hamas must put an end to violence, recognise past agreements, and recognise Israel's right to exist. At the same time, Israelis must acknowledge that just as Israel's right to exist cannot be denied, neither can Palestine's. The United States does not accept the legitimacy of continued Israeli settlements. This construction violates previous agreements and undermines efforts to achieve peace. It is time for these settlements to stop.[33]

With a strong claim of even-handedness, Obama committed his administration and himself as a person to a two-state solution whereby Palestine and Israel could live together as co-equal:

> On the other hand, it is also undeniable that the Palestinian people, Muslims and Christians, have suffered in pursuit of a homeland. For more than 60 years they have endured the pain of dislocation. Many wait in refugee camps in the West Bank, Gaza, and neighbouring lands for a life of peace and security that they have never been able to lead. They endure the daily humiliations large and small that come with occupation. So let there be no doubt: the situation for the Palestinian people is intolerable. America will not turn our backs on the legitimate Palestinian aspiration for dignity, opportunity, and a state of their own.[34]

Needless to say, however, a two-state solution requires a tough American policy towards Israel, an endeavour which Obama has found thorny indeed. Among the most important requirements of the two-state solution are:

1. a complete, rapid and guaranteed end to Israeli military occupation, presence, remote control, blockade and siege from all the territories occupied in June 1967 including east Jerusalem;
2. land occupied by Israeli settlers/settlements to be returned to Palestine as well as the existing infrastructure and full compensation to Palestinians for loss of use of their land during the period it was colonised;
3. the departure or integration of settlers into the Palestinian state; no right for Israel to insist on ruling anyone within the Palestinian state;
4. guaranteed free movement without Israeli interference between the West Bank and Gaza Strip and full Palestinian control over its airspace, water, land, electromagnetic spectrum, borders, immigration and commerce; and
5. full political and economic sovereignty and equality for the Palestinian state.

These conditions of full sovereignty seem remote as we consider the milieu in the region following the events of 2011, and particularly the ongoing crises in relations between the Obama administration and Netanyahu's regime. The crises were precipitated at the end of March 2010 during a visit by Vice-President Joe Biden, a devoted friend of Israel. Biden was met by the unexpected announcement from the Israeli Interior Minister of his government's intention to build 1,600 units in occupied Arab Jerusalem. Secretary of State Hillary Clinton described the announcement as an 'insult', while White House senior advisor David Axelrod described the situation as an 'affront' to the USA. Journalist Pat Buchanan titled his article on the subject 'The Poodle gets kicked'. Akiva Eldar, noted Israeli journalist, titled an article in *Ha'aretz*: 'Netanyahu and Obama at point of no return.' He began his article this way:

> The strife between Israel and the United States concerns something far bigger than the proximity talks with the Palestinians. As far as President Barack Obama and his senior advisers are concerned, Prime Minister Benjamin Netanyahu is to blame for nothing less than damaging the standing of the US in the Middle East and the Muslim world.[35]

Another journalist echoed a similar concern when he wrote the following in the *New York Times*:

> You can't have rapprochement with Muslims while condoning the steady Israeli appropriation of the physical space for Palestine. You can't have that rapprochement if US policy is susceptible to the whims of Shas, the Sephardic ultra-Orthodox party in Netanyahu's coalition that runs the Interior Ministry and announced the Biden-baiting measure. The Israeli right, whether religious or secular, has no interest in a two-state peace.[36]

After the contacts between Netanyahu and Obama became acrimonious in Washington, and as AIPAC was publicly urging the Obama administration not to push Netanyahu towards the settlement freeze, Netanyahu decided to return to Israel on 25 March after a disastrous meeting with the US President. According to press reports, Obama humiliated Netanyahu by leaving the meeting abruptly: 'I'm going to the residential wing to have dinner with Michelle and the girls,' he is alleged to have said, adding: 'I'm still around... Let me know if there is anything new.'[37] The Israeli daily newspaper *Ha'aretz* said: 'The Prime Minister leaves America disgraced, isolated and altogether weaker than when he came.'[38]

Obama's Vice-President, Biden, was no less antagonised by Netanyahu's behaviour. When Biden was embarrassed by the announcement of the 1,600 new homes in East Jerusalem, the administration reacted. According to the Israeli daily *Yedioth Ahronoth*, Biden engaged in a private and angry exchange with the Israeli prime minister. Biden reportedly told Netanyahu the following:

> This is starting to get dangerous for us.... What you're doing here undermines the security of our troops who are fighting in Iraq, Afghanistan and Pakistan. That endangers us and it endangers regional peace. [It] could have an impact on the personal safety of American troops fighting against Islamic terrorism.

The message couldn't be plainer: Israel's intransigence could cost American lives.[39]

The injection of the US Army into foreign policy issues in the Middle East added a new and interesting dimension to the story. Obama knew that he could not take on the Israeli lobby alone, particularly when Nancy Pelosi and her Congressional troops stood ready to provide Israel with whatever it needed and accommodate her decisions no matter the impact on US national security in the region. He may have speculated that the Israel lobby could find its match only when the US 'military lobby' was mobilised. Is it the only possible counterweight to Israel's American friends? Here is another illustration of the significance of the military lobby:

> There are important and powerful lobbies in America: the NRA, the American Medical Association, the lawyers – and the Israeli lobby. But no lobby is as important, or as powerful, as the US military. While commentators and pundits might reflect that Joe Biden's trip to Israel has forever shifted America's relationship with its erstwhile ally in the region, the real break came in January, when General David Petraeus sent a briefing team to the Pentagon with a stark warning: America's relationship with Israel is important, but not as important as the lives of America's soldiers. Maybe Israel gets the message now.[40]

And yet, the Washington conference on nuclear weapons, hosted by Obama on 12–13 April 2010, provided another test of Obama's resolve to deal with Israel when US national interest was at stake. When asked about Israel's nuclear programme at the Washington conference, Obama at first refused to address the Israeli dimension, preferring, instead, to talk about the USA and its commitment to reducing American nuclear weapon stockpiles. Here is how he diverted attention away from the question:

> Initially you were talking about US behaviour, and then suddenly we're talking about Israel. Let me talk about the United States... I do think that as part of the NPT [Non-Proliferation Treaty], our obligation, as the largest nuclear power in the world, is to take steps to reducing our nuclear stockpile. And that's what the START treaty was about, sending a message that we are going to meet our obligations... as far as Israel goes, I'm not going to comment on their program.[41]

Despite that initial reluctance to include Israel in his calling for compliance with the Nuclear Non-Proliferation Treaty (NPT), Obama hinted broadly that the USA was calling on all nations to sign the NPT, emphasising that he was following US policy:

> What I'm going to point to is the fact that consistently we have urged all countries to become members of the NPT. So there's no contradiction there... And so whether we're talking about Israel or any other country, we think that becoming part of the NPT is important. And that, by the way, is not a new position. That's been a consistent position of the United States government, even prior to my administration.[42]

The One-State Solution

Within a few years, Palestinians will constitute the majority in all the territories today controlled by Israel. Already, the prospects of a workable and durable two-state solution are doubtful. Even if Palestinians could be made to accept a truncated state in 15 or 20 per cent of their historic homeland, would that hold when they form say two-thirds of the total population? Nadia Hijab wrote the following about the growing belief in the single state:

> Ehud Olmert's nightmare is at hand. Not only does the former Israeli prime minister now really have to fight those corruption charges. He also faces the realisation of his fears that the Palestinians might give up on a two-state solution in favour of a struggle for equal rights that would mean, as he put it, the 'end of the Jewish state'. Yo, Ehud, that struggle is a growing movement, and it isn't a threat to Jews – on the contrary, Jews are very much a part of it. Just last weekend in Boston, American

and/or Israeli Jews accounted for nearly a third of the 29 speakers at a conference organised by TARI (Trans Arab Research Institute) with the William Joiner Center at the University of Massachusetts. This is the second major public conference on how to achieve a single democratic state for Palestinians and Israelis. The first was held in London in November, and a third is slated for Toronto in June.[43]

Ultimately it must be admitted that at the core of this conflict – like in Northern Ireland – is a lack of equality and a gross imbalance of power and rights, and any solution, whether based on one state or two, cannot work unless it guarantees equality. Oslo, aside from the substantive flaws in the initial agreement and subsequent accord, was doomed because of the vast asymmetry in power between Israel and the Palestinians, made even greater by the USA's robust support for Israel. Given the above, what resources of power are American negotiators and the President prepared to bring to bear to ensure Israel is willing to make meaningful concessions, bearing in mind that no president has ever brought sufficient pressure to bear? Will the President use the financial resources the USA provides to Israel as a means of enforcement and pressure? Is the President willing to anger and confront pro-Israel constituencies who cannot countenance any American policy except one that simply endorses whatever an Israeli government puts forward? Will the USA stop using its veto power in the UN to protect Israel from international scrutiny? If it becomes apparent to President Obama that a two-state solution is unworkable or unachievable, will he be prepared to put democratic alternatives on the table? Finally, if the process fails, will the President be prepared to give a full account of why it failed?

Showdown at the UN

Having failed to persuade Netanyahu to stop building Jewish settlements in the Palestinian OT, and feeling the pressures of the pro-Israel lobby, Obama, in his address of 21 September 2011 to the UN General Assembly, pre-empted the bid submitted on 23 September 2012 by Mahmoud Abbas, President of the Palestinian Authority, for full Palestinian membership in the international organisation.

In his address to the General Assembly, Obama characterised the Palestinian demand as an attempt to avoid hard negotiations and was bound to fail as a 'short cut' to the conflict. Of course, it can be argued that more than four decades of occupation and two decades of so-called negotiations under US auspices can hardly be considered a 'short cut'. Nevertheless, he made the founding of a Palestinian state conditional on Israel and the Palestinians settling their differences. In so doing, he gave the occupier the power to veto the establishment of such a state and subjected the Palestinian right to self-determination to the approval of a third party: an anomaly in international law.

Considering the present situation, it seems to many that the peace process has reached a dead end. Given these circumstances, hopes for a meaningful two-state solution have all but vanished. Time has arrived for both Palestinians and Israelis to re-evaluate the situation.

Notes

1. See Ilan Pappé, *The Ethnic Cleansing of Palestine* (Oxford: One World, 2008).

2. Baruch Kimmerling, *Politicide, Ariel Sharon's War against the Palestinians* (London: Verso, 2003).

3. Tanya Rienhart, 'Why academic boycott: a reply to an Israeli comrade' (Baruch Kimmerling), 19 May 2002, available at www.mediamonitors.net/tanya13.html. See also *The Road Map to Nowhere: Israel/Palestine Since 2003* (London & New York: Verso, 2006).

4. For an Israeli act that amounts to a war crime during the war on Gaza, see 'Amnesty details Gaza war crimes', BBC News, 2 July 2009.

5. International Crisis Group, 'Gaza's Unfinished Business', *Middle East Report*, No. 85, 23 April 2009.

6. For a discussion of these plans, see Naseer Aruri, *The Obstruction of Peace, the US, Israel and the Palestinians* (Monroe, Maine, 1995); and Naseer Aruri, *Dishonest Broker, The US Role in Israel and Palestine* (Boston: South End Press, 2003).

7. Aruri, *Dishonest Broker*, pp. 129–30.

8. See Samih Farsoun and Naseer Aruri, *Palestine and the Palestinians: A Social and Political History* (second edition) (Boulder, Colorado: Westview Press, 2006), pp. 361–5.

9. See Nir Hasson, 'Israel planning 50,000 housing units in East Jerusalem', *Ha'aretz*, 11 March 2010.

10. See H. Ashrawi, 'Barak's political exports: used goods to Arafat and a snub to Clinton', *Miftah*, available at www.miftah.org. See also R. Malley, 'Fictions about the failure at Camp David', *New York Times*, 8 July 2001.

11. See Kathleen Christisson, 'Anatomy of a frame-up: Camp David redux', *Counterpunch*, 15 August 2005. Available at www.counterpunch.org/christison 08152005.html.

12. *Washington Post*, 23 May 2005.

13. Ibid.

14. Simha Flapan, *The Birth of Israel: Myths and Realities* (New York: Pantheon Books, 1988), p. 223, citing Record of the Knesset, Vol. 1, 1949, Session 43.

15. Michael Palumbo, *The Palestinian Catastrophe: The 1948 Expulsion of a People from their Homeland* (London/Boston: 1987), p. 145.

16. *Jerusalem Post*, 30 March 2007.

17. John Dugard, 'Apartheid and occupation under international law', Hisham B. Sharabi Memorial Lecture, Washington, DC, The Palestine Centre, 30 March 2009.

18. 'Carter wants Hamas off US terror list', Press TV, 17 June 2009. Available at www. presstv.com/detail.aspx?id=98331&sectionid=351020202.

19. Ibid.

20. For details, see David Rose, 'The Gaza bombshell', *Vanity Fair*, April 2008.

21. Yossi Verter, 'Assassinating Annapolis', *Ha'aretz*, 15 November 2007.

22. Arnaud De Borchgrave, 'Jitters over expected Israeli air attack. Gulf states get set for a raid on Iran's nuclear sites', 17 April 2009. Available at www.washingtontimes. com/news/2009/apr/17/jitters-over-expected-air-attack.

23. Akiva Eldar, 'US: Palestinians need not recognise Israel as Jewish state before talks', *Ha'aretz*, 19 April 2009.

24. Ibid.

25. Roger Cohen, 'Clinton's Mideast pirouette', *Sunday New York Times*, 26 April 2009.

26. Ibid.

27. Jason Koutsoukis, 'Obama's stance worries Israelis', 18 April 2009. Available at www. theage.com.au/world/obamas-stance-worries-israelis-20090417-\aa90.html?page=-1.

28. Jason Koutsoukis, 'Obama refuses to meet Netanyahu', *The Muslim Observer*, 18 April 2009.

29. Eldar, 'US: Palestinians need not recognise Israel as Jewish state before talks'.

30. Ibid.

31. Ibid.

32. 'Mitzpim' literally means lookouts, but has connotations linguistically and geographically with prison towers from which to keep track of the Palestinians.

33. See text of Obama's speech in 'White House Blog. The President's speech in Cairo: a new beginning', posted by Jesse Lee on 4 June 2009.

34. Ibid.

35. *Ha'aretz*, 28 March 2010.

36. Roger Cohen, 'The Biden effect', *New York Times*, 15 March 2010.

37. Giles Whittell and James Hider, 'Binyamin Netanyahu humiliated after Barack Obama dumped him for dinner', *Times on Line*, 26 March 2010.

38. *Ha'aretz*, 29 March 2010.

39. Petraeus briefing: 'Biden's embarrassment is not the whole story', posted by Mark Perry, 13 March 2010, Foreign Policy Website.

40. Ibid.

41. www.ynetnews.com/articles/0,7340,L-3875661,00.html.

42. Ibid.

43. Nadia Hijab, 'Olmert's nightmare: the growing belief in a one-state solution', *Counterpunch*, 8 April 2009.

CHAPTER 6

Israel's War on Gaza: Zionism's Pyrrhic Victory?

Nancy Murray

Introduction

For 23 days beginning on 27 December 2008, Israel used its high-tech military force against a besieged people without a regular army and no way to defend itself. In Operation Cast Lead's immediate aftermath, both sides claimed victory.

Hamas, which (along with other militant groups) had fired some 8,000 crude rockets and mortars into Israel since April 2001, causing 21 Israeli deaths,[1] was not dislodged as the ruling party in Gaza. It retained its ability to fire rockets into Israel and appeared to have enhanced its political standing. But too many lives were lost and too much damage was done for its claim of victory to seem more than a rhetorical flourish, especially since the blockade remained tightly in place following Israel's unilateral ceasefire, and military strikes by the IDF continued.

Israel's military triumph was a foregone conclusion: according to the Palestinian Centre for Human Rights, 1,434 Palestinians were killed, including 960 civilians,[2] while only 13 Israelis were killed, among them three civilians and soldiers who died as a result of 'friendly fire'. Both the military and propaganda phases of Operation Cast Lead were long in preparation,[3] and designed to offset the damage to the IDF's reputation and morale caused by its bruising encounter with Hezbollah in 2006. By incurring minimal casualties in Gaza, the IDF demonstrated that it has retained its overwhelming military edge. It had other reasons to declare victory. It was able to act with virtual impunity, as foreign governments and the United Nations declined to intervene.[4] Furthermore, Gaza offered a rare 'live' testing ground for experimental weaponry and forms of urban warfare.[5]

However, Israel's exercise of what it called its 'right to self-defence' caused an upsurge of anger in neighbouring countries and globally that has not subsided given the collective punishment represented by the ongoing blockade. During the war, popular protest spanned the globe, with major demonstrations taking place from the USA and South America, across Europe and the Middle East, to Korea and Japan. Turkey, Israel's close regional ally, issued a strong rebuke, while Qatar cut its trade relations. Prince Turki Al-Faisal, the influential and highly pragmatic former Saudi intelligence chief and ambassador to the USA, declared: 'Today we are all Palestinians and we seek martyrdom for God and for Palestine.'[6]

Israel's war on the people of Gaza did not end with its unilateral ceasefire. As the Gaza Strip remained tightly besieged, with Israel barring the entry of sufficient food, fuel and other basic necessities, as well as material and equipment for the repair of essential infrastructure and the thousands of destroyed homes, the Gaza Freedom March, Viva Palestina and the Free Gaza Movement have brought together thousands of people from dozens of countries in an attempt to break the siege. Human rights organisations and a 50-person delegation of European Members of Parliament, politicians and former ministers sounded the alarm about the 'dire' humanitarian crisis in Gaza and the danger of allowing the situation to continue.[7] On 28 January 2010, 54 Members of the US Congress took the unprecedented step of sending a letter to President Obama, urging him to take action to end this 'de facto collective punishment' and to 'press for immediate relief for the citizens of Gaza'.[8]

Although the USA, as Israel's key protector, stood firm, providing arms, fuel and political and diplomatic backing for the Gaza War, and condemning the Goldstone Report in both Congress and the United Nations,[9] Israel's 'success' in Gaza could eventually prove both short-term and illusory. Indeed, its vulnerability was underscored by the intense global outcry and diplomatic crisis that followed its deadly 31 May 2010 attack on the Turkish ship the *Mavi Marmara* and the five other boats attempting to reach Gaza with humanitarian aid. This chapter will explore opportunities within the USA to make the war on Gaza a 'pyrrhic victory' for Zionism, a military adventure whose long-term costs outweigh any short-term benefits. A change in perceptions of Zionism that makes it seem as dispensable and detrimental to justice and co-existence as Jim Crow segregation and South African apartheid came to appear could prepare the way for 'one state' as an eventual outcome.

The Changing Landscape

'I would like Gaza to sink into the sea,' Israeli Prime Minister Rabin told a delegation from the Washington Institute for Near East Policy visiting Jerusalem on 2 September 1992. He added: 'but that won't happen, and a solution must be found'.[10]

At the time of writing, the possibility of Gaza sinking into the sea seems less remote than the 'solution' of Israeli Jews and Palestinians sharing a single state. The first is inexorably approaching, as the rapid melting of glaciers is resulting in an estimated 40 years before the Mediterranean intrudes into coastal communities, polluting water resources and making huge areas of land unsustainable.[11] The second solution seems as difficult to conjure up out of the rubble to which the Gaza Strip has been reduced as the notion that the massive destruction can be put right by hauling tens of thousands of tons of cement and building materials through rudimentary tunnels, even as Israeli war planes continue to pound them and Egypt builds a seven-to-ten-mile-long metal wall 60 feet underground along its border with Gaza in an attempt to foil them.[12] The rightward shift of the Israeli electorate and the projection that the population of the densely packed Gaza Strip is likely to double within 20 years[13] make it seem highly implausible that Israel would in the foreseeable future agree to share a polity with those against whom it has long been successfully practising what Baruch Kimmerling has called 'politicide' – the destruction of the political and national existence of the Palestinian people in order to deny them self-determination.[14]

It is not just 'one-state' that is now beyond the horizon. The war on Gaza, which intensified the bitter rift between Hamas and Fateh and brought Palestinian Authority police armed with long clubs on to West Bank streets to prevent solidarity demonstrations, dealt (in the view of several commentators) a death blow to the notion of a two-state solution, with Gaza and the West Bank forming the 'single territorial unit' which the 1993 Declaration of Principles defined them to be.[15] The one-state appears to be ruled out by Israel's 'facts on the ground' in the West Bank, by the 'Greater Israel' mind-set of Israel's government and, increasingly, the higher echelons of its military establishment, and by a fractured Palestinian leadership that has no vision of how to achieve Palestinian sovereignty in a state alongside Israel. Meanwhile, some West Bank technocrats have bought into Netanyahu's notion that 'economic development' for the West Bank can be an alternative to self-determination. The first newsletter of the Palestine Development Fund states that building 'a sustainable Palestinian economy' is becoming a 'reality'.[16] Its pages feature a 'conceptual design' of an imaginary housing development resembling a Palestinian Har Homa, and another of spiral tower blocs in a futuristic Ramallah, without a single mention of checkpoints and closures and other obstacles of occupation.

Long after Israel called a unilateral temporary ceasefire in deference to the inauguration of President Obama, Gaza remained a sealed-off 'prison' whose residents were living in unspeakable conditions. While the PA sought to ensure that it would control medical, food and other supplies provided for Gaza by international agencies, and Israel barred the entry of essential supplies,[17] as many as 160 Palestinians died in the thousand or so tunnels through which food and supplies have been smuggled from Egypt.[18] The impact of the siege a year after Israel's ceasefire was detailed by Harvard University researcher Sara Roy, who cited Amnesty International figures that 90–95 per cent of Gaza's water was 'unfit for drinking' and no more than 41 truckloads of construction materials were permitted into Gaza between the end of the war and December 2009, while Gaza's industrial sector alone needed 55,000 truckloads for reconstruction.[19]

Meanwhile, the prison in which Gazans were trapped was steadily shrinking, as Israel enforced a 300-metre 'buffer zone' along the 30 miles of Gaza's perimeter, putting 30 per cent of its best agricultural land off-limits to its farmers, and 20 per cent of its total territory beyond the reach of its 1.5 million people. Protest marchers were shot at and injured by Israeli snipers using live ammunition. On some occasions, farmers were shot who are well outside the 'buffer zone', and Israeli tanks and bulldozers crossed into Gaza to destroy farming land, which made the outlook for food production increasingly grim. The sea was also off-limits, as Israel maintained its naval blockade and was reportedly appropriating natural gas resources from Gaza's territorial waters for its own use.[20]

The dire humanitarian situation did not deter the Obama administration from carrying on with the Bush administration's policy of refusing to deal with Hamas while making an effort to prop up Mahmoud Abbas, whose term of office according to one interpretation of Palestinian election law ended in early January 2010.[21] As the administration explored ways to detach Syria from the league of 'extremists' and stem Iranian influence in the region, it did not seem prepared to back up critical words with action as Israel accelerated its settlement drive and takeover of East Jerusalem. With a further 73,000 new homes for settlers planned for the West Bank according to a Peace Now report,[22] and the announcement of 1,600 new units for East Jerusalem chilling US/Israel relations during Vice-President Joseph Biden's visit, Israel appeared confident that 'Greater Israel' was within its grasp, and that its security would be guaranteed by the 'security wall', ongoing arms transfers from the USA and, if Avigdor Lieberman's party got its way, the potential 'transfer' of those of its Palestinian citizens who refuse to take a loyalty oath to the Jewish state. The vaguely worded Military Order 1650 (13 April 2010) threatened any so-called 'infiltrator' who did not have a 'lawfully' held permit to reside in the West Bank with prison and expulsion, including to the Gaza Strip.

In addition, as envisaged under the Oslo Accords, Palestinians were expected to take up their 'law and order' responsibilities. In Jericho, a US general, Lieutenant General Keith Dayton, oversaw the training of Palestinian security forces in state-of-the-art facilities, with US$10 million from American taxpayers. The general, who wanted to 'have a well-trained battalion based in each of eight West Bank cities when he is through', said his trainees 'now feel like they're on a winning team, that they are building a Palestinian state'.[23] Or perhaps eight city-states?

Today, there seems nothing more on offer to Palestinians than an archipelago of miniature South African-style Bantustans in the West Bank and a deeply impoverished, teeming concentration camp on the Gaza Strip. But this is not inevitable. Finding Palestinian leaders to sign off on such a 'solution' could be forestalled if the Fatah-Hamas accord brokered by Egypt in early May 2011 proves to have staying power. And with the melting away not only of glaciers, but also of the global economy and military certainties, a sea change could well occur in Western – and American – attitudes towards an ever-expansionist Zionist state that will eventually put one-state on the agenda as an outcome worth exploring. Indeed, a first step was taken by General David Petraeus, when he told the US Armed Services Committee on 16 March 2010 that the Israeli–Palestinian conflict 'foments anti-American sentiment, due to the perception of US favouritism for Israel' and that 'Arab anger over the Palestinian question limits the depth of US partnerships and governments... and weakens the legitimacy of moderate regimes in the Arab world'.[24] At a time of such a dramatic transformation of the economic landscape, the impunity with which Israel has been permitted to operate may not survive a cost–benefit analysis that weighs ongoing uncritical US support for a regime increasingly condemned for its 'apartheid' practices against the need to shore up regional alliances, reduce instability, encourage cooperation in the allocation of increasingly scarce resources and avoid expensive new military disasters.

How can we begin to get from here to there? The forced retreat from executive branch circles of the tight band of neocons who made loyalty to Israel a patriotic duty as they shaped the policy agenda of the Bush administration, the advent of a president committed in rhetoric at least to restoring the nation's badly tarnished international reputation, and the troubling TV and internet images of Israel's Gaza onslaught and draconian blockade, combine to give those of us who are working for Palestinian rights an opening to do some re-framing of our own. I would like to focus on three ways we can take advantage of that opportunity.

First, we can tell Gaza's story in a way that lays bare what Israel's occupation has meant for Gazans and all Palestinians, and help Americans to understand that, to quote Nir Rosen, 'a Zionist Israel is not a viable long-term project'.[25] We must take encouragement from polls over the last few years that indicate that the public is not nearly as solidly pro-Israel as is commonly supposed, with new political opportunities offered by the ascendancy of the Democratic Party.[26] Second, recognising that there can be no movement forward as long as Hamas is seen as nothing more than a 'terrorist' organisation, we should be prepared to counter this simplistic image and expose how Israel's most fervent supporters have conflated Hamas and 'terrorism' to stoke domestic fears, and undermine fundamental tenets of the US legal system. Third, while Palestinians within the West Bank, Gaza, Israel and the Diaspora struggle to overcome crippling internal divisions and unite around a common political vision, the solidarity movement can build momentum by articulating straightforward, hard-to-refute demands that resonate with an American public craving a return to the rule of law and respect for human rights. The call for 'Freedom, Justice and Equal Rights for All', encompassing what are regarded as basic American values, could eventually make a 'one-state' solution seem a logical outcome for an otherwise intractable and far too costly problem.

I will look at each of these points in turn.

Telling Gaza's Story

An internal document from Combined Jewish Philanthropies (CJP) sets out the need to raise US$2.4 million for work in Boston to fight the 'growing, well financed campaign of anti-Israelism in many places around the world, even in the United States, involving religious leaders, academics, political leaders, media and ordinary citizens' using strategies that include 'boycotts, divestment and propaganda campaigns'. Claiming that much more must be done to win hearts and minds for Israel among the Jewish community, among businessmen and community leaders, in the media and especially on campus, the document states that 'support for Israel rests on a weak foundation', with many Americans possessing a 'subtle confusion about how they feel about the different players' in the conflict:

> While many Americans do have positive feelings about Israel as an American ally, the public is constantly exposed to a barrage of images from the media that portray Israel as a war-torn country steeped in military aggression where the average citizen is mired in conflict with neighbours. Within this context Israel is often portrayed as the aggressor against an underdog victim rather than as a party in pursuit of peace.[27]

The document is dated February 2008 – many months before the 'barrage of images' from Gaza. For the most part, the US mainstream media in late December 2008 and early January 2009 kept its focus on Israel as a victim (if not exactly an underdog), fighting a battle of 'self-defence' against the aggression of 'terrorists' on its borders.

But as in the case of Israel's 2006 attack against Lebanon, televised and internet images of the magnitude of the destruction have raised doubts and fed a desire to know more. The CJP must have been deeply worried by the proliferation of forums, teach-ins, lectures, church services and meetings, vigils, demonstrations, op-eds, videos, blogs, websites and other opportunities to lead audiences beyond 'subtle confusion' to a factual understanding of what Israel's creation and its relentlessly dominating presence have meant for the people of Gaza (and all Palestinians). 'Breaking the siege' visits to Gaza by such well-known figures as the writer Alice Walker and former Congresswoman Cynthia McKinney, as well as the 'fact finding' missions of Congressional Representatives Keith Ellison (Democrat, Minnesota), former representative Brian Baird (Democrat, Washington) and the then Senator John Kerry (Democrat, Massachusetts), and Vermont Senator Patrick Leahy's comparison of Gazans to his Irish ancestors fighting for their land, surely compounded the anxiety.[28] And the growing number of Jewish voices condemning Israel's war and its relentless settlement expansion in the West Bank must be particularly unsettling. How, for instance, can the outspoken Henry Siegman be dismissed as a 'self-hating' Jew when his biography includes 15 years as executive director of the American Jewish Congress and a stint as national director of the Synagogue Council of America?

One measure of the anxiety over how Israel is perceived is the near-hysterical vitriol directed at the South African jurist Richard Goldstone, who headed the UN investigation into Operation Cast Lead that found both Israel and Hamas guilty of war crimes. Goldstone has had a long involvement with Israeli institutions and has been described by his daughter Nicole as a 'Zionist' who 'loves Israel'.[29] After a year and a half of intense vilification, and shortly after the Human Rights Council resolved that the Goldstone Report should be sent to the UN General Assembly with the recommendation that it ask the Security Council to transmit it to the International Criminal Court for possible war crimes prosecutions, Goldstone himself threw Israel a lifeline by writing that 'if I had known then what I know now, the Goldstone Report would have been a different document', and then clearing Israel of the charge that it had deliberately targeted the 29 members of the al-Simouni family who were killed when their house was shelled by the IDF. He contended in his *Washington Post* op-ed that an Israeli investigation had revealed that their killing was not intentional, but rather a 'consequence of an Israeli commander's erroneous interpretation of a drone image'.[30]

Israel's supporters and the mainstream media insisted that Goldstone's alleged 'change of heart' in this one instance was a thorough vindication of Israel. But on the same day as the US Senate voted unanimously for the 'discredited' Report to be withdrawn, its co-authors – Christine Chinkin, Colonel Desmond Travers and Hina Jilani – issued a strongly worded statement to the *Guardian*, declaring that 'nothing of substance has appeared that would in any way change the context, findings or conclusions' of the Report and condemning the 'extraordinary pressure placed on members of the fact-finding mission [who] began our work in May 2009'.[31]

The Goldstone op-ed may have given the CJP and organisations like it a springboard to denounce the Report as a 'blood libel' and portray Israel as 'among the world's moral nations',[32] but Gaza's story still offered many opportunities to, in the CJP's words, 'discredit and de-legitimise the very concept of a Jewish state'. There are some obvious parallels with the American experience. While seventeenth- and eighteenth-century settlers regarded themselves as a chosen people sent from the Old World to create a 'new Jerusalem' in the wilderness, nineteenth-century European immigrants regarded it as their 'right' (in the words of the newspaperman John O'Sullivan, who coined the term 'Manifest Destiny') to spread 'democracy, freedom and industry' from sea to sea. The mentality behind the phrase attributed to Indian fighter General Phil Sheridan – 'the only good Indian is a dead Indian' – resulted in the reduction of the indigenous population from an estimated 1 million at the start of European colonisation to 300,000 by 1900.

Granting native people's citizenship in 1924 did not prevent the federal government from continuing to remove land from 300 Indian reservations that had been established across 27 states. As late as the 1960s, the US Congress passed laws abolishing over 100 tribal governments, enabling land that had been held in trust for reservations to be sold to non-native Americans.[33] Given its own long record of dispossessing indigenous peoples, it is not surprising that Congress shows such little concern about Israel's ongoing land appropriations in the West Bank.

But for demographic and cultural reasons, sections of the American public are likely to be more receptive to the Palestinian story now and in the future than in previous years and increasingly out of step with Congressional views. President Obama's election has not shaken the social and economic structures that are the legacy of 'white supremacy', but it has demonstrated how far the mind-set of the nation has moved since the days of Jim Crow segregation and the 'one drop' rule. Although an often virulent anti-Arab racism has been a stock in trade of Hollywood films and sections of the media since well before 9/11, it is difficult to imagine the explicit racism endemic in what Zionist leader Ze'ev Jabotinsky called Israel's 'colonising adventure'[34] finding an easy acceptance among the young people who were the backbone of Obama's campaign. Through the lens of Gaza's story, the treatment of Palestinians as so clearly 'less than' human can resonate with white Americans longing to transcend their own racial history. How can Zionism be supported when, by subjecting generations of Palestinians to the most humiliating and brutal repression, it appears to rule out the possibility of *any* lasting solution that does not involve the total submission of the indigenous population?

There are other reasons why the American public may increasingly turn away from the kind of 'racist triumphalism' implicit in the Zionist project that was memorably captured in words spoken by IDF Chief of Staff Raphael Eitan in 1983: 'When we have settled the land, all the Arabs will be able to do about it will be to scurry around like drugged cockroaches in a bottle.'[35] The USA is poised to become a 'majority minority' nation whose largest ethnic group, Hispanics, had their own encounter with dispossession and exile when they lost the land that is now Texas, New Mexico, Nevada, California and parts of Colorado, Arizona and Utah to those who believed the entire continent was divinely ordained to be a 'white man's country'. Furthermore, many newcomers understand what it means to be refugees. Many come from countries that had their own liberation movements, and some know about the role Israel played in their repression.[36] Several prominent African Americans, including many veterans of the anti-apartheid movement who are aware of the close ties between Israel and apartheid South Africa, have long embraced the Palestinian cause and are increasingly prepared to stand up against Israel's actions.

We have, then, many potential allies to whom we have never systematically reached out and many possible points of connection, including the loss of land, homes and country, personal encounters with racism, and a visceral understanding of why and how, against all the odds, human beings find ways to resist their systematic dehumanisation. The extreme nature of Israel's blockade and war – which killed the per capita equivalent of 300,000 Americans, the majority of them civilians – gives us the opportunity to debunk its propaganda and probe the purpose behind such ferocity. A starting point is Robert Fisk's observation. 'The existence of Gaza,' he writes, 'is a permanent reminder of those hundreds of thousands of Palestinians who lost their homes to Israel.'[37] As he points out, were it not for the 'Nakba', 80 per cent of Gaza's residents could be living in parts of Israel now reached by Hamas' home-made rockets.

The war on Gaza gives us the opportunity to talk about the Nakba, when 200,000 Palestinians fled from their villages and took refuge among the 80,000 residents in what was in 1948 Egypt-controlled Gaza. It also enables us to describe the lives of refugees, driven into exile and denied the right of return reaffirmed annually by the UN General Assembly since 1948 (and until 1993 by the USA), and now numbering nearly a million Gazans who are barricaded just miles from their former homes. And it allows us to take the measure of Israel's long-term intentions. For how could Israel possibly anticipate living in peace alongside a people whom it did not just dispossess, but subjected to a version of 'shock and awe' that is guaranteed to leave a population stricken with post-traumatic stress disorder and longings for revenge? And if a form of co-existence were indeed an eventual goal, how could such a war be conceived against a people who had already been weakened by an economic blockade that, since June 2007, had deprived Gazans of all but 12 basic items – with just enough of them permitted to enter to keep the population alive? Electricity and fuel were severely rationed, and cement, soap, many medical supplies, potable water and raw materials were kept out altogether as Israel made Hamas-ruled Gaza a laboratory for finding the breaking point of human beings.[38]

On 4 November 2008, the former Irish president and head of the UN Human Rights Commission, Mary Robinson, who was one of the few foreigners to be permitted to enter Gaza that month, told the BBC that it was 'almost unbelievable' that the world did not care about what she called 'a shocking violation of so many human rights... their whole civilization has been destroyed. I'm not exaggerating.'

On this same day, the Israeli army entered Gaza and killed six Hamas members, breaking the six-month truce between Hamas and Israel that was due to expire in December. On 15 December 2008, shortly before Israel launched its war, an article in the UK *Sunday Times* was headlined: 'Gaza families eat grass as Israel locks border.'

As commonly understood, the emotive term of 'genocide', implying the systematic massacre of an entire people, is far removed from the Gaza context. But 'genocide' has another meaning under international law. It was defined by the 1948 Genocide Convention, and reiterated in the 2002 Rome Charter of the International Criminal Court, as:

> *any* [emphasis added] of the following acts committed with intent to destroy, in whole or in part, a national, ethnical, racial or religious group, as such: killing members of the group; causing serious bodily or mental harm to members of the group; deliberately inflicting on the group conditions of life, calculated to bring about its physical destruction in whole or in part.[39]

When we see Israel's war and blockade as the latest, most violent chapter of Israel's six-decade-long project of destroying Palestinian resistance to dispossession, it is difficult to dismiss out of hand charges of 'genocide' levelled at Israel on 14 January 2009 by UN General Assembly head Father Miguel d'Escoto Brockmann, as well as by some Israelis, including historian Ilan Pappé and commentator Michel Warshawsky. What else explains the systematic destruction of practically the entire infrastructure of Gaza – most government buildings, clinics, hospitals and ambulances, university buildings and schools including the American School in north Gaza, thousands of homes, the sewage and water infrastructure and water wells, fishing boats, industrial facilities, the only cement packaging factory in Gaza and all cement mixer trucks, the only operating flour mill, food and drink factories, chicken farms and more than 100,000 chickens, as well as the massive bulldozing of agricultural land and the killing of sheep and goats by snipers from a distance of 700 metres?[40]

The war on Gaza and its terrible prelude and aftermath offer many opportunities to take on Israeli propaganda. After Israeli Defence Minister Ehud Barak was widely quoted asking what Americans would have done if they had for seven years been bombarded with Mexican rockets fired from Tijuana to San Diego, Randall Kuhn of the Jewish Alliance for Justice and Peace in Denver used the Tijuana–San Diego analogy to brilliantly skewer Israel's policies towards Palestinians, from 1948 to the present.[41] After describing how 'San Diego expelled most of its Hispanic, African American, Asian American, and Native American population… and forcibly relocated them to Tijuana', Kuhn described the system of repression established to control them, and their attempts at resistance:

> Okay, now for the unbelievable part. Think about what would happen if, after expelling all of the minorities from San Diego to Tijuana and subjecting them to 40 years of brutal military occupation, we just left Tijuana, removing all the white settlers and the soldiers? Only instead of giving them their freedom, we built a 20-foot tall electrified wall around Tijuana? Not just on the sides bordering San Diego, but on all the Mexico crossings as well…[42]

He wrote about the closures and the patrolling of the air space and waters, and then:

> Would you be at all surprised to hear that these resistance groups in Tijuana, even after having been 'freed' from their occupation but starved half to death, kept on firing rockets at the United States? Probably not. But you may be surprised to learn that the majority of people in Tijuana never picked up a rocket, or a gun, or a weapon of any kind.[43]

He concluded by stating, 'This is a sound analogy to Israel's military onslaught in Gaza,' and urged Americans to take a stand.

Another way of countering Israel's depiction of Palestinians as terrorists whose rockets demanded a harsh military response is to talk about the first intifada. Before the rockets there were the stones.

The first intifada was born in December 1987 in Gaza's Jabalyia refugee camp – much of which was destroyed in the attacks 21 years later. With stones hurled by children serving as the kind of provocation and pretext that Hamas' Qassam rockets were later to be, Israeli defence minister Rabin called for 'force, might and beatings' to put down what was essentially an unarmed uprising of the entire population.

Despite the fact that there was no way the first intifada could be portrayed as a 'war' between two sides, and that demonstrations, marches, strikes, graffiti and confrontations with the IDF involving stones, burning tyres and raised Palestinian flags were the methods of struggle, the cumulative results were not much different from the massive bloodletting to come. Some 1,200 Palestinians perished, including at least 300 children, while more than 130,000 Palestinians were injured, tens of thousands were arrested and prisoners were systematically tortured. The entire population of the Gaza Strip spent days and even weeks under a round-the-clock curfew, leading David Nyhan, a *Boston Globe* columnist, to write in disbelief:

> How do you put 700,000 people under house arrest? What kind of exasperation, what poverty of imagination, what weariness of mind and deadening of soul can persuade one of the world's supposedly enlightened governments to adopt such a policy? How do you lock up a population as big as South Dakota's?[44]

And along with the repression came the steady growth of the kind of anti-Arab expression that spanned the spectrum from dehumanisation to the desire for extinction. It came from the mouths of children: Zion Ben Kna'an, a school headmaster, reported driving in a bus near a West Bank settlement with children of the fourth and fifth grades:

> On the way, in front of the bus, two four or five-year-old Arab boys were fighting. One of them fell down in the road. The children in the bus shouted at the driver: 'Run him over, he is an Arab, crush him.'... The general atmosphere among these children is that this is our land and that the Arab is not a human being. He is a primitive stone thrower who must be wiped out.[45]

It came from the mouths of youths who would shortly be joining the army. After two Palestinian workers were burned to death in the Tel Aviv suburb Or Yehuda, when the hut in which they were locked for the night was set on fire, the newspaper *Yediot Aharonot* quoted a 16-year-old resident of the town as saying: 'What does it matter if an Arab burns? What does an Arab matter at all? It's not a human being. I wouldn't care if more than 2,000 burned!'[46] It was sometimes given an official imprimatur.

On the wall of the office of a Senior Officer of the Civil Administration in the Gaza Strip, near the routine announcements of the Israeli army offices, photographs, a Swiss calendar and 'wise' sayings of sages about 'what is love', the following poem was also hanging:

> Yes, it is true that I hate Arabs
> I want to take them off the map
> Yes, this is all [my] work.
> My life passes pleasurably
> One shoots a bullet and a head is flying.
> It is a pleasure to feel when the bullet touches [it]
> Knocks into the head and [the head] splits.
> Then I feel liberated and even [feel] a pleasure
> To see how the head is flying off.

There are beautiful places in the Territories
There is sea and sand and many palms
It is a pity that there are Arabs there too...[47]

For the next two decades, the trajectory was set: Israel's policies inflicted on the Gaza population 'conditions of life, calculated to bring about its physical destruction in whole or in part'.[48] In 1992, before the first Hamas suicide bombing, Israel began to subject the Gaza Strip to closure, cut off its residents from access to the West Bank and started importing foreign workers to replace Palestinian labour. 'We must see to it that Palestinians do not swarm among us' was how Prime Minister Rabin justified tightening the closure in 1993.[49] According to the former deputy mayor of Jerusalem, Meron Benvenisti, closure had become a means for 'institutionalising an apartheid regime here with much in common with the Black Homelands of South Africa'.[50] The most long-lasting result for the Gaza Strip of the Oslo Peace Process that got underway with the signing of the Declaration of Principles in September 1993 was its deepening isolation and the catastrophic decline of its economy.

The destruction of the people and infrastructure of Gaza accelerated during the second intifada, when Israel's actions against Palestinians were framed as an essential part of the global 'war on terror'. At least 3,000 Gazans (out of a total of 4,700 Palestinians) and nearly 500 Israelis were killed between 29 September 2000 and 26 December 2008, according to B'Tselem figures. After Israel removed its settlers from the Gaza Strip in the summer of 2005, it could attack that area with increasing impunity, as it did in Operation Summer Rains (June 2006) when it destroyed the only power plant in the Gaza Strip, plunging it into darkness and jeopardising the functioning of hospitals, water and sewage systems, and Autumn Clouds (November 2006). 'The figures speak for themselves,' writes the Israeli-born academic Avi Shlaim. 'In the three years after the withdrawal from Gaza, 11 Israelis were killed by rocket fire. On the other hand, in 2005–7 alone, the IDF killed 1,290 Palestinians in Gaza, including 222 children.'[51] Hamas' success in the January 2006 legislative election, and total takeover of the Gaza Strip following the June 2007 clashes, set the stage for the 'humanitarian implosion' of the 18-month-long siege, followed by the war on the entire people of Gaza which has not yet ended.

The Role of Hamas

One of the biggest hurdles faced by proponents of a one-state solution is overcoming the interpretation of the 'war on terror' as an ideological struggle between moderates and extremists, in which radical Islam – like Nazism before it – seeks the annihilation of the Jews and world domination. The term 'terrorism' has long been manipulated to serve US interests around the globe, as Edward Herman and Gerry O'Sullivan have described; and for decades before 9/11, Palestinians and the PLO were demonised within the US as 'terrorists' as a way of undermining political support for their cause. According to Herman and O'Sullivan, Israeli Prime Minister Benjamin Netanyahu established the Jonathan Institute in 1979 in order to convince the USA that the Soviet Union was sponsoring Palestinian terrorists, who should accordingly be killed before they can act.[52]

Following the attacks of 9/11, the very existence of an Israeli 'occupation' was airbrushed away in prevailing US discourse, or made to seem as 'well intentioned' as that which the US military was imposing on Iraq. With each suicide bombing or rocket attack on Israel, post-9/11 America was reminded of just how much the two peoples have in common and why they had to stand together in the battle against terrorism, whose leading sponsor was now alleged to be Iran.

Totally buried was any understanding of terror as a tactic of the weak in a struggle against foreign domination, used by liberation movements throughout history, including Zionism.[53] On the anniversary in 1991 of the founding of the terrorist 'Stern Gang', which then Prime Minister Yitzhak Shamir helped lead, he gave a revealing radio interview. 'Personal terrorism is a way of fighting that is acceptable under certain conditions and by certain movements,' Shamir stated. 'We believed in what we did… Therefore it was correct.'[54] But the Palestinian struggle for self-determination, whether or not it involved terrorism, could not be justified because 'they fight on land that is not theirs, that is the land of the people of Israel'. Shamir concluded that there are 'many Arab countries in the Middle East' where they can go and live.

In the twenty-first century, thanks to the efforts of Daniel Pipes, whose Middle East Forum website hosts Campus Watch, Islamist Watch and the Middle East Quarterly, Steven Emerson of the Investigative Project on Terrorism, Daniel Horowitz of FrontPage Magazine and the Freedom Center, and numerous pro-Israel organisations of the radical right, Palestinians are no longer depicted as fighting for land. Instead, their struggle is a front in the battle of global jihad, which has the single-minded aims of killing all Jews and destroying America and the West.

This interpretation was given its fullest expression in the award-winning, fear-inflaming film *Obsession: Radical Islam's War Against the West*, which was made in 2006, promoted by CNN and Fox, and then distributed by the shadowy Clarion Fund[55] to 28 million homes by direct mail and as an insert in 70 newspapers in the run-up to the 2008 presidential election. The film features, in addition to the usual talking heads (Pipes, Emerson and Dershowitz), Khalid Abu Toumeh, who is described only as a 'Palestinian journalist' (he is in fact an Israeli citizen who writes for the *Jerusalem Post*), and Walid Shoebat, who is identified as a 'former Palestinian terrorist'. On his website's home page, Shoebat states:

> Israel was the solution for the world's greatest refugee problem that went on for two thousand years... The Israeli Arab conflict is not about geography but about Jew hatred... The Arab refugee problem was caused by Arab aggression and not Israel. Why should Israel be responsible for their fate?[56]

In the film, Palestinian nationalists are seen as the direct heirs to Hitler, with 'Islamofascism' the new Nazism of our time. Hezbollah, Hamas and Iran are presented as purveyors of the most malicious anti-Semitism, who teach their children nothing but hate, seek the death of all Jews and threaten the USA itself. Hamas, it is said, 'has the largest infrastructure of all terrorist organisations on our soil today'.

This interpretation of Hamas' intent, reinforced with anti-Semitic statements from its Charter, has been steadily promoted by pro-Israel groups and their Congressional allies. On 22 May 2006, Representative Gary Ackerman (D-NY), speaking as one of the 205 Congressional co-sponsors of the Palestinian Anti-Terrorism Act of 2006, gave voice to the kind of disinformation that must be countered if American foreign policy towards Israel and Palestine is ever to be made more 'even-handed':

> And those forces of evil, whether they be called the Nazi Party or the Hamas Party, each of which came to power in uncontested democratic elections, each of which have in common the destruction of an entire people... how do we compromise with the notion of administrations and evil forces whose goal is the destruction of another people?[57]

While Representative Ackerman accuses Hamas of aiming at Israeli's destruction, it is the Palestinians who are actually being destroyed. And the Palestinian election of January 2006 was hardly 'uncontested,' as Ackerman says. Not only did the Bush administration urge the Palestinian Authority to hold an election in the interests of 'democracy-building,' it gave the PA US$2.3 million for this purpose, 'which many observers allege was designed to bolster the image of President Abbas and his Fateh Party'.[58] The election itself was, in Jimmy Carter's assessment, 'orderly and peaceful', with Hamas winning 76 of the 132 Parliamentary seats. The majority of Hamas legislators and several ministers, including the minister of education, were subsequently arrested by the IDF and imprisoned in an attempt to force Hamas to release the captured Israeli soldier Gilad Shalit, with no sign of US protest.

The ready acceptance in the USA that the results of the Palestinian exercise in democracy should not be allowed to stand was over a decade in the making.

By the early 1990s, before Hamas turned to suicide bombing in April 1994 in retaliation for Baruch Goldstein's murder of 29 Muslims who were praying in Hebron's Ibrahim Mosque, and before it had been listed in the USA as a terrorist organisation (1995), Daniel Pipes, Steven Emerson and an array of like-minded organisations were campaigning for the Justice Department to investigate Hamas' fund-raising activity in the USA.[59] The January 1993 arrest of Muhammad Salah, a naturalised American grocer from Chicago, when he was attempting to enter Gaza carrying humanitarian funds, was used both to deflect attention from Israel's mass expulsions of 415 suspected Hamas members into Lebanon's 'Valley of Snakes' the previous December and to ratchet up opposition to Hamas in the USA. Salah, labelled a senior Hamas commander, was tortured until he confessed and then spent five years in an Israeli prison. On his return home, he was branded a 'specially designated terrorist' by the US government and lived under draconian restrictions. In 2006–7, he was subjected to a Kafkaesque trial in a Chicago courtroom that was closed to the public, its windows covered with black crepe paper while federal agents barricaded the doors. Disguised Israeli agents were permitted to testify under code names, a violation of the Constitution's Sixth Amendment. Although acquitted by the jury of terrorism charges, Salah was sentenced by the judge to 21 months in prison and a US$25,000 fine for making statements 'calculated to protect Hamas'. His lengthy ordeal and the extraordinary way the US justice system was manipulated and long-accepted legal norms (including the inadmissibility of evidence obtained under torture) were undermined in the joint US–Israel effort to criminalise resistance to the Israeli occupation have been described at length by his lawyers, Michael Deutsch and Erica Thompson.[60]

A similar distortion of the legal process occurred in a case involving alleged 'terrorist funding' to Hamas by the Texas-based Holy Land Foundation for Relief and Development. At one point the largest US Muslim charity, the Holy Land Foundation had sent funds to the occupied territories for schools, medical clinics and orphanages. In December 2001 the FBI raided its Texas office, seizing assets of US$5 million and its organisational records. After a jury in 2007 declined to bring guilty verdicts, a new trial was held in 2008 and the jury convicted five of the Foundation's former officials. Both trials featured secret evidence and a secret Israeli witness as well as a list of nearly 300 'Unindicted Co-conspirators and/or Joint Venturers', among them well-known US organisations such as the Council on American Islamic Relations (CAIR), which now have to fight to clear their names.[61]

It is not just the media; Congress and the courts have also held up Hamas as a major terrorist threat. Hamas also features prominently in post-9/11 programmes purporting to train citizens on how to spot 'terrorists' within the USA. One such programme, called CAT Eyes (Community Anti-Terrorism Training Initiative) was widely promoted among neighbourhood watch groups in the Boston area and across the country. Developed by US and Israeli military personnel, its training video includes a map of the USA dotted with 'Hamas cells'. Half of the 'significant historical dates' that it lists as 'likely to trigger al-Qaeda attacks' relate to Israel, leaving the trainee with the implicit message that Israel and the USA need to stand shoulder to shoulder against al-Qaeda and all terrorists.[62] Another company with close ties to Israel, Security Solutions International (SSI), has used some of its considerable funding from the US Department of Homeland Security to give 'homeland security professionals' (police, sheriffs and intelligence analysts) training in Israel where they learn about 'suicide terror'; 15 such training missions were held between 2005 and 2009.[63]

Part of our task, then, is to roll back the 'war on terror' propaganda paradigm that equates Palestinian violence against Israel with al-Qaeda's 9/11 attack on the USA and the possibility of future attacks on the 'homeland'. A good place to start is the piece by Henry Siegman, 'Gaza: the lies of war'. He writes that:

- 'Hamas is no more a "terror organisation" (Israel's preferred term) than the Zionist movement was during its struggle for a Jewish homeland';
- it was Israel, and not Hamas, that broke the truce, giving Israel its pretext to attack on 27 December 2008;
- Hamas was ready to back a Palestinian state being formed within the 1967 borders that would exist alongside Israel; and
- Israel was determined to destroy Hamas because it believes 'that its leadership, unlike that of Fateh, cannot be intimidated into accepting a peace accord that establishes a Palestinian "state" made up of territorially disconnected entities over which Israel would be able to retain permanent control'.[64]

Certainly there is ample evidence that Hamas, which is deeply woven into Palestinian society and susceptible to popular opinion, is considerably more open to making compromises with Israel than Israel is ready to compromise with Palestinians. Many commentators have described the way Hamas has left the ideological confines of its Charter to embrace pragmatism very much at odds with its reputation in the USA. Hamas has on numerous occasions accepted 'a state within the 1967 borders and a truce' – in the words of the leader of its political bureau, Khalid Mish'al.[65] Its founder, Sheikh Ahmad Yassin, who was assassinated by an Israeli helicopter gunship in March 2004, told journalist Roger Gaess in 2002 that 'my own best vision for Palestine is of a land for Christians, Jews, Muslims – a state where everyone has equal rights'.[66] According to the co-founder of Hamas, Ismail Abu Shanab, who was killed by five missiles in August 2003:

> Hamas is focusing on an agenda for Israel's withdrawal from the lands taken in 1967, the establishment of a Palestinian state and a solution for the refugees – and the only solution to the refugee problem is UN Resolution 194. If these things are implemented, the Palestinians will be satisfied... The new Palestine can have good relations with Israel, as well as with the rest of our neighbours.[67]

Ismail Haniyeh who continues to serve in Gaza as Prime Minister of the Palestinian National Authority, told Lally Weymouth of the *Washington Post* that 'if Israel declares that it will give the Palestinian people a state and give them back all their rights then we are ready to recognise them'.[68]

Remarks like these may not change many minds within Israel, and US policy-making circles may not for some time have ready access to the kind of independent thinking represented by former US Ambassador Charles Freeman, who was subjected to a smear campaign by Israel's hard right supporters that caused him to withdraw his nomination for the position of chair of the National Intelligence Council.[69] Still, it is encouraging that a group of former top officials have written to the Obama administration urging it to engage with Hamas.[70] State Department officials had met with Hamas leaders before March 1993 when Israel insisted that they stop doing so and the push to add Hamas to the list of terrorist organisations went into high gear. According to the *New York Times* on 2 October 2001, as the Bush administration planned its 'war on terror', members of the State Department debated whether to include Hezbollah and Hamas on a list of terrorist organisations with a global reach, since they did not directly threaten the USA and their inclusion complicated the task of building alliances.

'We want to be part of the international community,' a Hamas leader, Ghazi Hamad, told the Associated Press a week after Israel announced an end to Operation Cast Lead:'I think Hamas has no interest now to increase the number of crises in Gaza or to challenge the world.' [71] It is up to us to ensure that this kind of message reaches the American public.[72]

Building the Movement

The viability of Zionism as a colonising ethno-nationalism that transcends borders has long been in doubt. In October 1991, former Secretary of State Henry Kissinger reportedly told a closed meeting of 250 Jewish millionaires that unless Israel agreed to relinquish a major portion of the occupied territories, 'it will become a replica of South Africa... If Israel keeps insisting on getting everything, it will lose everything.'[73]

Sixteen years later, on the date marked across the globe as the International Day of Solidarity with the Palestinian people, Israeli Prime Minister Olmert echoed the master of realpolitik: 'If the day comes when the two-state solution collapses, and we face a South African-style struggle for equal voting rights (also for the Palestinians in the territories), then, as soon as that happens, the State of Israel is finished.'[74]

That day is fast approaching. The analogy with apartheid South Africa has gained considerable momentum since the publication in 2006 of Jimmy Carter's book, *Palestine: Peace Not Apartheid*. Launched at the University of Toronto in 2005, Israeli Apartheid Week in 2010 was observed in nearly 60 cities, 11 of them in the USA. Israel's supporters claim the term 'apartheid' – 'separation' in Afrikaans – cannot be applied to a democratic state that extends citizenship and participation in political life to the Palestinians within its pre-1967 borders, no matter how 'separate and unequal' their lives may be. Those supporters cannot dismiss out of hand the extent to which Israel's practices match the 'inhuman acts' constituting the 'crime of apartheid', as specified in the 1973 International Convention on the Suppression and Punishment of the Crime of Apartheid, which was listed as one of 11 recognised crimes against humanity in the 2002 Rome Statute establishing the International Criminal Court.

By 2007, Israel's domination of the West Bank and Gaza Strip could no longer be described as a simple military occupation, according to the prominent South African jurist and UN Special Rapporteur, John Dugard. He wrote in a January 2007 report to the United Nations that he has been forced to broaden his framework of analysis to include 'colonialism, apartheid and foreign occupation', stating that Israel's occupation 'contains elements of all three... What are the legal consequences when such a regime has acquired some of the characteristics of colonialism and apartheid? Does it continue to be a lawful regime?'[75]

Three years later, in the aftermath of Operation Cast Lead, former American Jewish Congress head Henry Siegman wrote despairingly that:

> Israel has crossed the threshold from 'the only democracy in the Middle East' to the only apartheid regime in the Western world... The democratic dispensation that Israel provides to its mostly Jewish citizens cannot hide its changed character. By definition, democracy reserved for privileged citizens – while all others are kept behind checkpoints, barbed-wire fences and separation walls commanded by the Israeli army – is not democracy but its opposite.[76]

The growing focus on conceiving of Israel as a colonising, 'apartheid' regime comes at a time when many Americans want the Obama administration to return to what they see as basic American values of fairness and respect for human rights and the rule of law. Broad revulsion at the practices of the Bush administration that violated both international and US law and that have given the USA record low approval ratings, especially in the Middle East,[77] offers us the opportunity to shine a spotlight on Israel's pattern of human rights abuses – including the use of torture techniques so similar to those employed in CIA 'black sites', Bagram and Guantanamo – and to demand that the US government observe its own laws (the Arms Export Control Act, PL 80–829 and the Foreign Assistance Act of 1961, PL 87–195) by cutting off its massive military support to Israel.[78]

By shaking what the Boston Combined Jewish Philanthropies described as the 'weak foundation' of support for Israel among the public, we can eventually get the message to our elected officials that their uncritical support of Israel has a domestic as well as international cost. The same message must be taken to corporations and other institutions that do business with Israel's regime of 'colonialism, apartheid and foreign occupation'.

In the words of Omar Barghouti: 'Our South Africa moment has arrived.'[79] The war on Gaza gave a vigorous push not just to street protests and acts of civil disobedience at Israeli embassies and on college campuses, but to an expansion of the campaign of 'boycott, divestment and sanctions' called for in 2005 by 171 Palestinian civil society organisations. South Africa has continued to set the pace. It moved beyond the stage of issuing resolutions when the South African Transport and Allied Workers Union refused to unload the cargo from an Israeli ship docked at Durban in February 2009. In Brazil, a significant movement is being built against a free trade agreement with Israel, and in Europe and Canada, strides have been taken in the call for an academic and cultural boycott of Israel as well as in the boycott of Israeli products and divestment.

The USA has seen the launch of new product boycotts, including one aimed at Motorola for its role in protecting the settlements, and Boycott, Divestment and Sanctions (BDS) resolutions have been introduced at several universities. On 7 February 2009 at Hampshire College – the first American campus to divest from apartheid South Africa – Students for Justice in Palestine declared victory in their campaign to have the college divest from corporations supporting Israel's military occupation. But after an attack on the college spearheaded by Alan Dershowitz, officials stated their actions had nothing to do with the Israeli occupation (*Boston Globe*, 22 February 2009). More than 800 professors, students and alumni had signed the petition calling for divestment in a college with an enrolment of only slightly more than 1,300 students.

A year later, Dershowitz and AIPAC pulled out the stops to overturn the action of the student Senate at the University of California (UC) at Berkeley. On 18 March 2010, the Senate voted 16:4 in favour of a bill calling for divestment from General Electric and United Technologies because they produced weapons that were used to commit war crimes in the West Bank and Gaza. Despite passionate support for divestment from Archbishop Tutu and four other Nobel

Prize winners, elderly Holocaust survivor Hedy Epstein, UN Special Rapporteur Richard Falk, Naomi Klein and many Israelis, the Senate ultimately failed to overturn the veto of the bill imposed by the student council president.

What does all this add up to? The immediate battle may have been lost at Berkeley, but the UC example is proving contagious, and opponents of BDS are going to have an increasingly difficult time dealing with all the brush fires to come. When combined with the rupture in some trade and diplomatic relations that Israel faced as a result of the Gaza War, with ongoing demands for war crimes investigations from international bodies and human rights organisations, and with Israeli military commanders potentially facing legal problems when they travel abroad, the negative exposure is starting to have an impact. An article in the Israeli newspaper *Maariv* (6 May 2010) reported that 'Israeli diplomats stationed in the US have significantly reduced the number of public lectures that they give to students, as a result of the frequent heckling', and the same thing was happening in the UK. According to Shir Hever, in a posting on the website of the Alternative Information Center in Jerusalem, 'Israelis are beginning to see the power of BDS'.[80] To make his case, he quotes from four articles that appeared in an Israeli business magazine, *The Marker*, concluding that 'if the momentum is maintained and strengthened, Israeli businessmen may decide to move their headquarters away from Israel, or to begin to put pressure on the Israeli government to begin respecting international law, and ending the occupation'.

The 2005 BDS appeal by Palestinian civil society organisations went beyond a call to maintain 'boycott, divestment and sanctions' until the occupation had ended. It stated:

> These non-violent punitive measures should be maintained until Israel meets its obligation to recognise the Palestinian people's inalienable right to self-determination and fully complies with the precepts of international law by: 1. Ending its occupation and colonisation of all Arab lands and dismantling the Wall; 2. Recognising the fundamental rights of the Arab-Palestinian citizens of Israel to full equality; and 3. Respecting, protecting and promoting the rights of Palestinian refugees to return to their homes and properties as stipulated in UN resolution 194.[81]

This is not a call for the establishment of a Palestinian state alongside Israel, but for the dissolution of the discriminatory, expansionist Zionist project. The kind of polity that would be erected in its aftermath is left unspecified.

Drawing on the example of the African National Congress in building international support behind its slogan, 'one man, one vote', we need to craft a shorthand version of this call and embed it in our solidarity work in a way that resonates with Americans who long to close the book on 'war on terror' excesses, and reaffirm the values they believe the country stands for. What kind of convincing opposition can be mounted to the demand for 'freedom, justice and equal rights for all'? Without specifying any particular political arrangement, this slogan tacitly evokes some kind of 'one-state' democratic framework in which the values of liberty and equality would be respected. Who could object to that?

Much depends on the extent to which we can make Palestine *the* moral issue of the twenty-first century, just as the fight against apartheid in South Africa was the moral issue of the closing decades of the twentieth century. If Palestinian groups fire rockets indiscriminately at civilians, actions condemned as 'war crimes' by Amnesty International and the Goldstone Report, our job will be harder, as Israel's supporters will continue to insist that its aggression against Palestinians is a necessary front in the 'war on terror', in which the survival not just of Israel as a Jewish state, but of Jews as a people, is at stake.

Israel's supporters have long laid claim to the moral high ground, endowing its army with a unique 'purity of arms'. But in the Goldstone Report and elsewhere, the truth has been coming out. Both the Israeli and US press have published leaked testimonies given by IDF soldiers about the permissive rules of engagement in the Gaza War that led to the deliberate killing of women and children who posed no threat. 'What's great about Gaza – you see a person on a path, he doesn't have to be armed, you can simply shoot him,' explained a squad commander.[82] Actions like these were allegedly encouraged by the 'religious rabbinate' whose 'message was very clear: We are the Jewish people... God brought us back to this land and now we need to fight to expel the non-Jews who are interfering with our conquest of this holy land.'[83]

Has the 'overcoming Zionism' moment also arrived?[84] In his widely circulated *Los Angeles Times* op-ed, Ben Ehrenreich describes the Gaza War as a turning point:

> The problem is fundamental: Founding a modern state on a single ethnic or religious identity in a territory that is ethnically and religiously diverse leads inexorably either to politics of exclusion (think of the 139-square-mile prison camp that Gaza has become) or to wholesale ethnic cleansing. Put simply, the problem is Zionism... If two decades ago comparisons to the South African apartheid system felt like hyperbole, they now feel charitable. The white South African regime, for all its crimes, never attacked the Bantustans with anything like the destructive power Israel visited on Gaza in December and January... the characterisation of anti-Zionism as an 'epidemic' more dangerous than anti-Semitism reveals only the unsustainability of the position into which Israel's apologists have been forced... Establishing a secular, pluralist, democratic government in Israel and Palestine would of course mean the abandonment of the Zionist dream. It might also mean the only salvation for the Jewish ideals of justice that date back to Jeremiah.[85]

Given the vastly unequal balance of forces and the unwillingness of the Obama administration to exert significant pressure on Israel, it is not at the moment clear how the journey to a 'secular, pluralist, democratic government in Israel and Palestine' or any kind of shared polity can be pursued on the ground in a meaningful way. But with the alternatives Bantustans or barbarism, it is surely a future worth striving for.

Notes

1. The Report of the United Nations Fact Finding Mission on the Gaza Conflict (known as the Goldstone Report), September 2009, Chapter XXIV.

2. Palestinian Centre for Human Rights, Press Release, 12 March 2009. These figures were used in the 20 March 2009 report given to the UN Human Rights Council by UN Special Rapporteur Richard Falk. Immediately following Israel's ceasefire, the UN Office for the Coordination of Humanitarian Affairs and the ICRC used the figures provided by the Palestinian Ministry of Health – 1,314 people killed, of whom 512 were women and children, and 5,450 wounded. The Goldstone Report cited a variation in numbers of Palestinians killed, from 1,166 (the figure provided by the Israeli government) to 1,444 claimed by Gaza authorities.

3. According to an article headlined 'Israel claims success in the PR war' (*Jewish Chronicle*, 31 December 2008), Israel's new forum of press advisors (the National Information Directorate) began developing a PR strategy for warfare in Gaza at least six months ago: 'The international media were directed to a press centre set up by the Foreign Ministry in Sderot itself so that foreign reporters would spend as much time as possible in the main civilian area affected by Hamas rockets.' Foreign reporters were barred from Gaza during the war.

4. Israeli Prime Minister Ehud Olmert boasted about making Condoleezza Rice abstain from a UN resolution calling for a halt to the fighting which she herself had helped draft (*New York Times*, 13 January 2009).

5. There has been an outcry, including from Amnesty International, over the use of white phosphorus against civilians in densely crowded neighbourhoods and wide-spread reports that Israel used the GBU-39 'small diameter bomb' or Dense Inert Metal Explosives (DIME) bomb, causing the kind of extreme ripping injuries doctors had never seen before. On 9 September 2008 the Defense Security Cooperation Agency issued a press release stating that Israel had requested 1,000 of these bombs (developed by the Air Force Research Lab and the Lawrence Livermore Lab and manufactured by Boeing), and recommended (and soon received) Congressional approval: 'It is vital to the US national interests to assist Israel to develop and maintain a strong and ready self-defense capability.' For an overall analysis of what the war achieved – and failed to achieve – for Israel, see Anthony Cordesman, 'The "Gaza War": a strategic analysis', Final Review Draft, 2 February 2009: www.csis.org/component/option,com_csis_pubs/task,view/ id,5250. Chapter XII of the Goldstone Report found that Israel had been 'reckless' in its use of white phosphorous in built-up areas, that the flechettes fired by the Israeli army are 'particularly unsuitable for use in urban settings where there is reason to believe civilians may be present', and that there was a 'strikingly high percentage of patients' who suffered injuries consistent with DIME munitions. The Mission did not investigate allegations that depleted uranium weapons were used.

6. *Daily Telegraph*, 7 January 2009.

7. In the words of British MP Clare Short, if nothing is done for the people of Gaza, 'a deprived and traumatized generation fuelled by hatred and a desire for revenge will become a ticking time-bomb in the explosive caldron of the Middle East'. From *Eyewitness Report: The Tragedy that is Gaza Today and the Role of the EU*, European Campaign to End the Siege of Gaza Delegation, January 2010.

8. See http://middleeast.about.com/od/usmideastpolicy/qt/congressional-letter-gaza-siege.htm.

9. On 4 November 2009, the US Congress condemned the Goldstone Report as an unjust attack upon Israel by 344:36 despite the fact that it also found Hamas guilty of war crimes for its attacks on civilians. The following day the UN General Assembly voted 114:18 to accept the Goldstone Report. On 26 February 2010 the UN General Assembly voted 98:7 to keep the Goldstone Report alive by giving both Israel and Hamas a five-month extension to do their own independent investigations into its war crime allegations. Standing with the USA and Israel in opposition to the UN resolution were only Canada, Macedonia, Micronesia, Nauru and Panama.

10. *Yedioth Ahronoth*, 4 September 1992.

11. See 'Climate change: a new threat to Middle East security', Friends of the Earth Middle East; UN Climate Change Congress, 16 December 2007, UN Office for the Coordination of Humanitarian Affairs.

12. On 6 May 2010 the BBC reported that Gazans had successfully cut through the multi-million dollar steel barrier using blow torches.

13. This is the projection of the Harvard School of Public Health's Gaza 2010 Project. Arnon Soffer, a professor at Haifa University and former advisor to Ariel Sharon, made the following observation about Gaza in an interview published in the *Jerusalem Post* on 10 May 2004: '... when 2.5 million people live in a closed-off Gaza, it's going to be a human catastrophe. Those people will become even bigger animals than they are today, with the aid of an insane fundamentalist Islam. The pressure at the border will be awful. It's going to be a terrible war. So, if we want to remain alive, we will have to kill and kill and kill. All day, every day... If we don't kill, we will cease to exist. The only thing that concerns me is how to ensure that the boys and men who are going to have to do the killing will be able to return home to their families and be normal human beings.'

14. Baruch Kimmerling, *Politicide: Sharon's War Against the Palestinians* (London: Verso, 2003).

15. See, for example, Tariq Ali writing in the *London Review of Books* ('LRB contributors react to events in Gaza', 15 January 2009); and Haidar Eid, 'Gaza 2009: Culture of resistance vs. defeat', *Electronic Intifada*, 11 February 2009.

16. *Investment News*, Issue 1, Palestine Development Fund, February 2009.

17. The report that Mercy Corps had been trying in vain for more than seven weeks to ship 90 tons of macaroni into Gaza stunned even some Members of Congress. 'Is someone going to kill you with a piece of macaroni?', Rep. Brian Baird (D-WA) asked shortly after visiting Gaza. Dion Nissenbaum, 'Israel blocks pasta shipment to Gaza and tensions boil', 26 February 2009, McClatchy Newspapers.

18. Not all of the deaths have been caused by tunnel collapses. On 21 February 2009, the Ma'an news agency reported that Egyptian forces had shot gas canisters into the tunnels, killing five men. The Associated Press reported a similar incident on 29 April 2010, which took the lives of four Palestinians.

19. Sara Roy, 'Gaza: treading on shards', *The Nation*, 17 February 2010.

20. Noam Chomsky, *Hopes and Prospects* (Chicago: Haymarket Books, 2010).

21. See Palestinian Centre for Human Rights Position Paper, 'Controversy over end of presidential term in office': www.pchrgaza.org/Interventions/p_p_president's.htm.

22. 'Peace now: government plans to enlarge settlements', *Jerusalem Post*, 2 March 2009.

23. *New York Times*, 27 February 2010.

24. Statement of Gen. David H. Petraeus, US Army Commander, US Central Command, Before the Senate Armed Services Committee, on the Posture of US Central Command, 16 March 2010.

25. Nir Rosen, 'Gaza: the logic of colonial power', *The Guardian*, 29 December 2008.

26. In a University of Maryland survey of identified Republicans and Democrats in 2007, 58 per cent of Republicans and 80 per cent of Democrats said the USA 'should not take either side' in the Israeli–Palestinian conflict; *Middle East Policy*, winter 2008, pp. 94. A Ramussen Reports poll surveying Americans about Israel's attack on Gaza found the public 'closely divided over whether the Jewish state should be taking military action against militants in the Gaza Strip' – 44 per cent in favour to 41 per cent against, with Democratic Party supporters opposing the Israeli offensive by a 24-point margin. Glenn Greenwald, 'More oddities in the US "debate" over Israel/Gaza', *Salon*, 2 January 2009. The following year, in March 2010, a Zoghby International Poll (*Huffington Post*, 27 March 2010) found that 65 per cent of Americans had a favourable view of Israel and 29 per cent had an unfavourable view, compared to 71 per cent and 21 per cent the year before. Democrats held a 42 per cent favourable and 49 per cent unfavourable view.

27. CJP Jewish Boston Connected, Israel Advocacy Strategic Planning Subcommittee Final Report, February 2008.

28. Senator Patrick Leahy was speaking on 9 March 2009 during a debate on an Amendment (SA 629) to the Omnibus Appropriations Act that would have blocked Palestinians from being resettled into the USA. Senator John Kerry also testified against the Amendment shortly after his return from the Gaza Strip.

29. *Jerusalem Post*, 16 September 2009.

30. Richard Goldstone, 'Reconsidering the Goldstone Report on Israel and war crimes', *Washington Post*, 1 April 2011.

31. 'Goldstone report: statement issued by members of UN mission on Gaza war', *Guardian*, 14 April 2011.

32. Barry Shrage, 'A time for truth and a time for action', CJP website, 5 April 2011.

33. See Stephen Pevar, *The Rights of Indians and Tribes*, ACLU, 1992.

34. 'If you wish to colonise a land in which people are already living, you must provide a garrison for the land, or find a benefactor who will maintain the garrison on your behalf. Zionism is a colonising adventure and, therefore, it stands or falls on the question of armed force', Ze'ev (Vladimir) Jabotinsky, 'The iron law' (1925), in the Shahak Papers, No. 31, 'Collection on Jabotinsky', p. 16.

35. *New York Times*, 14 April 1983.

36. See Benjamin Beit-Hallahmi, *The Israeli Connection: Who Israel Arms and Why* (New York: Pantheon Books, 1987); Jane Hunter, *Israeli Foreign Policy: South Africa and Central America* (New York: South End Press, 1987); Jan Pieterse, 'Israel's role in the Third World: exporting West Bank expertise', *Race & Class*, winter 1985.

37. Robert Fisk, 'How easy to de-humanize Palestinians', *Independent*, 4 January 2009.

38. This was the theme of a devastating report issued by a coalition of human rights groups (including Amnesty UK, Care International UK, Christian Aid, Medecins du Monde, Oxfam and Save the Children UK) on 6 March 2008: 'The Gaza Strip: a humanitarian implosion'.

39. Convention on th Prevention and Punishment of the Crime of Genocide, adopted by Resolution 260(III) A of the UN General Assembly on 9 December 1948. Rome Statute of the International Criminal Court: www.preventgenocide.org/law/icc/statute/part-a.htm.

40. The devastation and legal findings relating to the various categories of destruction are detailed in the Goldstone Report.

41. *Washington Times*, 14 January 2009. Randall Kuhn and his piece are featured in *The Link*, April–June 2009.

42. *The Link*, April–June 2009, p. 5.

43. Ibid.

44. *Boston Globe*, 17 May 1989.

45. *Davar*, 13 December 1988, translated by Israel Shahak.

46. *Yedioth Ahronoth*, 17 August 1988, translated by Israel Shahak.

47. *Ha'aretz*, 16 June 1989, translated by Israel Shahak.

48. Convention on the Prevention and Punishment of the Crime of Genocide, adopted by Resolution 260(III)A of the UN General Assembly on 9 December 1948.

49. *New York Times*, 9 April 1993.

50. *Ha'aretz*, 4 April 1993.

51. Avi Shlaim, 'How Israel brought Gaza to the brink of humanitarian catastrophe', *Guardian*, 7 January 2009.

52. Edward Herman and Gerry O'Sullivan, *The Terrorism Industry: The Experts and Institutions that Shape our View of Terror* (New York: Pantheon Books, 1989), p. 104.

53. It wasn't until the summer of 2008 that an act of Congress was passed taking the African National Congress off the US list of terrorist organisations. Before then, Nelson Mandela had to secure a visa waiver to enter the USA.

54. *Mid East Mirror*, 5 September 1991.

55. The Clarion Fund, revealed to have close ties to a New York-based Orthodox Jewish organisation, Aish Hatorah, that reportedly backs the Israeli settler movement, was founded by the film's co-writer and producer, Raphael Shore, a Canadian Israeli. Adam Shatz in the *London Review of Books*, 9 October 2008.

56. See www.shoebat.com.

57. House Session – CSpan Video Library: www.c-spanvideo.org/videoLibrary/clip.php?appid=593065799.

58. Jeremy Sharp and Christopher Blanchard, CRS Report for Congress: US Foreign Aid to the Palestinians, 27 June 2006.

59. See Will Youmans, 'The new Cold Warriors', in Elaine Hagopian (ed.), *Civil Rights in Peril: The Targeting of Arabs and Muslims* (New York & London: Haymarket Books and Pluto Press, 2004); Kenneth Katzman, 'Hamas's foreign benefactors', *Middle East Quarterly*, June 1995.

60. Michael Deutsch and Erica Thompson, 'Secrets and lies: the persecution of Muhammad Salah', *Journal of Palestine Studies*, Part I, 37(1) (Summer 2008) and Part II, 38(1) (Autumn 2008).

61. For a critical account of what the 'war on terror' has meant for Muslim charities, see OMB Watch, 'Muslim charities and the war on terror: top ten concerns and status update', March 2006; and OMB Watch and Grantmakers Without Borders, 'Collateral damage: how the war on terror hurts charities, foundations, and the people they serve', July 2008: www.ombwatch.org/node/3578.

62. See http://cateyes.us.

63. See www.homelandsecurityssi.com/ssi/component/option,com_frontpage/Itemid,1.

64. Henry Siegman, 'Gaza: the lies of war', *London Review of Books*, 29 January 2009.

65. *Al Hayat*, 12 October 2006.

66. 'Interviews from Gaza, what Hamas wants', *Middle East Policy*, December 2002, p. 106.

67. Ibid., p. 109.

68. 'We do not wish to throw them into the sea', Ismail Haniyeh interview, *Washington Post*, 26 February 2006.

69. The White House declined to intercede when pro-Likudnik neocons, led by former AIPAC official Steve Rosen (now under indictment for passing classified documents to

a foreign country), implied that Charles Freeman might have received illicit funds from Saudi Arabia. Freeman had long been critical of Israel's policies toward Palestinians and the US–Israeli relationship. According to Stephen Walt: 'This outcome is bad for everyone, including Israel. It means that policy debates in the United States will continue to be narrower than in other countries (including Israel itself), public discourse will be equally biased, and a lot of self-censorship will go on. America's Middle East policy will remain stuck in the same familiar rut, and even a well-intentioned individual like George Mitchell won't be able to bring the full weight of our influence to bear' (11 March 2009, foreignpolicy.com). Others believe the hounding of Freeman might prove something of a 'Waterloo' for Israel's hard-line US supporters. See Robert Dreyfuss, 'Is the Israeli lobby running scared?', 15 March 2009: www.truthout.org/031609C.

70. *Boston Globe*, 14 March 2009. Signing the letter were Brent Scowcroft, Zbigniew Brzezinski, Paul Volcker, Lee Hamilton, Thomas Pickering, James Wolfensohn, Carla Hills, Theodore Sorensen, Chuck Hagel and Nancy Kassebaum Baker.

71. Steven Gutkin, 'Hamas officials signal willingness to negotiate', Associated Press, 29 January 2009.

72. However, following the June 2010 US Supreme Court decision in the 'material support to terrorism' case *Holder v. Humanitarian Law Project*, any kind of action coordinated with Hamas – such as placing an op-ed in a US newspaper – can now lead to a prison term of up to 15 years. See http://ccrjustice.org/holder-v-humanitarian-law-project.

73. *Yediot Ahronot*, 8 October 1991.

74. Interview, *Ha'aretz*, 29 November 2007.

75. Report of the Special Rapporteur on the situation of human rights in the Palestinian territories occupied since 1967. John Dugard, 29 January 2007, Human Rights Council (advance edited version), p. 22.

76. Henry Siegman, 'Imposing Middle East peace', *The Nation*, 25 January 2010.

77. A Zobgy International poll conducted in six Arab states revealed that two-thirds of those surveyed had a 'very unfavourable' attitude toward the USA and 95 per cent named Israel and the USA as the two countries that posed the 'biggest threat' to them. *Boston Globe*, 15 April 2008.

78. For the extent of US military aid to Israel, see Robert Bryce, 'Gaza invasion: powered by the US', *Salon*, 31 January 2009; and www.endtheoccupation.org.

79. Omar Barghouti, 'Our South Africa moment has arrived', *The Palestine Chronicle*, 18 March 2009: http://palestinechronicle.com/view_article_details.php?id=14921.

80. Shir Hever, 'Israelis are beginning to see the power of BDS', 2 March 2009: www.alternativenews.org/content/view/1605/381.

81. 'Palestinian civil society calls for boycott, divestment and sanctions against Israel until it complies with international law and universal principles of human rights', 9 July 2005: www.bdsmovement.net/?q=node/52.

82. Ethan Bronner, 'Soldiers' accounts of Gaza killings are raising furor in Israel', *New York Times*, 20 March 2009.

83. Ethan Bronner, 'A religious war in Israel's army', *Week in Review, New York Times*, 22 March 2009.

84. See Joel Kovel, *Overcoming Zionism: Creating a Single Democratic State in Israel/Palestine* (London; Ann Arbor, MI; Toronto: Pluto Press and Between the Lines, 2007).

85. Ben Ehrenreich, 'Zionism is the problem', *Los Angeles Times*, 15 March 2009.

PART II

Ideologies and the Idea of a Historic Settlement

CHAPTER 7

Deconstructing the Zionist Settler Narrative and Constructing an Alternative

Gabriel Piterberg

Introduction

The subject of an alternative narrative is addressed in this chapter in three steps. First, the conceptual framework within which the history of Zionism and the Israel/Palestine conflict ought to be understood – namely comparative settler 'colonialism' – is outlined. The currently prevailing hegemonic narrative is then explained and illustrated, showing how it is germane to a vision of a solution based on two ethnic communities that forever remain exclusive of each other. Finally, two rather different fields of intellectual activity, which offer guidance on how to think about an inclusive and porous – though by no means idyllic – historical narrative of Israel/Palestine from the 1880s until the present, are discussed.

The issues discussed in this chapter are much more weighted towards a review of the Zionist Israeli side than the Arab Palestinian one. One reason for this is that Zionist Israel is immeasurably the more powerful and influential party, though this is meant neither to imply that the Palestinians have been passive objects – even if they are undeniably the weaker side – nor to exempt them from being held accountable for their history. The other reason is that while this author has substantial knowledge of the history and culture of the Palestinian people, he has the relative advantage of a thoroughly intimate acquaintance with Zionism and Israel.[1]

Let me begin with what I cannot and do not wish to do. Since I am a scholar who writes on the intellectual and literary history of the Ottoman Empire, and on the intellectual and literary history of Zionism and Israel/Palestine, I am unable to produce a think-tank style of analysis, which would, as such, be useful for political negotiations. I do not wish to construct a narrative that would look like the outcome of an Oslo-type negotiation, in which each side supposedly budges a little so that 'compromise' can be reached. The victim of such a futile exercise is bound to be historical truth.

Comparative Settler Colonialism

The best way to understand in depth the history of Israel/Palestine in the past century or so is what is called in this chapter comparative settler colonialism. The expansion and conquests of Europe that had begun in 1500 produced two kinds of related but clearly distinguishable forms of colonialism. One was metropole colonialism, in which Europeans conquered and ruled vast territories, but administered and exploited them without the presence of Europeans seeking to make these territories their home: British India is a good example. When Gandhi famously told the British viceroy that once the Indians had got their act together, the question was when, not whether, the British would leave, he was conveying an important characteristic of metropole or franchise colonialism: eventually the colonisers must leave and they invariably do leave. The other type was settler colonialism, in which the conquest by European states brought with it substantial waves of settlers who with the passage of time sought to make the colonies their national patrimony. This process entailed a kind of relationship with the indigenous people that could range from dispossession to elimination, or from slavery (of mainly 'nativised' Africans) to cheap labour, depending on the land and labour formations of a given settler society. Settler colonialism can be said to have begun in earnest with the English – and later Scottish Presbyterian – settlers in Ireland in the second half of the sixteenth century, and continued with the settler colonies in what would become Virginia and New England in the seventeenth century. Unlike the colonisers of the metropole or franchise type, the settlers came to stay and carved out a national home for themselves, even if in certain cases (French Algeria and Kenya, for instance) they were forced to relinquish their project. It is within the burgeoning field of comparative settler colonialism that I seek to place the Zionist colonisation of Palestine and the state of Israel. This obviously means that the Israeli–Palestinian struggle is not just between the national communities vying for the same piece of land, but one between a national community of settlers and their descendants and a national community of indigenous people.

The achievements of the comparative study of settler colonialism have been at once scholarly and political. Many settler projects gave birth to powerful nation-states, which have asserted their hegemonic narratives nationally and internationally. The comparative field not only acutely refutes these narratives through evidence and interpretation, it also creates a language that amounts to a transformative alternative to the way in which these settler societies narrate themselves in their own words and dominate others. Three fundamentals of hegemonic settler narratives are thus undermined:

1.　the uniqueness of each settler nation;
2.　the privileging of the intentions and consciousness of settlers as sovereign subjects; and
3.　the putatively inconsequential presence of natives to the form and contours of settler societies.

To take uniqueness first, there is something deeper in the comparative approach than what the act of comparing obviously entails. This something is akin to what Benedict Anderson calls (in another but intimately related context) the modularity of nationalism.[2] The comparative studies of settler nations undercut the claim to uniqueness not because they find all settler nations identical; in fact, many of these comparisons result in underscoring historical specificity as much as similarity. What they do, however, is to offer a language that identifies a white settler trajectory when it sees one and renders it reminiscent of other trajectories. This is true not only for studies explicitly intended to make a comparative argument, but also for those that are solely concerned with one case.

The exponents of comparative settler colonialism are not oblivious to intentions; nor do they suggest that intentions do not matter. In his masterful book on the United States of America and South Africa, *White Supremacy*, the late George Fredrickson attributes much explanatory importance to the fact that the intention in creating the Cape colony in the mid-seventeenth century by the Dutch East India Company was to have a secure trading post on the way to the Indian Ocean, whereas the intention in establishing the English colonies in Ireland at the end of the sixteenth century and in what would become Virginia and New England in the early seventeenth century was to create pure settlements and exclude the local population.[3] The idea is therefore not to ignore intentions, but the persistently structural and predominantly material investigation overrides intentions and, crucially, leads to emphasising results. This sort of examination could, for example, substantially change the way many look at what in today's world would be called ethnic cleansing during the 1948 war in Palestine. Instead of the rather obsessive concern with whether or not there was an Israeli master plan to cleanse Palestine from its Arab presence, it might be asked whether the structural logic embedded in the type of settler nationalism, which the notion of a Jewish nation-state implies, explains the cleansing; it also might be asked whether cleansing-as-result is not, empirically and ethically, as important as cleansing-as-intention (or absence thereof).

The third fundamental, whether the presence of indigenous people is consequential to how settler societies were shaped, is possibly the most subtle and the one that exposes the exclusionary, or segregationist, nature of white liberalism and perhaps of multiculturalism too. As will be shown later, this fundamental is the most crucial obstacle to an alternative narrative. The more liberal versions of hegemonic settler narratives may admit that along the otherwise glorious path to nationhood, bad things were done to the indigenous people and, where applicable, to enslaved Africans; they may even condemn these 'bad things' and deem them unacceptable. At the same time these narratives, by the very way in which they are conveyed, deny the possibility that the removal and dispossession of indigenous peoples and the enslavement of others is an *intrinsic* part of what settler nations are – indeed the most pivotal constituent of what they are – rather than an *extrinsic* aberration or going astray of something essentially good, or an extrinsic issue that required attention and action. The point is not whether settler nations are good or bad, but the extent to which the act of exclusion in reality is congruous with the hegemonic rendering of that reality. The exclusionary fundamental that inheres in these white hegemonic narratives lies not in the denial by the sovereign settlers of the wrong they had done to those whom they disinherited or enslaved (though this happens too), but in the denial that the interaction with the dispossessed is the history of who the settlers collectively are. To be brutally candid and sweeping, what is denied is the extent to which the non-white world has been an intrinsic part of what is construed as European or Western history.

The comparative study of settler societies is not at all a subaltern studies project. It does not seek to salvage the voice of the dispossessed victims of settler colonialism and reassert it, nor does it adhere to a post-colonial methodology or register. In fact, the chief subject matter of most of these works is the settlers themselves more than either the metropoles or the indigenous peoples. But this subject matter is described in terms of its incessant interaction with the peoples who were either dispossessed and removed or used for labour. There cannot by definition be in this type of analysis a history of the institutions and ideologies of the settler societies that is not simultaneously a history of the settler–native relations. The history of white supremacy throughout Fredrickson's oeuvre is not a trajectory within the larger American or South African histories; in a very consequential way, the history of white supremacy *is* the history of these settler societies. Similarly, there cannot in this work be a history of private property (as the subject of legal studies and political theory) in early modern England that is not at the same time a history of land-appropriation first in Ireland and then east of the Appalachians. Analogously, and as will be discussed in greater detail below, there cannot be a history of the cooperative settlements and settlement theories, which is one trajectory in the hegemonic Israeli narrative, that is separable from another trajectory in that narrative; namely, 'the Arab problem'. For what shaped the cooperative settlements and made some theories more pertinent and applicable than others was precisely what the Zionists called the Arab problem, or the consequential existence of indigenous people who, from a settler vantage-point, were a problem. Arabs are completely absent from kibbutzim and moshavim, from the mitzpim (literally lookouts) that mushroomed in the wake of the state project which sought to 'Judaise' the Galilee, not only from post-1967 settlements in the occupied territories. This absence is the single most important fact for the history of the foundation of all Zionist settlements in Palestine – urban and rural, private and cooperative – as well as for what they are.

One of the most important things to bear in mind when we want to understand the nature of the 'Nakba', the Israeli occupation, the separation barrier and so forth, is that the creation of a nation-state out of a settler society is not just a foundational event but a continuing process. It is worth remembering the observation made by one of the most outstanding writers on settler colonialism, the Australia-based scholar Patrick Wolfe: '[t]he determination "settler-colonial state" is Australian society's primary structural characteristic rather than merely a statement about its origins... invasion is a structure not an event.'[4]

The Zionist Israeli Hegemonic Narrative

Three fundamentals of hegemonic settler narratives have been mentioned: the uniqueness of each settler nation; the exclusive primacy accorded to the settlers' subjectivity; and the denial of the fact that the presence of the colonised has been the single most significant factor in determining the structure and nature of the settler society. The Zionist Israeli narrative is a particular case of that general depiction. Its three fundamentals accordingly are:

- the alleged uniqueness of the Jewish nation in its relentless search for sovereignty in the biblically endowed homeland;
- the privileging of the consciousness of the Zionist settlers at the expense of the colonised, and of the intentions of colonisation by the settlers rather than the consequences for the indigenous Palestinians; and
- the denial of the fact that the presence of the Palestinian Arabs on the land destined for colonisation was the single most significant factor that determined the shape which the settlers' nation took.

This is articulated in the way Zionist scholars, and following them many others, present the history of Palestine from the beginning of Zionist settlement in the 1880s until 1948 and beyond. One of the most frequently used terms is the dual society paradigm. What is meant by dual society is that two completely separate and self-contained entities emerged in Palestine: the Jewish Yishuv and the Palestinian Arab society. Each developed according to its own trajectory, which is explicable – in the former case – by a combination of European origins and Jewish essence. Each trajectory is unrelated to the other, and the only meaningful relations were those of a struggle between two impregnable national collectives (if the national authenticity of the Palestinians is not altogether denied). It cannot be sufficiently stressed that what is denied is not the mere presence of Arabs in Palestine, nor in some cases even the fact they were wronged and treated unjustly, but rather the fact that their presence and resistance were consequential to the very essence of the Zionist colonisation project and the Israeli nation-state. It is clearly the ultimate scholarly articulation of the empty land concept.

This hegemonic is articulated in the work of the foremost Zionist Israeli historian of her generation, Anita Shapira. Her scholarly accomplishments have earned her the affectionate title of the Princess of Zionism. In recent years she has published a series of important essays on central issues relating to Zionism and Israel, such as the negation of exile and the Holocaust. Here we will examine her pronouncements on the place and use of the Bible. Shapira is significant at two intimately related levels: she is a foremost scholar of Zionist and Israeli history; and the intrinsic position from which her scholarship is conceived makes her also a foremost Zionist Israeli thinker. Her work offers insight on the use of the Bible, and reiteration and elaboration of Zionist Israeli ideology. The reiteration and elaboration, it is argued, is not just of a national ideology, with which Shapira would presumably agree, but of a national *settler* ideology, to which she might object. It is important to point out that politically she is part of the so-called peace camp – that is, the dovish antipode of the Zionist consensus – and staunch supporter of the Oslo process and the two-states path.

Shapira has written on the place of the Bible in Israeli culture and identity, and on Ben-Gurion's massive Bible project (what she aptly terms 'Bibliomania'), in the 1950s and early 1960s.[5] Within the confines of an intrinsic position, Shapira's overarching argument regarding collective Zionist Israeli culture and identity is perceptive and correct. That culture and identity, she observes, was based on a biblical and archaeological Israeliness, which could be sustained only as long as the community consisted primarily of the early Zionist settlers and their offspring. Once the tremendous demographic change had become consequential, Israeliness waned and the concomitant ascendancy of Jewishness began. The Bible was pivotal in the phase at which Israeliness reigned supreme and, except for the settlers in the post-1967 occupied territories, it was marginalised by the ascent of Jewishness. At no point in these essays does Shapira pause to wonder how the Arab citizens of the state were supposed to fit in a collective identity based either on Old Testament-guided Israeliness or *Shoah*-driven Jewishness.

As for Ben-Gurion, Shapira's observation is clear. His interest in the Bible or in Jewish history was limited at best, and he did not even share the fascination of his Second Aliyah peers in the book; his rhetoric was devoid of Biblical themes. The change in Ben-Gurion's attitude to the Bible had begun in the late 1930s and was complete as soon as the 1948 war had been decided and the state came into being. It went hand in hand with the pivotal role he envisaged for the army in the process of nation formation – especially in 'melt-potting' the immigrants from the Middle East and North Africa – and in the forging of a national ethos.

Shapira's texts on these issues rest upon a presupposition that makes them, concurrently, a scholarly contribution to the place of the Bible in Zionist Israeli history and culture, and a contribution to Zionist Israeli ideology. The presupposition is that the resort to the Bible, and the ways in which this has been done, is immanently and insularly Jewish as well as obviously Jewish, in the sense that no demonstration of how exactly it is so is felt to be necessary. Three related things are consequently occluded:

1. the 'return' to the Old Testament in this particular fashion is not organically or immanently Jewish but Protestant and has a history that is indebted to the Reformation;
2. there are other settler societies (and colonial ventures in general) which have resorted to the Old Testament/Bible in comparable ways and for comparable purposes; and
3. the resort to the Bible is not just part of a national project, but part of a national-colonial, or national-settler, project, for in the land of Israel there were not only fauna and flora, valleys, ravines and mountains, but also Arabs.

Let me address here the final implication of her presupposition, and remind the reader again of the third fundamental of hegemonic settler narratives, whereby the presence of indigenous people is extrinsic to the nature and institutions of the settler nation. To her credit, Shapira is highly cognisant of the Palestinian presence and of the 1948 'Nakba'. Few scholars on her side of the political spectrum are earnestly willing to engage in debate with the 1948 historians and other critical scholars. Her own observations often evince a critical distance, as indicated by the examination of the Bible as a source of a national mythology and narrative. The point is the compartmentalisation of the sacred and the profane that is so emblematic of this consciousness and imagination. The profane is the appropriate realm for discussing such things as the conflict, the treatment of the Palestinians, the attitudes to 'the Arab problem' and the image of the 'Other'. The sacred is the temple where (among other things) 'we' discuss 'our' identity and the infatuation with 'our' Bible. That the infatuation with the

Bible as a central – if contested – ingredient of Israeli identity, and the presence of natives of whose claims and presence the land must be emptied, actually collapse into one history is inconceivable. And it is inconceivable precisely because of the depth to which this compartmentalisation runs, the extent to which the ontological gap between who we are (intrinsically) and what we do (extrinsically) is presupposed to be real and unbridgeable. However, if one were to take away the imperative of the Judeo-supremacy that underlies the settler nation-state (and is achieved by excluding and distancing the Palestinian Arabs from it physically and discursively), one would be left with very little non-fragmented Jewish Israeli identity.

Shapira's compartmentalisation of 'the Palestinian problem', which is one thing, and the place of the Bible in 'our identity', which is quite another, is amply exemplified in her texts. It reaches a crescendo with the passage from the Mandatory period to the 1948 war and the 1950s. Especially striking are Shapira's allusions to what is called the 1948 generation (*Dor Tashah*) – those who were born in Palestine, fought in the 1948 war and within that discourse 'delivered' the state. Sometimes it is also referred to as the Palmach generation. She laments their alienation from the Bible after 1967, as a result of its appropriation by the religious right and later by the post-Zionists. For Shapira this represents the alienation from the Bible of a whole social stratum she calls humanist Zionism. Here is their vantage point, which she represents so faithfully:

> Moreover: the romanticism of the land of the Bible was associated in the imagina-
> tion of... the natives and disciples of the Land of Israel, the 1948 generation, with
> the country's virginal image before the War of Independence: the cactus bushes,
> water wells, stone houses embedded in a mountain's slope, gown-wearing figures
> who as it were belonged to the days of the patriarchs, camel convoys, tents, and
> other images that were actually associated with the Arab Eretz-Israeli landscape,
> which they saw as a reflection of the patriarchs' way of life in the land of Canaan.
> Lo and behold, in all places reached by Israeli progress the cactus bushes and water
> wells have disappeared. In lieu of treks concrete roads have been spread, and in
> lieu of camels moving at leisurely pace cars are zooming by. In lieu of the stone-
> houses that are one with the landscape, white ones with red tiled roofs tear up the
> harmony. Israeli modernisation has made the marks of the biblical past [*ha-`avar
> ha-miqrai*] disappear... Thus then, the renewed encounter with the land of the Bible
> after 1967 was one that gave birth to foreignness and did not rekindle the sense of
> mastery [*tehushat ha-adnut*] over the country, which was an integral part of the
> mental texture of the 1948 generation.[6]

The passage is fantastically illustrative in a multifaceted fashion. Perhaps it should be remembered that Shapira does represent faithfully and eloquently the voices of the 1948 generation and of the so-called peace camp of the past three decades; the point is that for the most part she reproduces these voices rather than critically examines them. Thus goes unnoticed the fact that constructing Arab Palestine as a remnant of the Bible's patriarchal era, through which 'the sense of mastery over the country' is obtained, is a typically settler, and more generally colonial, mechanism for emptying the designated homeland from its indigenous people as well as its history. What should be brought to the fore most clearly is that the state of mind earlier termed compartmentalisation now becomes a sort of schizophrenia when expressed by Shapira and the socio-political class she represents. Those who cleansed Arab Palestine, it might be recalled, who razed the rural landscape that included the stone houses so at one with it, the cactus bushes and water wells, those who built the white houses with red tiled roofs and have been dwelling in them, are precisely those who have been lamenting the disappearance of the Bible-like rural Palestine: the 1948 generation.

In a similar fashion, Ben-Gurion's utter obsession in the 1950s with the Old Testament in general and the Book of Joshua in particular was not just a central component of nation-state building in the conventional sense, as Shapira would have us believe. It was a central component of settler nation-state building, a process in which the emptying of the geography from the indigenous Palestinians in 1948, the fact that this looked to Ben-Gurion like the re-enactment of the Book of Joshua, and the need to fill the void created by the 'Nakba' with biblical significations, are all related things that collapse into one narrative. There is no biblical Israeli collective identity that is not inextricably bound with the biblical, settler-like, emptying of the land of its native inhabitants.

The gist of the preliminary thought of this chapter on an alternative narrative grows out of a concrete and detailed critique of the hegemonic one. This is done by unearthing the ways in which that hegemonic narrative perpetuates the false portrayal of two communities that have always been in conflict but autonomous of each other. The dialectic result of this critique should not be a honeyed narrative but one that brings to the fore the extent to which these two communities, through settler/indigenous conflict, have actually shaped each other (alas mostly for the worse), and therefore may have a common historical narrative rather than two separate ones.

Where Alternatives Can Be Sought

I shall now survey two possibilities that may inform the ways we can think about an alternative narrative. I intentionally allude to two quite different spheres of intellectual creativity. What they have in common is that they collapse dichotomies, and insist that even (or perhaps precisely) in situations of conflict, polarities do not have discrete and unrelated histories; on the contrary, their trajectories are mutually shaped and should be understood within one historical narrative, however complex that narrative might be.

History and Sociology of Pre-1948 Palestine

Earlier, the notion of the dual society paradigm was presented as one of the foremost articulations of the Zionist Israeli hegemonic narrative. For the history of pre-1948 Palestine, that narrative has been convincingly demolished and alternatives have been put forth in two masterful studies, one by historical sociologist Gershon Shafir[7] and the other by historian Zachary Lockman.[8]

The most important assumption that underpins the dual society paradigm, and correspondingly the one most thoroughly dealt with by Shafir, is the purported extrinsicality of the indigenous Arab society and of the conflict with it to the nature of the settler nation. Explicitly working within the framework of comparative settler colonialism, he shows that the formative period of the early Zionist colonisation of Palestine was shaped by the interaction with the indigenous Palestinians. Even though he does not study the latter directly, they are constantly present in the formation of the settler community which cannot be otherwise understood. In Shafir's historical-sociological thesis, in other words, there cannot be a narrative of the settler project that is not inextricably also a narrative of settler-indigenous relations.

Shafir begins by simultaneously listing the main features that are historically specific to Zionism and to the Zionist colonisation of Palestine in comparison to other frontiers of settlement and other movements of colonisation, and by anticipating that the type of colonisation that within a short while prevailed was that of the pure settlement colony. He insists that while this historical specificity 'gave Zionist colonisation a particular cast', it has 'not eliminated its fundamental similarity with other pure settlement colonies'. He then adds a category to the taxonomy created by D. K. Fieldhouse and George Fredrickson, which he calls the *ethnic* plantation colony. It was 'based on European control of land and the employment of local labour. The planters, in spite of their preference for local labour, also sought, inconsistently and ultimately unsuccessfully, massive European immigration. Algeria was an example of this hybrid type.'

Shafir's counter-narrative is focused on the initial – and in his interpretation foundationally formative – period of Zionist settlement in Palestine. It rests on the distinction between two stages of colonisation (each comprising finer distinctions that we do not need to consider here), which overlap with the first two waves of Jewish immigration, known in Zionist parlance as the First Aliyah (1882–1903, 20,000–30,000 immigrants) and Second Aliyah (1904–14, 35,000–40,000 immigrants). During that period roughly 425,000 Palestinian

Arabs lived in Palestine. The crucial moment that shaped the First Aliyah came when, after early failures and supplicating to the Rothschilds, Baron Edmond de Rothschild entered the fray. Assisted by French experts, he reorganised the First Aliyah colonies on the model of French agricultural colonisation in North Africa. These colonies became ethnic plantations based on vineyards, which relied on a large, seasonal, unskilled and cheap Arab labour with a much smaller and better-paid Jewish labour force and Jewish planters. The passage from the first to the second stage occurred around 1900, when Rothschild ended his money-pouring involvement. This meant, among other things, that land accumulation came to a temporary halt because Rothschild had disappeared and the World Zionist Organization (WZO), which Herzl had founded in 1897, was still at the phase in which it opposed land accumulation prior to having a state on the basis of an international charter.

The arrival of the Second Aliyah immigrants – eventually the founders of labour Zionism and the state of Israel – in that context signalled a shift from the land as a sphere of colonisation to that of labour, and the concomitant shift from the ethnic plantation to that of pure settlement. This is an original observation by Shafir that does not always get the notice it deserves: what is perhaps the most crucial step in the process of the Israeli nation-state formation out of a pure settlement colony emanated not from land as a *lieu de colonisation* but from that of labour. The shift occurred after the customary attempt to lower the standard of living in order to compete in the labour market against the Palestinian Arab workers had failed. In 1905, members of what was at that point one of the two labour Zionist parties, Hapoel Hatzair (The Young Worker), forsook the strategy of downward wages for the purpose of market competitiveness, and instead launched the campaign for 'conquest of labour'. The goal was to conquer all jobs in Palestine for Jews, but especially in Jewish plantations, without lowering wages. This was accompanied by a demand from the Jewish planters to oust their Arab workers and hire Jewish ones instead for reasons of national colonisation rather than economic considerations.

As such, the struggle for 'the conquest of labour' was unsuccessful; its pivotal importance lies in its having engendered the appearance of the pure settlement colony as a state of mind and as the only way of institution – and nation-state – building. It 'transformed the Jewish workers into militant nationalists who sought to establish a homogenous Jewish society in which there would be no exploitation of Palestinians, nor will there be competition with Palestinians, because there would be no Palestinians'. From that crucial juncture the workers' leadership moved back to continue the colonisation of land, through an alliance with a changing WZO and its two colonising agencies: the Palestine Land Development Agency (1909) and the Jewish National Fund (1901). In this venture the actual settlers were guided by the three German Jewish master-experts of settlement: Arthur Ruppin, Otto Warburg (a member of the famous banking family) and Franz Oppenheimer.[9] By the 1920s, the first cooperative settlements were founded and with the arrival of more immigrants, colonisation through various forms of cooperative settlement (kvutza, kibbutz and moshav, all created from 1908 to 1921) gained momentum. In 1920 the final and most powerful labour institution was established: the Histadrut. This was a multifaceted organisation that consisted of a trade union, a settlement section, a construction and industrial arm, and health, consumption and finance divisions. More than any other single institution, the Histadrut was the nation-state in the making. It is a common mistake leading to complete misunderstanding to see in the Histadrut only a trade union in the European mould. It is also not a coincidence that the position that made Ben-Gurion the uncontested leader of labour Zionism in the 1920s, and catapulted him to the leadership of the WZO and Jewish Agency in the 1930s, was that of the Histadrut's secretary general.

Shafir observes:

> The Second Aliyah revolution against the First Aliyah did not originate from opposition to colonialism as such but out of frustration with the inability of the ethnic plantation colony to provide sufficient employment for Jewish workers, i.e. from opposition to the particular form of their predecessors' colonisation. The Second Aliya's own method of settlement, and subsequently the dominant Zionist method, was but another type of European overseas colonisation – the 'pure settlement colony' also found in Australia, Northern US, and elsewhere. Its threefold aim was control of land, employment that ensured a European standard of living, and massive immigration... This form of pure settlement rested on two exclusivist pillars: on the WZO's Jewish National Fund and on the... Histadrut. The aims of the JNF and the Histadrut were the removal of land and labour from the market, respectively, thus closing them off to Palestinian Arabs.[10]

Lockman does not take the path of comparative settler colonialism, but the alternative he offers to the Zionist-Israeli narrative and what he rejects in it bring him very close to Shafir. Lockman too discards what I have been calling the third fundamental of hegemonic settler narratives: the unwillingness to accept that what determined the nature of settler nations was first and foremost their interaction with the people whom they had colonised, rather than any civilisational or national essence. The method and language Lockman develops are those of *relational* history. In the mid-1980s an interesting forum was convened at the New School for Social Research, in search of agendas for writing radical history; it revolved around the four heavyweights of British Marxism – Eric Hobsbawm, Christopher Hill, Perry Anderson and E. P. Thompson. Anderson had three suggestions: to enhance the role of theory; to draw attention to the possibility of alternative outcomes on the margins of what eventually occurred in certain historical junctures; and to write relational histories.

By relational history, Anderson means something that is simultaneously different from comparative history (which he endorses) and non-national in its unit of analysis. He calls for a history 'that studies the incidence – reciprocal or asymmetrical – of different national or territorial units and cultures on each other', a history that 'is a reconstruction of [such units'] dynamic inter-relationships over time'.[11] Lockman's turn to relational history is inspired by Anderson's pronouncement, which he adapts to his own research. Lockman studies the interaction between Labour Zionism's institutions and individuals, and Arab workers and their organisations, in Palestine in the period 1906–48. He shows not only how these two communities interacted with and shaped each other, but also how they were constituted within the same context of late Ottoman and then Mandatory Palestine. Concerning the Jewish side of his relational study, Lockman perceptively follows the tension within Labour Zionism between a commitment to a universal solidarity based on class (in which increasingly marginalised groups within that camp genuinely believed) and a national commitment to the Zionist project as a whole. By doing so he necessarily brings to the fore possibilities that might have existed as this particular history unfolded, even if they did not materialise (this is Anderson's second suggestion for radical history, which Lockman does not mention).

These marginal (or marginalised) possibilities emerge in Lockman's narrative whenever some sort of joint Jewish–Arab organisation or solidarity was weighed vis-à-vis the Zionist commitment solely to Jewish colonisation by the historical protagonists themselves, especially by the railway workers in the years 1919–25. He is a subtle historian, so the retrospective knowledge of failure, while there, does not spoil the story's unfolding. If, however, we were to juxtapose Shafir's work to Lockman's, the conclusion would have to be that by the time the Histadrut was founded (1920) and as it gained power, the principle of pure settlement had overwhelmingly won the day, and the groups for which class and labour solidarity across ethnic lines were paramount were very marginal. Can one in this light seriously contemplate possibilities that existed on the margins? The answer is not simple and is rather grim. Essentially, as Lockman might agree, Shafir's structural explanation is correct and compounded by the benefit of historical perspective: it is palpably clear that the pure settlement structure was perpetuated and grew exponentially in scope and might, and that therefore any universalist solidarity that breached the settler/indigenous fault-line did not stand a chance.

And yet there is much sense in what Lockman does in both scholarly and political terms. Concerning historical writing in the narrower sense, the inclusion of possibilities that existed on the margins fashions a nuanced portrayal of the past that heeds the experience of the historical actors themselves, whether they endeavoured to make these possibilities come true or fought tooth and nail to foil them. But in the wider significance that 'doing' history has, the highlighting rather than discarding of possibilities on the margins is one of the main things those of us in pursuit of radical history and politics have at our disposal. To use Walter Benjamin's language, in this world in which the state of emergency is the rule rather than the exception, the recovery of a collection of possibilities – unrealised, but real possibilities nonetheless – is perhaps not *all* we have, but much of it. In the repository to which radical history and politics turn for inspiration, this collection of Benjaminian pearls must surely occupy a special place.

Poetry, Politics and Ethics

In the previous section I searched for possibilities to recount the modern history of Israel/Palestine as one narrative, in which the settler and indigenous communities shape each other in ways that are far from idyllic, in the academic disciplines of history and sociology. Similar possibilities can be sought also in poetry and ethics.

Avot Yeshurun (1904–92) is the nom de plume of Yehiel Perlmutter, an avant-garde and oppositional Jewish Israeli poet. The literal meaning the poet chose for himself is 'the fathers are looking [at us]'. He was born in the western Ukraine in 1904 and spent his childhood in his grandfather's home in Poland, a home imbued with Hasidic culture. He immigrated to Palestine in 1925, where for some time he wandered in rural Mandatory Palestine, employed as a construction worker, swamp-dredger and fruit-picker; later, in Tel Aviv, he became a labourer in a brick factory and a print shop. His family perished in the *Shoah*. Avot Yeshurun died in 1992. Although he was strongly attacked and marginalised by the Labour Zionist and then Israeli establishment, including many of the country's intellectual elite, it seems that in recent years some young literary scholars have become not only interested in his poetry but also fond of Avot Yeshurun's persona. For oppositional Israelis, however few, his poetry is a beacon of light.

Yeshurun's poetry is radically dissenting in a variety of ways, which a recent study by Haggai Rogani analyses with much insight.[12] Let me highlight two pivotal features that make Avot Yeshurun's poetry such a remarkable site for thinking about an alternative narrative: poetic language and mode of remembrance. Yeshurun invented a poetic language that subverted the Hebrew purism of the nascent modernist Hebrew poetry and, more generally, of the language purism that was one of the cultural foundations of the Zionist Israeli community of settlers. What he conceived alternatively was a mélange, a challenging tapestry, which draws on several languages: Hebrew (both modern and liturgical),

Yiddish, Arabic and Aramaic. The Arabic, it should be clarified, was not the high written language, the *fusha*, which Yeshurun did not know, but the particular spoken Palestinian *'amiyyeh*, or dialect, which he mastered. Yeshurun's poetic language was synthetic, in the sense that it created new mixed words and crossed grammatical morphologies. The latter was especially true of Arabic and Hebrew, whose proximity facilitates this reciprocal movement.

After the events of 1945 and 1948, Yeshurun began to remember with a vengeance. His poetry from the 1950s on, and especially in that decade, is underlain by a unique kind of remembering. And it was this that challenged the underlying presuppositions of the hegemonic culture and incurred the establishment's wrath. For Yeshurun did not just poetically inscribe the destruction of Arab Palestine; a few others did that as well, in both prose and poetry. Yeshurun transgressed the settler fundamental emphasised so far in this chapter: thou shall not bring the indigenous into the sacred domain of who thou art. Yeshurun lamented the perishing of his family and of European Jewry more generally, and remembered them. The point is that he did so through *first* lamenting the Palestinian catastrophe of 1948 and remembering the rich texture of the vanished community, and through castigating himself and his own community for having perpetrated that catastrophe. From the settler perspective his sin was threefold:

1.   the mere talk about the cleansing;
2.   the creation of memory in which settler-self and indigenous-other are inseparably intertwined; and
3.   the fact that the act of remembering is initiated by full identification with the indigenous demise.

This was done in a language that collapsed sacrosanct dichotomies and violated conventions, and through an understanding of Jewishness and Judaism whose register was purely ethical, innocent of ethno-religious (let alone national) exclusive identity.

This chapter ends with two quotations of Avot Yeshurun. One is the draft of a letter he wrote in the early 1950s. It has been unearthed very recently by *Mitaam* (*On Behalf*), a journal for literature and radical thought whose chief editor is Yizhak Laor, Yeshurun's admirer:

> In the wake of the War of Independence small groups of young poets sporadically appeared in Israel. In stark contrast to the previous generation's poetry, which addressed the private from the vantage point of the social collective's togetherness, these young poets addressed the public out of their private self. The former spoke in the language of plural yearnings, the latter in the language of singular yearning; the former wrote on the pity of mother and father, the latter writes on self-pity.

To the catastrophe of the Jewish People in Europe they were hearing witnesses; and to the disaster of Palestine's Arabs they were seeing witnesses. Neither had any echo in their poems. Their fathers, who had immigrated as pioneers, told them, as the Shoah came, what had happened to the Jews there, in Europe. But they occluded and didn't tell nor made them cognisant of what had happened here, in front of their own eyes, to the Arabs. None of that elicited a single intervention in their poems. Just yesterday the Arabs would bring to their homes the 'mishmish', and on the morrow – 'mafish'. They were, and are no more.[13]

And now a poem's stanza, in my translation:

You received letters from the West, and here they rang from the East? Over there the township declines daily, over here the Arab village declines daily? Steps of camels rang? Din-dan. Did you hear? Can't hear? How come Jews' ears don't hear? Have you ever come to know the Arabs? Our *Shoah* we have cried for, theirs we haven't? There's war now? Such a handsome generation. No more.

Conclusion

This chapter put forth preliminary thoughts on the possible path towards a one-state narrative in three steps. The first was to show why the framework of comparative settler colonialism is the most valid interpretation of the history of Israel/Palestine from the 1880s until today. It was argued that this framework yields not only a truthful rendering, but also one in which the history of the indigenous and settler communities cannot perforce be comprehended separately but as inextricably intertwined constituents of a single narrative. Moreover, the comparative settler approach neither masks nor harmonises the harshly conflictual nature of that narrative.

The second step deconstructed the ideological underpinnings of the hegemonic narrative. I showed how the false consciousness, whereby the impregnability of the two communities and the extent to which their historical trajectories are two parallel narrative lines that shall never meet, is authoritatively conveyed as an objectively truthful state of affairs. I stressed the fact that the meta-narrative has emanated, on the Zionist Israeli side, not from the intransigent right (which may or may not endorse all or parts of it) but from Labour Zionism and the Israeli Liberal peace camp. It should by now be clear why this narrative is so germane to what that camp has been calling partition, then territorial compromise, and most recently a two-state solution.

The third step was an attempt to contemplate ways of thinking about the land and its history that see the contours and fate of the communities as strongly related to one another, as parts of one whole. Neither the excellent studies by

Lockman and Shafir nor Avot Yeshurun's iconoclastic poetry explicitly advocate a joint political framework as the solution for the tragedy of Israel/Palestine. However, in ways that are scholarly, aesthetic and ethical, they imply that the fate of these two communities is one and indivisible.

Notes

1. All translations from Hebrew are mine.

2. Benedict Anderson, *Imagined Communities: Reflections on the Origins and Spread of Nationalism* (revised edition) (London: Verso, 1991).

3. George Fredrickson, *White Supremacy: A Comparative Study of American and South African History* (New York: Oxford University Press, 1981).

4. Patrick Wolfe, *Settler Colonialism and the Transformation of Anthropology. The Politics and Poetics of an Ethnographic Event* (London: Cassell, 1999), p. 1.

5. Anita Shapira, 'Ben-Gurion and the Bible: the creation of a historical narrative?', *Alpayim*, No. 14, 1997, pp. 207–31; and Anita Shapira, *The Bible and Israeli Identity* (Jerusalem: Magnes Press, 2006). Both texts are in Hebrew.

6. Shapira, *The Bible and Israeli Identity*, pp. 23–4.

7. Gershon Shafir, *Land, Labour, and the Origins of the Israeli–Palestinian Conflict, 1882–1914* (Cambridge: Cambridge University Press, 1989).

8. Zachary Lockman, *Comrades and Enemies: Arab and Jewish Workers in Palestine, 1906–1948* (Berkeley: University of California Press, 1996).

9. On Oppenheimer and Ruppin, see Gabriel Piterberg, *The Returns of Zionism* (London: Verso, 2008), pp. 78–88.

10. Gershon Shafir, 'Zionism and colonialism: a comparative approach', in M. N. Barnett (ed.), *Israel in a Comparative Perspective* (Albany: State of New York University Press, 199), p. 235.

11. For this conference on radical history, see Piterberg, *The Returns of Zionism*, pp. 67–8.

12. Haggai Rogani, *Facing the Ruined Village: Hebrew Poetry and the Jewish Arab Conflict 1929–1967* (Haifa: Pardes, 2006), pp. 64–8. In Hebrew.

13. *Mitaam: A Journal for Literature and Radical Thought*, Vol. 9 (March 2007), p. 6.

CHAPTER 8

In the Golden Age of Constantinian Judaism: The Future of the Indigenous Jewish Prophetic: Israel, Ethnic Particularism and Universalist Values

Marc H. Ellis

To be asked at this point in history to address the interplay of ethnic particularism and universal values in the context of any nation, people or religious community is difficult. The interplay of ethnic particularism and universal values among Jews, Judaism and the state of Israel in the present day is an almost impossible task. At least within the United States of America, if not globally, such a subject is almost forbidden. It is best to leave unstated the obvious sensibility – that there is a case for Jews and Judaism to claim a rightful place among the particularities of the world. Better still is to leave the primal identity of the people Israel, Jews and Judaism behind, and proceed immediately to the politics of ethnic cleansing and a universalism devoid of particularity.

As a person who travels and lectures internationally, I have experienced this near impossibility of speaking about Israel, Jews and Judaism in their particularity. Speaking to different audiences, their palpable impatience with such talk often prompts an anger that runs deeper than the merely political. In the Middle East, there is great suffering, and Israel the state is seen and continues to be seen as an engine of that suffering. We speak now after Gaza, but in recent years we were speaking after Lebanon and in years before we also spoke after Lebanon, after each war, incursion and invasion, leading back to and before 1948.

To speak of Jewish particularity in any positive way is thus to enter into an international minefield. Yet what issues into crisis is often a double-edged sword, and the fight for Palestinian freedom is also to engage in a particular struggle and its concomitant claims of particularity. It might be awkward to maintain that the struggle in Israel/Palestine is a struggle of mobilised particularities; it might be easier to see the struggle as one between a Jewish particularity and Palestinian universality. However, the latter analysis misses the complexity of the contending parties and also passes by the potential solidarity between Jews and Palestinians.

Thus to acknowledge that the discussion of particularity and universal values is endlessly complex, this chapter offers what might be seen as a contrarian position on the one-state/two-state debate – or another way of approaching whatever position one holds.

Constantinian Judaism and Holocaust Denial

The difficulty in addressing the possibility of an affirmative Jewish particularity is well earned. The Jewish establishment – what the author calls Constantinian Judaism – has been advocating Jewish particularity as a clarion call with the expected results: a new and sustained Jewish militarism that is focused in the Middle East but is also global in reach.

Here the state of Israel is held high as the fulfilment of Jewish destiny and identity, with the Holocaust ever-invoked. Indeed, in this view of Jewish particularity, it is the Holocaust that grounds the state of Israel, which itself is the culmination of more than a millennium of anti-Semitism. In Constantinian Judaism, Jewish identity is fashioned around this anti-Semitism, the Holocaust and the state of Israel. Even the rituals of Judaism are harnessed to these sensibilities, events and the state. That the militarisation of Jewish life hides a colonial and imperial reality in fact is only possible because the factual nature of Jewish colonialism and imperialism are themselves hidden from sight. The colonial and imperial aspects of contemporary Jewish life are so well disguised that the promoters of Constantinian Judaism – as well as the consumers attached to Constantinian Judaism as a way of life – are largely ignorant of what they affirm, promote and enable. This is why Constantinian Jews are livid at the portrayal of their own power as colonial and imperial. Could contemporary Jews actually evidence these aspects which they have been accused of for so many centuries?

Here lies the crossover between myth and reality, and the answer to why the question of ethnic particularism and universal values is more complicated than is initially evident. Today any person of conscience would deride ethnic particularism and choose universal principles. But of course that has been a consistent criticism of Jews, perhaps the longest-running criticism of any collective that has survived the millennia. And no doubt this long-standing criticism has crept into the discussion among those who, in a progressive way, decry ethnic particularism and uphold universal principles. This has gone so far as a principled denial of the Holocaust or at least the extent of it, as seen in the current news of a renegade Catholic bishop being brought back into the Roman Catholic Church. It has also been introduced in the Israel/Palestine debate by such a group as Deir Yassin Remembered, founded in America, which sees the discussion of the Holocaust as primarily a smokescreen for support of Israel. The prevalence of Holocaust-focused agendas is to some puzzling, for its consistent and prominent place makes it appear that its continual reaffirmation is necessary – as if the Holocaust wasn't a historical fact.[1]

In Holocaust denial, the Holocaust becomes a venue for the critique of ethnic particularism gone wild. It feeds a view that the world must combat this ethnic particularism as a conspiracy to be rooted out. Can this virulent form of ethnic particularism be addressed in a normative way, by the forces within the Jewish community – Jews of Conscience – who affirm a Jewish particularity even as they struggle against the colonial and imperial identity that has subsumed it? Or is it impossible to be a Jew except in name only without an attachment in some way or another to a Constantinian Jewishness – because Constantinian Jewishness is the only way of being Jewish?

These distinctions are crucial because if you identify Constantinian Judaism as the only way of being Jewish no matter what affirming Jews say or do with their identity, then Jews assume a place in the identity cosmos different from all others, as if other nations, peoples and religions do not have similar struggles. On the contrary, if we understand that Jewish particularity can go either way, toward a militarism or toward a universalism within its own particularity – like other nations, peoples and religions – then the struggle can be seen as a common struggle within and across boundaries and borders.

If we thus see the trajectory of particularism and universalism as struggles of those who seek empire and those who seek community, then particularity may be seen in a more positive light. In this light, even universalism can be seen as a particularism on the move. For how can any one person or community be truly universal unless they recognise their own boundaries as the foundation for crossing those borders and boundaries? That is why much of the rhetoric of universalism lacks content and critique: by assuming that one's enlightened universalism is void of particularism, the universal becomes an abstraction that likewise hides its own culpability.

If Jews and Judaism are in the docket of global public opprobrium, do the judges that come from Islamic and Christian perspectives, or Marxist, Enlightenment or modern perspectives, escape the judge's gavel? Particularism, ethnic or otherwise, when unleashed with power at its side, is as dangerous as a universalism that has power as its fulcrum. Thus the issue may lie somewhere other than the distinction between the particular and the universal. But at the same time hasn't this debate endured for centuries now and haven't Jews always been at the centre of this discussion, at least in the West?[2]

The Prophetic as the Indigenous of the People Israel

Ethnic particularism, even when it emphasises universalism, can be problematic at the least. But isn't any identity formation intrinsically a problem? We all come from somewhere, born into and formed within localities, geographic and cultural, bound to social, political and ideological configurations beyond our control. Our options are therefore both developed and constrained by birth. At the same time, most if not all of these constraints – one might also see them as roots – also open up to a wider and equally particular worldview. Constraints and roots, closing down and opening: this is the rhythm of our lives and the world around us.

Israel the people, as differentiated from Israel the state, has always struggled with constraint and rootedness, an opening within and beyond both. If one reads the Hebrew Bible, it is all right there – the sense of being chosen as a particular people, of being called as a people by a God of liberation, to be alone among the nations as well as being a light unto them.

The narrative is complicated: the people Israel does not arise as one people, called together as already formed. Rather, Israel as a people comes into being in a struggle for liberation in which a series of disparate tribes come together, form a common memory of oppression and together pursue a common destiny. In the Bible, that destiny is to be found in the Promised Land, but only if a new way of being in the social and political realm is developed, instituted and maintained. With social, political and economic justice at its core, Israel is liberated from oppression in order to demonstrate that there is a different way of living the collective life.[3]

To facilitate a different way of collective living, a Sabbatical dynamic is established where every seven days, seven years and in the 50th year, a levelling of accumulated social, political and economic injustice is commanded among the people Israel and with those who accompany Israel. The stakes could not be higher: Israel's relation to itself and to God is on the line. If Israel models the society it was liberated from with its hierarchies, class divisions and slaves, then its ability to claim God and its special place among the nations is jeopardised. The biblical language is extremely strong here. If Israel becomes like other nations in its social, political and economic injustices, the Promised Land will devolve into war, anarchy and debauchery. Ultimately, Israel will be exiled from the land.

Thus the particularity of the people Israel is founded in the bond around justice and a God of justice with many twists and turns. Still, the central point of the narrative is the prophetic which, rather than the land, is the indigenous of the people Israel. Here we find the prophets of Israel come one after another, in the Bible and today. The prophet is the one that constantly reminds the people

Israel, often at great personal cost, of the vocation of Jewish particularity. This vocation is at the heart of Israel and ultimately everything that Israel does comes under that purview. The land can become a home, ritual can be appropriate and uplifting – if justice is being pursued and accomplished. A backsliding Israel is an admonished Israel. A permanently backsliding Israel is a punished Israel; each is bereft of God. Only in exile, where Israel's sins are recounted and repented for, can God reappear as Israel's shield, a reappearance heralded by the suffering of the prophets, who also proclaim the vision of Israel restored.[4]

Progressive Jews and the Limits of Jewish Dissent

Surveying the contemporary Jewish landscape, the opposition to Constantinian Judaism comes in two forms: that of Progressive Jews and Jews of Conscience.

In the main, Progressive Jews uphold the reality of contemporary Jewish life as revolving around the Holocaust–Israel axis. Progressive Jews see the Constantinian Jewish establishment as using the Holocaust to support policies of the Israeli government against Palestinians, thus perverting the lessons of the Holocaust toward power. The Holocaust remains as the centre and because of Jewish suffering in the Holocaust, Jews need an empowered state of Israel. Within that empowerment, Palestinians have a right to their own state alongside Israel.

The imperative placed on Jews for an empowered state is also imposed on Palestinians; because of historic Jewish suffering, Palestinians must embrace the Jewish need for a Jewish state. Once that acceptance is signalled and practised, Jews can render justice to the Palestinians within that framework. Though Progressive Jews recognise that this is not complete justice, within the context of Jewish needs, this is what is available. Once adopted, mutuality across the Israel–Palestine divide can evolve, since in this view the Jewish state of Israel can only be secure if the Palestinian state recognises Israel as a Jewish state and is also demilitarised. Mutuality will lead to new forms of cooperation, so much so that Israel will become the military protector of the fledgling Palestinian state. Indeed, any threat from other Arab countries to Palestinians would be met by the Israeli Defense Forces.

In its publishing history and its stance today, this is the essence of the argument of the Progressive Jewish movement's flagship magazine, *Tikkun*. With its editor, Michael Lerner, Tikkun is both a magazine and a movement, publishing its magazine monthly and establishing Tikkun communities around the nation, holding conferences and articulating positions on the Israeli–Palestinian conflict. Though in a sustained and vehement argument with the Constantinian Jewish establishment, Tikkun has also defined the parameters of legitimate dissent on the issue of Israel–Palestine, for both Jews and non-Jews.

For years the Tikkun litmus test for dissent included recognising the Holocaust as a defining event for world history and Israel as a Jewish state, demanding Palestinian recognition of both, and limiting the discussion of the history of the Israeli–Palestinian conflict to the post-1967 era. Off-limits for discussion were, among other things:

- the establishment of the state of Israel and the original dispossession of the Palestinians;
- the right of the Palestinians to return to the internal borders of what became the state of Israel;
- the discussion of punitive policies toward Israel, such as a freeze on aid from the USA, the withdrawal of American military guarantees to protect Israel, any movement toward divestment and boycotts aimed at Israel;
- charges that Israel was creating an 'apartheid' system, and any other comparison of Israeli behaviour with other unjust governments; and
- any comparison between Israeli policies with ethnic cleansing of the early years of the Nazi regime (i.e. before the Holocaust and its horrors swung into action).

Whether voiced by Palestinians, Jews or others, any of these assertions were deemed anti-Semitic by Tikkun and Jewish Progressives in general.[5]

As a voice of dissent among Jews, at least in the USA, Tikkun from its founding in 1986 usurped older left-of-centre views among Jewish dissidents; even today it still seeks to define the acceptable parameters of Jewish dissent. Clearly, Tikkun has also moved with the times, expanding its critique of the Constantinian Jewish establishment and beginning to consider some alternative critiques of the state of Israel. Though continuing to be patronising toward the Palestinian, Tikkun has become less so over time.

On the one hand, each step of Tikkun's evolution has coincided with changing public opinion in the USA and around the world, in particular that what can and cannot be said in public about Israel–Palestine is not determined only by Jews. On the other hand, each step that Tikkun has taken has been calculated to both move forward as well as hold back criticism of the state of Israel and of Jews themselves. In doing this, Tikkun has actually protected the Constantinian Jewish establishment and functioned as an enabler of both the establishment and the state of Israel. Whether this is conscious or not is beyond the author's purview or ability to discern. What is important is how criticism functions in the public realm: the same standards applied to those who critique Jewish particularity must also be applied to those who defend it. In the end, Tikkun and Progressive Jews in particular have functioned as a left-wing of Constantinian Judaism, as have such groups as Peace Now and Rabbis for Human Rights.

Jews of Conscience as the Continuation of the Indigenous Prophetic

The struggle with the indigenous prophetic of the people Israel is longstand-ing, beginning with the biblical narrative. Even before the liberation struggle in Egypt, the Israelites were grumbling. Was it better to leave Egypt for an unknown future or remain as slaves? The desert wandering was no different, with a consideration of Israel's destiny at the heart of their journey. Some wanted to turn back to Egypt or, at the very least, install new leadership. Others wanted to forge ahead without delay. Even Israel's discussion and sometimes argument with God was characterised by this back and forth. God, too, partici-pated in this dialogue, sometimes acting unilaterally, other times changing his own course. Especially decisive were God's extensive and combative discussions with Moses, where Moses alternately demanded action from God against his rebellious people and defended them against God's actions.

To assert that the indigenous of the people Israel are the prophetic is not at all to claim that Jews as a people (historically or in the present), when involved with the state, act prophetically in a collective way. Just the opposite: the depth of the prophetic is the very reason for the intense and continuing struggle against it. If the prophetic is not found at the Jewish core, why the constant denial of it? With regard to Progressive Jews and the prophetic, they, as the left-wing of Constantinian Judaism, should be seen as trying to express the prophetic while at the same time fearing its implementation. The desire to articulate the prophetic as central to Jewish life even while also keeping the lid on it has a long history within Jewish life.

Still, Progressive Jews have been challenged in a new and bold way by Jews of Conscience.[6] Though this challenge has been building for some years now, and has existed in various manifestations in other periods of Jewish history, includ-ing in relation to the founding and expansion of the state of Israel, a formative moment in the history of dissent occurred in the wake of the 2001 ascension of Sharon as Prime Minister and the Palestinian uprising already in progress. Among other things, this uprising saw the introduction of helicopter gunships and fighter aircraft against the Palestinian population.

Soon thereafter the construction of the separation barrier began. Though many of these policies had through other means been used by Israel previously, this time period saw an escalation and in effect a culmination of the history of Israel's birth and expansion. By 2000, more and more Jews saw the possibility of a two-state solution diminished, if not foreclosed altogether. At the same time, any claim to Jewish innocence and redemption, trumpeted by the Constantinian Jewish establishment or guarded by Progressive Jews, was impossible to main-tain. The struggle between Constantinian Judaism and Progressive Jews, as limited as it was, was seen as a fig leaf for a more serious and deeper struggle.

What was coming into view was the end of Jewish history as it had been known and inherited.[7]

There has been dissent within Jewish history about power wielded by the people Israel. Rarely has there been prophetic protest against the use of Israel's power against others. In the contemporary period, Jews of Conscience face all of these problematics, including the power used against them by progressive forces within the Jewish community. If there ever was a community assaulted on all fronts and in exile, it is the Jews of Conscience. It is difficult to know even where to start in parsing out the multiple sources. My own way of imaging the predicament of Jews of Conscience is that of a small group of intensely committed Jews travelling into exile, and with them they carry the covenant.

What constitutes the substance of the covenant carried by these Jews of Conscience into exile? Of course, we have the traditional content of the covenant, the indigenous prophetic, the foundation of Jewish particularity; we have within it as well the contemporary challenges: the Holocaust and the birth and expansion of the state of Israel; their task is to disassociate Jewish identity from the violence that permeates it, a violence associated with empire, colonialism and imperialism.

The journey of Jews of Conscience is multi-layered, linked to a difficult history and an ominous present. On the one hand, the behaviour of the state of Israel is destroying Jewish history; on the other, Jews of Conscience carry the fears of Jewish history on their shoulders. The world continues to be a dangerous place for Jews and the state of Israel may have increased that danger. Part of the danger is the desire among some to erase Jewish particularity altogether. Also, Jews of Conscience in their exile are increasingly separated from the broader currents of Jewish communal life, threatening Jewish particularity from within.

If we are at the end of Jewish history as we have known and inherited it, this exile may be the last in Jewish history. Jews of Conscience are entering unchartered territory – what might be called the New Diaspora. Here there is a gathering of exiles from around the world and it is questionable whether, in an ethos that thinks of itself in universal principles, any one particularity will survive even Jewish particularity. This is true even though the New Diaspora is impossible without the gathering of the shattered fragments of the many particularities that make up its wholeness.

Jewish Particularity, the Holocaust and Israel/Palestine

What is the difference between Constantinian Judaism, Progressive Jews and Jews of Conscience with regard to Jewish particularity and universal principles?

On the Constantinian Jewish side, Jewish particularity is exclusive. Operating from the perspective of the Holocaust and an eternal anti-Semitism as the foundation, an empowered state of Israel as a response to the Holocaust is its goal. For those Constantinian Jews who live outside of Israel, primarily in the USA, economic and political ascendancy within the USA is paramount, both for their own flourishing and for that of the Jewish people in and outside of Israel. Constantinian Jews choose empire as their vehicle to pursue these goals; their world is narrowed to the USA, Israel and parts of Europe, though Europe mainly used a negative trope for the projection of American and Israeli power.

If Europe is a Jewish graveyard, the USA and Israel guarantee Jewish survival; the rest of the world is out there, either unimportant or counter to these interests. Thus Jewish particularity is American–Israel-centric. Palestinians function both as a warning that the European graveyard may be augmented in the East – the spectre of another Holocaust – as well as to reinforce the sense that those outside of Europe are menacing to the 'civilised' world. The coupling of Palestinians and 9/11 is simply one more example of this multi-layered lesson coming from the Holocaust that is deemed antithetical to America's own security and interests. Ultimately, Jewish particularity must be mobilised and militarised in a hostile world.[8]

Among Progressive Jews, Jewish particularity is also exclusive, though that exclusivity is less prominent and joins with other communities with which Progressive Jews seek to encounter and work. This exclusivity, coupled with solidarity, allows Progressive Jews to continue to assert Jewishness as defining even as they share and borrow aspects of American culture. This is true as well in Israel, as many Progressive Jews who articulate public positions on issues Jewish and political were born and raised in the USA. Like the European Jews who took a lead role in creating Israel, Progressive Jews in Israel see themselves and Israel itself as Western, European and American; they just happen to live geographically in the Middle East.

As are Constantinian Jews, Progressive Jews are American-centric, living within and benefiting from the American empire. Though their positions on many of the broader issues are liberal and more, supporting women's rights, critiquing neoconservative politics and the like, the Leftist critique prominent among Jews in the early part of the twentieth century, mostly found in various kinds of Communist and Marxist sensibilities, are now softened. Thoroughly ensconced in the American empire reality, yet feeling uneasy within it, the critique popular among Progressive Jews is a soft one, ameliorating aspects of American empire and spreading its wealth to those without it. This includes its understanding of Israel as a country deserving of American support and necessary to the future of all. Israel here is also Western, imbued with American ideals, which in the USA have not yet been fully realised. Those outside of the American paradigm – Arabs in general and Palestinians in particular – are being schooled in these American values, with Jews as their sometimes flawed teachers. The unfortunate aspect of the Israeli–Palestinian crisis is that Palestinians and Arabs are slow learners; Israel, with its flaws, remains a model for them.

The Jewish particularity of Progressive Jews is filled with Americana and the Israeli kitsch that was so prominent after the 1967 War. Most Progressive Jews came of age during this time period. The exploration and disappointment with both sensibilities demands a reaffirmation, even a refounding of these values, which can happen with this type of Judaism (at least its potential) they grew up in: Jews as innocent. If Progressive Jews can recapture Jewish life as essentially the encapsulated good, with America also struggling toward that goodness in the fight for civil rights and the protests and final ending of the Vietnam War, couldn't Israel also recapture its glory days of the pre-1967 War and the fight for survival found within the war itself? The Progressive Jewish sense of its prophetic mission resides here: to recapture goodness and innocence of Jewish, American and Israeli history, all of which represent the best possible future for the world, if only Jews, Americans, Israelis and everyone else in the world receive and embody this message. Thus Progressive Jews are evangelical in their Jewish particularity, spreading their Good News to the world, including to the Constantinian Jewish establishment that has lost its way.[9]

Can the Jewish particularity of Jews of Conscience be markedly different than those of Constantinian and Progressive Jews? Since Jewish particularity is defining and since members of all three groupings grew up within the similar communal understandings of history and the present, the differences among them cannot be as great as might, at first consideration, seem. In fact, the same experiences, even with varying interpretations, shaped the contemporary Jewish groups we are exploring. Thus the differences found among them are nuanced and, though important, cannot hide equally important commonalities. If the possibilities within the differences can be appreciated and highlighted, it should not surprise us that when the chips are down, the limitations of all three groups might come to the fore.

On the question of Israel–Palestine, the marked differences between Constantinian Jews, Progressive Jews and Jews of Conscience are crucial markers of possibility and limitations. With Constantinian Jews, Israel is a remarkable and innocent flowering of Jewish history; Progressive Jews see Israel as a remarkable and innocent enterprise that has gone wrong, threatens to continue down that path or, with the application of Jewish ethics, could – must – be righted again. Despite the evidence that Israel, as a state, operates like a state, like any other state, Progressive Jews cannot accept this as a final verdict. Is this because it would also throw into question Jewishness as a particularity unlike other particularities?

Jews of Conscience go further than Constantinian or Progressive Jews, back to 1948 as the war for a state of Israel that ethnically cleansed the Palestinian population – an ethnic cleansing that has continued under various guises since the formation of the state of Israel and continues apace. Over the years, Jews of Conscience have split with Progressive Jews over the issue of Israel, signalling a deepening fissure within Jewish particularity itself. Whereas Progressive Jews see innocence as the centre of Jewish history – the formation of the state of Israel was part of that 'innocent' stream but is now interrupting it; hence the need to 'correct' the new trajectory of the state – Jews of Conscience are losing faith in Jewish innocence and in the possibility of correcting the trajectory of the state of Israel.[10]

Yet in struggling against the tide of Constantinian Jewish power and Progressive Jewish rhetoric, Jews of Conscience also stake out a place where Jewish particularity can be embodied, despite (or perhaps because of) their increasing distance from anything identifiable as such. In this way, distance from a skewed and violent Jewish particularity, now widely viewed as culpable, might be the only way of embodying Jewish particularity in our time. Stripping everything identifiably Jewish away, and moving as far into exile as possible, would it not then be appropriate simply to leave Jewish life completely and any issue connected with it? Especially since the cost is so high, what with the power of Constantinian Judaism and the delegitimising and often hurtful rhetoric that Progressive Jews apply to them. At the same time, Jews of Conscience are on the losing end of all their concerns. Israel has triumphed, we do live in the Golden Age of Constantinian Judaism and Progressive Jews will continue to fight for their ascendancy as the next Jewish establishment regardless of the facts on the Jewish ground – for where else can Progressive Jews go with their rhetoric except toward Constantinian Judaism?

After Gaza: The (Un)Future of the Indigenous Prophetic

So if American and Israeli interests – matched with massive investments from Jews outside Israel, and tied to the violence found in all of them – have penetrated the centre of Jewish life, becoming its essence, without which Jews would not know how to continue on, why should Jews of Conscience identify as Jews, when they are considered by other Jews as non-Jews or self-hating Jews? They may even begin to think of themselves in that light.

Should Jews of Conscience think this way? In some sense, Constantinian and Progressive Jews are not mistaken; Jews of Conscience have seen their understanding of what it means to be a Jew unravel, compelling their exile – an unravelling plain for both Constantinian and Progressive Jews to see. If the entire history of Israel is not recognised for what it is, if the crushing of the Palestinian uprisings in 1987 and 2000 did not make things clear, then the 2006 Lebanon war and the 2008–9 invasion of Gaza should do so. But if too much is invested in a certain conception of Jewish particularity, then the twisting and bending of Jewish history, ancient or contemporary, will handle diversions from this conceptual essence. In this way, Constantinian and Progressive Jews are both involved in reducing the cognitive dissonance between what is asserted and what is done in the name of that particularity. If Jews of Conscience recognise that the reduction of that cognitive dissonance is no longer possible, except through a sophisticated maze of hypocritical assertions and projections that exist within the Jewish particularity of our time – a hypocrisy violative at its core of the indigenous prophetic that Jews have carried through history – is there any other option than becoming less and less Jewish, and thus more and more (un)Jewish?

The trappings of Jewish life from ritual to wealth to power have overwhelmed Jews on both sides of the aisle. With Progressive Jews seeking a middle path, they move to and fro, but the end time has arrived – or so Jews of Conscience feel. A choice needs to be made and it is no longer between the self-assertion of Constantinian Judaism and the rescue of Jewish particularity promoted by Progressive Jews. Jews of Conscience see this dichotomy as false and, at any rate, unsustainable. Having broken with available options palatable to Constantinian Jews, to live within this unravelling is all that is left for them.

It is indeed strange that the indigenous Jewish prophetic is no longer recognised as Jewish at all by normative Jewish discourse. Too often, Jews of Conscience, while railing against the Constantinian and Progressive Jews who deride them, nonetheless internalise their definitions of what is Jewish and what is not. Distanced from normative Jewish life and resources, they are also separated from those who might mentor them in their journey. The life Jews of Conscience are leading, and the exile they have entered, continues, but the meaning of that exile with regard to the deepest aspects of their being remains unarticulated. Still, the yearning to name one's experience is strong: next to the indigenous prophetic, the longest tradition of the people Israel is naming our journey – in exile.

Here we come to an intriguing juncture. It is within the indigenous prophetic and the naming of Israel's destiny that the final breakdown of the dichotomy of ethnic particularism and universal values is found. This is also where the Jewish 'problem' is exposed as a sham. For without the prophetic there is no meaning in the world, and without the indigenous prophetic being spoken and lived by those within the community who gave the prophetic to the world, where would Jews and others be?

Indeed, the prophetic has spread far and wide. Israel's indigenous prophetic is increasingly carried by others, especially in the various liberation movements around the world. Perhaps ironically, after so long a history of recrimination and discrimination, it is Christians who are today reinvigorating the prophetic at the very time that the prophetic is being lost to Jewish life. In the long history of the people Israel, the prophetic has been submerged but never lost; just when the funeral procession is gathering, the prophetic comes back to life. Jews of Conscience are thus heirs to a long history of prophetic revival. What is new in our time is that this prophetic revival is happening in concert with the flourishing of the prophetic among those who once derided it. Perhaps that is too wide a berth, for the prophetic being carried by Christians is largely influenced by Third World Christians who were themselves subjugated and humiliated by their Christian conquerors. To see Christianity in league with the prophetic, Third World Christians have turned toward the indigenous prophetic of the Hebrew Bible – thus creating a very different kind of Christianity.[11]

So a new solidarity is on the horizon, or could be, between Jews of Conscience and Christians of Conscience. Could Muslims of Conscience also be included in this new configuration? With variations attendant to their evolving particularity, the indigenous prophetic of the people Israel is carried forward. Again, in a striking and unexpected way, Christians and Muslims of Conscience, in exile from their own Constantinian communal formations, are places where Jews, searching for their own prophetic, can glimpse what was their birthright. In sum, the Jewish prophetic is now spread to other particularities, can rebound back to Jews of Conscience in exile, then return once again to Christians and Muslims of Conscience. This scenario posits a very different geography than what passes for interfaith dialogue in the present. The latter in reality is an ecumenical 'deal', where the representatives of Constantinian formations of Jewish, Christian and Muslim faith communities come together to forge an alliance that as often as not together punishes dissidents within each tradition.

The (un)future of the indigenous Jewish prophetic can be found in solidarity of people of conscience across religious lines – and secular lines as well. If all religions tend toward Constantinian formations, with people of conscience embracing the prophetic, so too secularity in its modern form has its Constantinian formations and dissenters. Including secular folks of conscience helps to discipline Jews, Christians and Muslims of Conscience who are also prone to a Constantinianism on the Left. At the same time, religious people of conscience ask questions of secularity and its tendency to absolutise their (un)beliefs as much as believers absolutise their own beliefs.

The 2008–9 Israeli invasion of Gaza, as was the case with the 2006 invasion of Lebanon, raises the questions addressed here to another level. Most of the history of Israel/Palestine since 1948 has been a series of 'afters'. Is Gaza so different?

The question of the solution of the Israeli–Palestinian crisis is as far away, or even farther still, than ever. At this moment of stalemate, is it even more important to suggest a solution as a way to envision a future?

To frame the question though, as two-states or one-state is misleading; neither will come into being in the foreseeable future. In reality there is in effect one state even if not declared, and that is Israel, which stretches from Tel Aviv to the River Jordan. And so, advocates of a one-state solution must engage with the reality that transforming the present situation into a unitary state, with a radically different power structure to that which currently prevails, will encounter myriad difficulties. Controlling this land as well as sharing control of Gaza with Egypt, the only question that remains is what will happen to the millions of Palestinians within Israel's control? The three remnant Palestinian populations within Israeli control – the Palestinian citizens of the state of Israel, the Palestinians in Jerusalem and the West Bank, and the Palestinians of Gaza – exist within the vortex of Israeli control. There is no power to challenge Israel's control of the area in question and only a catastrophe could change the equation of power to any significant degree. Such a catastrophe is conjectured as a possible missile strike against Tel Aviv or another Israeli population centre, but even here the Israeli response would be overwhelming, as it would envelop the region in a kind of war the Middle East has yet to see. Politics aside, the moral and ethical question is whether a Jew or anyone else could wish such a catastrophe on Israel as a way to teach a lesson this nation has been unwilling to learn on its own.[12]

Here the relationship of ethnic particularism and universal values take on a different dynamic. If Jews, because of ethnic ties, could not wish such a catastrophe on Israel, could Jews, in light of universal values, sanction such hope in order to rescue the Palestinians? The clash between the two devolves when the reality of mass death stalks the unthinkable, which, paradoxically, is eminently possible.

In such a situation, what should Palestinians hope for? Their future lies in the empowerment of their own ethnic particularism, even if couched in universal values. To win their freedom, they need to be able to sacrifice their universal sensibility – even to ultimately achieve it. Whether they would survive an attempt at victory is a question that requires consideration well in advance.

What is more likely in the long run is a civil rights movement of some Jews and Palestinians that will reach a small percentage of both populations, but just enough to build coalitions and a political base so as to modify the separation of Jews and Palestinians. The inclusion of Jews and Palestinians in some areas of economic and civic life might then influence the political realm. Into what formulation and just how such coalescence might occur is anyone's guess, but this slow process is more likely to gain a foothold than outdated or unreasoned proposals. In the meantime, the suffering of the Palestinian people will continue. At the same time, Israel will remain insecure, on the verge of catastrophe and militarised to the extreme. The Jews and Palestinians that remain in Israel/Palestine will be those who cannot leave.

During these years the Golden Age of Constantinian Judaism will flourish, Progressive Jews will vanish and Jews of Conscience will move deeper and deeper into exile. Jews of Conscience will exist in a community of varied exiles from different religions and cultures, including Palestinians. Contrasted with a militarised Israel and suffering Palestinian population, this community will develop an inclusive relationship that comes from sharing a universe of shattered and fragmented particularities. With these various particularities encountering one another, a new understanding of universal values might emerge. The new universal may include parts of former ethnic particularities and parts of what was known as universal values. Here Jews will play their more familiar minority role; the question then will be how and whether Jewish particularity will survive. Will Jews continue to identify as Jews? In the Golden Age of Constantinian Judaism, will Jewish identity continue and in what form? The rebellion against Constantinian Judaism may lead to a flowering of another form of Jewish identity; it may also lead to the abandonment of any identification with Jewishness itself. This Jewish exile may be the last exile in Jewish history. If it is, will the indigenous of the people Israel, the prophetic, then disappear?

Placed alongside the suffering of the Palestinian people, the disappearance of the Jewish prophetic might seem a misplaced concern. Yet if that prophetic, so important in world history, is no longer carried by the people who have embodied it throughout history, and is lost, could it also postpone (if not destroy) the slim chance of a Middle East where Jews and Palestinians embrace one another in equality and justice?

Notes

1. See the article by Dan McGowan, the head of Deir Yassin Remembered, 'What does the Holocaust really mean?', *Dissident Voice*, 27 February 2009. Available at www.dissidentvoice.org.

2. For the author's most recent exploration of this theme, see *Judaism Does Not Equal Israel* (New York: New Press, 2009).

3. A fascinating discussion of the origins of ancient Israel can be found in Norman Gottwald, *The Tribes of Yahweh: A Sociology of the Religion of Liberated Israel, 1250–1050* (London: Sheffield Academic Press, 1999).

4. A still seminal work on the prophets is Abraham Joshua Heschel, *The Prophets: An Introduction* (New York: Harper, 1962).

5. *Tikkun*, the magazine, was first published in 1986. If you follow the journal, especially Michael Lerner's editorials, you will find the attitudes discussed. Look especially at the issues surrounding the 1993 Oslo Accords.

6. Since this naming of Jews of Conscience is fairly new, the parameter of the community is in flux. But to help visualise those Jews who historically and in the present belong to this community, we might include people like Martin Buber, Judah Magnes, Hannah Arendt, Noam Chomsky and Sara Roy.

7. My understanding here is that the Palestinian uprising that began in 2000 was the last gasp of the progressive Jewish Left regarding Israel. This also exposed the limitations of Progressive Jews as the left wing of Constantinian Judaism. When Israelis started dying in greater numbers – that is, proportionally – than in earlier clashes, the idea vanished that Palestinians would simply act the way Progressive Jews wanted them to. For the author's early articulation of this situation, see 'The mural-colored wall: on separation and the future of Jews and Palestinians in Israel/Palestine and the Diaspora', *Chicago Journal of International Law*, 5, Summer 2004, pp. 271–85.

8. The outpouring of literature linking 9/11 and the resurgence of anti-Semitism is instructive in this regard. For the revival of the theme of anti-Semitism in the post-9/11 literature, see Phyllis Chesler, *The New Anti-Semitism: The Current Crisis and What We Must Do About It* (San Francisco: Jossey-Bass, 2003).

9. The author writes about this in the third edition of *Toward a Jewish Theology of Liberation: Into the 21st Century* (Waco: Baylor University Press, 2004). See the final chapter: 'The coming of evangelical Judaism'.

10. See Ilan Pappé, *The Ethnic Cleansing of Palestine* (London: One World, 2007).

11. One of the first expressions of this prophetic Third World theology can be found in Gustavo Gutierrez's *A Theology of Liberation: History, Politics, and Salvation* (Maryknoll: Orbis, 1973).

12. On the Israeli matrix of control in the West Bank, see Jeff Halper, *Obstacles to Peace: A Reframing of the Palestinian-Israeli Conflict* (third edition) (Jerusalem: Palestine Mapping Center, 2005).

CHAPTER 9

Challenging the Consensus Favouring the Two-State Model

Ali Abunimah

In November 2008, a blue ribbon group of former US officials sent a document to then President-elect Barack Obama entitled, 'A Last Chance for a Two-State Israel–Palestine Agreement'. The paper, authored by bipartisan establishment luminaries including former National Security Advisers Brent Scowcroft and Zbigniew Brzezinski, warned the incoming president that the next 'six to twelve months may well represent the last chance for a fair, viable and lasting solution'.[1]

The document emphasised a number of points that have become conventional wisdom in peace process circles, and appeared to shape the approach of the new Obama administration: that Israel/Palestine peace is a US 'national interest', and that securing such a peace would rob Middle East 'extremists' of the ability to use the plight of the Palestinians to recruit for their causes. Scowcroft – the lead author – and his colleagues called for early and active US engagement, faulting the administrations of Presidents Bill Clinton and George W. Bush for waiting too long during their own terms and doing too little. The recommendation that the President name a high-level special envoy to oversee Palestinian–Israeli and Syrian–Israeli negotiations was taken up almost immediately, with Obama's appointment of former senator and Northern Ireland mediator George Mitchell.

The prevailing view in Washington was encapsulated in this statement:

> There is a cliché – one that has the merit of truth – to the effect that 'Everyone knows, more or less, what the peace treaties will say; the hard part is getting to the signings'. There has been no shortage of unofficial, bilateral drafting of 'treaty' language – this is hardly a 'wheel' to be 'reinvented'. Indeed, the outline of an Israeli–Palestinian accord was crafted during the dying days of the Clinton administration. Yet getting to the end-game will be anything but easy.[2]

The idea that 'everyone knows' what 'peace' would look like is accepted as true merely because it is repeated often. This perhaps explains why almost the first year of Obama's presidency was focused on process. On the one hand, the USA tried to persuade Israel to freeze construction of settlements in the occupied West Bank in exchange for gestures toward normalisation with Israel by Arab states – and on the other, it continued the Bush administration policy of providing financial and military support to the Palestinian Authority regime led by Mahmoud Abbas, specifically to carry out 'security coordination' with Israel. In other words, the PA's job under both Bush and Obama administrations was to wipe out real or suspected centres of resistance, but especially the political, military and social infrastructure of Hamas which won the January 2006 Palestinian legislative election. The Obama administration continued the Bush administration's tacit support for Israel's punishing blockade of the Gaza Strip, depriving 1.5 million Palestinians of basic rights and necessities.

Paradoxically, the Scowcroft paper also acknowledged that the 'dispute between the two [Israeli and Palestinian] sides is too deep, and the discrepancies of power between them too vast, for them to solve their conflict without the US acting as a determined outside and even-handed advocate and facilitator'. The most important step the USA could take, the document argued, would be for the USA itself to publish its own outline for a 'fair, viable and sustainable agreement, based on principles that both Israel and the Palestinians have previously accepted by signing on to UN Security Council Resolutions 242 and 338, the Oslo Accords, the 2003 Road Map, and the 2007 Annapolis understandings'.

The parameters proposed in the Scowcroft document were likely to form the basis of any US peace plan issued by the Obama administration (or behind the scenes 'mediation') and indeed closely reflected the positions expressed by Obama before and after his election.[3] They are worth reproducing in full:

(1) Two states, based on the lines of June 4, 1967, with minor, reciprocal, and agreed-upon modifications as expressed in a 1:1 land swap, to take into account areas heavily populated by Israelis in the West Bank;

(2) A solution to the refugee problem consistent with the two-state solution, that does not entail a general right of return, addresses the Palestinian refugees' sense of injustice, and provides them with meaningful financial compensation as well as resettlement assistance;

(3) Jerusalem as home to both capitals, with Jewish neighbourhoods falling under Israeli sovereignty and Arab neighbourhoods under Palestinian sovereignty, with special arrangements for the Old City providing each side control of its respective holy places and unimpeded access by each community to them;

(4) A non-militarised Palestinian state, together with security mechanisms that address Israeli concerns while respecting Palestinian sovereignty, and a US-led

multinational force to ensure a peaceful transitional security period. This coalition peacekeeping structure, under UN mandate, would feature American
leadership of a NATO force supplemented by Jordanians, Egyptians and
Israelis. We can envision a five-year, renewable mandate with the objective of
achieving full Palestinian domination of security affairs on the Palestine side of
the line within 15 years.

What is immediately noticeable is how similar these parameters are to those
proposed by Israeli Prime Minister Benjamin Netanyahu in a much-publicised
June 2009 speech grudgingly accepting the concept of a two-state solution.[4]
Netanyahu's proposal raised ire in the Arab world for demanding that any
Palestinian state be 'demilitarised', and that Palestinians renounce refugees'
right to return and recognise Israel as a 'Jewish state'.

The Scowcroft paper does not call on Palestinians to declare their recognition of Israel as a 'Jewish state', but concern for maintaining a Jewish majority
and thus Israeli Jewish supremacy lies behind the document's insistence that 'a
formula must be found to protect Israel from an influx of [Palestinian] refugees'.
An approach that had any concern for international law and refugee rights or
any awareness of a Palestinian sense of the injustice would seek to protect the
rights of Palestinians against Israel's refusal to respect them. But that is not the
case here; the Scowcroft document recommends that the USA endorse and adopt
Israel's rejectionist position on refugee rights as 'fair'.

Similar problems arise with the position on borders and Jerusalem, where the
document elaborates that the 'aim' of any adjustment to the 1967 line 'will be
to incorporate large settlement blocs within Israel while preserving Palestinian
contiguity...'. This would resolve the issue of settlements only to the extent that it
would just legitimise decades of Israeli colonisation. In Jerusalem, the document
states, 'the formula of Israel governing Jewish neighbourhoods and Palestine
governing Arab neighbourhoods largely works'. Translated into practice, this
would mean that Israel would retain all of the massive settlements it has built
in and around East Jerusalem since 1967. The notion that Palestinians would
be 'compensated' for settlements in and around Jerusalem with desert land near
Gaza is roughly equivalent to proposing that France could be 'compensated'
for the seizure of Paris with an equally-sized piece of uninhabited countryside
elsewhere.

Last but not least, the 'independent' Palestinian state would remain occupied
over the long term by a US-led NATO force including Egyptian, Jordanian and
Israeli troops. In other words, instead of ending the Israeli occupation, large
numbers of foreign troops would be brought in to replace some but not all of the
Israeli occupation forces. 'Robust' foreign forces, the paper elaborates, would
remain in Palestine 'for a period of indeterminate length assisting Palestinian

authorities in executing their responsibilities in the security sphere and helping them build capacity in order eventually to act without outside assistance'. All of this falls under the heading 'Addressing Israel's security challenges'. Thus the very architecture of the imagined Palestinian state is built around meeting Israel's needs, not restoring Palestinian rights.

The Scowcroft document distils a broader Western approach to countries as diverse as Bosnia, Kosovo, Iraq and Afghanistan. In each of these cases, US-led Western military intervention (either direct invasion or UN-sanctioned 'multi-national' missions) were followed by the establishment of a nominally independent and sovereign local regime, backed by and subservient to the intervening powers. The ostensible goal of the Western presence has always been to assist the local government to stand on its own two feet. Yet in each case, the US-led intervention has turned into a long-term presence. None of the local governments has managed to establish the capacity or legitimacy broad enough to survive a Western withdrawal.

The Scowcroft paper – to the extent that it does represent US establishment thinking about Palestine – is an endorsement of a Western-backed and dependent state, with the trappings of sovereignty, but no actual independent control of its borders, airspace, resources or even its politics. Efforts to put this strategy in effect in Palestine were in fact started by the George W. Bush administration immediately after Hamas won the 2006 election. With US encouragement, Mahmoud Abbas' defeated Fateh faction refused to relinquish power over the Palestinian Authority or control of its security forces. The USA armed and trained Palestinian militias to maintain Abbas in power and attempt to crush Hamas.[5] By maintaining this police, the Obama administration kept a simmering Palestinian civil war going.

The parameters proposed by the Scowcroft group bear no resemblance to what any significant group of Palestinians would consider a 'fair, viable or sustainable' settlement.[6] In effect, they ask Palestinians to accept as final and permanent the outcomes of what a large body of scholarship describes as the 1948 ethnic cleansing of Palestine, and more than four decades of Israeli colonisation in the West Bank since 1967.

Under extremely restrictive conditions, some Palestinians may be permitted under this plan to continue to live in their country in something called a 'state', as long as it does not interfere with Israel's 'security needs'. Meanwhile, millions of Palestinian refugees would have to abandon their rights to go home in order to maintain Israel's status as a 'Jewish state'. The fate of almost 1.5 million Palestinian citizens of Israel – who face in some extreme quarters calls for their expulsion – is not even mentioned. Moreover, they are totally incompatible with a long-established body of international law and United Nations resolutions which protect fundamental Palestinian rights.

Palestinians obviously consider this unfair and unworkable, and in addition to resembling the strategies in other Western-occupied countries, it appears to be a repeat of the failed Oslo accords. But because the consensus has declared the ideas as 'fair, viable and sustainable', there is apparently no need to examine who might legitimately resist or oppose them. Whenever similar 'solutions' have been seriously proposed – for example, at the failed 2000 Camp David summit, or informally in the 'Geneva Initiative' – they have generated enormous popular resistance from Palestinians, not only among the refugee Diaspora, but also in the West Bank and Gaza, whose residents would presumably stand to gain the most from the establishment of a Palestinian state.[7] These parameters do not express a broad-based consensus on how to resolve the Palestinian–Israeli conflict. Rather, they represent a consensus among peace process industry insiders and operators about how to produce ambiguous formulas that simulate a commitment to emancipating Palestinians from occupation, while creating the conditions for its perpetuation.

The extensive foreign military presence and the emphasis on building up security forces as the fundamental institutions of the putative Palestinian state reflect an implicit understanding that a great deal of force would be required to impose such a settlement. As mentioned, the Scowcroft document – like many of the conventional analyses it represents – admits no legitimate opposition. It does recognise that among the 'obstacles' to a 'successful' outcome would be certain 'external negative influences' defined as 'Syria and Iran [which] through their support for Hamas, other Palestinian "rejectionist" groups, and Hezbollah, actively aim to keep Israeli and Palestinian talks from reaching closure'. The new Palestinian state from its birth would be at war with its own people. It is notable that Scowcroft and Brzezinski were widely portrayed as being anti-Israel or pro-Palestinian – so much so, that Obama could not afford any public association with them lest he offend his pro-Israel supporters. This is what has become of the vaunted 'two-state solution'.

Rather than a means to liberate Palestinians and restore their rights, the goal of the 'two-state solution' today seems to many observers to be precisely the opposite: to contain Palestinians and force them to give up fundamental rights so that Israel can remain a 'Jewish state'.

This chapter is not intended to suggest that everyone who advocates a two-state solution is participating in some sort of conspiracy, or consciously wishes to deprive Palestinians of their rights. Some people have a genuine belief that it represents the most 'pragmatic' path to peace. It is argued elsewhere that the accepted wisdom that partition is the most pragmatic and realistic solution is not supported even by mainstream academic theories on conflict regulation.[8] Yet a major attraction of the two-state solution is that it appears to require only the formal ratification of a partition that already happened and that resulted in a reality of two already existing and distinct geographical-political entities. One of these entities is the 'Jewish' state of Israel, and the other a Palestinian state-in-waiting whose statehood merely awaits declaration. The fiction of an already achieved but somehow suspended partition has been constantly reinforced in post-Oslo discourse through, among other means, the abandonment by Western-backed Palestinian elites of the language of national resistance and liberation in favour of 'state-building', despite the fact that Palestinians in the West Bank and Gaza Strip remained under deepening military occupation for long years after the Oslo Accords were signed. We also witnessed the rhetorical transformation of the PA into a 'government' (especially after the January 2006 elections).

At the same time the 'Palestinian people' has been gradually downsized to exclude any group that might interfere with the two-state plan as described here: the Diaspora and its refugees and Palestinian citizens of Israel. Most notably, after Hamas countered a US-backed coup attempt and took over the Gaza Strip in June 2007,[9] the 1.5 million Palestinians in Gaza were effectively excluded from having any voice in Palestinian affairs and it became common for peace process insiders to talk about establishing a West Bank-only state. Palestinian elites who benefited from Oslo answered dissenters with appeals to 'pragmatism' and 'realism' despite the reality that their own assertions that a Palestinian state was in the process of being built were little more than fantasy.[10] Massive international donor funding has been targeted at the West Bank and Gaza Strip to reinforce the notion that a Palestinian state was already under construction, while in fact such funding indirectly subsidised the ongoing Israeli presence.[11]

The failure ever to arrive at the stated destination of two states 'living side by side in peace' could always be explained by outside factors: the assassination of Rabin, the idiosyncrasies and even the unwelcome longevity of Arafat, the corruption of Olmert, 'extremists on both sides' and so on. These convenient explanations meant that evangelists of the two-state solution could always avoid having to re-examine their fundamental assumptions and they could continue to claim that other than a few issues that would not divide 'pragmatists', the dirty work of partition had already been done.

But if an alien were to come from another galaxy and view historic Palestine from above without knowing anything about the 1967 lines, they would not see an existing partition along those lines. Rather, they would see a reality of physical segregation throughout historic Palestine. The 1967 line may have political salience, but it does *not* divide Palestine into ethnically homogenous, compact and economically viable units. Israel's settlement project was designed to make sure of that.

Zionism cannot long be appeased or satisfied with a two-state solution that would leave 1.5 million Palestinians of Israel inside the Jewish state. This is why so many Israelis – represented by the likes of Avigdor Lieberman – now support the 'transfer' of Palestinian citizens of Israel. Indeed, the history of early partitions in Palestine, India, Cyprus and the Balkans suggest that a repartition of Palestine today would not produce peace. It would probably spark a renewed bout of ethnic cleansing aimed at removing Palestinians from inside Israel, especially from the Galilee.[12] Already today, Jewish supremacists have imported precisely the intimidation and settlement tactics they have used to displace Palestinians in the West Bank to the hearts of Palestinian communities in Acre, Jaffa Um al Fahm and other cities inside Israel's pre-1967 boundaries.[13]

What emerges from this analysis is that there is nothing inherent in a two-state solution or even a one-state solution that Israel rejects. Indeed, geographer and former Israeli Deputy Mayor of Jerusalem, Meron Benvenisti, describes Israel/Palestine already as a 'de facto bi-national state'.[14] It is clear that there is only one power that exercises all the attributes of sovereignty in historic Palestine today, and that is the Israeli state. It is this fact that makes moves towards both a more meaningful two-state solution or a radically different secular unitary state a difficult endeavour.

In Israel there has never been a consensus supporting a full withdrawal from the 1967 occupied territories. The only consensus has been for the continued expansion of Israeli settlements in the West Bank – to the extent that embracing a two-state solution could allow Israel to maintain overall control; while shedding responsibility for the Palestinians (as the Scowcroft plan implied), Israeli leaders will embrace it. At the same time, Israel has fiercely resisted a two-state solution in any form that it feels would challenge Israeli Jewish domination and control. What Israel objects to then is equality in any form.

Many Palestinians supported the two-state solution not because they believed it would be the most just solution, but because they believed promises that it would allow them to enjoy some form of free existence. Over two decades after the 1991 Madrid Conference, it is clear that has not been the case. The constant mantra by international officials that they are committed to the peace process should be taken for what they are: commitment to an endless process that absolves them of responsibility to take any effective or politically costly action to check Israeli violations of international law, human rights, and regular massacres and war crimes. As long as any cornered Western politician can say 'I support the peace process', they are let off the hook.

Israel's December 2008/January 2009 war which killed more than 1,500 Palestinians – the vast majority of whom were civilians – in the Gaza Strip brought the situation in Palestine to a turning point. It clarified that despite Israel's relentless attempts to destroy them, it is not Palestinians that cannot survive, but Israel as a Jewish state. Israel was created through the ethnic cleansing of Palestinians, and is maintained only through constant violence and discrimination directed at three groups of Palestinians:

1. Most visibly, Palestinians in the occupied Gaza Strip and West Bank who are subjected to extreme forms of violence, dehumanisation, collective punishment and imprisonment.
2. Palestinian citizens of Israel – the survivors and descendants of those ethnically cleansed in 1948. They live inside Israel's pre-1967 boundaries and face mounting incitement, demonisation and threats of expulsion.
3. Palestinian refugees – who are prevented from returning home for the sole reason that they do not fit Israel's ethno-racial criteria: they are not Jews.

But despite the oppressive conditions they live under, there are more Palestinians in Palestine than ever before. Today, the population of historic Palestine (Israel, the West Bank and Gaza Strip) is 11 million people. Just over 5 million are Israeli Jews, just over 5 million are Palestinians, and the remainder is neither. This is of course not counting millions more Palestinians who are in involuntary exile.

So today it is Israel that needs the fig leaf of a two-state solution to cover up the reality that in historic Palestine, the Israeli government is in danger of becoming a minority regime, at which point it could understand its only option to maintain power through coercive means. Such a state can never hope to gain legitimacy. In this scenario, to maintain the status quo, Israel will have to wage escalating Gaza-style military attacks on a regular basis in an attempt to subdue the Palestinian population.

Increasingly, Palestinians have concluded that the responsibility and opportunity falls on them and a mobilised global civil society collectively to provide a way out. They are taking stock of assets which they see as:

1. the moral justness of the Palestinian cause rooted in universalism, which contrasts with a Zionism rooted in communalism and tribalism;
2. the reality that Palestinians are not only the indigenous people of the land, but will soon once again be the majority, reinforcing their claim to set the agenda for the country's future as a unified, democratic and inclusive state for all who live in it; and
3. global support for the Palestinian cause, including from a highly-educated and motivated Diaspora.

Each of these assets is only useful if utilised through a number of complementary strategies.

Palestinians and their allies have come to understand the importance of building support for a universal vision for Palestine. The 2007 'One State Declaration', issued in English, Arabic, Hebrew and Spanish, was one attempt to do that.[15] Others have built on it, taking it as it was intended as a starting point for discussion and debate. They have declared that equality must be at the centre of their vision, in terms not merely of rights written into a constitution, but of an actual redistribution of power and resources which results in an empowering of the country's Palestinian population.

Notes

1. The report is published by the US/Middle East Project whose president is Henry Siegman. Available at www.usmep.us/usmep/wp-content/uploads/official-a-last-chance-for-a-two-state-israel-palestine-agreement1.pdf.

2. Ibid., p. 9.

3. See Ali Abunimah, 'President Obama and the prospects for Israeli–Palestinian peace: an analysis', Palestine Center Information Brief No. 169, 17 November 2008. Available at www.thejerusalemfund.org/ht/d/ContentDetails/i/3172.

4. See 'Full text of Netanyahu's foreign policy speech at Bar Ilan', Ha'aretz, 14 June 2009. Available at www.haaretz.com/hasen/spages/1092810.html.

5. For an excellent account of this US strategy in practice, see Paul McGeough, Kill Khaled: The Failed Assassination of Khalid Mishal and the Rise of Hamas (New York: The New Press, 2009); especially Chapters 21–6.

6. See Ali Abunimah, 'One voice: manufacturing consent for Israeli apartheid', Electronic Intifada, 1 May 2009. Available at http://electronicintifada.net/v2/article10497.shtml.

7. See the author's book One Country: A Bold Proposal to End the Israeli–Palestinian Impasse (New York: Metropolitan Books, 2006), especially Chapter 1.

8. Ali Abunimah, 'A curious case of exceptionalism: non-partitionist approaches to ethnic conflict regulation and the question of Palestine', Ethnopolitics, Vol. 10, Issue No. 3–4 (September–November 2011), pp. 431–44.

9. See David Rose, 'The Gaza bombshell', Vanity Fair, April 2008. Available at www.vanityfair.com/politics/features/2008/04/gaza200804.

10. See Joseph A. Massad, The Persistence of the Palestinian Question: Essays on Zionism and the Palestinians (London: Routledge, 2006).

11. See Anne Le More, International Assistance to the Palestinians after Oslo: Political Guilt, Wasted Money (London: Routledge, 2008); and Islah Jad, 'NGOs: between buzzwords and social movements', in Development in Practice, Vol. 17, Nos 4–5, August 2007.

12. See Abunimah (2011), op. cit.

13. Ali Abunimah, 'The Arab–Jewish clashes in Acre and the connection to Israeli's extremist settlers', The Palestine Center, 15 October 2008. Available at www.thejerusalemfund.org/ht/d/ContentDetails/i/2250.

14. Meron Benvenisti, 'The case for shared sovereignty', The Nation, 18 June 2007, pp. 11–14.

15. See Various Authors, 'The One State Declaration', Electronic Intifada, 29 November 2007. Available at http://electronicintifada.net/v2/article9134.shtml.

CHAPTER 10

A Blueprint for a One-State Movement: A Troubled History

Ilan Pappé

The demise of the Oslo Accord at the very beginning of the twenty-first century gave special impetus to the old–new idea of a one-state solution. It seems to be with us again and the interest in it is growing by the day. And yet it does not appear as an item on the agenda of any actor of significance on the Palestine chess board. Neither major powers nor small political factions endorse it as a vision or strategy, let alone as tactics for the future. Its attractiveness, however, is undeniable given the failure of the alternative solutions. This seems to be the appropriate moment to ponder about its past history and its future trajectory.

This chapter is not intended to recap the faults of the two-state solution, nor to argue the advantages of the one-state solution. Both tasks have been taken on by other contributors to this book in a way that does not need further elaboration. The purpose here is first to remind readers that although the idea today is hypothetical, theoretical and quite abstract, it used to be a concrete plan, strategy and a vision. Second, based on this historical recognition, the chapter argues it is time to transform the idea once more into a real political plan that would be carried on by a popular movement for change in Israel and Palestine. One cannot doubt that there is a new impulse inside and outside of Palestine for a regime change. There is now a constant search for changing the present realities whereby the authority of the state of Israel extends over the whole of historic Palestine, and this authority is ethnically biased, discriminatory and oppressive towards its Palestinian citizens and subjects. It is by and large a non-violent impulse for equality and a craving for normality that should be translated into a powerful agent of change for the sake of the Palestinians and Israelis alike.

A Troubled History

The one-state solution has a troubled history. It began as a soft Zionist concept of Jewish settlers, some of whom were leading intellectuals in their community, who wished to reconcile colonialism and humanism. They were looking for a way that would not require the settlers either to return to their homelands or to give up the idea of a new Jewish life in the 'redeemed' ancient homeland. They were also moved by more practical considerations, such as the relatively small number of Jewish settlers within a solid Palestinian majority. They offered bina-tionalism within one modern state. They found some Palestinian partners when they appeared in the 1920s, but were soon manipulated by the Zionist leader-ship to serve that movement's strategy and then disappeared to the margins of history. In the 1930s, notable members among them, such as Yehuda Magnes, were appointed as emissaries by the Zionist leadership for talks with the Arab Higher Committee. Magnes and his colleagues genuinely believed, then and in retrospect, that they served as harbingers of peace, but in fact they were sent to gauge the impulses and aspirations on the other side, so as to defeat it in due course.[1] They existed in one form or another to the end of the Mandate. Their only potential ally, the Palestine Communist Party, endorsed their idea of binationalism for a while, but in the crucial final years of the Mandate the party adopted the principle of partition as the only solution – admittedly due to orders from Moscow rather than out of a natural growth of its ideology. So by 1947, there was no significant support on either the Zionist or Palestinian side for the idea. It seems that there was no genuine wish locally or regionally to look for a solution and it was left to the international community to look for one.

The appearance of the one-state solution as an international option in 1947 is a chapter of history very few know about or bother to revisit. The scope of this chapter does not allow for expansion on this, but it is worth remembering that at one given point during the discussions and deliberations of the United Nations Special Commission on Palestine (UNSCOP), February to November 1947, those members of the UN who were not under the influence of either the USA or the USSR – and they were not many – regarded the idea of a one-state in Palestine as the best solution for the conflict. They defined it as a democratic unitary state, where citizenship would be equal and not on the basis of ethnic-ity or nationality. The indigenous population was defined as those who were in Palestine at that time, nearly 2 million people of whom about two-thirds were Palestinian. When their idea was put as a minority report of UNSCOP (the majority report was the basis for the famous or infamous United Nations General Assembly Resolution 181 of 29 November 1947), half of the then UN members of the General Assembly supported it, before succumbing to pressure by the super powers to vote in favour of the partition resolution.[2] It is not surprising in hindsight that people around the world who, unlike the Western powers, did not view the creation of a Jewish state at the expense of the Palestinians as the best compensation for the horrors of the Holocaust would support the unitary state. After all, the Jewish community in Palestine was made up of newcomers and settlers, and constituted only one-third of the overall population.[3]

So Palestine was partitioned between Israel, Jordan and Egypt. But the idea was kept alive when the Palestine Liberation Organisation (PLO) came into being. Its version of a one-state was of a secular and democratic one, although unsympathetic towards the possible presence of Jewish settlers who arrived after 1948, and was attractive enough to inspire a small anti-Zionist group – Matzpen – in Israel to accept it for a while. The Arab world, in words and through the Arab League, seemed to stand behind the idea. This was the vision of the liberation movement until the 1970s, when lack of success, pragmatism and a growing realisation of how powerful Israel had become following unconditional American support in the climate of the Cold War, forced a change of position. Since Soviet support for the PLO did not match the US commitment to Israel, the Palestinians had to consider new ideas about the future. Thus came into being the Movement for the Liberation of Palestine's (Fateh) Stages Program. This was a willingness to consider a two-state solution. Initially, the plan was presented as a temporary means to bring peace and justice to Palestine, but later it was portrayed as a strategy and perhaps even as a vision.

The idea of a two-state solution, however, did not germinate on the Palestinian side. It was always the preferred solution of pragmatic Zionism. This, also known as mainstream Zionism, was upheld by the Jewish community in Palestine since the late nineteenth century and its basic ideas have continued to guide the Israeli political system until today. The power of the two-state solution depends much on the power of pragmatic Zionism. Those who are presently regarded as pragmatic Zionists are defined as such due to their support of the two-state solution. Since the support has only to be verbal and non-committal, even right-wing parties in Israel, despite their declared ideology of a Greater Israel (i.e. the pursuit of a one-state solution with exclusive Jewish presence and rights), can endorse it. This was recently demonstrated by Benjamin Netanyahu's pledge to such a solution made only to allow the continued strategic alliance between an allegedly more critical American administration and a more hawkish Israeli government.

But because the two-state solution is so closely connected to the fortunes of pragmatic Zionism, it is important to recap the historical record of this mainstream Zionist force. The leaders and movements who represented pragmatic Zionism were responsible for the 1948 dispersal of Palestinians, the military rule imposed on the Palestinians inside Israel for almost 20 years, the creeping colonisation in the West Bank in the last 40 years and the repertoire of oppressive policies against the people of Gaza in the last eight years. And the list of course is longer, and new chapters of oppression and dispossession are added to it by the day. Yet the total identification of pragmatic Zionism with the two-state solution and, before it, with territorial compromise with Jordan (i.e. the Jordanian option) equated it in the eyes of the world with 'peace' and 'reconciliation'. As transpired clearly during the days of the Oslo Accord, the discourse of two states and peace provided a shield that enabled the pragmatic Zionist governments to expand the settlement project in the West Bank and escalate oppressive policies against the Gaza Strip.

Looked at from a different angle, pragmatic Zionism was the only actor on the ground that gave substance to the idea of two states, whereas the PLO, even when it endorsed the idea, had to accept the Zionist interpretation of it. The relevant international actors and the USA in particular followed this Zionist interpretation as they still do today. This interpretation meant that the two-state solution is based on a total Israeli control of the whole of what used to be Mandatory Palestine: its airspace, its territorial waters and its external borders. It includes a limited measure of Palestinian sovereignty within those parts of Palestine that Israel is not interested in (i.e. the Gaza Strip and less than half of the West Bank). This sovereignty would also be limited in essence: a demilitarised government would have little say in defence, foreign and financial policies.

It seems that even a fragile Arafat twice realised what this hegemonic interpretation of the two-state solution meant – once before signing in Cairo the Oslo B Agreement and then for the second time during the Camp David summit of 2000. In the first instance, it was too late (literally minutes before the ceremony) and there was no outlet. On the second occasion he had time to ponder more profoundly and refused to accept this Israeli dictate.

But the potency of this Zionist interpretation of the two-state solution, which is still to this very moment the only one in town, is waning. This is the main reason for the re-emergence of the one-state solution. The latter was kept alive by those who always believed in it as the only moral, not just political, settlement that contains and answers all the outstanding problems involved in the ongoing conflict. Issues such as the refugees' right of return, the colonialist nature of Zionism and the need to accommodate the multi-religious and multicultural fabric of society seem to have no room in the two-state solution. They were the 'desperadoes', those who reluctantly endorse the one-state solution since they despair of implementing a two-state solution. They regarded the new geopolitical realities Israel created on the ground as irreversible and they recognised there is no will on the Israeli side to accept a truly independent and sovereign Palestinian state alongside Israel.

Thus, despite its troubled history, the one-state idea is still with us today. And yet it remains on the margins and attributed to naive daydreamers. From this very brief and admittedly somewhat esoteric description, it is clear that only a significant erosion in the validity of the two-state solution can revert attention back to the concept of a one-state solution, in whatever form. However, it is important to stress early on that the idea was kept alive not by those who despaired of the chances of a two-state solution, but rather by those who did not lose faith in the moral validity of the concept and its political feasibility. These very few feel vindicated in the last decade by the many that joined them as 'new converts', as the demise of the two-state solution becomes clearer by the day.

As these words are being written, it is mainly a large number of individuals, and not even NGOs, who stand firmly behind the idea. They are visible and have advanced the case of the one-state solution significantly in recent years by structuring the discussion and airing the outstanding issues beyond slogans and ideals. The final boost to this intellectual and public activity was the appearance of several coherent books, the authors of which contributed to this volume and who with other writers joined efforts to disseminate the concept, and root it deeply in the public discourse and mind.[4] But as mentioned, there are no political parties upholding this idea, and although an intuitive survey of the scores of NGOs working on the ground in Israel, Palestine and in the exilic communities indicates a wide support in Palestinian civil society for this idea, none of the present governmental and non-governmental actors have officially taken a stance of support.

A political movement has first and foremost to clarify its position vis-à-vis those in power; or, put differently, it has to decide whether it wishes to substitute the powers that be, or influence them. In the former case, the One State Movement (OSM) can only act by becoming a party, a faction or whatever term one uses these days in the abnormal reality on the ground in Palestine, where a sovereign state exists alongside an occupied, stateless enclave and highly controlled community.

But there is another option which may be a necessary, preliminary stage before a clearer decision on strategy is taken. For this, one has to adopt a more fluid definition of the concept of a movement than the one usually appearing in the more professional literature. The movement we are looking for is a vehicle that represents certain impulses, hopes and a vision. As such, its main task is to translate popular, or bottom-up, demands in the political realm which are ignored by the political and media elites in a given society. In our particular case, it wants those in power to examine urgently new options for salvaging an escalating catastrophe.

There are two paradoxes that would have to be dealt with early on. One is that it takes a long time to build a movement, and the reality on the ground demands from every activist urgency and immediate activism to thwart the continued oppression. The second one is that quite often a public demand directed at the political elite is engendered and propelled by growing suspicion of, and total lack of confidence in, that very political elite, without necessarily showing enthusiasm for replacing it.

These are given constraints and it is not suggested here that we can reconcile the paradoxes. We can just be aware of them. There is a way around it as another similar effort to create a movement has shown us. This is the BDS movement: the movement of Boycott, Divestment and Sanctions against Israel. It is a call for using a very drastic non-violent action against Israel, the purpose of which is to stop the present policies on the ground, such as the Gaza incursions and killings in January 2009, but also at the same time engender a general discussion about the nature of the regime and its international legitimacy. It also relates to the second paradox mentioned above by not wishing to play a role among the political elite, but forcing that same elite to take a stance on the issue given the failure of all the other strategies of the struggle. It began a few years ago as a brainchild of a small number of individuals and grew to significant proportions when it was fully endorsed by civil society in the occupied territories, and thence supported widely by Palestinians around the world and inside Israel.[5]

Before remarking further on the two options open for the OSM – whether to build a political movement per se or to engage in establishing a wide following for the one-state idea – there is a preliminary issue that has to be addressed. This refers to the problems arising from the formation of the new coalition that now pushes the idea forward. As mentioned, it is made of long-standing believers in the idea and 'desperadoes' joining late in the day due to their frustration in the inability of implementing the two-state solution. This is not the healthiest of coalitions to advance a concept that is still utopian and unaccepted by the political elites and mainstream media. Motivation and inspiration are not likely to be found among the 'desperadoes'. This was very clear, for instance, in the contribution to the March 2009 Boston conference on the one-state of Meron Benvenisti.[6] But his and others' valuable deconstruction and explication of what is wrong with the two-state solution and their engagements with realpolitik can benefit the OSM enormously.

If a minimal basis for cooperation can be found – and again judging from the evidence so far this is not something one can take for granted – the next stage is to direct the efforts of persuasion towards 'state sceptics' who, although they are not oblivious to the chaotic reality on the ground produced by a constant adherence of the international community to the two-state solution, still do not find the courage to support the one-state solution. It is really a question of how to enlarge both the core group of the movement and its base of support. The effort should be to elasticise the concept so as to increase its attraction to its maximal optimum. We are arguably more or less there, at that stage, after the Boston March 2009 conference. As noted before, it is from here that we should weigh the two possible options: playing by the rules the political elites set; or working through the popular networks to change public discourse and the political elites' orientations.

The nature of politics, especially in the West, has been evolutionary and not revolutionary ever since the Second World War. Sticking to formulas is thus in the nature of such political systems and unless catastrophes prove such formulas to be dead, for all intents and purposes political elites are not likely to deviate from them. Let alone when the issue is not the highest on their agenda, or even when it is prominent among their concerns, it is only for a very short span of time. Thus, even very visible indicators of the impossibility of implementing a two-state solution of any kind, or one that can only be unilaterally accepted by Israel, are not likely to produce a dramatic change of orientation or policy. This means that the first option explored above, of impacting a change of policy towards a one-state solution (OSS) from within the political elites is premature and is likely to result at this stage in total disappointment and a dangerous transformation of the One State Movement (OSM) into a quixotic voyage into oblivion.

Therefore, the more viable option is the one that does not play a part yet in the political elite game, but prepares the ground for the inevitable earthquake that would also force the politicians and principal actors to take a different stance. A movement in this respect is literally an attempt to move people's mindsets, attentions and recognitions. This can be seen as a three-pronged effort: reintroduce the past into the equation; deconstruct the essence of the present peace process; and prepare products that translate the concept of one-state into a tangible reality in the future.

Re-selling the Past

The struggle over memory in the case of Palestine seems to be the most important achievement in this century for anyone committed to the Palestine cause. The convergence of industrious Palestinian historiography with the new revelations made by revisionist historians in Israel transformed not only the research agenda of academia, but also the public discourse among the activists. It was in many ways the exposure to the full picture of what occurred in 1948 that expanded the spectrum of peace activists, and members of Palestinian solidarity committees, so that it included the 1948 events. Even President Obama in his June 2009 Cairo speech acknowledged a Palestinian suffering that extended over 60 years.

The struggle over past memory is highly relevant to the debate about a one-state solution. Only the historical perspective reveals the reductionist nature of the two-state solution: the fact that 'Palestine' refers to only one-fifth of the land

and about one-third of the Palestinians. A deeper historical recognition exposes the Zionist movement as essentially colonial in nature. It not only shows that Palestinians were forced to flee – or ethnically cleansed in the modern parlance – in 1948 and never allowed to return, but also that the ideology that produced this policy is still operative today. An Italian journalist and writer described the narrative employed hitherto to justify the raison d'être of a two-state solution to a historical narrative that explains the French Revolution as a violent juncture that has no origins or any background information.[7]

The unified Palestinian experience from the late nineteenth century and up to 1948 has been replaced by discrete experiences due to the fragmentation of the people and the bisection of the land. But these new disjointed experiences, without exception, relate to what happened in 1948. In other words, whether you live in Ramallah, London, Yarmouk or Nazareth, your present predicament is a direct result of what occurred in 1948. Moreover, the ideology that produced 1948 is the one that retains refugees in their camps today, discriminates against Palestinians inside Israel, and oppresses those under occupation in the West Bank and aggressive containment in the Gaza Strip. Seen from that perspective, a two-state solution is a small lid trying to cover a huge boiling pot and whenever it attempts to cover the pot, it fails utterly. A conflict is concluded when the right lid can be put firmly on the past to bring its horrors to a closure.

At the academic and civil society level, this realisation is solid and has created the fertile ground for the discussion about a one-state solution. Unfortunately, this is not the case with the mainstream media and political arena in the West or in the Arab world. As the acceptance of the narrative that stretches the origins of the issue into the late nineteenth century and to 1948 is not immediately recognised as a political stance, this effort may have a better chance of success at this stage than a straightforward recognition of the one-state solution.

In other words, what should be hammered in is that what the 'desperadoes' call the facts on the ground that gradually made the desired two-state solution impossible were not an accident. They are the outcome of a strategy aimed at granting the state of Israel control over all of Mandatory Palestine. This strategy was and is the corner stone of pragmatic Zionism and it divided the land into two territories: the one that Israel rules directly; and in it, the one it wishes to implement what Shimon Peres coined as 'maximum territory and minimum Arabs'. What was and still is presented by Western journalists and politicians as a fundamental debate inside Israel about peace and war, of retaining the territories or withdrawing from them, is in effect a debate about what is 'maximum territory', what are the means of achieving it, as well as how one attains the target of 'minimum Arabs'. Unmasking the paradigm of parity, the charade of a genuine debate in Israeli society and revealing the strategy behind Israeli policy in the last 40 years is a task the OSM should take upon itself in the near future.

Deconstructing the Peace Process

The biggest contemporary obstacle for putting forward the one-state solution as a viable option is the raison d'être of the 'peace process' in the last 40 years, which is firmly based on the vision of two states. It is so powerful that even some of the bravest and most committed colleagues in the struggle for Palestine endorse it in the name of realpolitik. In order to confront it successfully with the modest means that a One State Movement has and will have, it is important to recognise the premises that underlie the raison d'être of the peace process, as they are still governing today the Obama administration, the Palestinian Authority, the so-called peace camp in Israel, and large sections of the political and media elite in the West.

The peace process began immediately after the June 1967 War ended and, while the early initiators were French, British and Soviet, it soon became an attempt to impose a Pax Americana. The basic American assumption underlying the 'peace' effort was an absolute reliance on the balance of power as the principal prism through which the possibilities of solutions should be examined. As Israeli superiority was unquestioned after the war, it meant that whatever Israeli politicians and generals devised as a peace plan soon became the basis for the process as a whole. Thus the Israeli political elite constantly produced the common wisdom of the peace process and formulated its guidelines according to its own concerns. These American–Israeli guidelines were drafted in the first years after the 1967 occupation and crystallised as a vision for a new geopolitical map for historical Palestine. Pragmatic Zionism dictated that the country would roughly be divided into two spheres: one that Israel controls directly as a sovereign state; and the other in which Israel rules indirectly while giving the Palestinians limited autonomy.

The principal American role was to present to the world these dictates in a positive manner such as 'Israeli concessions', 'reasonable behaviour' and 'flexible positions'. Until this very moment, either out of ignorance or self-interest, successive American administrations have adopted a perception of the conflict that caters solely to the internal Israeli scene and one which disregards totally the Palestinian perspective.

This hegemonic American–Israeli presence produced five guidelines that so far have not been challenged politically or diplomatically by the Quartet,[8] and whoever manages the peace process and all the histrionics around it. The first guideline relates directly to the struggle over memory mentioned above. It states that the 'conflict' began in 1967 and hence the essence of its solution is an agreement that would determine only the future status of the West Bank and the Gaza Strip. Such a perspective confines a settlement to 22 per cent of Palestine.

The second guideline is that everything visible in those areas is divisible and that such divisibility is the key for peace. So even the remaining 22 per cent of Palestine has to be divided for the sake of peace. Moreover, the peace agenda meant that not only should the 1967 occupied areas be divided, but also its people and natural resources.

The third guideline is that anything that happened until 1967, including the consequences of 1948 and the Palestinians' displacements, is not negotiable. This pushed out of the agenda the refugees' issue, where it remains to this very day.

The fourth guideline is an equation between the end of the Israeli occupation and the end of the conflict. Namely, once some kind of Palestinian eviction or control over their remaining territory would be agreed upon, the conflict would be declared as solved for all intents and purposes.

The fifth and last guideline is that Israel is not committed to any concession until the Palestinian armed struggle ends.

In 1993, these five guidelines were translated into the Oslo Accord, when a Palestinian partner seemed to accept them in principle. This was repackaged again in Camp David 2000 and in both cases, after trials and tribulations, rejected by the PLO and the PA. But these are still the agreed-upon principles for the peace process.

The task here is twofold. The first is to associate in the public mind the present reality, which is accepted by international observers as representing a human catastrophe of unimaginable dimensions, as the inevitable outcome of this peace process and its principles – thus exposing it as a political act that provided international immunity for a policy of colonisation and dispossession. It is true that this policy has escalated dramatically since 2000, but it is not true that the escalation is the result of the collapse of the peace process – it is the result of the raison d'être of the process.

As a movement of a sort, the OSM has the academics, journalists and activists who possess the means of disseminating this knowledge through books, journals and public meetings whenever the current affairs of Palestine and Israel are discussed. A media monitor of sorts is already working, but not in a professional or systematic way, although it is much more timidity than ignorance that prevents intelligent and knowledgeable journalists and politicians from exposing the 'peace process'. Pragmatic Zionism did not wish to control directly the populated Palestinian areas in the West Bank and the Gaza Strip, did not dare to expel them and did not wish to give them more than limited autonomy.

The second task is to bring to the fore the Palestinian voices that were directly affected by this Israeli policy in the last 40 years within a paradigm of analysis that highlights the connection between their sufferings and the charade of peace. In other words, the debate is not only about whether the road taken so far was right, but also a claim against those who drove down that road that they contributed directly to the continued misery of the Palestinians in the occupied territories. This would mean challenging the very agenda of the Palestinian Authority, which claims that peace with Israel under the old premises will bring an end to the suffering of the occupied people, while the counter argument should be that it is having precisely the opposite effect: deepening the occupation and perpetuating Israeli control.

This deconstruction of the peace process should not remain an academic exercise. It should have some immediate practical implications. The first was already mentioned: a systematic challenge of the media coverage of the peace process in the West. Second, it should help to transform the nature of the peace activity in Western civil societies, and for that matter among the peace groups still active in Israel as well. These activists until recently were loyal to both the paradigm of parity and the logic of the two-state solution as the vision of peace. Thus, peace activity for years was based, as the peace process itself, on the paradigm of two equal narratives that needed mediation and bridging. Hence both the EU and the major funding bodies in the West were financing and encouraging the phenomenon of 'kissing cousins' meetings. Similarly, Western activists believed their main mission was to bring the two sides together on a neutral, namely Western, ground. This noble impulse gave unintentional support for the official peace process and presented it as a reflection of a wider wish among Western societies.

The OSM can be a pinnacle of a new orientation and effort of this impulse of Western civil societies to transform the reality in Palestine. Instead of facilitating futile encounters, which are unnecessary anyway as they can take place at any given moment on the ground, they can provide venues for strategising the campaign for changing the policies of Western governments, and for pondering of a more genuine and comprehensive solution to the conflict.

Desegregating the activity of civil society in the West, as well as inside Israel, illustrates the very essence of a one-state solution when the OSM is still in its embryonic stage. An activity around themes, and not according to national, religious or ethnic identity, can be the unique contribution of the OSM. But again, themes can sound too abstract and fluid for a movement that seeks desperately to change the public mind after years of being conditioned by a distorted historical narrative, manipulated media coverage and a destructive futuristic vision. Thus the themes should be closely connected to tangible products. The last part of this chapter explores some of these themes and products.

Preparing for the Future: The Modular Model

In its present form, the One State Movement is made of individuals from all walks of life who can bring to the fore their activism and professionalism before the vision would be taken more systematically by NGOs and political parties. It is time to expand the activity beyond the big conferences which heralded so far successfully the idea and exposed the fallacies of the two-state solution model. There are more areas for investigation that the OSM can focus on.

The first is a survey of attitudes towards the one-state idea. So far no one has attempted such a survey, and despite the obvious weakness of such an instrument, this is a precondition for any future campaign of disseminating the idea and recruiting others for it.

The second one is the formation of working teams, very much on the basis of the 'Taqawim' that were preparing, in earnest but in vain, for the creation of an independent Palestinian state in the Orient House during the Madrid Conference days. These teams should prepare the practical products emanating from a future political outfit for Palestine and Israel in whatever form it will appear: a constitution, an educational system, curricula and textbooks, basic guidelines for an economic system, the practical implications within a state of a multicultural and multi-religious society, and so on. For some of these aspects of statehood there is no need to invent the wheel, as the 'Taqawim' were quite good in covering them; for others inspiration should be found elsewhere in history, other geographies and human thought.

A particular project that would have to be considered is a serious contemplation about the future of the Israeli Jewish settlements. For the Taqawim, it was clear that a future Palestinian state meant one without these settlements. In the case of the one-state solution, this is a different matter. This chapter does not propose a way out of it, but only points out the need to discuss it now and not later.

The making of these end products in the most practical way, such as a prototype constitution, an educational curriculum, laws of citizenships for all (indigenous, returnees and new immigrants), land and property ownership regulations (including compensations and absentee properties) and similar projects, can give substance to the idea of the one-state beyond slogans and the deconstruction of the two-state solution.

The last project for the OSM before it hopefully becomes a potent, popular and political movement is a focus in small teams and later in front of larger audiences on the question of dissemination of and instruction in the idea. Palestinian NGOs inside and outside, the few NGOs in Israel that are still engaged in the struggle against the occupation, the Palestine Solidarity Campaigns and Committees, and all the other NGOs in Western societies and around the Arab and Muslim worlds can be recruited to take a firmer stand on the issue.

The struggle for one-state need not be predicated on a need for close cooperation with official PLO, Hamas and Palestinian Authority representatives. There is also no need to adopt the discourse or dictionary of these organisations. This will allow the OSM to envision peace and reconciliation in a less limited and more inclusive way. One doubts whether Arab regimes would help, apart from heads of state who came openly in support of the idea. On the other hand, the South Africa government and NGOs have already shown a greater enthusiasm for the idea than any other state actor on the international scene. With these limitations in mind, and with these potential partners, the voice of the OSM should be heard at all times.

This can be done, despite the profound knowledge that popular support for the idea depends crucially on a total disintegration of the two-state solution and that this scenario in turn is beyond the power of the One State Movement. While waiting for developments beyond our control and influence, we should prepare as if this moment is around the corner and assume that millions of desperate Palestinians, Israelis and whoever cares about them in the world would soon look for an alternative to the paradigm that informed so disastrously the peace process in Palestine and Israel. Activism, scholarship, dissemination of information, persuasion, protest and solidarity are the most powerful weapons powerless people have. Let us use them wisely for the sake of a noble vision and the only solution for the Palestine issue.

Notes

1. See Ilan Pappé, *A History of Modern Palestine; One Country, Two Peoples* (Cambridge: Cambridge University Press, second edition, 2006), pp. 115–16.

2. The author has written on the minority report in Ilan Pappé, *The Making of the Arab–Israeli Conflict, 1947–1951* (London and New York: I.B.Tauris, 2001), pp. 16–46.

3. United Nations Archives, UNSCOP Verbatim Report in United Nations General Assembly Files, Second Session, August–November 1947 files.

4. See Ali Abunimah, *One Country; A Bold Proposal to End the Israeli–Palestinian Impasse* (New York: Holt McDougal, 2007); Ghada Karmi, *Married to Another Man: Israel's Dilemma in Palestine* (London: Pluto Press, 2007); Joel Kovel, *Overcoming Zionism: Creating a Single Democratic State in Israel/Palestine* (London: Pluto, 2007); and Jamil Hilal (ed.), *Where Now for Palestine? The Demise of the Two States Solution* (London: Zed Books, 2007).

5. The website of that campaign is www.pacbi.org.

6. See Meron Benvenisti, 'The binationalism vogue', *Ha'aretz*, 30 April 2009. This was written as a response to the March 2009 Boston conference declaration.

7. The Italian journalist and writer Paolo Barnard is the senior political correspondent of Radiotelevisione Italiana, Italy's national public service radio and television broadcasting organisation. He recorded on YouTube seven short clips titled 'Palestine-Israel: the missing narratives', May 2009.

8. A four-member committee established in 2002 to mediate the Israeli–Palestinian conflict. The committee is made up of the United Nations, the USA, Russia and the European Union.

PART III

Practicalities in the Search for a Resolution of the Conflict

CHAPTER 11

The Rights of Palestinian Refugees and Territorial Solutions in Historic Palestine

Susan M. Akram

Introduction

Perhaps the single most critical component of a solution to the Israeli–Palestinian conflict is the resolution of the Palestinian refugee problem. Since the refugees are the majority of the Palestinian population, it is impossible to craft a political solution that will have durability without redressing their legitimate rights. But this overly simplistic conclusion begs a series of questions that go to the heart of what makes this such a complex conflict. These questions must be examined under some objectively defensible standard before deciding what territorial compromises can or should be made in the final agreements. In contrast to political solutions, international law can provide objectively defensible standards, and is thus an indispensable measure against which the justice and durability of post-conflict agreements can be assessed.

This chapter addresses the territorial implications of the rights of Palestinian refugees in the Israeli–Palestinian conflict as measured under international law. The chapter focuses only on the central issues, addressing the questions: how do rights of return, property restitution and compensation affect the claims to state territory? Concerning self-determination in the territory of former Palestine, which people are entitled to self-determination – Palestinians, the 'Jewish people', Israeli Jews or Israelis? And over which territory are the 'people' entitled to exercise their self-determination? These questions can only be answered in very summary fashion in this chapter, but the main legal principles and sources that provide the framework to address these questions are set out and examined here.

Background to the Palestinian Refugee Right of Return

When the Palestinian refugee exodus began in the 1947–8 conflict, the General Assembly established the United Nations Conciliation Commission for Palestine (UNCCP) by Resolution 194 of 11 December 1948.[1] Resolution 194 described the refugees for whom the UNCCP would provide international protection and, in paragraph 11, set out the required legal formula for resolving the refugee problem: return, restitution of properties and compensation.[2] The UNCCP was unable to achieve what it was entrusted to do, either in terms of an overall settlement of the conflict between the parties, or in accomplishing the return of the refugees and restitution of their properties;[3] however, the principles set out in Resolution 194's paragraph 11 have been reaffirmed each year by the General Assembly.[4]

A year after the UNCCP was established, the General Assembly passed Resolution 302(IV), of 8 December 1949, setting up another international organisation relating to the Middle East conflict, the United Nations Relief and Works Agency for Palestine Refugees (UNRWA).[5] The UNRWA's mandate was strictly humanitarian: to provide for the refugees' subsistence needs until the durable solution set out in Resolution 194 could be implemented.[6] The UNRWA had a mandate only towards that sub-category of the refugee population that met its needs-based definition: Palestinians normally residing in Palestine before the 1947–8 conflict who had lost their homes or livelihood, and were now residing in one of the five areas allocated for the UNRWA's operations.[7] Later amendments expanded this definition to the descendants of refugees from 1948, and to Palestinians displaced in 1967 and their descendants.[8] In 2009, more than 7.4 million people were refugees or internally displaced out of a total Palestinian population of about 10.1 million. The refugee figure includes 6 million of the original 1948 refugee population, of which 4.67 million are registered with the UNRWA, which provides them with humanitarian assistance.[9] The UNRWA-registered refugees are not, however, the total refugee population to be taken into account, as it is the entire refugee population which has suffered loss of rights, which is seeking redress, and for which a final settlement must be found.

Palestinian Refugee Right of Return: To Where?

The most obvious source to determine *to where* Palestinians have the right to return is Resolution 194 itself. The formula of paragraph 11 in Resolution 194 incorporated what was already customary international law, and has become a stronger set of principles through widespread state practice to the present.[10] This paragraph means that Palestinian refugees must be permitted to return to their precise homes and lands if they so choose. Only return to place of origin is an absolute obligation on a state, since no state is obliged to absorb or resettle a refugee in a place not of their origin.[11] Paragraph 11 makes return, restitution of property and compensation equally enforceable, according to the refugee's own choice.[12] Paragraph 11's binding requirements that Palestinian refugees have an absolute right to return to their original places of origin, and obtain full restitution and compensation for properties taken or destroyed, reflect the drafters' intent to preclude political solutions that fail to meet the legally required durable solutions for Palestinians.

Critics often challenge whether Resolution 194 incorporated the state of the law on return at the time it was passed. The right of return was firmly entrenched in customary law by 1948.[13] When the original draft of paragraph 11 was submitted to the General Assembly, the US delegate confirmed that no new rights were being created. He commented that the formula 'endorsed a generally recognised principle and provided a means for implementing that principle'.[14] The first priority in paragraph 11, because it involved the strongest and most well-defined rights under international law, was to implement the refugees' right to return. The precise location where the refugees had the right to return was also spelled out: 'to their *homes*'.[15] Since absorption in host states and resettlement in third states are neither rights of the refugees nor obligations on any of the states concerned, they were not mentioned in the first part of paragraph 11 at all. The second part of the paragraph explains that the role of the UNCCP is to facilitate durable solutions for the refugees: first, on implementing the legal rights of the refugees and the concomitant obligation on Israel to accept them back to their homes; second, on finding solutions for those refugees *not choosing to return home* within other states that might be willing to accept them as a matter of discretion.[16]

Aside from the specific source of right of return for Palestinian refugees, the right of return in general represents a complex interrelated set of rights grounded in distinct bodies of treaty and customary international law. The right of return is found in the major treaties and rules that protect individuals and groups in times of armed conflict under humanitarian law and the laws of war;[17] it is found in treaties and principles governing issues of nationality and state succession;[18] and it is found in the core human rights conventions governing state obligations in both war and peacetime,[19] particularly in refugee provisions. In all of the provisions in which aspects of the right of return are found, no distinction is made between its applicability to individuals or groups.[20] Since 1948, the evidence is overwhelming that the right of return for refugees – as an aspect of nationality, humanitarian, human rights and specifically refugee law – has become one of the strongest of existing state obligations.

The widespread incorporation of the principle of return to place of origin in international treaties and regional instruments has been reinforced by incorporation in peace agreements and state practice in virtually every part of the globe.[21] This expansion in the law is also reflected in state practice as millions of refugees have returned to their countries and homes of origin on the basis of bilateral and tripartite agreements involving both states and specialised agencies like the Office of the UN's High Commissioner for Refugees (UNHCR).[22] Over the course of the last decade, approximately 12 million refugees returned or were repatriated around the world.[23] That trend has continued to the present, as the UNHCR has highlighted the 'one-millionth return' to places like Afghanistan and Bosnia and Herzegovina.[24] That is not to say that in all cases repatriation has been informed by a respect for the law; states continue to forcibly repatriate or *refoule* (the norm of *non-refoulement* – forcible return to persecution, to torture or risk to life or freedom – is by now widely-accepted as a customary norm of international law, binding on all states, whether parties to a treaty incorporating the norm or not) refugees contrary to their legal obligations.[25] Nevertheless, the fact remains that the vast majority of refugees who returned home since the 1990s have done so of their own volition,[26] and few states question their right to return. Even in especially difficult cases like Bosnia and Herzegovina, the problem is not so much whether or not refugees have a right to return, but rather over the location of return within the state itself.[27]

Palestinian Property Restitution: Rights and Claims

Restitution of property and (only when restitution is impossible) compensation for lost or damaged property are the required forms of reparation for persons who have suffered violations of their housing and property rights. The principle that restitution is the required remedy for violations of international law has been firmly entrenched since 1928, stemming from the Permanent Court of International Justice (PCIJ) decision, *Chorzow Factory (Indemnity) Case*.[28] In *Chorzow Factory*, the PCIJ established that for wrongful property taking, specific restitution must be made – that is, return of the property itself to the victim – in order to undo the harm caused by the violation, and only if restitution were not possible should a state pay compensation equal to the value of restitution.[29]

Many voluntary repatriation agreements have explicitly or implicitly affirmed the right of returning refugees and internally displaced persons to restitution of housing, land and property. Examples of repatriation agreements including the right to restitution of housing and property are those in Kosovo,[30] Croatia,[31] Kuwait,[32] Angola,[33] Rwanda,[34] Mozambique and Zimbabwe,[35] the DRC,[36] Afghanistan,[37] Eritrea and Ethiopia,[38] and Bosnia and Herzegovina.[39] The 1995 Dayton Agreement, which ended the conflict in Bosnia and Herzegovina, contains the most specific incorporation of restitution and return rights for displaced persons and refugees of any agreement to date. It created an international mechanism to enforce restitution of property, and compensation for property that could not be restored.[40] In the Bosnian situation, no compensation was paid, as the remedy for property claims has exclusively been specific restitution.[41] Of particular note are the agreements in Mozambique, Guatemala and Tajikistan, which entitled returnees to repossess former lands and homes, whether or not they had previously possessed official title.[42]

In 2004, the International Court of Justice examined Israel's expropriation of Palestinian land and destruction of property in its Advisory Opinion on *The Legal Consequences of the Construction of the Wall in the Occupied Palestinian Territory*.[43] The Court cited the *Chorzow Factory* principles, concluding that Israel had an obligation to return the land and other property seized from any person during the Wall construction, and to compensate such persons if specific restitution was materially impossible.[44] The ICJ placed obligations on Israel to make reparations for land takings that violated international law under principles that are applicable to all Palestinian victims of land expropriations, whether as a result of the recent wall construction, or as a result of confiscations dating from 1948 to the present.[45]

As the drafting history leading to the passage of Resolution 194 and the Resolution's language itself make clear, 194 incorporated binding law on restitution at the time it was passed.[46] The Resolution has been affirmed yearly by the General Assembly, and has only been strengthened by incorporation of its principles in human rights instruments, international jurisprudence and state practice since then.

Claims of Self-determination: Jews and Palestinians

By 1920, the League of Nations recognised that self-determination was a legal right of communities with 'unresolved territorial sovereignty'.[47] The League of Nations was entrusted with supervising the terms of the Mandates over Syria, Lebanon, Iraq and Palestine.[48] Of these League-supervised Mandates, Palestine was among those closest to independence.[49] Britain had already recognised Palestinian citizenship and issued Palestinian passports under Mandate regulations.[50] Palestinians were officially documented by the British Civil Administration in Palestine in July 1921 as consisting of 700,000 people, overwhelmingly Arab. Four-fifths of the population were Arab Muslims, 77,000 were Arab Christians and 76,000 were Jews. Of the Jewish population at the time, the British Report stated: 'Almost all have entered Palestine during the last 40 years.'[51]

The British interpreted the Balfour Declaration as committing them to allowing immigration of Jews to Palestine and free access to Jewish religious sites, but not the establishment of a Jewish state.[52] Britain could not – consistent with her legal obligations under the Mandate – promise Palestine to European Jewish immigrants. The concept of self-determination was incorporated into the Mandate system, through which sovereignty was placed in the hands of the local populations, while the Mandatory was entrusted to bring the territory to independence in accordance with the wishes of the indigenous populations.[53] The native Palestinians, as other Arab populations in the Mandatory areas, had overwhelmingly and consistently expressed their demands for independence in a definite territorial area.[54] The interpretation of Balfour as committing Britain to a 'national home for Jews in Palestine', as opposed to a 'national homeland for the Jewish people in Palestine',[55] is the most consistent with the language and purpose of the Mandate treaty, and Britain's powers under it. As the King-Crane report noted:

> For a national home for the Jewish people is not equivalent to making Palestine into a Jewish State; nor can the erection of such a Jewish State be accomplished without the gravest trespass upon the civil and religious rights of existing non-Jewish communities in Palestine.[56]

The Report noted with concern 'that the Zionists looked forward to a practically complete disposition of the present non-Jewish inhabitants of Palestine'.[57]

Who has the Right to a State, and Where?

The United Nations has recognised the Palestinians as a people since the 1947 Partition Resolution – the people entitled to claim sovereignty in the 'Arab state' whose contours were defined in the Resolution.[58] From Resolution 181 onwards, UN resolutions have incorporated increasingly clear language about the de jure status of the Palestinians as a people entitled to self-determination in a sovereign state.[59] The ICJ, in its *Advisory Opinion on the Legal Consequences of the Construction of a Wall in the Occupied Palestinian Territory*, has affirmed that the Palestinian people are entitled to self-determination, pointing out that Israel itself has recognised that Palestinians are so entitled.[60] The UN has also, in both general terms and those specific to Palestinians, affirmed the right of people denied self-determination to the use of force to regain their rights, consistent with the UN Charter.[61]

Turning to Israeli and Jewish claims to self-determination, Israel proclaimed her state on behalf of 'the Jewish people', a concept and definition that grants rights to and within the state on an extraterritorial basis.[62] Israel has enacted laws granting 'nationality' to Jews only, and reserved superior rights – including rights to use and own land and property in Israel – to Jews only.[63] Israel's institutionalised preferencing of Jews is through the legal definition of 'Jewish national', as opposed to non-Jewish citizens who can never become nationals of the Israeli state, and hence never entitled to rights equal to Jews.[64] Israel's proclamation of her state as that of the 'Jewish people' recognises extraterritorial rights of persons who have no connection to the territory of Israel over those with historical and uninterrupted connection to the territory. Such a concept contravenes basic principles of customary law on nationality and state succession.[65] Moreover, 'Jews' as a 'nationality' were not recognised as the 'people' entitled to self-determination in the Jewish state under the Partition Resolution.[66] Nor has the concept of the 'Jewish people' ever been juridically recognised as a national entity with rights to self-determination.[67] On the other hand, the people entitled to national status in the 'Jewish state' defined under Resolution 181 included both Jews and Arabs already residing there,[68] all of whom were to be granted equal rights under a constitution to be implemented in each state, which had to meet the requirements of the UN Charter.[69] UN treaty bodies and the ICJ have affirmed that Israeli violations of the non-discrimination provisions in treaties Israel has ratified, as well as in the UN Charter itself, stem from the definition of the 'Jewish people' as a nationality concept, and the denial of self-determination of the Palestinians.[70] In other words, the legal consensus is overwhelming that the legal preferencing of Jews over non-Jews that stems from Israel's nationality law is a violation of customary and treaty law to which Israel is bound.

Contours of the Palestinian State: Territory and Borders

If the Palestinian people are entitled to self-determination and a sovereign state as a matter of international law, and the right to use force to obtain those rights, the territory in which such rights may be exercised must be defined. The only Israeli borders with international recognition are those in the Partition Resolution. Israeli expansion to territory beyond those borders may be recognised as de facto borders, but since the acquisition of territory by use of force is a fundamental violation of the UN Charter,[71] borders beyond those allocated to the 'Jewish state' in Resolution 181 cannot be recognised. As for later Israeli expansion, prolonged belligerent Israeli occupation of the 1967 territories is manifestly illegal under the UN Charter, international consensus and customary law – as affirmed by the ICJ's *Wall Opinion* in 2004.[72] United Nations Security Council (UNSC) Resolution 242 of 22 November 1967, which all parties have incorporated into the framework for official negotiations from Madrid onwards, reiterates the 'inadmissibility of the acquisition of territory by war', and requires the 'withdrawal of Israeli armed forces from territories occupied in the recent conflict'.[73] At a minimum, then, the Palestinian right to self-determination includes the territories occupied in 1967, all of the West Bank and Gaza, including all the area currently illegally occupied by Jewish settlers.[74]

What Consequences Do Refugee Rights Have on the Definition of Territory?

The conclusions that can then be drawn are that:

- under international law Palestinians who fled as refugees in the 1947–9 and 1967 conflicts possess the right to return to the homes they occupied at the time, as well as to full restitution of their properties and compensation for properties that cannot be returned;
- Palestinians are a recognised national population with a collective right to self-determination, to be exercised at least within the 1967 borders of the West Bank and Gaza;
- Israel is belligerently and illegally occupying those territories and East Jerusalem, and illegally operating settlements there; and
- both Palestinians and Israeli Jews living in Israel have the right to self-determination on a non-discriminatory basis.

Refugee law and precedent show that to be durable, refugee solutions require respect and implementation of return as the central principle, followed by host and third states offering resettlement to refugees not choosing to return on a discretionary, burden-sharing basis.[75] Until the state of origin implements the right of return, no other state is required to accept refugee resettlement. In the Palestinian case, law and precedent require that all refugees choosing to return to their place of origin are entitled to do so, and their property must be returned to them. But return and property restitution do not require a particular territorial outcome; mass refugee return has been implemented post-conflict in situations where the former state boundaries have remained the same, as well as to successor states, and to new territorial configurations.[76] An individual right of return is to the home, the place of origin, not to a defined political space. The same is true of property restitution: what is required is return of title and physical possession of property. However, the disposition of that property is at the discretion of the rightful refugee owner, which is an entirely separate matter from the nationality or citizenship of the owner. Hence mass property restitution has been implemented post-conflict in situations where the individual has physically returned to repossess their property, as well as where the individual has sold, rented or deferred possession while secondary occupant claims were addressed.

The collective claims of self-determination are more complicated than individual ownership rights, in the sense that the law recognises the former rights in both the Palestinian people as well as in Israeli Jews. However, what is important is that the right devolves on Israeli Jews – Jews habitually resident in Israel – not to the Jewish people. Since there has never been legal recognition of a 'Jewish state', international law recognises the rights of those Jews residing in Israel who have acquired rights in the territory, but only on an equal basis and without discrimination towards Palestinians. The Palestinian national entity comprises both refugees and others whose rights to their land and nationality accrue to them as indigenous residents of the territory of Palestine. As long as these principles are met, these respective rights can be exercised in a single state, in two states, in a confederated union of states or any of a number of other territorial configurations.

Notes

1. G.A. Res. 194(III), ¶ 11, UN Doc. A/RES/194(III) (11 December 1948).
2. Id.
3. Susan M. Akram and Terry Rempel, Recommendations for Durable Solutions for Palestinian Refugees: A Challenge to the Oslo Framework, 11 Palestine Y.B. Int'l L. 1, 19–22 (2000–1).
4. See *UN Comm. on the Exercise of the Inalienable Rights of the Palestinian People*, Resolutions and Decisions of the General Assembly and the Security Council Relating to the Question of Palestine, UN Doc. A/AC.183/L.2 (and addenda 1–28); see also United Nations Information System on the Question of Palestine, The Question of Palestine and the United Nations, ch. 5, 2, DPI/2276 (2003), available at www.un.org/Depts/dpi/palestine.
5. G.A. Res. 302(IV), UN Doc. A/1251 (1949).
6. Id., ¶¶ 2–3.
7. Id., ¶ 7; see also Econ. Survey Mission for Mideast, UN Conciliation Comm'n for Palestine, Interim Report, UN Doc. A/1106, available at http://unispal.un.org/pdfs/A1106.pdf.
8. Technically, the UNRWA's mandate has never been formally amended to include 1967 refugees; instead, the General Assembly has repeatedly authorised the UNRWA to provide assistance 'on an emergency basis and as a temporary measure' to the 1967 displaced, bringing them under UNRWA's de facto mandate. See Lex Takkenberg, *The Status of Palestinian Refugees in International Law*, 82 (1998).
9. BADIL Res. Ctr. for Palestinian Residency and Refugee Rights, Survey of Palestinian Refugees and Internally Displaced Persons: 2006–2007, 43–4 (2007). For up-to-date figures on the number of refugees registered with the UNRWA, see UNRWA.org, UNRWA: Publication/Statistics, www.un.org/unrwa/publications/index.html (last visited 19 June 2009); http://www.un.org/unrwa/publications/index.html
10. For deeper analysis of the development of the right of return and restitution in customary international law, see John B. Quigley, *Repatriation of Displaced Palestinians as a Legal Right*, 8 Nexus 17, 18–19 (2003); Terry Rempel, *Housing and Property Restitution: The Palestinian Refugee Case, in* Returning Home, 275, 308–11 (Scott Leckie (ed.), 2003); Eric Rosand, *The Right to Return under International Law Following Mass Dislocation: The Bosnia Precedent?*, 19 Mich. J. of Int'l L. 1091, 1121–39 (Summer 1998); and *Housing, Land, and Property Restitution Rights of Refugees and Displaced Persons* (Scott Leckie (ed.), 2007).
11. Guy S. Goodwin-Gill, *The Refugee in International Law*, 322–3 (Oxford: Clarendon Press, 2nd ed., 1996).

12. Akram and Rempel, *supra* note 3, at 35–6.

13. W. T. Mallison and S. Mallison, *An International Law Analysis of the major United Nations Resolutions Concerning the Palestine Question*, 30, UN Doc. ST/SG/ SER.F/4, UN Sales No. E.79.I.19 (1979).

14. UN Conciliation Commission for Palestine, *Working Paper: Compensation to Refugees for Loss of or Damage to Property to be Made Good under Principles of International Law or in Equity*, ¶ 8, UN Doc. A/AC.25/W/30 (31 October 1949) (prepared by the Secretariat).

15. G.A. Res. 194(III), *supra* note 1, ¶ 11.

16. *Id.*, ¶ 11 ('Instructs the Conciliation Commission to facilitate the repatriation, resettlement, and economic and social rehabilitation of the refugees and the payment of compensation...'), ¶ 14 ('*Calls upon* all Governments and authorities concerned to co-operate with the Conciliation Commission and to take all possible steps to assist in the implementation of the present resolution...'); see also UN Conciliation Commission for Palestine, *Working Paper: Analysis of Paragraph 11 of the General Assembly's Resolution of 11 December 1948*, pt. 1, § 3, UN Doc. A/AC.25/W/45 (15 May 1950) (compiled by the Secretariat) ('There is no doubt that in using this term ["to their homes"] the General Assembly meant the home of each refugee... the refugees not returning are to be compensated for their property...').

17. For the right of return in humanitarian law, see Geneva Conventions of 1949, 6 UST 3114, TIAS No. 3362, 75 UNTS 31; 6 UST 3217, TIAS No. 3363; 75 UNTS 85; 6 UST 3316, TIAS No. 3364, 75 UNTS 135; 6 UST 3516, TIAS No. 3365, 75 UNTS 287. For analysis of the right of return under humanitarian law and the laws of war, see Gail Boling's analysis of the Hague Conventions in Gail J. Boling, *The 1948 Palestinian Refugees and the Individual Right of Return* (Bethlehem: BADIL Resource Center for Palestinian Residency and Refugee Rights, 2nd ed., 2007), pp. 28–32, available at www. badil.org/Publications/Legal_Papers/Gail-E-print.pdf.

18. See, for example, L. Oppenheim, *I International Law* (London: Longmans Green & Co., 7th ed., 1948), p. 598; see also Ian Brownlie, *The Relations of Nationality in Public International Law*, 39 Brit. Y.B. Int'l L. 284, 320 (1963); Guy Goodwin-Gill, 'Voluntary repatriation: legal and policy issues', in G. Loescher and L. Monahan (eds), *Refugees and International Relations* (Oxford, England: Clarendon Press; New York: Oxford University Press, 1989), pp. 255, 260.

19. See, for example, International Convention on Civil and Political Rights art. 12(4), 16 December 1966, G.A. Res 2200A(XXI), UN Doc. A/6316; International Convention on the Elimination of Racial Discrimination art. 5(d)(ii), 21 December 1965, 660 UNTS 195.

20. Although there is a very large body of literature on the right of return under international law, both general and particular to the Palestinian case, there are a few outstanding studies on the latter. The author has relied, in particular, on the following works: Mallison and Mallison, *supra* note 12; Boling, *supra* note 16; Kathleen Lawand, *The Right to Return of Palestinians in International Law*, 8 Int'l J. Refugee L., Vol. 8, 532 (October 1996); John Quigley, Mass *Displacement and the Individual Right of Return*, 68 Brit. Y.B. Int'l L. 65 (1997). The author has previously discussed these articles and the most important legal issues on the right of return in prior work: Susan Akram and Terry Rempel, *Recommendations for Durable Solutions for Palestinian Refugees: A Challenge to the Oslo Framework*, XI Palestine Y.B. of Int'l L., 1–71 (2000/2001); Susan Akram and Terry Rempel, *Temporary Protection as an Instrument for Implementing the Right of Return for Palestinian Refugees*, 22 B.U. Int'l L.J., 1–162 (Spring 2004).

21. See, for example, General Framework Agreement on Peace in Bosnia-Herzegovina (Dayton Peace Agreement) annex 7, ch. 1, art. 1, 14 December 1995, available at www. unhcr.org/refworld/docid/3de495c34.html; Agreement on Resettlement of the Population

Groups Uprooted by the Armed Conflict in Guatemala princ. 1, 17 June 1994, available at www.usip.org/library/pa/guatemala/guat_940617.html; Declaration and Concerted Plan of Action in Favour of Central American Refugees, Returnees and Displaced Persons, 31 May 1989, UN Doc. CIREFCA/89/14; Declaration and Comprehensive Plan of Action (Comprehensive Plan of Action Concerning Indochinese Refugees), 26 April 1989, UN Doc. A/CONF.148/2; Agreement on a Comprehensive Political Settlement of the Cambodia Conflict pt. 5, art. 20, ¶ 1, 23 October 1991, UN Doc. A/46/608-S/23177.

22. Between 1997 and 2007, an estimated 11.4 million refugees have returned home, 7.3 million with the help of the UNHCR. UN High Comm'r for Refugees, 2007 UNHCR Statistical Yearbook, at 37 (2008), available at www.unhcr.org/statistics.

23. Id.

24. See, for example, News Stories, UN High Comm'r for Refugees, 'Afghan family joins 1 million who have gone home from Iran' (2 September 2004); Press Release, UN High Comm'r for Refugees, 'One millionth returnee goes home in Bosnia and Herzegovina' (21 September 2004).

25. UN High Commissioner for Refugees, Measuring Protection by Numbers 11 (2006), available at http://www.unhcr.org/publ/PUBL/4579701b2.pdfwww.unhcr.org/publ/PUBL/4579701b2.pdf.

26. It is estimated that 12 million refugees were repatriated in the 1990s. Khalid Koser and Richard Black, 'The end of the refugee cycle?', 2, 3, in *The End of the Refugee Cycle* (Richard Black and Khalid Koser (eds), New York: Berghahn Books, 1999); Oliver Bakewell, *Returning Refugees or Migrating Villagers? Voluntary Repatriation Programmes in Africa Reconsidered* 1 (UN High Comm'r for Refugees, Working Paper No. 15, 1999), available at www.unhcr.org/3ae6a0c40.pdf; while Refugees International estimates 2.5 million returns were involuntary over the 14-year period of 1989–2002. M. Lynch, Refugees Int'l, Forced Back 26 (2004), available at www.reliefweb.int/rw/lib.nsf/db900SID/LHON622KA4/$FILE/refintl_forced_back_may2004.pdf.

27. For this general assertion, see Office of the United Nations High Commissioner for Refugees, the Problem of Access to Land and Ownership in Repatriation Operations 14 (May 1998). On Bosnia and Herzegovina specifically, see Marcus Cox and Madeline Garlick, 'Musical chairs: property repossession and return strategies in Bosnia and Herzegovina', in *Returning Home*, 65 (Scott Leckie (ed.), Ardsley, NY: Transnational Publishers, 2003); Walpurga Englbrecht, 'Property rights in Bosnia and Herzegovina: the contributions of the Human Rights Ombudsperson and the Human Rights Chamber towards their protection', in *Returning Home, supra*, at 83.

28. Factory at Chorzow (F.R.G. v. Pol.) 1928 P.C.I.J. (ser. A) No. 13 (13 September 1928).

29. Id., at 47. 'The essential principle contained in the actual notion of an illegal act – a principle which seems to be established by international practice and in particular by the decisions of arbitral [sic] tribunals – is that reparation must, as far as possible, wipe out all the consequences of the illegal act and reestablish [sic] the situation which would, in all probability, have existed if that act had not been committed. Restitution in kind, or, if this is not possible, payment of a sum corresponding to the value which a restitution in kind would bear; the award, if need be, of damages for loss sustained which would not be covered by restitution in kind or payment in place of it – such are the principles which should serve to determine the amount of compensation due for an act contrary to international law.'

30. Protocol on Voluntary and Sustainable Return, Kosovo-Serb.-UN Interim Admin. in Kosovo art. 1, 6 June 2006, available at www.unmikonline.org/docu_QL.htm (click on link to Protocol of Returns).

31. Basic Agreement on the Region of Eastern Slavonia, Baranja, and Western Sirmium (The Erdut Agreement), Croat.-Serb. ¶ 9, 12 November 1995, as reprinted in *Housing,*

Land, and Property Restitution Rights of Refugees and Displaced Persons, 37 (Scott Leckie (ed.), Cambridge UK; New York: Cambridge University Press, 2007).

32. S.C. Res. 674, ¶ 8, UN Doc. S/RES/674 (29 October 1990).

33. Memorandum of Understanding between the Governments of the Republic of Angola and the UNHCR for the Voluntary Repatriation and Reintegration of Angolan Refugees art. 4(4) (14 June 1995), as reprinted in *Housing, Land, and Property Restitution Rights of Refugees and Displaced Persons*, 51 (Scott Leckie (ed.), 2007).

34. Tripartite Agreement on the Voluntary Repatriation of Rwandese Refugees from Tanzania art. 10, 12 April 1995, as reprinted in *Housing, Land, and Property Restitution Rights of Refugees and Displaced Persons*, 51 (Scott Leckie (ed.), 2007).

35. Tripartite Agreement between the Government of the Republic of Mozambique, the Government of Zimbabwe and UNHCR for the Voluntary Repatriation of Mozambican Refugees from Zimbabwe art. 8, ¶ 5, 22 March 1993, available at www.unhcr.org/refworld/docid/3ee884a74.html.

36. Tripartite Agreement on the Voluntary Repatriation of Congolese Refugees from Tanzania, Dem. Rep. Congo-Tanz.-UNHCR, art. 10, 27 August 1991, available at www.unhcr.org/refworld/docid/3ee84d5b4.html.

37. Joint programme between the Government of the Islamic Republic of Iran, the Transitional Islamic State of Afghanistan, and the UNHCR for Voluntary Repatriation of Afghan Refugees and Displaced Persons, art. 8, sec. 4, 16 June 2003, as reprinted in *Housing, Land, and Property Restitution Rights of Refugees and Displaced Persons*, 55 (Scott Leckie (ed.), 2007).

38. Agreement between the Government of the Federal Democratic Republic of Ethiopia and the Government of the State of Eritrea arts. 2 and 5, 12 December 2000, available at www.usip.org/library/pa/eritrea_ethiopia/eritrea_ethiopia_12122000.html.

39. Dayton Peace Agreement, *supra* note 20, at annex 7, ch. 1, art. 1.

40. Id., at ch. 2.

41. Paul Prettitore, *The Right to Housing and Property Restitution in Bosnia and Herzegovina: A Case Study* 14 (BADIL Res. Ctr. for Palestinian Residency and Refugee Rights, Working Paper No. 1, 2003).

42. Scott Leckie, 'New directions in housing and property restitution', in *Returning Home*, 3, 18–19 (Scott Leckie (ed.), 2003).

43. Legal Consequences of the Construction of a Wall in the Occupied Palestinian Territory, Advisory Opinion, 2004 ICJ 136 (9 July).

44. Id., ¶¶ 152–3, at 198, ¶ 163(3)C, at 202. 'By fourteen votes to one, Israel is under an obligation to make reparation for all damage caused by the construction of the wall in the Occupied Palestinian Territory, including in and around East Jerusalem...' id., at ¶ 163(3)C.

45. Id. at ¶¶ 87–8, 91–101, 114, 118 (establishing the principles by which Israel is liable for wrongs perpetrated against the Palestinian people, beyond simply the issue of the barrier).

46. UN Conciliation Commission for Palestine, *Working Paper: Analysis of Paragraph 11 of the General Assembly's Resolution of 11 December 1948*, UN Doc. A/AC.25/W/45 (15 May 1950) (compiled by the Secretariat).

47. Report of the International Committee of Jurists Entrusted by the Council of the League of Nations with the Task of Giving an Advisory Opinion upon the Legal Aspects of the Aaland Islands Question (The Aaland Islands Case), 1920 League of Nations O.J., Special Supp. No. 3, at 5–6.

48. Article 22 of the League of Nations Covenant stated that these 'communities' were to be 'provisionally recognised [as independent nations] subject to the rendering of administrative advice and assistance by a Mandatory until such time as they are

able to stand alone'. League of Nations Covenant art. 22, 28 June 1919, as reprinted in *Documents on the Arab–Israeli Conflict*, Vol. 1, 23 (M. Cherif Bassiouni (ed.), 2005), UN GAOR, UN Doc. A/297 (1947), also available at http://avalon.law.yale.edu/20th_century/leagcov.asp.

49. *Documents on the Arab–Israeli Conflict, supra* note 47, Vol. 1, 93.

50. Palestinian Citizenship Order in Council, 1925, S.R. and O., No. 25.

51. Herbert Samuel, 'British Interim Report on the Civil Administration of Palestine during the Period July 1, 1920–June 30, 1921', as reprinted in *Documents on the Arab–Israeli Conflict, supra* note 47, Vol. 1, 47.

52. Statement of British Policy in Palestine from Mr Churchill to the Zionist Organisation (The Churchill White Paper), 1922, Cmd. 1700, available at http://avalon.law.yale.edu/20th_century/brwh1922.asp.

53. Dietrich Rauschning, 'Mandates', in 10 *Encyclopedia of Public International Law*, 288–9 (Amsterdam; Oxford: North-Holland Publishing Co., 1987); for more in-depth discussion of sovereignty in the mandatory system, see also Musa E. Mazzawi, *Palestine and the Law* (Reading, UK: Ithaca Press, 1997), pp. 29–79.

54. Mazzawi, *supra* note 53, at 23; see also 'The American King-Crane Commission of Inquiry Report', in *From Haven to Conquest* (Walid Khalidi (ed.), Washington, D.C.: Institute for Palestine Studies, 1971), pp. 213–14.

55. See W. T. Mallison, Jr., *The Zionist-Israel Juridical Claims to Constitute 'The Jewish People' Nationality Entity and to Confer Membership in it: Appraisal in Public International Law*, 32 Geo. Wash. L. Rev. 983, 996 (1963–4).

56. Henry C. King and Charles R. Crane, 'The American King-Crane Commission of Inquiry Report', 1919 § II, ¶ 3 (28 August 1919), reprinted in *From Haven to Conquest* (Walid Khalidi (ed.), 1971), pp. 213, 215.

57. Id.

58. The Partition Resolution refers to the Arab and Jewish communities living in Palestine as the 'two Palestinian Peoples', G.A. Res. 181 (II), part. III, ¶ 1(b), UN Doc. A/RES/181(II) (29 November 1947).

59. G.A. Res. 3237(XXIX), UN Doc. A/RES/3237(XXIX) (22 November 1974) (inviting the PLO in an official observer capacity to participate in the UN); G.A. Res 3089(XXVIII), UN Doc. A/RES/3089(XXVIII) A-E (7 December 1973) (linking implementation of the rights of Palestinian refugees to return to their homes and property to realisation of Palestinian self-determination); G.A. Res 2672(XXV), UN Doc. A/RES/2672(XXV) A-D (8 December 1970) (stating that the General Assembly 'recognises that the people of Palestine are entitled to equal rights and self-determination, in accordance with the Charter of the UN'); G.A. Res 2649(XXV), UN Doc. A/RES/2649 (30 November 1970) (expressing concern that the people of South Africa and Palestine were being denied the right to self-determination due to 'alien domination'); G.A. Res 2535(XXIV), UN Doc. A/RES/2535(XXIV) A-C (10 December 1969) (affirming 'the inalienable rights of the people of Palestine').

60. Legal Consequences of the Construction of a Wall, *supra* note 42, at ¶ 118 ('As regards the principle of the right of peoples to self-determination, the Court observes that the existence of a "Palestinian people" is no longer in issue. Such existence has moreover been recognised by Israel...').

61. G.A. Res. 3236(XXIX), UN Doc. A/RES/3236(XXIX) (22 November 1974) (affirming 'the right of the Palestinian people to regain its rights by all means in accordance with... the Charter of the United Nations').

62. 'This right is the natural right of the Jewish people to be masters of their own fate, like all other nations, in their own sovereign State.' Declaration on the Establishment of the State of Israel (14 May 1948), available at www.mfa.gov.il/MFA/Peace+Process/Guide+to+the+Peace+Process/Declaration+of+Establishment+of+State+of+Israel.htm.

63. Sourad R. Dajani, Ctr. on Housing Rights and Evictions, BADIL Res. Ctr. for Palestinian Residency & Refugee Rights, Ruling Palestine 56–64 (2005).

64. Id.

65. See Gail J. Boling, *The 1948 Palestinian Refugees and the Individual Right of Return* (2nd ed., 2007), pp. 44–6, available at www.badil.org/Publications/Legal_Papers/ Gail-E-print.pdf; W. T. Mallison, Jr., *The Zionist-Israel Juridical Claims to Constitute 'The Jewish People' Nationality Entity and to Confer Membership in it: Appraisal in Public International Law*, 32 Geo. Wash. L. Rev. 983, 1052–60 (1963–4).

66. G.A. Res. 181(II), *supra* note 57.

67. Mallison, *supra* note 65; states such as the USA have, in fact, explicitly rejected juridical claims to a 'Jewish People' nationality. Id., at 1065–6.

68. G.A. Res. 181(II), *supra* note 57, at part 1, § C, ch. 3, ¶ 1.

69. Id., at § B, ¶ 10(d).

70. Int'l. Convention on the Elimination of all Forms of Racial Discrimination, Comm. On the Elimination of Racial Discrimination, *Concluding Observations: Israel*, ¶¶ 16–17, UN Doc. CERD/C/ISR/CO/13 (14 June 2007); UN Econ. and Soc. Council, Comm. on Econ., Soc., and Cultural Rights, *Concluding Observations: Israel*, ¶ 16, UN Doc. E/C.12/1/Add.90 (23 May 2003).

71. Legal Consequences of the Construction of a Wall, *supra* note 42, at ¶ 87.

72. Id., at ¶¶ 74, 78.

73. Id., at ¶ 117.

74. This conclusion is reinforced by UNGA 2625(XXV), the 'Principles of International Law Concerning Friendly Relations', which describes equal rights and self-determination of peoples as necessarily precluding actions impairing the territorial integrity or political unity of sovereign states. G.A. Res. 2625(XXV), UN Doc. A/RES/2625(XXV) (24 October 1970).

75. See United Nations High Commissioner for Refugees, Executive Committee (EXCOMM) Conclusion No. 5(XXVIII), 1997 *Asylum*; United Nations High Commissioner for Refugees, EXCOMM Conclusion No. 15(XXX), *Refugees Without an Asylum Country* (1979); United Nations High Commissioner for Refugees, EXCOMM Conclusion No. 18(XXXVI), *Voluntary Repatriation* (1980); United Nations High Commissioner for Refugees, EXCOMM Conclusion No. 40(XXXVI), *Voluntary Repatriation* (1985); United Nations High Commissioner for Refugees, EXCOMM Conclusion No. 67(XLII), *Resettlement as an Instrument of Protection* (1991).

76. Examples of implementing right of return to new configurations and territory include the Dayton Peace Agreement, *supra* note 21 (Bosn. and Herz.); Protocol on Voluntary and Sustainable Return, *supra* note 30 (Kosovo-Serb.). Examples of implementing right of return to the same territorial states include Memorandum of Understanding; *supra* note 33 (Angl.); Agreement on a Comprehensive Political Settlement (Cambodia).

CHAPTER 12

The Geographic and Demographic Imperatives of a Single State

Salman H. Abu Sitta

The history of the Palestinians' conflict with the Zionist movement and later on Israel is full of landmarks, the three key ones perhaps being: the 1897 founding (in Basle, Switzerland) of the World Zionist Organization which set the stage for the ongoing conflict; the 1948 establishment of the state of Israel in Palestine; and the war of June 1967 which resulted in the Israeli occupation of what was left of Palestine. Common to all these eventful landmarks has been the Palestinians' gradual loss of control over the land and the rise of the Palestinian Diaspora.

There is a sense of permanence in all of this. During the long period of the conflict, Zionism can be seen to have had three objectives which are still very much in force, namely: occupying and acquiring the land of Palestine; creating a demographically Jewish state; and replacing any 'Arab' link to the land with a 'Jewish' history, memory and identity.[1] Myths have been propagated reinforcing these ideas such as: Palestine is a land without people; there is no such thing as Palestinians, they do not exist; the Palestinians left their homes and country in 1948 on Arab governments' orders; refugees may not return to their ancestral villages which no longer exist and their former sites have been built over; and so on.[2]

In spite of all this, the Palestinians consider themselves a significant and important cultural community in the region. They view themselves as prime players in Middle East events. For them the stalemate between the force of the occupying power and the determination of the occupied people has produced a myriad of possibilities and a rapidly changing dynamic situation. Meanwhile, they accept that death and destruction will continue to wreak havoc on both sides until a settlement is reached. Clearly this is a state of affairs that cannot continue. But to end it requires what Palestinians accept as durable justice.

While there are a number of grave social, political and military elements which at this historical juncture will not allow for a settlement equitable to the

Palestinians, it is the position of this author that the most intractable among them relates to the status of the Palestinian refugees. A solution that does not respect the Palestinian right of return condemns more than half of the Palestinian people who presently live outside the borders of historic Palestine to a dim and uncertain future, and permanent exile. Such a solution is bound to be unstable and temporal. Of all the permanent status issues in the Israeli–Palestinian negotiations, such as borders, Jerusalem, settlements, security arrangements and water resources, Israel has adopted the most uncompromising position on the question of the repatriation of refugees, invoking security threats, ethnic-religious balances and Zionist doctrinal beliefs. More central to the Israeli position is the contention that the refugees' original places of residence have been taken over by the Jewish citizens of Israel and it is geographically not possible to repatriate even a reasonable number of the more than 5 million Palestinian refugees.

This chapter focuses on one dimension critical to the resolution of the Palestinian refugee issue. It does not analyse the issues of political and existential arguments on both sides as to why the right of return of the Palestinians should be either implemented wholesale, curtailed or prevented. Though they are very important elements in the attempt to bring to the fore the argument for a one-state solution, political, emotional and security concerns of both sides will not be looked at. Instead this chapter will concentrate on the more practical, physical and logistical elements. It proposes to demonstrate that it is feasible to repatriate a large number, if not all, of the Palestinians in the *shatat* (exile) to their original places of residence and rebuild Palestine into one country. Any resulting dislocations will be manageable. To substantiate this thesis, three elements are considered: the land of Palestine; the people of Palestine; and the law of the land.

The Land

Palestine is a well-documented country. The Byzantines had a detailed inventory of Palestinian villages in the fourth century. The Ottomans had detailed books of taxation and census since 1596. The British Mandate produced, in its short term of 30 years, voluminous data on Palestinian land and people that became the basis of United Nations records.

British records show that, at the end of the Mandate, Jewish ownership in Palestine reached 1,429 km^2 out of Palestine's area of 26,322 km^2. Thus, Jewish ownership was 5.4 per cent of the area of Palestine.[3] But this small percentage was dwarfed during the war of 1948–9 when, in a matter of a few months, Zionist forces captured 78 per cent of Palestine.[4] The division of land in 1948 is shown in Figure 12.1. It is important to recall that half of the refugees left or were forced to leave before Israel was declared on 14 May 1948, before the British

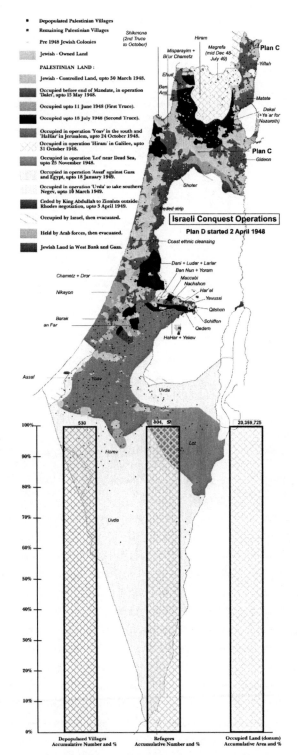

Figure 12.1 The Israeli conquest of Palestine in 1948/9 is shown at various stages of Israeli military operations.

Source: Salman Abu Sitta, *Atlas of Palestine 1917–1966*. London: Palestine Land Society, 2010, p. 90.

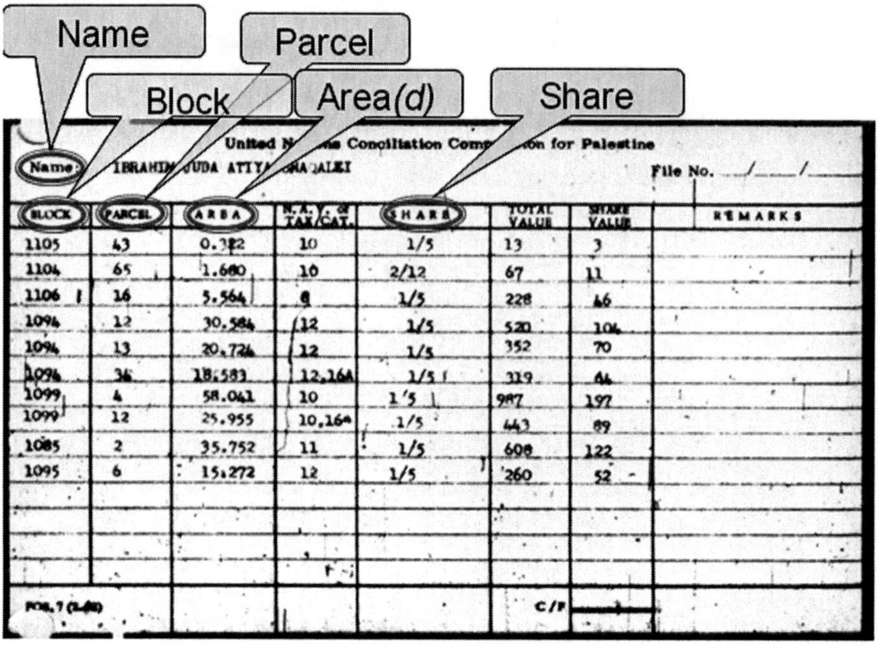

United N… Conciliation Com…on for Palestine

Name: IBRAHIM JUDA ATIYA …HA'QALEI File No. __/___/___

BLOCK	PARCEL	AREA	N.A.V. of TAX/CAT.	SHARE	TOTAL VALUE	SHARE VALUE	REMARKS
1105	43	0.322	10	1/5	13	3	
1104	65	1.680	10	2/12	67	11	
1106	16	5.564	8	1/5	228	46	
1094	12	30.584	12	1/5	520	104	
1094	13	20.724	12	1/5	352	70	
1094	36	18.583	12,16A	1/5	319	64	
1099	4	58.041	10	1/5	987	197	
1099	12	25.955	10,16A	1/5	443	89	
1085	2	35.752	11	1/5	608	122	
1095	6	15.272	12	1/5	260	52	

FOR. 7 (3-49) C/F

Figure 12.2 A typical record of one of 453,000 Palestinian land owners. All Palestine is Palestinian Arab except those areas (5.4 per cent) for which Jews possess legal title deeds.

Source: Records of the United Nations Conciliation Commission on Palestine. Sample Registration Card. A/AC.25/W.84, Identification and Valuation of Refugee Property/Methods by Land Expert – CCNUP – Working Paper, Jarvis Report, April 28, 1964.

Mandate ended and before any Arab regular soldier set foot on Palestinian soil during the warfare which ensued.

Eighty-five per cent of Palestinian inhabitants of the land that is now called Israel became refugees, and have remained so ever since. There are at the UN 453,000 records of individual Palestinian property owners defined by name, location and area (see Figure 12.2).[5] Given the detailed knowledge that exists of almost every parcel of land in Palestine, it is feasible to investigate what the Israelis did with the conquered Palestinian land.

David Ben-Gurion anticipated there would be an international demand on Israel to restore conquered lands and property to its original Palestinian owners. To avoid such a possibility, Ben-Gurion, then leader of the Provisional Government (later Israel's first Prime Minister), and the Zionist command approved a plan to prevent the return of Palestinian refugees to their homes and property which was later demanded by UN Resolution 194 of 11 December 1948. He ordered the demolition of several hundred Palestinian towns and villages, and entered into an agreement with the Jewish National Fund (JNF), an international Jewish organisation registered as a tax-exempt charity in the USA and Europe, for the JNF to enter into a sale contract for choice Palestinian

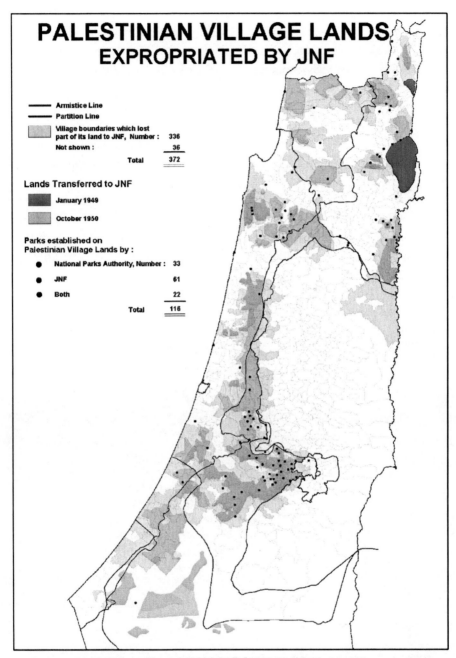

PALESTINIAN VILLAGE LANDS EXPROPRIATED BY JNF

	Armistice Line
	Partition Line

	Village boundaries which lost part of its land to JNF, Number :	336
	Not shown :	36
	Total	372

Lands Transferred to JNF

	January 1949
	October 1950

Parks established on Palestinian Village Lands by :

●	National Parks Authority, Number :	33
●	JNF	61
●	Both	22
	Total	116

Figure 12.3 AJNF confiscated 2,500,000 donums (1 donum = 1/4 acres) which belonged to 372 Palestinian villages, comprising 55 per cent of the registered refugees.

Source of parks' identification: Collated from tables featured in Noga Kadman, *Erased from Space and Consciousness – Depopulated Palestinian villages in the Israeli-Zionist Discourse.* Master's Thesis. Department of Peace and Development Research, Goteberg University, November 2001.

land adjacent to the armistice line, which was now under new ownership. This way, he would claim that this land was not under his control. The data for this deal is shown in Figure 12.3. The JNF had expropriated most of the property of 372 villages on which it established 116 parks under the slogan 'clean environment'.[6] The JNF planted parks, hiding the rubble of destroyed Palestinian homes, and the cactus plants which are still there to this day.

All the land acquired by the JNF during the Mandate and the Palestinian land seized by Israel is administered by the Israel Land Administration (ILA).[7] The area under the ILA varies according to various acts of expropriation, but it ranges from 18,775 to 19,508 km^2.[8] In order to examine the possibility of reconstructing Palestine after the destruction of its landscape and seizure of its land, consider the region bounded by the Jaffa–Tel Aviv–Jerusalem corridor in the north, and Gaza in the south. This corridor was subject to great changes in the last 60 years due to rapid urban expansion and the concentration of the population in this area. The selected region envelops the southern portions

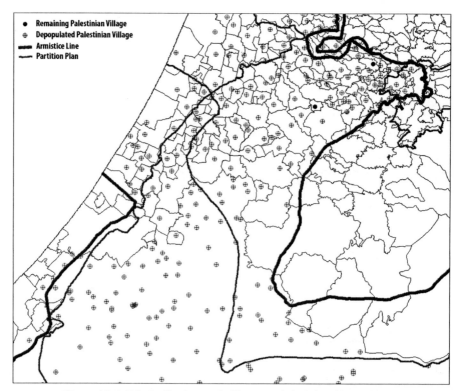

Figure 12.4 Ethnically cleansed villages and their land boundaries.

Source: Salman Abu Sitta, 'Mechanics of Expulsion: The Perpetual Ethnic Cleansing'. Lecture at SOAS, London, on January 15, 2011. Available at http://www.plands.org/speeches/017.html. Adapted from Fig. 19 A–E.

of Tel Aviv, Central Israel and the inhabited upper Israeli Southern District according to the current administrative division in Israel. Other areas are less problematic.

Figure 12.4 shows this region with its mostly Palestinian villages and their land area before 1948. All these villages, except two, were 'ethnically cleansed' by the Israelis in 1948. The population was expelled south towards the Gaza Strip and east towards the West Bank and Jordan. Their land was seized and used to expand urban development radiating from Tel Aviv to accommodate new immigrants.

Figure 12.5 shows the same region with the present Israeli urban expansion. It is very clear that most sites of depopulated villages are still vacant, contrary to frequent Israeli claims. The same figure shows the land confiscated by the JNF. The land is allocated to some kibbutzim in the area. As shown in Figure 12.15, the total rural population in the upper Southern District, which comprises the larger area of the selected region, is smaller than the population of one refugee camp in the Gaza Strip.[9]

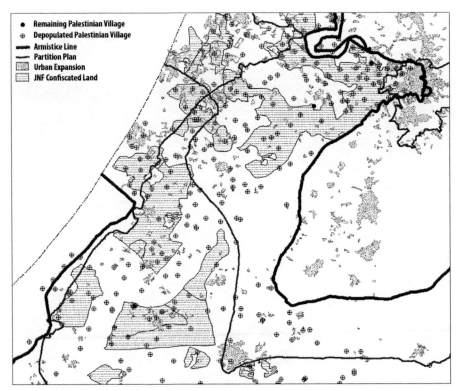

Figure 12.5 Same as Figure 12.4, showing that village sites are still vacant in spite of Israeli urban expansion. The figure shows JNF-confiscated Palestinian lands.

Source: As Figure 12.4.

This vast area of land, sparsely populated, with only marginal agricultural output, is not of any particular vital socio-economic importance to the large settled Israeli population elsewhere. A reason for holding onto it could be that it is to prevent the return of the land owners to their homes and to have it as a strategic reserve for the future. This reserve is now used to house and maintain Israel's military. Figure 12.6 shows the same region with some of the military and strategic locations and closed areas containing military bases, factories, training grounds, missile bases and weapons depots. The density of these sites is unmatched by any other country. Furthermore, any attempts to populate the Southern District with new immigrants has achieved limited success in spite of the strenuous efforts on behalf of the JNF.

The illustrations in Figures 12.4, 12.5 and 12.6 reveal the original cause of the problem, the reason for the continuation of the conflict and the possible ways to end it. This analysis of land use is not a mere conjecture. Israeli records confirm it. Land-use data in Israel in 1994 and as projected in 2020 (see Figure 12.7)[10] shows that 12 per cent of the Israeli land area contains most of the population, while 88 per cent is used as a reserve land for the military, or protected or closed

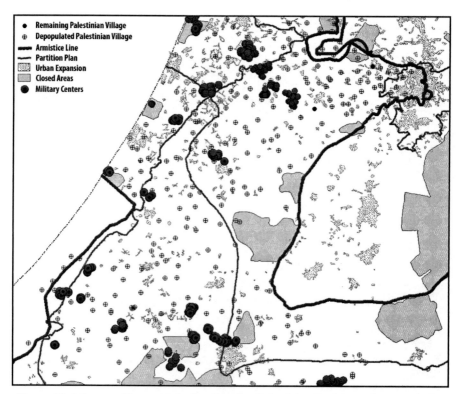

Figure 12.6 Same as Figure 12.4, showing that Palestinian land is used primarily for military purposes.

Source: As Figure 12.4.

Land Use	Km²	Per cent of total	Km²	Per cent of total	Per cent per group
	1994		2020		
Population centres	1,150	5	1,800	8	12
Spaces in centres	640	3	710	3	
Military	5,860	27	5,860	27	88
Open, protected	5,090	24	5,090	24	
Vacant	8,760	41	8,040	37	
Total	**21,500**	**100**	**21,500**	**100**	**100**

Notes: Total includes Golan (1,154 km²). Net Israel area 20,346 km².
Population centres: includes built-up areas, roads and railways within.
Spaces: includess army installations, bases and factories.
Military: includes camps, training, manoeuvrings and firing ranges.
Open protected areas: includes nature reserves, parks, panoramic scenes, forests, woods.
Vacant: includes uninhabited areas, mining, quarries, roads, railways and agriculture.
Cultivated area is 4,200 km² (1997) including irrigated land 2,000 km² (1979), reduced to 1,115 km² (2000).

Figure 12.7 Official classification of land use showing that 88 per cent of Israel is used for purposes other than human habitation.

Source: Adam Mazor, *Israel Plan 2020* (Haifa: The Technion, 1997). Adapted from Vol. 2, p. 188, Table 12.1 in the Hebrew edition.

areas, or vacant land. This includes 4,200 km² of cultivated land, which uses a colossal 70–80 per cent of the overall water consumption, while producing only 1.5 per cent of Israel's GDP.[11]

The People

The second element in the reconstruction of Palestine as one country is people. Today, there are about 11 million Palestinians who are living in the *shatat* or in historic Palestine. There are also 5.5 million Jews[12] who are mainly immigrants from or after the British Mandate period, including West Bank settlers, but now citizens of Israel. How did this come about?

Before the establishment of the state of Israel in 1948, there were 1,304 'villages' in Palestine, of which 956 came under Israeli rule[13] (Figure 12.8). Of these, 773 were Palestinian Arab villages. During the 1948–9 war the majority (674) were

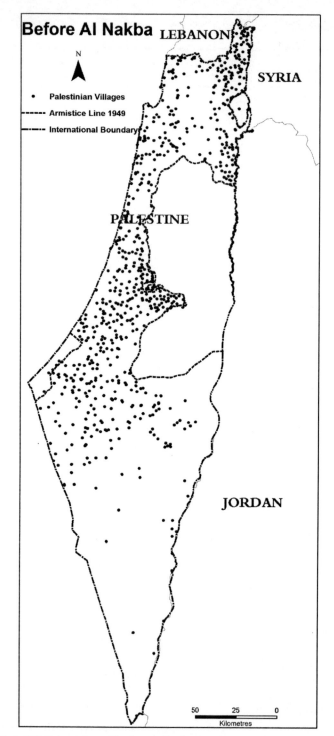

Figure 12.8 1,300 Palestinian villages in all of Palestine. Only 99 remained in the part of Palestine that became Israel. Others in that part were ethnically cleansed.

Source: Salman Abu Sitta, *Atlas of Palestine 1917–1966*. London: Palestine Land Society, 2010, p. 122.

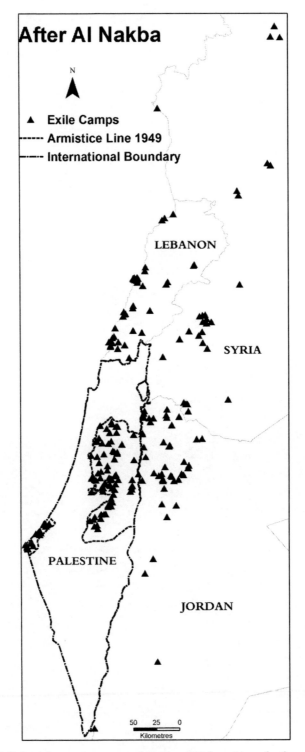

Figure 12.9 Palestinians were scattered in over 200 locations of refugee camps, not allowed to return home.

Source: As Figure 12.8.

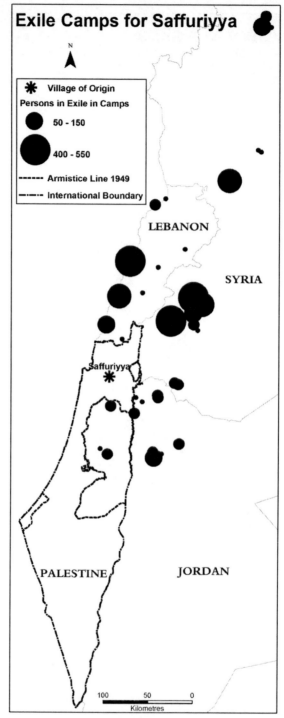

Figure 12.10 Those expelled from Saffuriyya village in Galilee sought refuge in adjacent regions, mostly Syria and Lebanon.

Source: Salman Abu Sitta, 'Mapping Palestine: for its Survival or Destruction?'. Lecture at Palestine Center, Jerusalem Fund, Washington DC, on April 28, 2011. Available at: http://www. plands.org/speechs/016.html. Adapted from Fig 19-C.

depopulated, with only 99 villages remaining. The inhabitants of depopulated villages were exiled into 602 locations, registered and served by the United Nations Relief and Works Agency (UNRWA) (Figure 12.9). Non-registered refugees live in various Arab and foreign countries. For registered refugees, UNRWA records show who they are, where they are from originally in Palestine and to where they were exiled.[14]

As an example, take the case of Saffuriyya, a village in Galilee (Figure 12.10). Some inhabitants found refuge in nearby Nazareth. The majority were expelled to Lebanon, Syria, Jordan and the West Bank. Given that they and their descendants are known, it is possible to construct how they would return from exile camps to their villages of origin. In other words, the process that took place in 1948 can be reversed with high reliability.

Another case is that of Jabaliya Camp in Gaza, which was greatly damaged by F16s and Israeli tanks in the December 2008 to January 2009 Israeli assault. The original villages of those people who took refuge in Jabaliya Camp – their *hamulas* (extended families), even their individual names – are known (Figure 12.11).

But Gaza has a special significance; 247 villages in the Southern District of Mandate Palestine (i.e. Gaza and Beersheba sub-districts) were depopulated and their inhabitants expelled to the tiny Gaza Strip (Figure 12.12). Here they live in eight camps in a strip which is 1 per cent of the area of historic Palestine, and cut off from land, sea and air contact from other Palestinian lands. The adjacent Israeli town of Sderot is built on the land of Najd village whose people are now refugees in Gaza, 2 km away. Today, 1.5 million people live in Gaza, now the most densely populated place on earth.

In order to assess the feasibility of a return of Palestinians to the territory of historic Palestine, an examination of the origin and distribution of the present occupants is in order. They can be classified into five categories:

1. Palestinians who remained at home;
2. Ashkenazi Jews of pre-1948 origin;
3. Jews from Arab countries who came in the decade post-1948;
4. Russians who immigrated after the demise of the Soviet Union; and
5. assorted European and American Jews who came intermittently, particularly after 1967.

This broad classification forms the basis of the author's research on immigration to Israel over the years,[15] and on the geographical distribution and placement of these immigrants. This research covered over 1,000 now-Israeli towns and villages. Of these, the findings indicate that fewer than 50 have a sizeable population. The rest are small settlements – kibbutzim and moshavim – each with an average population of 300–500 people. At the same time, the author studied

Figure 12.11 Jabaliya camp, pulverised by Israeli tanks and planes, is the temporary home of tens of ethnically cleansed southern villages.

Source: Salman Abu Sitta, *Atlas of Palestine 1917–1966*. London: Palestine Land Society, 2010, p. 149.

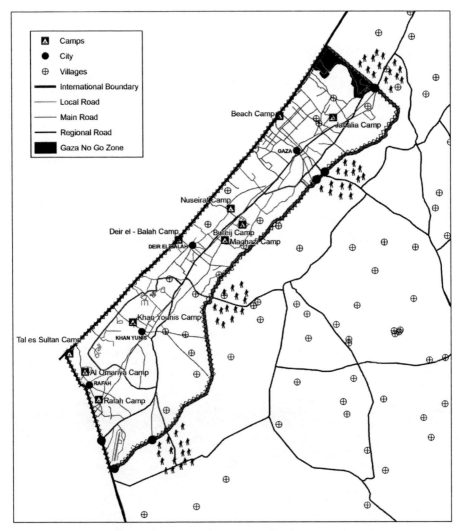

Figure 12.12 The besieged Gaza strip (1 per cent of Palestine) is the present home for 1.5 million people expelled from 247 villages.

Source: Salman Abu Sitta, 'Mechanics of Expulsion: The Perpetual Ethnic Cleansing'. Lecture at SOAS, London, on January 15, 2011. Available at http://www.plands.org/speeches/017.html. Adapted from Fig. 17 A, B.

the Palestinian population of 674 depopulated Palestinian towns and villages. Their home villages and their refugee camps were traced using the records of the UNRWA.[16] Based on the voluminous data collected, it was possible to chart a plan of return.

In the present Israeli Northern District, a sizeable percentage of the population is still Palestinian. Figure 12.13 shows both the present population and the possible accommodation of returning Palestinians. There does not seem to

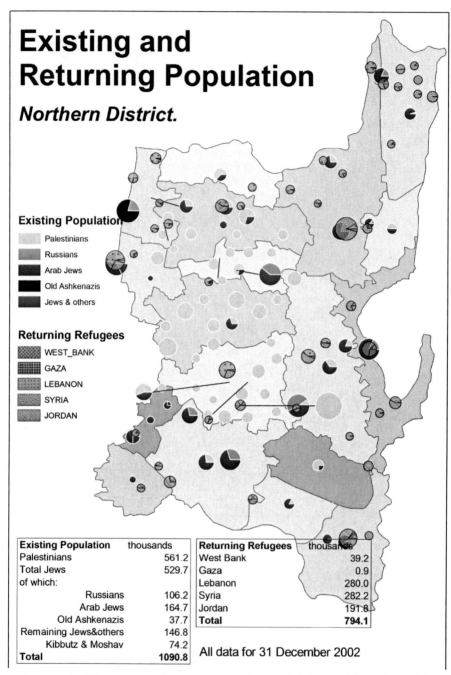

Existing and Returning Population

Northern District.

Existing Population

- Palestinians
- Russians
- Arab Jews
- Old Ashkenazis
- Jews & others

Returning Refugees

- WEST_BANK
- GAZA
- LEBANON
- SYRIA
- JORDAN

Existing Population	thousands
Palestinians	561.2
Total Jews	529.7
of which:	
Russians	106.2
Arab Jews	164.7
Old Ashkenazis	37.7
Remaining Jews&others	146.8
Kibbutz & Moshav	74.2
Total	**1090.8**

Returning Refugees	thousands
West Bank	39.2
Gaza	0.9
Lebanon	280.0
Syria	282.2
Jordan	191.8
Total	**794.1**

All data for 31 December 2002

Figure 12.13 The return of the expelled population of Galilee will be welcomed by their families who remained at home.

Source: Salman Abu Sitta, *Atlas of Palestine 1917–1966*. London: Palestine Land Society, 2010, p. 150.

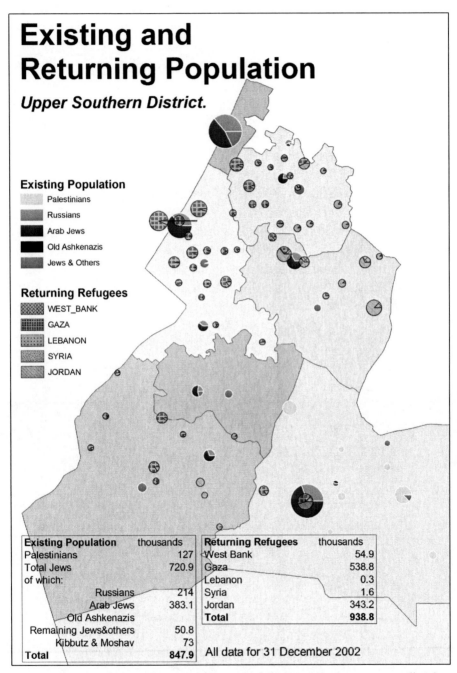

Existing and Returning Population

Upper Southern District.

Existing Population
- Palestinians
- Russians
- Arab Jews
- Old Ashkenazis
- Jews & Others

Returning Refugees
- WEST_BANK
- GAZA
- LEBANON
- SYRIA
- JORDAN

Existing Population	thousands	Returning Refugees	thousands
Palestinians	127	West Bank	54.9
Total Jews	720.9	Gaza	538.8
of which:		Lebanon	0.3
Russians	214	Syria	1.6
Arab Jews	383.1	Jordan	343.2
Old Ashkenazis		**Total**	**938.8**
Remaining Jews&others	50.8		
Kibbutz & Moshav	73		
Total	**847.9**	All data for 31 December 2002	

Figure 12.14 Total ethnic cleansing of the south left the south almost empty till today. Expelled Gaza refugees can literally walk home.

Source: As Figure 12.8.

be a problem of overlapping or overcrowding. Refugees can take a bus from their current refugee camps and return to live in their homes with their kith and kin. In any case, the restoration of Palestinian rights to return would have to be balanced by a right of Jews to remain in the area, largely in their existing homes.

The same exercise can be applied to the present Israeli Southern District, which is actually much less of a problem. Figure 12.14 shows the existing population classified as in the Southern District. With the exception of three originally Palestinian towns, now inhabited and expanded by Israeli Jews, all the rural Jews in this area (73,000) are hardly the equivalent population of one refugee camp in Gaza. The existing population and the returning refugees are almost the same number: 800,000 each. If Gaza refugees were to return, they could literally walk to where their homes had been within an hour. Housing for the returning Palestinians is also not a problem. The author researched this matter and found that more than adequate space was available for the Palestinians to rebuild and replace their houses.[17] Similar or larger projects were built in the Gulf where Palestinian engineers played a key role. It is evident, therefore, that

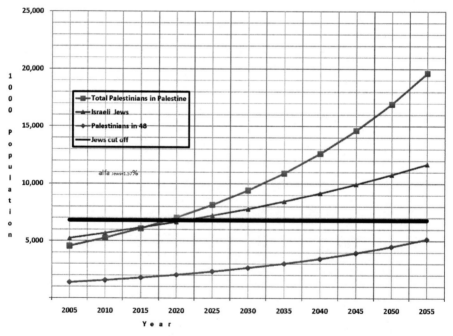

Figure 12.15 All projections show that Palestinians will be the majority at some place or time. Hence renewed ethnic cleansing plan is discussed publicly in Israel.

Source: Salman Abu Sitta, *Atlas of Palestine 1917–1966.* London: Palestine Land Society, 2010,
p. 152.

from the physical and logistical points of view, the whole process of repatriation and rehabilitation is quite manageable.

There is a prevalent attitude in Israel that calls the presence and growth of Palestinians in the country 'a demographic bomb'.[18] Figure 12.15 shows the Palestinian and Jewish population projection in Palestine. It shows the Jewish and Palestinian citizens of Israel as having a natural growth of 1.57 per cent until the year 2055. The top line shows total Palestinians living in the three regions – that is, Israel, the West Bank and Gaza – that form historic Palestine. The Palestinians in exile (not shown) who reside outside the borders of Palestine are approximately the same number. Anywhere between 2015 and 2017, Palestinians in all of Palestine will be equal to Israeli Jews. If a strict definition of a 'Jew' is applied, the Palestinians are probably already equal in numbers to Israeli Jews. In the year 2050, Palestinians will be around 17 million and Israeli Jews will be 11 million if the present trend continues without interruption. But this is not the point.

The Law

The third element in reconstructing Palestine, next to land and people, is the law that needs to prevail in the country and the mechanism by which it is applied.[19] For Palestine, international bodies and organisations, particularly the United Nations, have been involved in the issue for some 90 years. Their legal foundations and their policies and decisions can guide future actions. In them, the bases for establishing a democratic free government can be found in Article 22 of the Covenant of the League of Nations, the Universal Declaration of Human Rights and the Right to Self Determination. Though far from being optimal, UN Resolution 181 partitioning Palestine has some useful and necessary provisions to protect the political, civil, religious and educational rights of each group, whether Palestinian or Jewish. This should be a good basis from which an expanded formula can be developed for one country. Upholding UN Resolution 194, which has been affirmed by the international community over 135 times in the last 60 years, more than any other resolution in UN history, is also imperative. It has three main elements:

1.   it calls for the refugees to return;
2.   it provides them with relief until that happens; and
3.   most importantly, it provides a mechanism for their repatriation and rehabilitation. This mechanism is the UN Conciliation Commission for Palestine (UNCCP).

In the Lausanne negotiations, 1949–50, Israel managed to obstruct the refugees' return and rendered the UNCCP idle.[20] The only provision of relief that survived, represented by UNRWA, is still in operation. But the UNCCP is still legally valid and has its offices within the UN. Its annual routine report says every year: 'we are unable to facilitate the return of the refugees this year'.

In her writings, the noted legal scholar Susan Akram has outlined with much clarity the legal implications of applying the right of return.[21] It should be clear then that a legal framework for a reconstituted Palestine is available and needs to be applied, as it was in dozens of similar cases such as Kosovo, Bosnia, Abkhazia, Uruguay, Uganda, South Africa, Iraq and Afghanistan.[22] Needless to say, the real question that remains is whether or not the great powers that created the problem in the first place have the political will to enforce outstanding international resolutions.

Notes

1. See, for example, the works of Nur Masalha, *The Politics of Denial: Israel and the Palestinian Refugee Problem* (London: Pluto, 2003); *A Land Without a People: Israel, Transfer and the Palestinians* (London: Faber and Faber, 1997); *Expulsion of the Palestinians: The Concept of Transfer in Zionist Political Thought, 1882–1948* (Washington, DC: Institute of Palestine Studies, 1992); and *Imperial Israel and the Palestinians: The Politics of Expansion* (London: Pluto Press, 2000).

2. The Israeli narrative is challenged by a growing body of scholarship, including that of the 'new historians' in Israel. See, for example, Ilan Pappé, *The Making of the Arab-Israeli Conflict, 1947–1951* (London and New York: I.B.Tauris, 1992); Simha Flapan, *The Birth of Israel, Myths and Realities* (London and Sydney: Croom Helm, 1987); and Norman Finkelstein, *Image and Reality of the Israel–Palestine Conflict* (London: Verso, 1995).

3. *Village Statistics*, Palestine Government Printer, 1945; and *Survey of Palestine*, prepared in December 1945 and January 1946 for the information of the Anglo-American Committee of Enquiry, reprinted by the Institute of Palestine Studies, Washington, DC, 1991, Vol. 2, Table 2, p. 566.

4. For details, see Benny Morris, *The Birth of the Palestinian Refugee Problem Revisited, 1947–1949* (Cambridge: Cambridge University Press, 2004); and Ilan Pappé, *The Ethnic Cleansing of Palestine* (London: One World Publications, 2007). Morris maintains the Zionist view that the 'Nakba' was 'an accident of war'. Pappé maintains that ethnic cleansing was pre-planned. For graphic details of the Nakba, see Salman Abu-Sitta, *The Atlas of Palestine 1948* (London: Palestine Land Society, 2005).

5. See A/AC.25/W.84 of 28 April 1964, Working Paper Prepared by the Conciliation Commission's land expert [Frank Jarvis] on the Methods and Techniques of Identification and Valuation of Arab Refugee Immovable Property Holdings in Israel. Jarvis summarised on cards the Land Registry books and classified them by land owner. His work covered only 20 per cent of Palestine which was duly registered under the Land Ordinance (Settlement of Title) of 1928. This Ordinance was promulgated due to strong pressure by Zionists calling for a full survey of the land in Palestine to determine which land can be allocated to them. The Ordinance was based on the Australian Torrence method, which was a unique system combining both normal survey definition of land

plot boundaries and legal documentation of land ownership. It was applied from 1928 to 1947 covering mostly areas where Jews had land ownership. The rest, predominantly Arab, was defined by the Mandate as Arab or Jewish and registered accordingly on fiscal and taxation basis. The word 'Public' which appeared in Village Statistics denotes common land belonging to the village and was not taxable, such as grazing, woods or rocky areas, sometimes registered under the name of the High Commissioner. This is not to be confused with State Land, which was allocated for government disposal such as the granting of concessions. The latter area comprised only 1,179.8 km² (1945). The British left in a hurry without completing the implementation of 'Land Settlement' according to the 1928 Ordinance. Their hurried departure does not cause a major legal dispute of land ownership, as the Jews fully registered their land and the rest was recognised by all to be Arab owned.

6. See Noga Kadman, *Erased from Space and Consciousness-Depopulated Palestinian Villages in the Israeli–Zionist Discourse*, Master's thesis in Peace and Development studies, Department of Peace and Development Research, Göteborg University, Sweden, November 2001. See also JNF Report: www.plands.org/JNF%20Report1.pdf; and Michael R. Fischbach, *Records of Dispossession: Palestinian Refugee Property and the Arab Israeli Conflict* (New York: Columbia University Press, 2003), pp. 58–68.

7. A series of laws were promulgated to legalise the seizure of Palestinian land and escape international censure. See, for example, Geremy Forman and Alexander Kedar, 'From Arab land to "Israel lands": the legal dispossession of the Palestinian displaced by Israel in the wake of 1948', *Environment and Planning D: Society and Space* 22/6, December 2004, Vol. 22, pp. 809–30; Sabri Jiryis, *Settlers' Law: Seizure of Palestinian Lands* (Leiden: Palestine Yearbook of International Law, Vol. II, 1985), pp. 17–36; and Hussein Abu Hussein and Fiona McKay, *Access Denied: Palestinian Rights in Israel* (London: Zed Books, 2003), pp. 69–77.

8. Walter Lehn and Uri Davis, *The Jewish National Fund* (London: Kegan Paul International, 1988), p. 114. See also Abu Hussein, op. cit., pp. 135, 150.

9. See Figure 12.14 herein for population figures.

10. Two hundred and fifty Israeli and foreign experts met over several months to examine Israel's future by 2020. The result was 18 volumes of analysis. See Adam Mazor, *Israel Plan 2020* (Haifa: The Technion, 1997). Translated into Arabic by the Centre for Arab Unity Studies, Beirut, 2004. The table is adapted from Vol. 2, p. 188, Table 12.1.

11. Salman Abu Sitta, 'The feasibility of the right of return', in Ghada Karmi and Eugene Cotran (eds), *The Palestinian Exodus* (London: Ithaca, 1999).

12. According to the Israeli Central Bureau of Statistics (CBS), the population of Israel in September 2009 was 7,465,500, of which 5,634,300 were Jews, assuming that all Russians are Jews, 1,513,200 Palestinians including those in annexed Jerusalem, and 318,300 others, mostly foreign workers.

13. The figure of 1,304 'villages' as shown in British maps refers to all towns, primary villages, secondary villages, hamlets and Jewish settlements in Palestine during the Mandate. Of these, 956 were situated inside the Armistice Line of 1949. Another 183 were Jewish, leaving 773 Palestinian Arab 'villages' under Israeli rule. Of the latter, 99 remained intact and 674 were depopulated. Other scholars quote numbers less than 674 depending on their definitions. Benny Morris refers only to 369 towns and villages. Walid Khalidi listed 418 villages and excluded towns, smaller villages, hamlets and all of Beersheba district except for three villages. For the names and location of the total depopulated villages of all types, see Salman Abu Sitta, *The Atlas of Palestine 1948* (London: Palestine Land Society, 2005).

14. See, generally, www.unrwa.org. The UNRWA Registry gives detailed information about every refugee.

15. See Annual Statistical Abstracts, Central Bureau of Statistics, Israel.

16. Registered refugees at the UNRWA represent only 75 per cent of all refugees. Others did not register in 1949–50 because registration was based on need for food and shelter, which they did not require as they had their own resources.

17. Salman Abu Sitta, *From Refugees to Citizens at Home* (London: Palestine Land Society, 2001). Available online at: http://www.plands.org/books.htm.

18. Netanyahu expressed this view at the Herzliya Conference in December 2004. The extremist Avigdor Lieberman has publicly advocated the expulsion of Palestinian citizens of Israel. The debate about this issue is common in many sectors of Israeli society without fear of censorship or condemnation.

19. For examination of the legal background, see W. T. Mallison and S. V. Mallison, *The Palestine Problem in International Law and World Order* (Essex: Longman, 1986); and John Quigley, *Palestine and Israel: A Challenge to Justice* (Durham University Press, Durham, 1990).

20. Ilan Pappé, *The Making of the Arab-Israeli Conflict, 1947–1951* (London and New York: I.B.Tauris, 1992), p. 212.

21. The reader may refer to the contribution of Susan Akram to this volume.

22. For a variety of applications of property restitution in various areas of conflict, see www.badil.org/Solutions/restitutuion.htm.

CHAPTER 13

Mizrahi Feminism and the Question of Palestine: Two States or One?

Smadar Lavie

The Mizrahim

The modern state of Israel declared itself to be a homeland to a citizenry consisting of three major social groups. Of its 7 million citizens, about 20 per cent belong to a group that the government and popular culture term Arab Citizens of Israel, or Israeli Arabs. They prefer to be called Palestinian Citizens of Israel, Palestinian Israelis or Palestinians Residing in Israel. In Arabic they are called '1948 Arabs', shorthand for those who stayed in Palestine after the 1948 founding of the state of Israel. The second group is the Mizrahim (Orientals), who constitute 50 per cent of Israel's total population and about 63 per cent of the Jewish population. Their parents arrived in Israel mainly in the 1950s from the Arab and Muslim world, or from the former margins of the Ottoman Empire such as Morocco, Tunisia, Egypt, Yemen and Iraq, or even Turkey, Iran, Bulgaria and India.[1] Officially, the Israeli government terms them 'descendants from Asia-Africa', or 'Edot Hamizrah' (Bands of the Orient).[2,3] Mizrahim[4] is the coalitional term they use when advocating their rights before the ruling minority, the approximately 30 per cent of Israeli citizenry called Ashkenazim.[5]

The Ashkenazim originated in central and eastern Europe and spoke Yiddish. While their first organised immigration wave arrived in Palestine in 1882, most came after the Holocaust. Official Israeli terminology endows them with the appellation Kehilot Ashkenaz (Ashkenazi communities).[6,7] Most Mizrahim vehemently reject the identity descriptor 'Arab Jews', designated for them by diasporic anti-Zionist Mizrahi intellectuals. Yet while most Ashkenazim identify themselves first as Israelis and then as Jews, most Mizrahim identify first as Jews and only then as Israelis.

Official discourse camouflages the fact that the majority of Israel's citizenry is of Mizrahi origin. The Israeli population survey authority devised an all-inclusive demographic category, called *yelidei ha'aretz*, for those Israeli Jews 'born in Israel'. If one does not know the identity of the parents and grandparents of those born in Israel, then the proportions of Mizrahim and Ashkenazim seem more equal than they actually are. When younger Jewish Israelis are described as having been born in Israel, they lose their historical diasporic roots, which still define racial-ethnic zones of privilege. Because Mizrahi families had much higher birth rates than the Ashkenazim until the middle of the 1970s, it is evident that the majority of Jews born in Israel are Mizrahim.[8] Identifying this disparity, or its occlusion in the census, greatly clarifies the patterns of discrimination within the Jewish population.

Since the arrival of Ashkenazi Zionists in Palestine in 1882 and since 1948, the Mizrahim have been expected to relinquish their Arab or Mediterranean culture and family structure and their non-European mother tongues. After 1948, upon immigration, they were forced to reside in economically deprived border villages and development towns. The Mizrahim received government-sponsored training programmes for production-line jobs, while the Ashkenazim went to universities for professional training. Like the Palestinian Israelis, the Mizrahi majority has only a small minority of representation in all financial, legal and cultural institutions of the Israeli elite. This holds true not only in these institutions, but also in political movements such as feminism, where sharp divisions exist between Ashkenazi and Mizrahi feminists.

Ashkenazi Feminist Elitism

The emergence of Mizrahi feminism in the 1990s must be placed into the context of Ashkenazi elite domination of Israel's public sphere. These elite are an almost hermetically sealed group of families that ensures intergenerational transmission of financial assets and Ashkenazi Zionist pedigree. Upward mobility is almost impossible for those lacking proper genealogy, unless they have relatives, neighbours and close friends who can 'pull strings' for them.[9,10] Most of the public sphere is framed by a discourse focusing on security that muffles awareness of the rampant intra-Jewish racism by uniting Jews against the Arab enemy,[11] talking about the Palestinians as a demographic time bomb[12] or appealing to a shared Israeli masculinity.[13] The remainder of the sphere is saturated with US–European high and popular culture.

When Israeli Ashkenazi feminism arose in the 1970s, many of its members were middle-class Ashkenazim who had immigrated to Israel from English-speaking countries. Their activism included founding a system of shelters for battered women, rape crisis lines, courage-to-heal groups for incest survivors, and a prostitute rehabilitation movement and fighting against the commodification of women's bodies in commercials.[14] From the mid-1980s on, the space that middle-class Ashkenazi feminists had created for feminism in the public sphere was usurped by the *gvarot* (ladies) of the liberal Ashkenazi elite.[15] The upper-class Ashkenazi feminists had the wealth, leisure and Zionist pedigree to conduct full-time feminist advocacy through their fathers, husbands or other kinship ties. Among them were: Shulamit Aloni, wife of Reuven Aloni, a long-time member of the Labour Party establishment; Yael Dayan, Moshe Dayan's daughter; and the much younger Meirav Michaeli, niece of Mordechai Namir, one of the Labour Party's leaders.

Early Mizrahi feminists faced an uphill struggle in their efforts to carve out a place in the little space left in Israeli civil society devoid of militarism or the liberal feminist agenda. Mizrahi women's needs were met by neither group. The *gvarot* were insufficient to represent the welfare mother, the production-line worker from the hinterland company town or the woman who had just lost her job due to the economic downturn that followed the failed Oslo Peace Accords. They could not even represent the Mizrahi woman intellectual, who had neither the pedigree nor the relatives to secure her a tenure-track position in Israel's 'Ashkenazi Academic Junta'.[16,17]

Mizrahi Feminism

Mizrahi feminism is the only feminist movement in Israel that currently draws its membership from all segments of society, including intellectuals, artists, small business owners, fired factory workers and homeless welfare mothers.[18] The movement started when Mizrahi women wanted to bring immediate aid and long-term empowerment and social justice to disenfranchised women in their communities. They were inspired by the distinct voices of US feminists of colour who had emerged in the 1970s arguing that white feminism could not transcend the racism, ethnocentrism and privilege that typified the Western public sphere and its liberal feminist movements. Since American trends arrive in Israel about a decade later, in the mid-1980s a group of Mizrahi women met in Tel Aviv, upon the initiative of the feminist activists Ilana Sugavker, whose parents immigrated to Israel from Bombay, and Hanna Cohen, daughter of Iranian immigrants. Its members were Yemenis Yonit Mansour, Yael Zadok and Ronit Dagan-Timsit, Iraqis Ilana Shamai, Rutie Gur, Irit Daloumi and Shosha Goren, Egyptian Vicki Shiran and Iranian Zehava Goldstein. All were Zionists, but all criticised the Israeli feminist upper-class *Anglo-Saxiyot* ('Anglo-Saxons', Hebrew, feminine plural – Ashkenazi immigrants from English-speaking countries) and the US–UK Anglo-feminism influences on them. They criticised, too, the classism and racism faced by Mizrahi and Palestinian–Israeli women.[19] Though a Mizrahi discourse of resistance had existed in Israel since the 1920s, when the Yemeni labourers brought in as 'natural workers' unionised,[20] this was the first time that Mizrahi women identified themselves as a category.[21]

The major event of Israel's feminist non-governmental organisations (NGOs) since the late 1970s has been the Annual Feminist Convention. Until 1991, almost all the speakers and workshop leaders were Ashkenazi women, with the inclusion of a single token Mizrahi and a single token Palestinian–Israeli.[22] The Tel Aviv Women's Group used to joke, in the Audre Lorde[23] tradition of 'The master's tools will never dismantle the master's house', that Mizrahi women cleaned house and babysat for the Ashkenazi *gvarot* so that the *gvarot* could devote time to feminism.

In 1991 the Mizrahi group refused to remain token participants in the Annual Feminist Convention meetings and demanded proportional representation for each group of Israeli citizens: Palestinians, Mizrahim and Ashkenazim. It won this battle because, with the refusal of the obligatory single Mizrahi and single Palestinian to act as a fig leaf, the Ashkenazi feminists found their liberalist pluralism challenged.

In 1994 the Mizrahi feminists demanded that lesbians be added to the proportional representation paradigm. From then on, until early 2000, almost all Israeli non-academic feminist events were run by what is officially termed 'the quarter system', where each panel or workshop had an Ashkenazi, a Mizrahi, a Palestinian and a lesbian.[24,25] Israeli academic feminist events, on the other hand, remained almost exclusively Ashkenazi.

By 2000, many Ashkenazi feminists saw the problem as resolved and returned to the system of the all-Ashkenazi panel with a token Mizrahi and/or Palestinian. Mizrahi feminists tried to challenge this paradigm but were left without much success, because by then some of them felt conflicted by a sense of obligation to Ashkenazi NGO feminists, who had singled them out as 'good Mizrahim', or Mizrahim willing to accept these token diversity roles.

In response to the Al-Aqsa Intifada (2000–5), many Palestinian–Israeli individual feminist activists and NGOs boycotted Israeli feminist activists' events altogether. They objected to the fact that such events included Jewish feminists, mainly Ashkenazi, from settlements in the West Bank and Gaza, and Orthodox Jewish feminists, mainly Ashkenazi as well, who believe in the idea of a Greater Eretz Yisrael but lived within its pre-1967 borders.

The only event that still observes the official policy of the quarter system is Israel's annual feminist NGO convention. While Mizrahim and Palestinian Israelis seek to devote their energies to their own communities, Ashkenazi feminists have made a strategic choice to shift their focus to the question of Palestine.

Israeli Feminism and the Question of Palestine

The question of Palestine best illustrates the gulf between Ashkenazi feminists and the majority of Jewish Israeli women, who are disenfranchised Mizrahim. The term 'the question of Palestine', alludes to Edward Said's book of that title.[26] Yet for most Ashkenazi feminists, who conceive of themselves as representatives of all Israeli women, Palestine is to be found only in the West Bank and Gaza.[27] They are not alone in this view. The question of Palestine has developed into a legitimate subject of activism among feminists in the West – many of whom, particularly in the USA and Canada – are progressive Ashkenazi Jews.[28]

Most Ashkenazi Jews in the Diaspora are unaware of the vast socio-economic disparity that exists in Israel and throughout the Jewish world. While 15 per cent of world Jewry is Mizrahi, this group resides mainly in Israel. The 85 per cent majority of world Jewry that is Ashkenazi resides mainly in the Diaspora.[29] Historically, Diaspora Ashkenazi feminists have been willing to battle racism in their own societies. Progressive and radical Jews have always been at the fore-front of anti-racist struggles, whether in South Africa during the fight against apartheid or in the USA during the civil rights movement. Many Diaspora Ashkenazi feminists have consistently protested Israel's colonial practices towards non-Jews in the West Bank and Gaza. Nevertheless, because Mizrahi discourse on intra-Jewish racism has been suppressed, whether by the English language barrier that prevented it from travelling abroad or by severe censorship from Ashkenazi hegemony,[30] the extent of Israel's intra-Jewish racial divide is unfamiliar to most progressive Jews abroad.

Ashkenazi peace feminists focus on ending Israel's occupation of Palestine in the West Bank and Gaza, and some do concurrently fight for equal civil rights for Palestinian citizens of Israel. But this fight deflects their attention from their responsibility for and participation in the racial and economic oppression of the non-European Jewish majority citizenry within Israel. These feminists employ a discourse about the Palestinian as the external, homogenised, nationalist Other, who cannot be subject to the perennial Israeli debate about who is a Jew.[31] Palestinian women especially serve as Others for Ashkenazi feminists, who recognise and nurture this difference.

Such activism almost surely yields European or US funding. It is easier for the Ashkenazi peace *gvarot* to deal with Palestine as a specifically feminist issue, as this allows them to dialogue with the English-speaking, Western-bred, secular-liberal Palestinian nationalist elite. They need not engage with members of the lower classes of Palestinian women, who belong to Islamist movements such as Hamas, mainly as a result of their disillusionment with the exclusive NGO-isation and professionalisation[32] of cosmopolitan Palestinian feminism.[33]

The question of Palestine is a well-funded springboard for Israeli activism under the utopian platform of peace and co-existence. In Hebrew, *du-kiyyum* literally means 'co-existence'. It has become a shorthand description of a genre of Palestinian and Israeli get-togethers designed to process old grievances and encourage potentials for peace. Often, a professionally trained group facilitator aids the process. The meetings are held at elegant resorts, in beautiful natural settings meant to provide the relaxed atmosphere needed to allow past traumas to heal. The Israelis likely to participate come from the Ashkenazi upper-middle class. Outside Israel, these *du-kiyyum* get-togethers are conducted in English. This further limits the composition of participants, since, in the non-English-speaking world, English proficiency and upper-class cosmopolitanism often go together. In Israel, the *du-kiyyum* is habitually performed in Hebrew, the colonisers' language. Subaltern Palestinians speak it fluently. The Israeli participants are not likely to speak Arabic. Some Palestinians have given *du-kiyyum* the sardonic affectionate nickname '*dukki*'.[34,35]

These ritualised *du-kiyyum* dialogues with the upper-class feminist elite of Ramallah have permitted Ashkenazi feminists to justify their racial and class bias toward Mizrahi women with benevolence toward Arab Muslim and Christian women of the West Bank (far less than toward those of Gaza). They espouse the cause of the Palestinian women activists who are citizens of Israel, even while controlling much of the funding that goes to the Palestinian–Israeli feminist NGOs.

In an era where the public sphere has undergone NGO-isation and feminist NGOs have undergone professionalisation,[36] *du-kiyyum* is used as a magic key to unlock NGO funding for local projects. Funds flow to Israel for *dukki* feminism from the European Union as well as from Diaspora organisations and US Jewish women's groups. The *dukki*'s prestige brings in handsome budgets. In late 2002, the peace-and-dialogue movement received about US$9 million of US and EU tax-deductible donations.[37]

Almost all Israeli feminist NGOs are funded by the New Israel Fund (NIF) and Women-to-Women USA–Israel. These foundations espouse an enlightened, left-leaning form of Zionism and have influenced the scholarly political, cultural and social agendas of Israeli feminism and women's studies. In the realm of feminist activism, the NIF and its subsidiary, SHATIL,[38] have professionalised the NGOs by offering job opportunities at a time of job scarcity. But hired professionals must conform to role expectations, which has tended to depoliticise some activists. Aside from organisations' leadership, which is mostly comprised of Ashkenazim, the NIF metes out its funds into part-time positions held mainly by Mizrahi and Palestinian women. This practice confines many grass-roots women activists to jobs with fragmented hourly pay, devoid of benefits and labour rights.

In funding NGOs, the NIF has also enacted a Durkheimian division of protest labour. As Durkheim[39] classifies the manner in which hierarchies of different labours cohere into a social order, the NIF has created a hierarchy of gendered ethnic-national protests regulated by its funding policies. The progressive-liberal feminist elite is funded by the NIF and Women-to-Women USA–Israel to protest violations of the human and civil rights of Palestinians of the West Bank and Gaza, or even those of Israel itself. It employs the language of cosmopolitan human rights, including the discourse and the struggle of indigenous first nations. The funding agencies do not object when these NGOs use terms like 'racism' and 'apartheid' to describe the discriminatory ideologies and practices of the Israeli regime against Palestinians. The Israeli regime now allows even its Palestinian citizens to have their own tightly supervised human rights NGOs, also mainly funded by the NIF. They receive demonstration permits and conduct activism objecting to Israeli segregationist policies against them. Yet both the government and the funding agencies use the Palestinian–Israeli and Ashkenazi elite human rights NGOs as proof of their claim to enlightenment. The NIF vetoes any Palestinian human rights activism that would inform the Palestinian public about the racial divisions of Zionism or the oxymoronic concept of a democratic Jewish state.[40]

The NIF and Women-to-Women USA–Israel do not bestow even such confined protest and popular mobilisation privileges on Mizrahi NGOs. Instead, they have relegated these NGOs to the role of substituting severely truncated state welfare programmes. Feminist Mizrahi NGOs are funded mainly to help women re-enter the job market through workshops for starting small businesses – such as selling home cooking in a tight, highly professionalised catering market or embroidery in an exploitative market for ethnic crafts, already populated by Bedouin women who have their own collectives for embroidery and weaving. When the Mizrahi NGOs refuse to become charities or 'oceans of tears',[41] they are neutralised by the funders' threats of greatly reducing their grants.[42] In sum, as Racheli Avidov[43] argued, Mizrahi feminism has been transformed into a depoliticised subcontractor of mainstream Ashkenazi feminism.[44]

Until recently, Ashkenazi feminists have discredited Mizrahi feminists as *mitbakhyenot* (cry-babies),[45] while erasing their own colour and class differences from Mizrahi women under the guise of Jewish sisterhood.[46] The result has been an almost complete disjuncture between Mizrahi feminists and Palestinian–Israeli feminists, despite their similar structures of patriarchy and similar multiple axes of oppression, whether by Ashkenazi men and women or their own men. Mizrahi and Palestinian–Israeli feminists are able to establish dialogue only through the mediation of the Ashkenazi feminists, even when the Ashkenazim are physically absent during the dialogue.[47] Furthermore, the lack of English skills and/or elite educational experience abroad[48] makes it impossible for Mizrahi feminists to engage with the upper-class nationalist feminists of the Palestinian Authority.

The history of feminist activism and scholarship teaches us that progress starts at home. Palestinian feminists, particularly if Islamist, conduct their activism in keeping with the spirit of the old Jewish 'sages of blessed memory', who advised: 'Put the poor of your home before those of your town, and the poor of your town before those of the next town.'[49] In other words, use common sense and compassionate logic. Unlike the Israeli feminist *gvarot*, Palestinian feminists first work locally, putting their class privileges into action for the betterment of the disenfranchised in their own communities, and only then present this work to the international community and media.[50] Yet the question of Palestine enables the Ashkenazi peace feminists to avoid sharing their power, prestige and money with the Mizrahi internal Others of Israeli society. Mizrahi feminists see great irony in the contrast between Ashkenazi feminists' emphasis of human rights for the Palestinians and silence on human rights for the Mizrahim. This irony is but a small part of the practices and policies that have led the majority of Israeli women, Mizrahi women, to move farther to the right since 1977.[51]

Idiosyncrasies of Israel's Political Left and Right

The majority of Ashkenazim vote for the Israeli political left. The left agrees on a land-for-peace settlement of the Israeli–Palestinian conflict, but is divided among three factions. First, the Zionist Left voting bloc, consisting of the Labour Party and Meretz Party, and even the Kadima Party, espouses liberal to socialist Zionism.[52] Nevertheless, when in power, the Zionist Left has consistently carried out right-wing domestic social and economic policies. The bloc's affluent constituency has been composed of the Ashkenazi economic-political elite – industrialists, bankers, developers and high-tech businessmen.[53] A second group, the Post-Zionist Left, recognises the reality of the 1948 Nakba and conducts active demonstrations against Israel's 1967 occupation of the West Bank and Gaza, but does not differ from the Zionist bloc when it comes to its Ashkenazi elite-class interests. The third faction, the Anti-Zionist Left, is also of the Ashkenazi elite class, but traces its roots back to the European New Left of the 1960s. It favours transforming Israel from a Jewish state, where Jews have advantageous privileges of citizenship, into a secular state with equitable citizenship for all inhabitants, including the Palestinians who remained in what was declared to be Israel after the 1948 war. A minority within the Anti-Zionist Left believes that one-state Israel/Palestine ought to be formed from Israel, the West Bank and the Gaza Strip. None of these leftist movements has managed to attract the Mizrahim.

On the eve of the 1967 War, Michael Selzer[54,55] argued that all factions of the Ashkenazi left had aryanised the Jews more than those of the right had, by co-opting the then-fashionable counterculture discourse of peace and love to make solidarity overtures to the Palestinians. But the left, while romanticising the Palestinians, could not digest its own Jewish Arabs – the Mizrahim – as part of the conflict between Israel and its neighbours. Selzer points out that it treated them as the inassimilable excess of what the left termed 'the peace discourse'.[56] He concludes that unless the political left dismantles Israel's intra-Jewish apartheid system by de-aryanising Israel's Ashkenazi domination and hegemony, there will be no armistice, let alone peace, between Israel and the Arab world. Selzer goes on to say that the left has not 'realis[ed] how significant it is that the Ashkenazim have shown themselves incapable of living with their own Jewish brethren of Arab background'.[57]

In the 1977 election, the Mizrahim voted almost as a bloc for Menachem Begin, in order to reject the left wing's racial formations of Zionism and its inability to acknowledge the humiliation and discrimination to which the Mizrahim have been subjected under the reign of Labour Party governments since 1948. In 1959, Begin served as head of the right-wing Herut Party and operated far outside the liberal-socialist Zionist consensus. He became one of the most revered figures among many Mizrahim when he made a solidarity visit with the rebels of Wadi Salib, an overcrowded Haifa slum where North African Jews had risen up to protest the squalid conditions of their forced resettlement into an area whose Palestinian residents had been expelled by the left-wing Labour regime. Because of this visit, and especially because Begin was the first politician to acknowledge that discrimination against the Mizrahim was based on their non-Ashkenazi ethnic origins, the Mizrahim voted for the rightist Likud Party, successor to the Herut Party, for years thereafter. Wadi Salib was the first event to shape post-1948 Mizrahi consciousness.

In his 1977 landslide victory, Menachem Begin moved from underdog to Prime Minister, due in part to the early 1970s civil unrest sparked by the Mizrahi Black Panthers, a protest movement that took its name as a symbolic gesture to the eponymous Oakland movement. The Black Panthers were also in coalition with the budding late-1960s, New Left Anti-Zionist Ashkenazi movement. Starting in Jerusalem's pre-1967 border zone slums, their demonstrations swept through almost all Mizrahi ghettos in Israel's urban centres. These were suppressed by brutal police force, following the instructions of Prime Minister and Labour Party leader Golda Meir. Some Panthers were shot dead at short range by police snipers. Others were co-opted into establishment positions, and those who remained activists are still denied meaningful employment and housing by the Israeli regime. One mysteriously disappeared.[58] Just when they were about to embark on coalitional relationships with European New Left and

radical socialist groups, Israeli officials confiscated the passports of their delegation members. Israeli scholars and the public believe that the Black Panthers
movement led directly to the fall of the Labour Party and the transfer of power
to Begin and the right. The Israeli political right has held power since 1977,
except for short periods, and has carried out a policy that had been initiated by
the Labour Party – settling the West Bank and Gaza through colonial outposts
under the ideology of Eretz Yisrael.

A new generation of Mizrahi politicians aligned themselves with the Likud
Eretz Yisrael ideology and practice, and rose into lower-level municipal politics
as mayors. Then some went to the Knesset or obtained ministerial portfolios.
But this new cadre of Mizrahi politicians was still subservient to those with
Ashkenazi lineage in the Likud, who were popularly called *nesikhim* (princes).
The Mizrahi politicians advanced the political agenda of the *nesikhim* rather
than that of their own Mizrahi communities. It is interesting to note that these
Mizrahi politicians enjoyed repeated re-election even though they failed to
advance their own communities' interests.

Nevertheless, there were good reasons for the lower-class Jewish majority of
Israel to keep voting for the political right. Many Mizrahi families wanted to
escape the Mizrahi ghettos, especially when the cities in central Israel started
turning into real-estate bubbles that made housing there utterly unaffordable.[59]
In pursuing its goal to settle Eretz Yisrael, the Likud continued the policy of
creating viable single-family dwellings for lower-middle-class Israelis. It was
the Labour government that started devising a plan in which the only housing
upgrades available for poor people were to be found in large-scale settlements
like Ariel, Ma`ale Adumim or the newer expansion of Jerusalem's neighbour-
hoods to deep inside post-1967 occupied Palestine. Here, upscale-for-the-poor
projects bore names such as Pisgat Ze'ev (The Wolf's Peak)[60] or Neve Ya`akov
(The Oasis of Jacob). Since the mid-1980s, however, right-wing governments
of Israel not only invested in these settlements, but also initiated project
renewal in the Mizrahi ghettos throughout the country. Although the project
did not support enough new housing, it did establish community centres and
significantly improve the infrastructure, particularly electricity and sewage.
Furthermore, it was during the right-wing Israeli regimes that Mizrahi culture,
as long as it avoided connecting its own Arabness with that of the Palestinians,
embarked on a renaissance.[61]

During the 1993–9 Oslo years, brokered by the USA, the Israelis and
Palestinians negotiated Israel's gradual withdrawal from some of the territories it had seized from Jordan and Egypt in the 1967 War. One of the selling
points to the Israeli public was the promise of an immediate regional economic
boom, led by the globalised restructuring of the Israeli economy. The Labour–
MERETZ bloc, then in power, dismantled labour unions and outsourced

production to Egypt, Jordan, South Africa and Southeast Asia. The left elite invested in sweatshops abroad and employed cheap labour to replace Mizrahi and Palestinian–Israeli women production-line workers.[62] The Zionist Left leadership also started privatising the public sphere, and initiated the move to reduce welfare allowances for the needy. The Post- and Anti-Zionist Left did not protest, afraid of disturbing the peace process. The right deployed populist ethnic and social justice rhetoric to win the support of Israel's Mizrahim until 2003, when Benjamin Netanyahu slashed almost all the remaining Israeli welfare rights, exposing the rhetoric as hollow.

One of the slogans chanted in many demonstrations by all varieties of the Israeli political left is 'Fund the 'hoods [the Mizrahi slums and development towns] not the settlements [Israeli communities in the West Bank and Gaza]'. Rafi Shubeli[63] argues that the evocation of this catchphrase is illusory. He asks, since when has the Israeli Ashkenazi left fought for the Mizrahi poor or tried to provide a viable alternative to the avenues for upward mobility provided by an allegiance to the right? Ironically, the kibbutzim, the showcases of enlightened socialist Zionism, exploited Mizrahi development towns by hiring underpaid menial labourers with no rights.[64] Shubeli notes that the Ashkenazi left habitually depicts the Mizrahim as the atavistic chauvinistic masses. The left almost always chants the slogan 'Fund the 'hoods, not the settlements' in the context of the military occupation of the West Bank and Gaza, without acknowledging the fact that the Mizrahim are the silent majority of the West Bank and Gaza settlements. They do not chant that slogan in the context of the racism and poverty typical of lived experience in the slums of either Palestinian Nazareth or mixed Palestinian–Israeli upper Nazareth, let alone skid row in South Tel Aviv,[65] where they will travel half a mile to the ''hoods' only to eat inexpensive shish-kebabs of foie gras rolled into Iraqi pita-bread. Shubeli concludes that, in a sense, by using such a slogan, the left inflames one public (the Mizrahim) against the other (the Palestinians), due to its omission of the societal context having to do with the ethnic composition of either the slums or the settlements vis-à-vis the ethnic composition of the left.[66]

The left's Ashkenazi feminists responded to Israel's grave human rights violations during the first Intifada (1987–2003) and the Al-Aqsa Intifada (2000–5). In her writings, Gila Swirsky,[67] one of the founders of Women in Black and the Coalition of Women for a Just Peace, vividly evokes the brave feats of Israeli peace activists demonstrating in solidarity with the Palestinians of the West Bank during the Al-Aqsa Intifada – endangering their own lives as they distributed food to besieged villages, preventing with their bodies the uprooting of olive trees, or exposing themselves to physical and verbal violence from right-wing Israelis as they marched to crown Jerusalem with peace. Ashkenazi feminists have demonstrated more often than men; because of the combination of their gender and class privileges, it is less likely that the Israeli Defense Force (IDF) soldiers on active duty policing the West Bank, most of whom are Mizrahim, would attack them to stop the demonstrations.[68] Still, Ashkenazi feminists ignore the plight of their disenfranchised Mizrahi neighbours; rather, they can be found just across the street, in favour of what Swirsky[69] describes as 'TV crews from all over the world' who document their 'street theatre' protests against the occupation. These photograph well for the media in search of simplistic Israel/Palestine binaries. Concurrently, as Swirsky aptly puts it, these feminists continue to wonder why their groups 'remain largely invisible to the Israeli public'.[70]

The Ashkenazi left takes for granted the loyalty of the Mizrahim to the state. Indeed, Mizrahim continue to vote for the political right regardless of which party is in power. Similarly, Ashkenazi feminist scholarship and activism continue to ignore these class and race divisions within Israel.[71]

Mizrahi Feminist Predicament and Strategy

The Mizrahi predicament is complicated and driven by contradiction. It cannot be compared to the clear-cut situation of West Bank or Gaza Palestinians living under the daily atrocities of Israel's military might. It cannot even be compared with the daily acts of apartheid that Israel performs toward its own Palestinian citizens. G. Avivi argues that Mizrahim are situated between their own economic-cultural oppression and the Palestinian fight for national determination.[72] Most Mizrahim still believe in Zionism's utopian promise, even as they remain excluded from its economic and cultural power centres. They are not active in struggles to overcome their disenfranchisement. Avivi hypothesises that if the Mizrahim were to change loyalties in the Zionism versus Palestine equation, they would incur immediate losses to whatever gains they have made through the tenuous political-economic upward mobility that came with their Ashkenazification.[73]

Like all Jewish citizens of Israel, Mizrahim are obligated to serve in the military, an institution that facilitates upward mobility for Israeli Jews. Since the 1982 Lebanon War, however, actual combat has gradually become less attractive to Ashkenazim, who, due to their superior schools in affluent neighbourhoods, are eligible for the high-tech behind-the-lines units. Today, Mizrahim train for the majority of infantry and armoured corps front-line duty jobs. Higher casualties follow.[74] Avivi also points out that it is the Mizrahim who end up as targets when Palestinian suicide bombers explode. Suicide bombings are likely to occur on public transportation, which is frequented by Mizrahim who cannot afford to own private cars. Other favourable locations for suicide bombers are impoverished neighbourhoods, where residents are not affluent enough to collectively hire the patrolling services of privately run security companies and where official Israeli police rarely patrol, except for during drug raids.[75]

The Ashkenazim, whether on the right or left, have international, specifically American, connections in the World Zionist Organization and on Capitol Hill. Ashkenazi feminists on the left, funded by the NIF, have also appeared before the European Parliament and received more funding.[76] The Palestinians, too, have gradually won international recognition for the Nakba and their heroic struggle for a free and independent homeland. But the Mizrahim, despite their NIF-funded NGOs, have yet to gain international recognition as another regional problem. Only such recognition would persuade the NIF to allow the Mizrahi NGOs to change their focus from local soup kitchens to transnational and coalitional social justice activism for the benefit of the Mizrahi communities, thereby yielding a just and genuine peace process.

At present, Mizrahi feminist NGOs avoid publicly facing the question of Palestine. Their grass-roots advocacy work is funded by Diaspora Zionist sources, and Mizrahi feminist NGOs know that cutting these strings would provoke the Ashkenazi hegemony to inflict further losses on Mizrahi communities.[77] Furthermore, Mizrahi activists do not collaborate with Palestinian feminists of lower socio-economic status within Israel or the West Bank because of their affiliations with Hamas. All NGOs funded by the NIF are required to take minutes of their meetings, and these minutes are subject to possible inspection by the NIF and the State Registrar of NGOs. This places Mizrahi feminist NGOs in a predicament. These organisations are comprised of, remarkably, the same factions as those of the Ashkenazi feminists: Socialist Zionists, Post-Zionists and Anti-Zionists. Yet, although they do not agree with each other, any mention in the minutes of their actual discussions about the question of Palestine and international affairs would be interpreted by the NIF as an invasion of Ashkenazi turf, with consequences so dire that they dare not risk it.[78] The NIF or even the Registrar of NGOs could publicise the opinions of the Mizrahi feminists. If the Mizrahi community finds out about the feminists political opinions, it would likely reject their attempts to conduct projects for women in impoverished neighbourhoods. The community is concerned only with the harsh Mizrahi life of trying to get food, employment, housing and education. Therefore, Mizrahi feminists have agreed among themselves that silence is a wiser strategy.

The Mizrahi feminists' ability to challenge the regime is limited. They are threatened by the NIF with budget cuts whenever they include Mizrahi feminist consciousness in their project proposals along with the charity work. They must speak the language of practice in order to help disenfranchised Mizrahi women resolve their daily problems in dealing with the regime's authorities, which, by default, are Ashkenazi. Thus, they have avoided intellectual possibilities for reabsorbing Mizrahim into Arab space. They have not pointed out that the early

Ashkenazi–Zionist eugenic ideologies and practices against Mizrahim – such as forced sterilisation,[79,80] high-dose X-ray medical experiments without the subjects' consent[81] and the removal of Mizrahi babies for Ashkenazi adoption without the parents' consent[82] – connect to the treatment of Palestinians.[83] They have been silent about these Mizrahi/Palestinian similarities. Gingerly, even while acknowledging the solace of sorts that Mizrahi communities have found in the political right, Mizrahi feminists would have had to face their constituencies and explicate the interplay between the Mizrahi erasure of Arab memories, rooted in language and culture,[84] and the almost universal insistence by Israel's Ashkenazi left on a two-state solution.

Two States or One?

A two-state solution, combined with the flat denial of the Palestinians' right of return, is calculated to preserve Israel's Ashkenazi dominance and hegemony. Liberal-socialist and Post-Zionist Left leaders repeatedly say they are willing to swap land for peace – that is, give up Palestinian land that Israel occupied in the 1967 War. Giving up Gaza and the West Bank, however, would release the Israeli regime from its position as an occupier responsible for millions of Palestinian Arabs. Meanwhile, the separation barrier, planned and initiated during the short-lived government of Labour Party Prime Minister Ehud Barak with support from Meretz, and continued by Likud Prime Minister Sharon, is confiscating large areas of Palestinian land and water within the occupied territories, so that these will be inside the proposed new permanent boundaries of a smaller, more compact Israel. The objective is to restructure Israel into a Jewish-majority state, made possible by the presence of the Mizrahi population. If the leftist leadership can get elected on the peace ticket agenda, in spite of the Mizrahi anti-left vote, Israel's Ashkenazi hegemony and its democratic, peace-loving discourse will emerge, enabling Israel's rebirth as a Jewish state.

As this is written, the Israeli regime has nearly finished building the barrier that is to separate the Palestinian Authority of the West Bank and Gaza from pre-1967 Israel and the additional territories it occupied in 1967. Nevertheless, the barrier is an integral part of the 'two states for two peoples' solution.[85] Paradoxically, among pro-Palestine scholars and activists abroad as well as among a handful of post- to anti-Zionist scholars and activists in Israel itself, the idea of a one-state solution is experiencing a resurgence.[86]

While a one-state solution does not seem a viable option for the majority of Israeli Jews, Mizrahim and Ashkenazim alike, it is a powerful agenda because of its in-situ demographics. As it is, Jews of all ethnic varieties are already becoming a minority in the territory between the River Jordan and the Mediterranean coast.[87] The multiple strands analysed in this chapter point to the failure of Israel's feminist peace movement to work within the context of the Middle East demographics, cultures and histories, and the inability of the Mizrahi feminist movement to weave itself into the feminist fabric of the Arab world. From the Mizrahi feminist point of view, the assumption that only two peoples are involved here – Israelis and Palestinians – is not matched by reality. For the Palestinian feminists to continue using this binarism reaffirms the European racial domination and internal colonisation of Mizrahim. Given the demographics of Israel and Palestine, a one-state solution would be an Arab majority solution. If the Mizrahi feminists advocate it, they would alienate the right-wing Mizrahi communities. If they stay silent and merely watch it come to pass, there will probably be little or no space to enact equal rights for the Mizrahi citizens of this one state. In the Mizrahi activists' scenarios, a just escape from this paradox seems unattainable.

Conclusion

Although Ashkenazi feminists are known internationally for their valuable peace activism and human rights work, this chapter argues that from the Mizrahi perspective their critique and activism are limited, if not counterproductive. They have not been able to bring racial, social and cultural justice issues into the perpetual US-brokered political peace process. Further, their choice to pursue international activism, rather than to merge the struggle for a just peace with the struggle against the racism experienced by the Mizrahim, denies them the necessary demographic constituencies to change Israeli voting patterns from right to left. Despite the historical changes reviewed in this chapter, the Ashkenazi–Mizrahi distinction is a racialised formation so resilient it manages to sustain itself through historical challenges such as the upward mobility of Mizrahim after 1967, when West Bank and Gaza Palestinians replaced them as blue-collar labourers, and the mass immigration of Ashkenazim from the former Soviet Union in the early 1990s. Therefore, the Ashkenazi/Mizrahi formation has not remained a dichotomy frozen in time and space.

A window of opportunity for constructive Mizrahi–Palestinian–Arab feminist dialogue opened for a brief period after the 2006 Second Lebanon War. While the Israeli regime had endowed Ashkenazi left-wing kibbutzniks living in northern Israel with well-equipped air-conditioned underground shelters, it had failed to make corresponding provision for the neighbouring Mizrahi agricultural cooperatives and development towns. After the war, the Mizrahim in the north – including several long-term Mizrahi feminist activists – publicly acknowledged, with great bitterness, that they had been sacrificed for Israel's military adventure.

The 2009 Gaza operation carnage was portrayed to the Israeli public as a corrective measure for the defeat by Hezbollah in the summer of 2006. As a result, Barak's popularity rose from 12 to 70 per cent. Nevertheless, as in almost all of the Israeli elections after 1977, the Likud Party emerged victorious with the Mizrahi vote. Any possibility for Mizrahi-Arab feminist dialogue has been slammed shut.

Notes

1. Clare Louise Ducker, *Jews, Arabs, and Arab Jews: The Politics of Identity and Reproduction in Israel*, Research Paper, Institute of Social Studies, The Hague, Netherlands, 2005.

2. Smadar Lavie, 'Blow-ups in the borderzones: Third World Israeli authors' gropings for home', *New Formations*, No. 18, 1992, pp. 84–106.

3. The author provided all translations.

4. In English, Mizrahim are often mistakenly called Sephardim, derived from the Hebrew word, *sfaradim* (Spaniards). The Sephardim are descendants of the Jews who were expelled from Spain in 1492, and they constitute one group of the Mizrahim.

5. Ducker, *Jews, Arabs, and Arab Jews*.

6. Ibid.; Lavie, 'Blow-ups in the borderzones'; Ella Shohat, 'Sephardim in Israel: Zionism from the point of view of its Jewish victims', *Social Text*, 19/20, 1988.

7. Clare Louise Ducker's (2005) findings on Israel's demographics are the most recent and are quite similar to the previous findings mentioned in this article. She wrote her award-winning MA thesis, *Jews, Arabs, and Arab Jews: The Politics of Identity and Reproduction in Israel*, at the Hague Institute of Development. Ducker accounts for the large-scale post-Soviet immigration to Israel in the 1990s, yet she is careful to distinguish between the Asian and European post-Soviet Jewish and non-Jewish immigrants. The Central Asian post-Soviet immigrants to Israel are counted as Mizrahim. The visible and vocal post-Soviet immigrants to Israel, however, are the Ashkenazim. In almost all of the wide array of references substantiating the analysis in this article, the fact that race and class go hand-in-hand in Israeli society (i.e. the fact that the Mizrahi majority of Jews of darker hues is comprised mainly of the lower-middle class and down, while the Ashkenazi minority is largely middle class and up) is never disputed by any scholar of Israeli society in Hebrew. Such information about the accepted axioms of intra-Jewish racism rarely leaks out of Israel.

8. Ducker, ibid.

9. Brenda Danet, *Pulling Strings: Biculturalism in Israeli Bureaucracy* (Albany: State University of New York Press, 1989); Eva Etzioni-Halevi, *The Elite Connection and Democracy in Israel* (Tel Aviv: Sifriyat Poalim, 1993). In Hebrew.

10. While the author borrows the term from Brenda Danet (1989), that analysis of the Israeli 'pulling strings' culture falls within the ideological paradigm of Zionist or post-Zionist academic discourse, which takes for granted the racial formations of the Zionist project and therefore ignores the problem of intra-Jewish racism in Israel.

11. Sami Shalom Chetrit, *The Mizrahi Struggle 1948–2003: Between Oppression and Emancipation* (Tel Aviv: `Am `Oved, 2004). In Hebrew.

12. Ivgenia Bistrov and Arnon Sofer, *The State of Tel Aviv: A Threat on Israel* (Haifa: Department of Geography and Environmental Studies, University of Haifa, 2006).

13. Danny Kaplan, *David, Jonathan, and Other Soldiers: On Identity, Masculinity and Sexuality in IDF's Combat Units* (Tel Aviv: HaKibbutz HaMeuhad, 1999).

14. Hannah Safran, *Don't Want to Be Cute: The Struggle for Women's Voting Rights and the Origins of Israel's New Feminism* (Haifa: Pardes Publishing, 2006). In Hebrew; Barbara Swirski and Marilyn P. Safir (eds), *Calling the Equality Bluff: Women in Israel* (London: Pergamon Press, 1991).

15. While this term might seem archaic or offensive, *gvarot* was one of the standard Hebrew terminological categories dividing Jewish women in British Mandate Palestine after the 1920s. The other two were *po'alot* (workers), whether Ashkenazi or Mizrahi, and *'ozrot* (maids), who, by default, were all Mizrahi. See Smadar Lavie, 'Imperialism and colonialism: Zionism', in Suad Joseph (ed.), *Encyclopedia of Women in Islamic Cultures* (Leiden: Brill, 2007), Vol. 6, pp. 9–15.

16. Vardit Damri-Madar, 'My brothers, the Mizrahim', in *Azut Mezah: Mizrahi Feminism* (Jerusalem: ZAH: Students for Social Justice, 2002). In Hebrew, pp. 54–7; Smadar Lavie, 'Border poets: translating by dialogue', in Ruth Behar and Deborah A. Gordon (eds), *Women Writing Culture* (Berkeley: University of California Press, 1995), pp. 412–27; Smadar Lavie, 'Search the Mizrahi women', in *Women in Judaism: A Multidisciplinary Journal*, 3(1), 2002; Smadar Lavie and Rafi Shubeli, 'On the progress of affirmative action and cultural rights for marginalized communities in Israel', *Anthropology News*, 47(8), 2006, pp. 6–7.

17. The term 'Ashkenazi Academic Junta', or 'the Academic Junta', is commonly used by the non-academic Israeli public and indicates their estrangement from the impenetrable networks of the Israeli academic elite. See Israel Blachman, *Mizrahim in the Faculty of Israeli Research Universities*, Master's Thesis, Tel Aviv University, Tel Aviv, Israel, 2005. In Hebrew; Iris Zarini, *Capital and Networking: Socialization Processes of Mizrahi Women Professors in Israeli Academe*, Seminar Paper Submitted to the Open University, Israel, 2004. In Hebrew.

18. Vicki Shiran, 'The symmetrical self-representation: Mizrahi women's contribution to Israeli feminism', in V. Damari Madar (ed.), `*Azut Metzah* (Jerusalem: ZAH: Students for Social Justice, 2002), pp. 12–19. In Hebrew.

19. Ibid.

20. Pinhas Kapara, *From Yemen to Sha'arayim* (Rehovot: self-published book, 1978). In Hebrew.

21. Vicki Shiran, 'Feminist identity vs. oriental identity', in Swirski and Safir (eds), op. cit.; Vicki Shiran, 'Mizrahi women and other women', *Mizad Sheni*, 5/6, 1996, pp. 24–8. In Hebrew; Shiran (2002), op. cit.; Ella Shohat, 'Mizrahi feminism: politics of gender, race and multi-culturalism', *Mizad Sheni*, 5/6, 1996, pp. 29–33. In Hebrew.

22. Erella Shadmi, 'Yearning for fullness, yearning for power: preliminary notes on the lived reality of Ashkenazi women in Israel', in Yael `Azmon (ed.), *Will You Listen to My Voice? Women's Representations in Israeli Culture* (Tel Aviv: Hakibbutz Hameuhad, 2001), pp. 408–26.

23. Audre Lorde, 'The master's tools will never dismantle the master's house', *KLAF Hazak*, 10, 1993/4 (1979), pp. 16–17. In Hebrew.

24. Nurit Barkai, 'Actually, I was present at the 8th Feminist Conference', *KLAF Hazak*, 7, 1993, pp. 16–18; Yael Ben-Zvi, 'Conversation: the zone between darkness and whiteness', *KLAF Hazak*, 9, 1994, pp. 30–40; Vicki Shiran, 'Settling the bill: the 11th Annual Feminism Conference', *KLAF Hazak*, 15, 1995, pp. 43–9. In Hebrew.

25. Lesbianism is an identity more difficult to endure as a Mizrahi or a Palestinian than as an Ashkenazi because of the Arab patriarchal structure of taboo in both Mizrahi and Palestinian families. Mizrahi feminists noticed that having a lesbian representative doubled the Ashkenazi presence at feminist events. But because in hetero-normative Israel even Ashkenazi lesbians, with their class-race privileges, are still outcasts of sorts, the Mizrahi feminists decided to put pressure on the lesbians to have a proportional

representation within their group, rather than cancel the quarter system of representation (Shiran, ibid.).

26. Edward Said, *The Question of Palestine* (New York: Vintage, 1979).

27. Gila Swirsky, 'Feminist peace activism during the Al-Aqsa Intifada', in Nahla Abdo and Ronit Lentin (eds), *Women and the Politics of Military Confrontation: Palestinian and Israeli Gendered Narratives of Dislocation* (New York, Oxford: Berghahn Books, 2002), pp. 234–9.

28. Sherna Berger-Gluck, *An American Feminist in Palestine: The Intifada Years* (Philadelphia: Temple University Press, 1994); Andrea Dworkin, *Scapegoat: The Jews, Israel, and Women's Liberation* (New York: Free Press, 2002); Lynne Segal, *Making Trouble: Life and Politics* (London: Serpent's Tail, 2007); Philippa Sturm, *The Women Are Marching: The Second Sex and the Palestinian Revolution* (New York: Lawrence Hill Books, 1992); Elise G. Young, *Keepers of the History: Women and the Israeli–Palestinian Conflict* (New York: Teachers College Press, 1992).

29. Shlomo Swirski, *Israel: The Oriental Majority* (London: Zed Books, 1989).

30. Smadar Lavie, 'Transnational English tyranny', in *Anthropology Newsletter*, April 2006, pp. 9–10.

31. Smadar Lavie, 'De/racinated transcendental conversions: witchcraft, oracle and magic among the Israeli feminist left peace camp', *Journal of Holy Land Studies*, 9(1), 2010, pp. 71–80.

32. Sally E. Merry, 'Transnational human rights and local activism: mapping the middle', *American Anthropologist*, 108(1), 2006, pp. 38–51; Sangtin Writers and Richa Nagar, *Playing with Fire: Feminist Thought and Activism Through Seven Lives in India* (Minneapolis: University of Minnesota Press, 2006).

33. Islah Jad, 'Between religion and secularism: Islamist women of Hamas', in Fereshteh Nouraie-Simone (ed.), *On Shifting Ground: Muslim Women in the Global Era* (New York: CUNY Press, 2005), pp. 172–95.

34. Lavie (2006), op. cit.; Rafi Shubeli, 'It is not the occupation that corrupts', *Mizad Sheni*, 14/15, 2006, pp. 38–41.

35. I rely here on the brilliant discussion of this slogan provided by Rafi Shubeli, ibid.

36. Merry (2006), op. cit.; Sangtin and Nagar (2006), op. cit.

37. Yair Ettinger, 'Record demand for funding of Arab-Jewish get-togethers since the October uprising – but their practical side is negligible', *Ha'aretz*, 14 October 2003.

38. SHATIL is the acronym for Sherutei Tmikha v'Ye'utz l'Irgunim (Support and Consulting Services for NGOs, Hebrew).

39. Emile Durkheim, *Division of Labour in Society* (New York: Free Press, 1984).

40. In 2006, Palestinian NGOs based in Israel issued a joint document entitled 'The future vision for Palestinian Arabs in Israel'. The document can be found at www.knesset.gov.il/committees/heb/material/data/H26-12-2006_10-30-37_heb.pdf (accessed on 22 July 2010). It recommends that Israel become a state for all of its citizens, without privileging Jews over non-Jews. Some of the NGOs participating in this document are funded by the New Israel Fund. According to some of the signatories, whom I interviewed and who wish to remain anonymous, they received threats that the NIF would cut their funding and, therefore, their salaries, if they continue to initiate and participate in events that the NIF interprets as doing away with what it defines as Israel's Jewish democratic character.

41. 'Ocean of Tears' is a 1998 television series – researched, directed and produced by Ron Kahlili and Shosh Gabai – about the history of Mizrahi music. It derived its name from a Mizrahi pop tune by the same title. An Ocean of Tears is the ultimate act of *l'hitbakhyen* (see Note 45).

42. In 2002 and from January to March of 2003, Vicki Shiran (founder of Israel's Feminism of Colour) and I worked on the long-term budget of Ahoti (Sistah), a Mizrahi

feminist NGO. On 6 January 2003, as co-authors of the budget proposal, we defended it in the Jerusalem offices of the NIF. The woman in charge of funding Mizrahi NGOs refused to fund our efforts to raise awareness about feminist of colour, saying that it would be too divisive for Israel's feminist movement.

43. Racheli Avidov, *Postmodern Feminism in Israel: Mizrahi Feminism*, Master's Thesis, Haifa University, Haifa, Israel, 2004. In Hebrew.

44. The HILA NGO has been suggested for discussion as a beacon of an anti-Zionist feminist NGO. HILA, a Hebrew acronym for 'Parents for the 'Hood', works to raise Mizrahi and Palestinian parents' consciousness against the tracking of their children to vocational schools. While its founder is indeed an anti-Zionist Mizrahi feminist, my two decades of observations and interviews indicate that she has not dared go into the Mizrahi communities with her anti-Zionist viewpoints because no one will participate in her projects. Nevertheless, in the rush to create and reframe Mizrahi activist history in the form of scholarly discourse, anti-Zionist PhD students are presently sent from Western universities to study this one- to two-person NGO and give it equal weight to the larger Mizrahi NGOs such as the Mizrahi Democratic Rainbow or Ahoti. It is worth mentioning, however, that HILA is well connected to powerful anti-Zionist Mizrahi intellectual exiles outside Israel.

45. The Hebrew slang verb *l'hitbakhyen*, or 'to be a cry-baby', is value judgemental, and is used mainly in the Mizrahi–Ashkenazi context. *Livkot*, a verb derived from the same root – the three Hebrew letters *bet*, *khaf* and *heh* – but in another conjugation, means 'to cry' in standard Hebrew. *L'hitbakhyen* is a reflexive conjugation. Whenever Mizrahim evoke their history of inequality, based on the eugenics ideologies and practices of the Ashkenazi establishment or on this establishment's anti-Arab sentiments (Lavie, 2007, op. cit.), they are accused of being *mitbakhyenim* (cry-babies). The term is usually deployed by those articulating what is known as 'the Israeli discourse of pluralist enlightenment' as part of its 'Israeli (i.e. Ashkenazi) universalism vs. Mizrahi ethnic particularism' analysis of Israeli society (Reuven Abarjel and Smadar Lavie, 'A year into the Lebanon 2 War: NGO-ing Mizrahi–Arab paradoxes, and a one state vision for Palestine/Israel', *Left Curve*, 33, 2009, pp. 29–36). Good examples for the evocation of this verb are in the context of affairs such as the kidnapping of Yemeni babies from the 1930s to the early 1970s, and their subsequent selling for adoption to Ashkenazim (Shoshana Madmoni-Gerber, *Media Constructions of Public Sphere and the Discourse of Conflict: A Case Study of the Kidnapped Yemenite Babies Affair in Israel*, PhD dissertation, University of Massachusetts, Amherst, 2003), or the Ringworm Children Affair (David Belhassan and Asher Hemias, *The Ringworm Children* (DVD), directed by David Belhassen and Asher Hemias, Israel: Casque D'Or Films, 2004), where about 150,000 North African children, without their parents' consent, were irradiated with high-dose X-rays as part of an unauthorised medical experiment.

46. Vicki Shiran, 'Deciphering power, creating a new world', *Panim*, 22, 2002. In Hebrew.

47. Paula Ebron and Anna Tsing, 'In dialogue? Reading across minority discourses', in Ruth Behar and Deborah A. Gordon (eds), *Women Writing Culture* (Berkeley: University of California Press, 1995), pp. 390–411; Lavie (1995), op. cit.

48. Lavie (2006), op. cit.

49. Babylonian Talmud, Bava Metziah 71a.

50. Jad (2005), op. cit.

51. Lavie (2010), op. cit.

52. Because the Ashkenazi Zionist Left keeps moving to the right, the Kadima Party is now considered a leftist party. Kadima has no socialist roots, but, because its leaders promote the idea of a land-for-peace swap with the Palestinians, it is viewed as leftist.

53. Vera Reider, 'The right, for one, does not lie', *Mizad Sheni*, 14/15, 2006, pp. 32–7. In Hebrew; Shubeli (2006), op. cit.

54. Michael Selzer, *The Aryanization of the Jewish State* (New York: Black Star, 1967).

55. Michael Selzer is an Ashkenazi Jew whose parents emigrated from Europe to a part of colonial India that later became Pakistan.

56. Selzer, *The Aryanization of the Jewish State*, p. 94.

57. Ibid.

58. According to a January 2009 interview with Reuven Abarjel, one of the Jerusalem's Black Panthers co-founders, Black Panther Ovadia Harari was executed by Israeli police death squads from short range during a chase in May 1971. Black Panther Daniel Sa'il fled from Israel in 1975. He first went to France, and then Spain. Abarjel states that the rumours were that he broadcasted from the Iraqi radio anti-Israeli propaganda in Arabic and then returned to Spain. He then entered the Israeli consulate there and was never seen again (David Fischer, *They Buried Him Alive* (film), directed by David Fischer, Israeli TV, Channel 1, 1996). Another Panther, Ya`akov (Koko) Der`i, was violently beaten during the 1977 demonstrations. In the 1980s, when many Black Panthers were criminalised for their resistance activity and imprisoned at the Be'er Sheva Jail, they organised a revolt, of which Der`i was a key organiser. For the first time in Israel's history, prison guards shot tear gas and smoke grenades into the small cells of Jewish prisoners. In doing so, they targeted Der`i. Yehezkel Cohen, another Black Panther, was arrested for being a part of a mainly Ashkenazi group, Shining Path, which was blamed by the Israeli regime in collaboration against the state. The most celebrated prisoner from this group was an Ashkenazi kibbutznik, Udi Adiv. He was given special comfortable conditions in the prison. Cohen, the only Mizrahi in the group, was the one most exposed to torture, emerging from his long jail term with untreated broken bones. In addition, he lost his vision almost completely due to prison torture. See www.planetnana.co.il/r_aberjel10/0_a.r_dvar_hapanterim.htm (accessed on 9 January 2009).

59. The inflated prices of real estate in central Israel, where most employment is to be found, rose sharply in the early 1990s due to the large wave of immigration to Israel by former Soviet Union Ashkenazim, which the Labour Party leadership referred to as the white *aliya* (literally 'ascendance', also the term for Jewish immigration to Israel) that was to redeem Israel from Mizrahi-sation. The European former Soviet Jewish immigrants – as opposed to those from Central Asia – were given large governmental subsidies for rent or purchase of housing. They preferred to live in the central cities' slums so that they would be closer to employment and better education for their children than in Israel's hinterlands, where housing is better but schools and unemployment worse (Smadar Lavie, 'Arrival of the new cultured tenants: Soviet immigration to Israel and the displacing of the Sephardi Jews', 14 June 1991, *The Times Literary Supplement*, 4602, p. 11).

60. 'Pisgat Ze'ev' literally translates to 'The Wolf's Peak' – a name that romanticises the imperialist endeavour, given that the neighbourhood overlooks the majestic desert wilderness dropping sharply from the Ramallah mountain range into the below sea-level oasis of Jericho. However, it is also possible that the neighbourhood is named after Ze'ev Jabotinsky, one of the founders of the right-wing Herut Party, precursor to the present-day Likud Party.

61. Abarjel and Lavie (2009), op. cit.

62. Shimson Bichler and Jonathan Nitzan, *From War Profits to Peace Dividends: The Global Political Economy of Israel* (Jerusalem: Carmel, 2001). In Hebrew; Lavie (2010), op. cit.; Navit Zomer, 'Delta Textile closes its textile plant in Khurfeish: two hundred women workers will be laid off', *Yedi'ot Aharonot*, 30 July 2001. In Hebrew.

63. Shubeli (2006), op. cit.

64. Chetrit (2004), op. cit.

65. An eloquent analysis of the division of Tel Aviv into a 'White City' and a 'Black City' is provided by Sharon Rotbard, *White City, Black City* (Tel Aviv: Babel Publishing, 2005).

66. Compare Sarah Lebovitz-Dar, 'Oslo is still far removed from Ofakim', *Ha'aretz Weekly Magazine*, 1 February 2002. In Hebrew; and Nir Bar'am, 'Exposing the face of the left', *Ma'ariv*, 27 June 2003. In Hebrew.

67. Swirsky (2002), op. cit.

68. Yehudit Kirstein Keshet, *Checkpoint Watch: Testimonies from Occupied Palestine* (London: Zed Books, 2006).

69. Swirsky (2002), op. cit., p. 238.

70. Keshet (2006), op. cit., p. 238.

71. Lavie (2010), op. cit.

72. G. Avivi is the nickname of an incisive analyst who frequently writes talkbacks and forum entries in Kedma (Eastbound), the Mizrahi portal: www.kedma.co.il.

73. Ashkenazification is the process by which Mizrahim become second-rate Ashkenazim, as they wish to integrate into mainstream Israeli society but lack the phenotypical and historical privilege of coming from Europe.

74. Yagil HaLevi, *An Army of Others for Israel: Materialistic Militarism in Israel* (Tel Aviv: Yedi'ot Aharonot, 2003); and Yagil HaLevi, 'Materialistic militarism', *Mizad Sheni*, 14/15, 2006, pp. 42–7.

75. Abarjel and Lavie (2009), op. cit.; Amir Rappaport, 'Who gets attacked more? Palestinian terror hurts us all, but some populations are much more exposed to murderous attacks', *Ma'ariv*, 14 September 2003, pp. B2–3. In Hebrew; Erella Shadmi, 'The police: servant of the hegemony', paper delivered at Ashkenazim conference, Beit Berl College, Israel, 3 June 2004.

76. Nurit Peled-Elhanan, Speech on International Women's Day, the European Parliament, *ZNet*, 27 March 2005.

77. A good example of a possible future grass-roots Ashkenazi–Mizrahi–Palestinian devoid of Zionist funding can be found at www2.jewishsolidarity.info/en/petition (accessed on 18 March 2007).

78. See Note 13.

79. Yali Hashash-Daniel, *Sex/Gender, Class and Ethnicity in the Policy of Birth in Israel 1962–1974*, Master's Thesis, Haifa University, Haifa, Israel, 2004. In Hebrew; Sahlav Stoler-Liss, *Raising a Zionist Baby: An Anthropological Analysis of Parents' Guidebooks*, Master's Thesis, Tel Aviv University, Tel Aviv, Israel, 1988. In Hebrew; Sahlav Stoler-Liss, 'Mothers birth the nation: the social construction of Zionist motherhood in wartime in Israeli parents' manuals', *Nashim*, 6 (Fall 2003), pp. 104–18.

80. It is interesting to note that Sahlav Stoler-Liss (1998) meticulously documents Ashkenazi eugenics in her MA thesis written in Hebrew for Tel Aviv University, yet, when publishing her findings in English, she uses the less potent and more accepted tropology of building the new Jew's body.

81. David Belhassan and Asher Hemias, *The Ringworm Children* (DVD), directed by David Belhassen and Asher Hemias, Israel: Casque D'or Films, 2004.

82. Rafi Shubeli, 'The Yemeni children affair: an oriental imagination?', in Yossi Yonah, Yonit Na'aman and David Machlev (eds), *A Rainbow of Opinions: A Mizrahi Agenda for Israel* (Jerusalem: November Books, 2007), pp. 174–83; Shoshi Zeid, *The Child is Gone: The Yemeni Children Affair* (Jerusalem: Geffen Publishers, 2001). In Hebrew.

83. Abarjel and Lavie (2009), op. cit.; Lavie (2007), op. cit.

84. Lavie (1992), op. cit.; Ella Shohat, *Taboo Memories: Toward a Multicultural Thought* (Tel Aviv: Bimat Kedem, 2001). In Hebrew.

85. Abarjel and Lavie (2009), op. cit.

86. Ali Abunimah, *One Country: A Bold Proposal to End the Israeli–Palestinian Impasse* (New York: Metropolitan Books, 2006); Meron Benvenisti, 'How Israel became a bi-national state', *Ha'aretz*, 23 January 2010. In Hebrew; Yehuda Shenhav, *In the Trap of the Green Line* (Tel Aviv: `Am `Oved, 2010); Virginia Tilley, *The One-State Solution: A Breakthrough for Peace in the Israeli–Palestinian Deadlock* (Ann Arbor: Michigan University Press, 2005).

87. Abunimah, ibid.

PART IV

Mobilising for a Solution

CHAPTER 14

Mobilising Palestinians in Support of One State

George E. Bisharat

Introduction

The challenges of mobilising Palestinians in support of the one-state solution have rarely been systematically explored by supporters of this solution.[1] Proponents of the single state have, instead, focused primarily on how to overcome anticipated resistance from Israeli Jews. Considering the extent of Israeli Jewish opposition to the one-state idea, this focus is understandable.[2] Advocates of a one-state solution ('one-staters') may also have tacitly assumed that, as the advantages to Palestinians of their cherished goal are so obvious, Palestinian support for it need not be cultivated, but rather would grow naturally.[3] It is, however, a mistake to assume Palestinian support for the single-state concept, or to underestimate the breadth and, in some cases, the intensity of Palestinian opposition to it. The goal of this chapter, therefore, is to identify both the appeal of the one-state ideal to Palestinians, and the questions and concerns they may have over it, and to sketch how the appeals may be strengthened, and how the questions and concerns may be most effectively addressed.

This is a complex task. In fact, the roughly 11 million Palestinians today are geographically dispersed, deeply fragmented, and facing extremely diverse experiences and challenges that are, at least potentially, generative of different interests and outlooks.[4] Unfortunately, we know little about the current level of Palestinian support for the one-state solution; public opinion is difficult to track when the 'public' in question is strewn across state boundaries and, in some cases, lives in highly vulnerable political circumstances, where frank expression is not always prudent. There is some polling evidence from the occupied territories suggesting that support there for one state fluctuates between 25 and 33 per cent.[5] Evidence is more elusive regarding the perspectives of Palestinian citizens of Israel[6] and is virtually non-existent regarding the views of Palestinian refugees living outside of the borders of historic Palestine.[7]

It seems probable, however, that no single message or appeal will be effective for all categories of Palestinians and that – on the contrary – a 'one-size-fits-all' approach is likely to fail. Of course, a completely systematic approach to the challenge of mobilisation would assess Palestinians in all their diverse conditions and perspectives, and detail what appeals and organising approaches would likely be most effective for each sub-group. Such an effort is beyond the scope of this brief study, and thus there is a need to establish some priorities.

First, if mobilisation might be conceptualised as entailing phases of both *persuasion* – that is, convincing a group of the need to act in a particular direction – and *organisation* – that is, providing them with a concrete framework and instrumental means of moving forward – then the emphasis here will be on the phase of *persuasion*.[8] Second, this chapter will focus more on the *content* of persuasive messages than on the *means* of communicating with Palestinians in their various distinct living situations.[9] Third, while there are many categories and sub-groups of Palestinians – defined by class, gender, religion or sect, occupation, political affiliation and others – and, as noted, ideally one would systematically study all of them, and consider potentially distinct appeals for each one, this chapter will sample, albeit somewhat inconsistently, only from a few key categories. After addressing one reservation concerning the single state that may obtain to some extent among all groups of Palestinians – namely, the perception that it is 'utopian' and 'idealistic' but unattainable – it will be discussed how the one-state model may be presented most effectively to the three major segments of the Palestinian people (citizens of the state of Israel, residents of the Occupied Palestinian Territories and Palestinians living in exile outside of historical Palestine). The Palestinian political class is pivotal, so we will examine how to make headway on the one-state ideal with that group. Palestinian nationalists, loosely defined, are another important category that can reasonably be expected to have reservations about one state. Finally, Islamists, a powerful and ascendant force in Palestinian politics, may not resist the notion of a single state as such, but their vision of the character of that state may be considerably different than that promoted by most supporters of a single state. Thus, how to engage their support for a democratic and *egalitarian* one-state solution seems a necessary part of this discussion. Selections of these particular categories will be further justified as they are each discussed.

Persuasion entails identifying and building on support among Palestinians for a single state, but it also, and perhaps even more importantly, involves understanding and effectively addressing Palestinians' possible reservations concerning this goal. The discussion over the one-state solution, moreover, is not taking place in a vacuum. Rather, it is occurring in the context of alternatives, and unquestionably the other main alternative disposition is the two-state solution.[10] So the challenge, in some respects, is simultaneously one of persuasion in favour of the one-state model and dissuasion against the two-state model.

One final note is necessary before embarking on the substance of this discussion, and that concerns the *tone* in which proponents of one state attempt to persuade other Palestinians to support this goal. That tone, it seems, must be respectful, judicious and tolerant of differences if proponents seriously hope to gain substantial support. We must be able to acknowledge that there are bona fide concerns about the one-state solution – particularly regarding its attainability – and reasons to support a two-state solution that could lead Palestinians of good faith to conclusions different from our own. It would be completely counterproductive to impugn the motives or ridicule the logic of other dedicated and committed Palestinians when the realities are so complex, the prospects so speculative and the future ahead so unclear. One-state supporters situated outside of historical Palestine and possibly ensconced comfortably in the West are particularly vulnerable to delegitimation on the ground that we would not live the indefinite, but likely lengthy, suffering to which we would seem to be condemning other Palestinians as the inevitably long struggle for the single state unfolds. A healthy dose of humility and a collegial debate, on the other hand, afford better prospects of convincing sceptical minds.

Escaping the 'Utopian' Tag

Perhaps the single greatest challenge that proponents of a one-state confront in persuading Palestinians of its validity is the perception that, despite its clear moral or political advantages, the single state is 'utopian' or 'unrealistic', while the two-state solution, although imperfect and requiring compromises of principles, is 'realistic' and attainable.[11] This is a perception likely held by many Palestinians, wherever they are situated, and thus we will address it first. If, indeed, this perception were correct, proponents of one state would arguably be leading Palestinians (and Israelis, although the preoccupation of this study is Palestinians) into a dangerous diversion, which would sap strength from the effort to achieve two states and consign Palestinians to years, if not decades, of continued acute suffering.[12] Confronted with a choice between the tangible and relatively immediate relief that a two-state solution would seemingly provide the Palestinians, especially those suffering acutely under occupation in the West Bank and the Gaza Strip, and the distant and speculative goal of one state, many Palestinians – even those whose rights and interests might not be vindicated by the establishment of a Palestinian state – would seize the opportunity to alleviate the suffering of fellow Palestinians. This would be an entirely reasonable and compassionate response – and we bear the burden of showing why it is, nonetheless, mistaken.

There is no ready or definitive answer to this challenge. But two general, and perhaps slightly contradictory, responses seem due. The first involves accepting the propriety of subjecting political goals to a test of realism and working quickly and assiduously to meet that test. It is, perhaps, understandable for the time being that supporters of one state are still negotiating first principles, but very soon we must begin to propound a credible political programme for the future. This programme must be as definitive as possible with respect both to the end goal and, even more importantly, the path to achieve it. At the same time, supporters of one state must insist that the same standard of realism to which they have been subject also apply to the two-state solution.

The second response would involve re-framing the discourse surrounding solutions away from the language of 'possibility' and 'impossibility' altogether – language that some of us have been accustomed to using. We have argued, for example, that the two-state solution is 'no longer possible' or that the 'window of opportunity' for its realisation has now closed.[13] Currently it seems that this approach is simply not persuasive, and may indeed be self-defeating. For whatever the obstacles to the two-state solution are – at least one that a majority of Palestinians might be willing to accept – the obstacles to the one-state solution might seem to many Palestinians to be considerably greater, and little is accomplished by proving them both to be impossible.[14]

It seems more forthright to acknowledge that nothing – strictly speaking – is impossible, and the question instead is one of probabilities: what are the odds that a conjuncture of political forces could arise in the reasonably foreseeable future that would produce either a one- or two-state outcome? And how, by our own agency, can we 'make' or tip these odds in the direction we desire? Viewed in this way, the answer seems relatively clear: considering the vast military, diplomatic and economic power imbalance between Israel and the Palestinians at this time, any agreement between them will reflect this inherent underlying imbalance, and thus will be unjust to the Palestinian people. Imbalances, of course, can be offset by external actors. Yet at this point, it seems unlikely that the rhetorical shifts by the USA under President Obama presage a sufficiently significant re-alignment of real American power to offset the imbalance between Israel and the Palestinians in any serious way. The bitter truth, therefore, is that no solution that is likely to be accepted by a majority of Palestinians is at all imminent.

This does not mean, however, that no agreement is currently possible, but simply that its terms would indubitably involve surrender of substantial Palestinian rights. Current Israeli Prime Minister Benjamin Netanyahu, in his

May 2011 address to the US Congress, gave some inkling as to what sacrifices might be involved: demilitarisation, Israeli control of Palestinian airspace, recognition of Israel as the 'state of the Jewish people', abandonment of Palestinian refugees' right of return, Israeli annexation of all of Jerusalem, a permanent Israeli military presence in the Jordan Valley and more. To be sure, this Israeli list of demands may not be met in full, but certain of its elements would surely be incorporated into any agreement negotiated in the near term.

Hence what really seems to be at stake here is not which solution can be realised in the near future – because none is likely – but rather, what will be the platform for the next stage of the struggle for justice and peace in Israel/Palestine? Does a 'state', no matter how diminished, provide a haven for Palestinians, a place to affirm their national identity and enable them to consolidate gains while preparing for new forms of struggle? Or will the price tag, in terms of the formal and permanent surrender of core Palestinian rights, be too great? Given the current constellation of power, the latter seems the more likely outcome.

Despite this bleak outlook, we do have recourse, and that is to rely on the moral power of the one-state idea. We must be candid, however, that the struggle for justice and equal rights for all of the residents of Israel/Palestine in one state is still distant – perhaps even decades in the making. A single state offers the most promising framework for maximising the rights of the greatest number of Palestinian Arabs and Israeli Jews, as will become evident (at least with respect to Palestinians) in the next section.

One State and the Three Major Segments of the Palestinian People

In 1948, the Palestinian people were cleaved into two broad segments: those who managed to remain in their homes and homeland, eventually to become citizens of the state of Israel; and those who were less fortunate and driven by force or by fear into exile into the surrounding Arab countries, or into the remnants of Palestine which fell either under the control of Egypt (the Gaza Strip) or Jordan (the West Bank, including East Jerusalem).[15] In 1967, when Israel seized the West Bank and the Gaza Strip, yet a third category of Palestinians was created: those who still resided within the borders of historic Palestine, but as residents of territories militarily occupied and ruled by Israel and lacking any political rights. Thus it is possible to speak today – very generally – of the three major segments of the Palestinian people: citizens of the state of Israel, who today number approximately 1.2 million;[16] those 3.88 million or so who live under Israeli military occupation in the West Bank and the Gaza Strip;[17] and the other 5.2 million who live in exile outside of the borders of historic Palestine.[18] Needless to say, this is a somewhat crude breakdown, and there are substantial differences in the circumstances faced by Palestinians within each of these segments.[19] One implication of the widely varying circumstances of these three major segments of the Palestinian people is that the one- and two-state solutions have differential impacts on Palestinians depending on where they live and what challenges they face in life. Of course, not all Palestinians will simply support the solution that most immediately supports their narrow interests or which does the most to ameliorate the condition of the segment of which they are part. Such factors as political affiliation or ideology, or even basic sympathy for the plight of Palestinians facing more dire circumstances, might well trump self-interest in the judgement of many Palestinians considering the relative advantages of the one- and two-state solutions. Nonetheless, it is likely that where Palestinians are situated will greatly impact on how they view the future, and thus we must examine how these different groups stand to gain or lose through the two alternative solutions, for which purpose we examine the implications for Palestinian citizens of Israel, refugees and residents of the Occupied Palestinian Territories.

One State and the Palestinian Citizens of Israel

It should be clear that among the three segments of the Palestinian people, those 1.2 million who live under a regime of formal and informal discrimination as citizens of Israel have the least to gain by the two-state solution and the most to gain by the one-state solution.[20] Whether or not Israel's status as the state of the Jewish people is enshrined in an official agreement, the very purpose of the two-state solution would be to preserve Israel as a majority Jewish state (while also providing space for national expression for Palestinians elsewhere). The relaxation of tensions that would presumably follow such an agreement might permit marginal improvement of the position of Palestinian citizens of Israel, but this is by no means certain.[21] As Israeli law professor Ruth Gavison, speaking on the future of Palestinian–Jewish relations, stated in 2004:

> One of the fraudulent things about the Israeli–Jewish Left is the statement that yes, there will be equality. There will not be equality. There will be dispute. It will be better than [elsewhere] in the region; it will be better than in many other places; there will be a process; but there will not be equality...[22]

There are other worrying indications that the status of the Palestinian citizens of Israel could actually deteriorate in the aftermath of a two-state solution, particularly if accompanied by a substantial re-concentration of Israeli settlers from the West Bank into Israel. A glimpse of what could be in store was had, perhaps, in the October 2008 'pogroms' (a term employed at the time by the

Israeli press and some political leaders) against Palestinian residents of Akka, apparently in which former residents of Israeli settlements in the Gaza Strip – evacuated in 2005 – played a leading role.[23]

Yet it is not only the prospect of increased informal racism at the hands of individual Israeli Jewish citizens that is of concern. The last two Israeli foreign ministers, Tzipi Livni and Avigdor Lieberman, have either hinted at or openly advocated alternative means of disenfranchising Palestinian citizens of Israel in connection with a peace agreement. Livni, while campaigning for the office of Prime Minister in December 2008, offered that she would say to Palestinian citizens of the state: 'Your national solution is somewhere else.' At the very least, the statement seemed to imply that Palestinian citizens who did not accept the Jewish character of the state should leave for the Palestinian state or, perhaps, suffer the attenuation of voting rights within Israel in favour of a status akin to permanent residency. Current Israeli Foreign Minister Avigdor Lieberman has been much more frank, advocating land swaps with the Palestinian state that would put large Palestinian communities adjacent to the Green Line, such as Umm al-Fahm, under the jurisdiction of the Palestinian state, effectively denationalising their residents.[24]

In sum, then, the two-state solution would permanently segregate the Palestinian citizens of Israel from their fellow Palestinians and render their struggle for equality a purely internal Israeli matter, with uncertain but troubling prospects. In contrast, a single state founded on the fundamental principle of equal rights would end formal, institutionalised discrimination against Palestinian citizens. These Palestinians would no longer be a politically marginalised minority, but rather members of a unitary state that treats all its citizens as equals, and thus is able to defend itself against other forms of discriminatory governmental practices. Thus Palestinians hitherto separated would enjoy the opportunity to commingle, intermarry and engage economically without restriction with other Palestinians that have been spatially separated. Furthermore, because the single state would permit for the genuine realisation of the right of Palestinian refugees to return, Palestinian citizens of Israel could also look forward to the reconstitution of their families, torn asunder and separated for more than 60 years.

In terms of interests, therefore, the appeal of the one-state solution to Palestinian citizens should be very strong. Yet headway may nonetheless be difficult. Perhaps the greatest problem in establishing and broadening support for one state among Palestinian citizens of Israel may be overcoming the combination of despair and fear that they might logically be expected to feel. The despair would reflect Palestinian citizens' acute and intimate awareness of the solidity of the Israeli state, replete with its Zionist features, and their understanding of the strong commitment of Jewish Israelis to keeping their advantages in the current system intact. The fear would be a predictable response to Israeli repression, exemplified in the minds of many in the prosecutions and eventual harassment into exile of Palestinian Member of the Knesset Azmi Bishara – repression that may intensify if Palestinians begin to take effective actions in support of one state and to accrue momentum towards that goal. If so, more than any 'message' as such, what may be needed to spark greater open support of one state among Palestinian citizens of Israel would be an organisational effort and campaign to provide protection for those daring enough to speak out. To reiterate, however: not all Palestinian citizens of Israel can be expected to support one state simply because it promotes their interests more so than two states – ideology, political affiliation and other factors may militate otherwise.[25] We are speaking of tendencies and amenability to the one-state message only.

One State and Palestinians in Exile

Refugees living outside the borders of historic Palestine constitute another segment of the Palestinian people who, logically speaking, should be sympathetic to the call for one state. The reason is straightforward: the two-state solution is self-evidently unable to accommodate the Palestinian right of return. Even in the most generous versions of the two-state solution, such as the Geneva Initiative (an informal plan that Israel has never accepted), refugee return to their actual homes and villages within Israel would be token.[26] While return to the Palestinian state would be permitted, presumably without restriction, in practice – even assuming complete Israeli withdrawal from the West Bank – the land base and economy of the state would be insufficient to absorb large numbers of Palestinian refugees from exile. The Gaza Strip in particular is, at 4,010 persons per square kilometre, one of the most densely populated areas in the world today, and is in acute need of population relief.[27] The West Bank, less densely populated, nonetheless has limited arable land, and even fewer water resources, and thus it too could accept only limited numbers of refugees. As a matter of practice, then, relatively few Palestinians would be likely to immigrate to the new Palestinian state, in view of limited economic and life opportunities, and their 'right' to return would *effectively* have been nullified.

In any case, while 'return' to a Palestinian state in the West Bank and Gaza Strip would redress one dimension of the refugees' plight – namely, their statelessness – in legal and moral terms, this fails to address the real core of refugee rights, which involve the right to return to their *actual* homes and receive compensation for their losses, or (where that is not possible) to nearby alternative housing.[28] The single-state solution, in contrast, would open up much greater space for the actual realisation of the right of return, as refugees would be able to settle anywhere within the new state.

One State and the Residents of the Occupied Territories

There is little question that proponents of a single-state solution face a tough challenge in winning support among residents of the West Bank and Gaza Strip. These Palestinians have faced more than four decades of Israeli military occupation that has only grown more violent, brutal and repressive over time. The litany of abuse is quite familiar: thousands of Palestinians have been killed, and many more wounded, in Israel's periodic eruptions of violence; approximately 10,000 Palestinian political prisoners, including some minors, languish in Israeli jails, many held without trial; countless Palestinian detainees have been subjected to torture; thousands of homes have been demolished or sealed; Israel's siege of the Gaza Strip and its policy of closures and restriction of movement in the West Bank have disrupted economic and social life, stunted Palestinian children and reduced many Palestinians to penury.

Manifestly, these Palestinians acutely need and deserve relief from such dire circumstances, and were a credible opportunity to achieve it honestly presented, it would be very hard to deny it to them. Moreover, if residents of the West Bank and Gaza Strip wished never to lay eyes on Israelis, their persecutors, that would be an understandable human reaction to their suffering.[29] And indeed, the two-state solution, even in a diminished (and diminutive) version, is likely to afford them at least some measure of relief, although precisely how much would depend greatly on the actual terms of such a settlement.

Given the circumstances, it is striking that support for one state – as previously noted to range from 25 to 33 per cent, according to evidence from polls – is as high as it apparently is in the Occupied Palestinian Territories. Several responses by advocates of one state can bolster this support, in my view. First, an appeal to national unity and solidarity with other Palestinians must be made. The point must be stressed that any relief for residents of the occupied territories will, as we have seen, come at the expense of the permanent surrender of rights of Palestinian citizens of Israel and Palestinian refugees. At the same time, proponents of one state must devise a strategy that encompasses short-term relief for the residents of the occupied territories – strongly implying a moratorium on the exercise of the right to resist occupation violently and a disciplined resort to pure non-violence. The strategy must be capable of inspiring hope in West Bank and Gaza Palestinians that their sacrifices are not in vain, and instead are for the ultimate good of their people. They should be honoured and celebrated for their courage and *sumud* – or 'steadfastness'.

The Palestinian Political Class

The Palestinian political class – by which is meant officials of the PLO, or of the PA, and their close administrative and other associates, political party officers, union and professional association leaders and the like, mostly located today in the occupied territories – constitute a pivotal audience for proponents of a single-state solution. It is almost certain that some members of this group already support this solution.[30] However, beyond the occasional threat issued by high PA officials that Palestinians would begin to demand one state if a two-state solution were not in the offing, this group has offered no public support for the one-state ideal.[31]

The substantive points to be raised in attempting to win greater support for one state among Palestinian professional politicians may not be different than they would be for attempting to win the support of any other Palestinians. The reason for singling them out here, however, is because of their commanding role vis-à-vis vital Palestinian resources, tangible and intangible. These include the PLO embassies throughout the world, the permanent mission to the United Nations and the legally recognised right to speak on behalf of the Palestinian people before the international community. Such are key institutions, especially in the way they set standards for what constitutes acceptable support for Palestinians worldwide. More than once the phrase 'we cannot be more Palestinian than the Palestinians' has been voiced to justify a state's refusal to take a bold position on Palestinian rights. Were Palestinian officialdom's as yet unbending commitment to the two-state solution shifted, it might well release a significant reserve of international solidarity for the one-state solution that has been impeded from expression up to this point.

Speaking to Palestinian Nationalists

As we have noted repeatedly, the way Palestinians are likely to respond to appeals for one state is a function of multiple factors. One of them, surely, is political outlook or ideology – the set of ideas, values, ethics and beliefs that individuals employ in thinking about public life. As in most populations of similar scale, Palestinians hold highly diverse political perspectives and worldviews. Prudence would suggest that supporters of the one-state solution should not seek to overturn these worldviews in favour of a unitary ethical justification for this solution, but rather that they probe the various outlooks and traditions of thought held by Palestinians for elements that are compatible with or complementary to the one-state ideal.

Many Palestinians, wherever they are situated, and whether or not they are affiliated with a specific political party, are 'nationalists' in the sense they wish

their people to have a flag, their own passports, public holidays, national muse-
ums and an educational system that teaches their national narrative – in short,
to have their *identity* as a people affirmed and expressed within the framework
of an independent nation state. Others may further believe that after 60 years
of fragmentation, dispersal and repression, Palestinians need the protection of
an independent state to reconstitute themselves as a people – to rebuild their
economy, educational system, infrastructure and so forth, so as to be able to
participate in the global community from a position of greater strength.

Many Palestinian nationalists, loosely defined, might fear that in a single state
their people would be denied the opportunity for national self-expression, or at
least would be forced to share the 'public sphere' with Israeli Jews. Meanwhile,
they might also be apprehensive that Palestinians from the occupied territories
and from exile would be assimilated into a single-state society at approximately
the level of Israel's current Palestinian citizens – in short, as the new state's
permanent underclass. These are estimable concerns, and supporters of a single
state must, in some way, have a response.[32]

There is no escaping the fact that in a single state, Palestinians would not
enjoy exclusive control of the public domain, and instead would be obliged to
share it with Israeli Jews. On the other hand, this sacrifice would be made recip-
rocally by Israeli Jews. Moreover, for both peoples, lack of exclusive control
of the public and political domain is not tantamount to the negation of their
respective national identities. After all, constitutional arrangements are possible
that could enshrine and concretise the identities and interests of both peoples.
In short, 'half a loaf', while less preferable than a whole, is better than nothing.

Perhaps a new and more inspiring vision of Palestinian nationalism can be
engendered here as well. There was a time, in the not-too-distant past, when to
say that one was 'Palestinian' implied nothing about one's ethnic or religious
identity. Cannot pride be fostered in a re-emergence of that older, more ecumenical notion of 'Palestinian-ness'? Isn't the newer ethnically-based understanding
of what it means to be 'Palestinian' a distortion or deviation from tradition that
has been forced on Palestinians by their confrontation with Zionism? And have
not the Palestinians been diminished by being forced to assert just one facet of
themselves as their exclusive identity, and one that is, in some senses, the mirror
image of Zionism itself? Would it not venerate our deepest traditions of tolerance and hospitality to return to that broader understanding of who we are?

As to concerns that Palestinians would be submerged in the new unitary state
as a permanent underclass, these are not totally unjustified, but may be somewhat exaggerated. In the first place, the current position of Palestinian citizens
in Israel is not an accurate predictor of the future of other Palestinians in a very
different kind of single state. Their condition, on the contrary, is in significant
part the consequence of official Israeli discrimination and political vulnerability

as a minority of 20 per cent – factors that would be negated in the type of single state which is proposed here. In addition, Palestinians, particularly in the Diaspora, have invested heavily in education, and would enter the economy and bureaucracy of this unitary state with considerable entrepreneurial and other skills and experience.[33] In addition, with their linguistic, cultural, familial, social and economic ties to surrounding Arab countries, Palestinians returning to this new state would bring substantial assets and economic opportunities. This is not to say that the single state would immediately be a paradise of social and economic justice and equality. But Palestinians may not be as severely disadvantaged as imagined, and some would no doubt prosper.

Speaking to Palestinian Islamists

Palestinian Islamists have won their current prominent position in Palestinian politics by steadfast opposition to Zionism. Whatever one may think of their ideology (some aspects of which are clearly adverse to progressive values) and occasionally their military tactics (some of which violate international laws of war), Palestinian Islamists have demonstrated tremendous courage and willingness to sacrifice to defend Palestinian interests and advance their cause. They will not be disappearing from the political scene any time soon, and thus supporters of the one state must attempt to engage them.

Some Palestinian Islamists appear to support the idea of one state in Palestine in principle – but their vision of such a state differs from either the binational or secular democratic models supported by most proponents of the single-state ideal. The reference in the charter of Hamas to the land of Palestine as a 'waqf' – that is, inalienable – and to be held in trust for Muslims in perpetuity seems irreconcilable with any notion of sharing the land equitably between Palestinian Arabs and Israeli Jews.[34] And the notion in the same document that non-Muslim religious communities can only be safe and prosper in Palestine 'in the shadow of Islam' seems, on the face of it, to be a prescription for Muslim political supremacy.[35]

But these ideas, articulated in 1988, are perhaps not as fixed as they might first appear. Hamas has, over time, demonstrated strong pragmatic tendencies, evidenced in the organisation's support for a long-term hudnah or 'truce' in return for an end to Israeli military occupation of the West Bank and Gaza Strip. This stance, which is tantamount to an acceptance of two states, has been repeatedly articulated by Hamas political leaders.[36] It is hard to believe that Islamists would be less open to a one-state solution that, while imperfect from a doctrinaire perspective, responds far more comprehensively to Palestinian rights and interests than a mere end of Israeli occupation. It seems far more likely that

Hamas would respond as Hezbollah has done in Lebanon – that is, to enter the political mainstream as a rule-abiding party. When the will exists, moreover, there is ample scope within the Islamic legal tradition (*fiqh*) to justify the shifts that Hamas and other Palestinian Islamists might deem helpful and necessary on political grounds. For example, some contemporary scholars of the Islamic *fiqh* have argued that classical doctrines mandating exclusion of non-Muslims from positions of rule were, in fact, historically contingent – making room for the argument that the conditions justifying the doctrines have now expired, and there is no contemporary justification for them.[37] These positions cannot be foisted on Palestinian Islamists by outsiders, but respectful dialogue might help them locate the sources they need when the time is deemed appropriate by Islamists themselves.

Conclusion

The task of mobilising Palestinians in support of one state is substantial. Much attention has been properly focused on the greater challenge of persuading Israeli Jews to accept the one-state ideal; it would be a grave mistake to neglect the need to cultivate support among Palestinians. This chapter has, hopefully, identified some of the ways in which Palestinians can be approached and their support won. In the end, we should not underestimate the power of a moral idea to inspire and transform both peoples. As previously noted, there was a day when to say that one was 'Palestinian' implied nothing as to one's faith or ethnicity. We need to return to that day.

Notes

1. For example, two leading and otherwise excellent monographs on the issue – Ali Abunimah, *One Country* (New York: Metropolitan Books, 2006); and Virginia Tilley, *The One State Solution* (Ann Arbor: University of Michigan Press, 2005) – devote relatively little discussion to the question of Palestinian support for a single state, and still less to possible Palestinian objections to it. Abunimah treats Palestinian views on one state in ten pages of a chapter entitled 'Israelis and Palestinians thinking the unthinkable'. Tilley includes an appendix on Palestinian public opinion on one state, but her discussion of Palestinian perspectives is sprinkled sporadically throughout the text, and nowhere deals systematically with Palestinian qualms. Similarly, Joel Kovel's *Overcoming Zionism: Creating a Single Democratic State in Israel / Palestine* (Ann Arbor, MI: University of Michigan Press, 2007), which also advocates the one-state solution, has virtually no discussion of Palestinian reservations. Ghada Karmi's *Married to Another Man* (London: Pluto Press, 2007), while supporting a single state, includes a brief but forthright discussion of Palestinian objections to the single-state solution, including vehement opposition from some prominent Palestinian intellectuals, including the late Ibrahim Abu-Lughod.

2. According to a poll reported in *Ha'aretz* on 20 November 2003, 78 per cent of Israeli Jews oppose a single binational state. See Gary Sussman, 'The challenge to the two-state solution', *Middle East Reports*, 231, Summer 2004. Available at www.merip. org/mer/mer231/sussman.html.

3. This author has argued elsewhere that a single state provides the most promising framework for vindicating the fullest range of rights for the broadest numbers of both Palestinian Arabs and Israeli Jews. See George Bisharat, 'Maximizing rights: the one state solution to the Palestinian-Israeli conflict', *The Global Jurist*, 8(2), 2008.

4. The Palestinian Central Bureau of Statistics estimated the worldwide population of Palestinians at 10.6 million as of the end of 2008 in a special report issued on the 61st Anniversary of the Nakba of 1948. The breakdown of this population will be reviewed below. See Badil, Palestinian Central Bureau of Statistics, Special Report on the 61st Anniversary of the Nakba, 14 May 2009. Available at www.badil.org/Publications/ Press/2009/press506-09.htm.

5. Abunimah, op. cit., p. 165. Polls have been conducted regularly in the occupied territories by the Jerusalem Media and Communications Center, and can be viewed at the group's website.

6. Haifa University sociologist Sammy Smooha has conducted polling among both Israeli Jews and Palestinian citizens of Israel over a period of years, the results of which indicate strong support among Palestinian citizens for the two-state solution. For example, in 2007, 83.8 per cent of 'Arabs' favoured 'two states for two peoples'; Sammy Smooha, 'The position on two-state solution of the Palestinian–Arab and Jewish citizens in Israel', unpublished paper abstract, available at www.yorku.ca/ipconf/speakers. html#Smooha. Four 'vision documents' issued by leaders of the Palestinian community in Israel in 2007 also at least nominally accepted the two-state framework. On the other hand, these same documents called unequivocally for implementation of the right of return and full equality for Palestinian citizens of Israel – demands that are inconsistent with the concept of 'two states for two peoples', or with the maintenance of Israel as a Jewish majority and Jewish-dominated state. Polling research conducted by the Haifa-based Palestinian research institute Mada al-Carmel in 2005 affirmed the strong support for the right of return among Palestinian citizens of Israel; 70.3 per cent of those surveyed supported either granting Palestinian refugees the right of return to Israel proper or offering them the choice between return and compensation; Nadim Rouhana and Areej Sabbagh-Khoury, *The Right of Return and the Refugee Issue*, unpublished manuscript, on file with the author. In short, Palestinian citizens of Israel appear to support the two-state solution and yet also take positions that seem at odds with that end.

7. The only systematic recent effort to elicit the viewpoints of Palestinian refugees was the Civitas project, yet its focus was on issues of governance and representation, not final disposition options. See www.nuffield.ox.ac.uk/Projects/Civitas/index_english. aspx. There is, of course, demonstrable interest in the one-state idea among Palestinian intellectuals and activists in the Diaspora evidenced in articles, conferences, groups and declarations.

8. This is not because organisation is any less important than persuasion, but simply due to the fact that other contributors to this volume write on organisation. My choice to emphasise persuasion is intended to avoid overlap and promote complementarity.

9. In fact, the problem of how to communicate with Palestinians is substantial – again, due to their geographical dispersion, and the absence of any effective deliberative body within which matters of national interest may be raised and debated. The Palestine National Council, which once served this function (albeit never perfectly), has not met since 1997.

10. Israeli anthropologist and founder of the Israeli Committee Against Home Demolitions, Jeff Halper, has suggested a 'two-phase' solution, ultimately leading to a

Middle Eastern regional confederation joining Israel and the surrounding Arab states, but this is one of very few alternatives to either the one- or two-state solutions that has been publicly propounded; Jeff Halper, 'Paralysis over Palestine: questions of strategy', *Journal of Palestine Studies*, 34(2), January 2005, pp. 55–69.

11. For a good example of this, see Uri Avnery, 'The binational state: the wolf shall dwell with the lamb', *Counterpunch*. Available at www.counterpunch.org/avnery07152003. html.

12. One of the best articulations of this concern is Salim Tamari, 'The dubious lure of binationalism', *Journal of Palestine Studies* 30(1), October 2000.

13. This is a fairly common formulation among supporters of one state. For example, Virginia Tilley begins her study by saying: 'The Jewish settlements, always recognised by the international community as an "obstacle to peace", have accomplished their purpose: the territorial basis for a viable Palestinian state no longer exists. The premise for all present diplomacy – the two-state solution – has therefore become impossible.' Tilley, op. cit., p. 1.

14. As veteran Israeli journalist and political commentator Uri Avnery cleverly noted in a recent writing, those who support a single state after the demise of the two-state solution are like a middleweight boxer who, having lost the championship match, now wants to take on the heavyweight champion.

15. Originally these groups were about 154,000 and more than 800,000 respectively. See www.badil.org/Publications/Press/2009/press506-09.htm. There is by now a voluminous literature on the expulsion of the Palestinians in 1948. See, for example, Nur Masalha, *Expulsion of the Palestinians: The Concept of 'Transfer' in Zionist Political Thought* (Washington, DC: Institute for Palestine Studies, 1992); and Benny Morris, *The Birth of the Palestinian Refugee Problem Revisited* (Cambridge University Press, 2004). On the specific characterisation of the expulsion as an example of deliberate 'ethnic cleansing', see Ilan Pappé, *The Ethnic Cleansing of Palestine* (Oxford: Oneworld, 2006).

16. The Israeli Central Bureau of Statistics counted the Arab population of Israel as 1.45 million at the end of 2007; this figure, however, included 200,000–250,000 Arab residents of East Jerusalem, who are permanent residents, but not citizens of Israel; Israeli Central Bureau of Statistics, Israel in Figures 2008. Available at www.cbs.gov.il/www/publications/isr_in_n08e.pdf.

17. Ian Scobbie, 'An intimate disengagement: Israel's withdrawal from Gaza, the law of occupation and of self-determination', in E. Cotran and M. Lau (eds), *Yearbook of Islamic and Middle Eastern Law*, 11 (2004–5), Brill, 2006, pp. 3–31. The Gaza Strip remains 'occupied territory' within the meaning of international law notwithstanding Israel's withdrawal of its settlers and ground troops in August–September 2005. Israel continues to exercise 'effective control' over the region by patrolling its coastal waters, land borders and airspace, and by entering it at will to arrest and kill Palestinians. Israel also supplies the Gaza Strip with electrical power and fuels, and retains its population registry.

18. These population figures are derived from the Palestinian Central Bureau of Statistics. Needless to say, these are extremely broad and in some cases messy categories (e.g. 27.2 per cent of West Bank residents and 67.9 per cent of Gaza Strip residents are refugees, meaning that, even while living under Israeli military occupation, they share certain interests and experiences with Palestinians in the more distant Diaspora).

19. For example, Palestinians living in Lebanon without citizenship, and legally barred from over 70 professions and occupations, face vastly more daunting challenges than Palestinians in Jordan, who have been awarded citizenship and are able to enter occupations free of formal legal discrimination.

20. See Adalah, *Institutionalized Discrimination against Palestinian Citizens*, 2001; Human Rights Watch, *Second Class: Discrimination against Palestinian Arab Children*

in Israeli Schools, 2001; Nimer Sultany (ed.), *Citizens without Citizenship* (Haifa: Mada-Arab Center for Applied Social Research, 2003); and Susan Nathan, *The Other Side of Israel* (New York: Bantam Dell Pub Group, 2005). Adalah, the Legal Center for Minority Rights in Israel, has counted some 20 Israeli laws that explicitly favour Jews over non-Jews or otherwise discriminate against Palestinians. Apart from this de jure discrimination, Palestinian citizens also face de facto policy discrimination in the form of unequal access to benefits, employment, education and other services.

21. It is intriguing, for example, that the Israeli High Court's decision overturning discriminatory housing practices in Katzir was reached in the year preceding the outbreak of the Al-Aqsa Intifada and in a relatively hopeful atmosphere concerning the prospects for a peace agreement.

22. Quoted in Tom Segev, 'Can a "Jewish state" be for all its citizens?', *Ha'aretz*, 24 November 2004. Gavison, a former head of the Israel Civil Rights Association, and sometimes mentioned as a candidate for the Israeli High Court, had joined in a two-year project sponsored by the Israel Democracy Institute to develop a charter for Jewish–Palestinian relations. The project ended without conclusion as the group, composed of 12 Jews and eight Palestinians, was unable to reach agreement over whether Israel would remain a 'Jewish state' or a 'state of all its citizens'.

23. Yoav Stern and Yuval Azoulay, 'Livni tells Acre residents: don't take the law into your own hands', *Ha'aretz*, 9 October 2008.

24. Jim Teeple, 'New cabinet appointment tilts Israel to the right', *Voice of America*, 24 October 2006.

25. For example, Hadash, the socialist Israeli political party that draws substantial support from Palestinians, has consistently supported the two-state solution – while also calling for equal rights within Israel. See Alternative Information Center, 'Balad and Hadash: election campaigns take different directions', 27 February 2009.

26. Text of the Geneva Initiative is available at www.informationclearinghouse.info/article5019.htm.

27. Badil, op. cit.

28. On the legal foundations of the Palestinian right of return, see John Quigley, *The Case for Palestine* (Durham: Duke University Press, 2005).

29. Anecdotally, the author can report at least, this sentiment is quite strong among many Palestinians in the West Bank.

30. As former Negotiations Support Unit lawyer Michael Tarazi reported to Ali Abunimah, following the publication of his op-ed piece in the *New York Times* supporting one piece in October 2004, he was approached by a number of Palestinian Authority officials who agreed with his perspective, but declined to say so publicly. See Abunimah, op. cit., pp. 161–2.

31. For example, top Palestinian peace negotiator Ahmad Qurei stated in August 2008: 'If Israel continues to reject our propositions regarding the borders [of a future Palestinian state], we might demand Israeli citizenship.' See *Jerusalem Post*, 'Qurei: Palestinians might demand citizenship', 11 August 2008.

32. These concerns are expressed in different ways by Salim Tamari, op. cit., pp. 83–7; and Uri Avnery, 'A binational state? God forbid!', *Journal of Palestine Studies*, 28(4), 1999, p. 55.

33. As one observer noted: 'Education has been of mighty importance in Palestinian perception as well as in real-life strategies. Education has been seen as both a form of and a preparation for the struggle. It has been the sole source of social mobility and an opportunity to save refugees from current degrading circumstances.' Helena Lindholm Schultz, *The Palestinian Diaspora: Formation of Identities and Politics of Homeland* (London: Routledge, 2003), p. 132. Diaspora Palestinians have been extremely successful entrepreneurs in private enterprise and have made major contributions to state-building in

Arab countries, particularly in the Gulf. See Julianne Hammer, *Palestinians Born in Exile* (Austin: University of Texas Press, 2005).

34. Hamas Charter, Article 11. Available at www.thejerusalemfund.org/www.thejerusalemfund.org/carryover/documents/charter.html.

35. Hamas Charter, Article 6, available at www.thejerusalemfund.org/www.thejerusalemfund.org/carryover/documents/charter.html. Indeed, Ahmad Abu Lafi concludes that '… support for the idea of a binational state is unlawful from the perspective of the Shari'a'. Ahmad Abu Lafi, 'Islam and the binational state', in Mahdi Abdul Hadi (ed.), *Palestinian–Israeli Impasse: Exploring Alternatives to the Palestine-Israel Conflict* (Jerusalem: PASSIA, 2005), p. 298.

36. See, for example, Ahmad Yousef, 'Pause for peace', *New York Times*, 1 November 2006.

37. Sherman Jackson, 'Shari'ah, democracy and the modern nation-state: some reflections on Islam, popular rule and pluralism', *Fordham International Law Journal*, 27(1), 2004, pp. 77–108.

CHAPTER 15

Mobilising Israel and World Jewry for the One-State Solution

Norton Mezvinsky

Mobilising world Jewish opinion for a one-state solution in the foreseeable future will be a most difficult task. Opinion polls of Jews in the state of Israel and the USA, conducted by the most reliable pollsters, clearly indicate this difficulty. What those polls indicate about Jewish opinion in the state of Israel and the USA is most likely similar to Jewish opinion in other countries as well.

The following seven questions and answers typically illustrate Israel Jewish opinion regarding peace with the Palestinians. The first three are taken from a poll, conducted by the Harry Truman Research Institute between 25 August and 1 September 2008. The fourth is taken from a poll conducted by the B. I. Cohen Institute of Tel Aviv University between 1 and 3 December 2008. The fifth is taken from a poll conducted by the Tami Steinmetz Center for Peace Research in February 2009. The sixth and seventh are taken from a 25 July 2008 poll conducted by MarketWatch:[1]

1. 'What is the best solution to the conflict: a one-state or two-state solution?': 79 per cent responded in favour of the two-state solution; 11 per cent responded in favour of the one-state solution.
2. 'Do you support or oppose the mutual recognition of Israel as a state for the Jewish people and Palestine as a state for the Palestinian people as part of a permanent status agreement?': 71 per cent favoured such mutual recognition; 25 per cent opposed.
3. 'Do you support or oppose the Saudi initiative which calls for Arab recognition and normalisation of relations with Israel after it ends its occupation of Arab territories occupied in 1967 and after the establishment of a Palestinian state?': 38 per cent supported the Saudi initiative; 59 per cent opposed.

4. 'Do you agree or disagree with the following statement?: "In reality, most of the Palestinians do not accept the existence of the state of Israel and would destroy it if they could, despite the fact that the PLO leadership is conducting peace negotiations with Israel."?': 61 per cent agreed; 20 per cent disagreed.

5. 'Do you or do you not believe that negotiations between Israel and the Palestinian Authority will lead to an eventual peace between Israel and the Palestinians?': 34.4 per cent said yes; 63.7 per cent said no; 1.8 per cent had no opinion.

6. 'There are those who claim that in a situation with no significant progress, Israel could turn into a binational state, meaning that the Palestinians would relinquish their demand for a state and instead demand to live in Israel as citizens. In such a situation, two nations would live within the borders of Israel. In your opinion could a situation like this come about or not?': 26 per cent answered that this could come about; 71 per cent answered that it could not come about; 3 per cent were undecided.

7. 'Which situation do you view as preferable?': 74 per cent said the establishment of a Palestinian state alongside Israel, meaning two states for two people; 14 per cent said the establishment of a binational state, meaning one state for two peoples; 9 per cent said neither; 3 per cent were undecided.[2]

More recent is an Israeli poll, conducted as part of an in-depth study by the Institute for National Studies and revealed in a 17 June 2009 *Ha'aretz* article by Akiva Elder. This poll revealed that 64 per cent of the Israeli Jewish public supports a two-state solution. The percentage of Israel's adult Jewish population willing to accept the establishment of a Palestinian state as part of a final status arrangement rose from 21 per cent in 1987 to 61 per cent in 2006, and then fell to 55 per cent in 2007 and 53 per cent in mid-2009. This poll, however, is complicated in that it also reveals that the total idea of a Palestinian state and what it should entail is vague and contains negative connotations for many Israeli Jews. Only 15 per cent of Israeli Jews, according to this poll, support the removal of all West Bank settlements as part of a final status arrangement; 43 per cent favour evacuating only the small and isolated settlements. More than 40 per cent oppose any conditions; 60 per cent oppose any withdrawal from the Golan Heights, while 20 per cent are willing to return the Golan to Syria so long as the Jewish settlements there remain, Syria signs a peace treaty with Israel including full diplomatic and economic ties and demilitarisation of the heights, and Syria end its alliance with Iran and its support of Hezbollah, and expels all terrorist organisations – including Hamas.[3]

The following three questions and answers typically represent attitudes of American Jews. The first two are taken from polls conducted by the American Jewish Committee between 1993 and 2008. The third is taken from a poll conducted by B'nai B'rith on 10 January 2008:[4]

1. 'Do you agree or disagree with the following statement?: "The goal of the Arabs is not the return of occupied territories but rather the destruction of Israel."?': In 2007, 82 per cent agreed; the percentage of the same agreement had increased consistently year to year from 1993 when it was only 42 per cent.
2. 'Do you think there will or will not come a time when Israel and the Arabs will be able to settle their differences and live in peace?': In 2006, 38 per cent said will (changing to 37 per cent in 2007, 38 per cent in 2008); 56 per cent said will not (55 per cent in 2007, 56 per cent in 2008); 6 per cent were undecided (8 per cent in 2007, 6 per cent in 2008).
3. 'Do you support or oppose an Israeli withdrawal to the 1967 borders as a condition of peace with the Palestinians?': 26 per cent supported; 66 per cent opposed (2008).

Led by the Jewish Agency, an arm of the Israeli government, Zionist organisations have generally done an excellent job of propagandising for and convincing a majority of Jews that the state of Israel is a necessity. The Jewish Agency has maintained for many years that at least 70 per cent of Jews around the world see the demographically Jewish state of Israel as vital for Jewish identity. The Jewish Agency has continually proclaimed that its educational efforts are primarily designed for and aimed at the remaining 30 per cent of Jews.

For the Jewish Agency, Zionist education is the most critical aspect of Jewish continuity and effort. A majority of synagogues have classes, lectures and other programmes that allegedly illustrate and explain the connection between Zionism, Judaism and Jewishness. Rabbis' sermons give the same message. The underlying themes have emphasised, and continue to emphasise, that Zionism equals Judaism and that the state of Israel is the ultimate connection of Judaism's goals and ideals.

An understanding of the underlying reasons for the massive Jewish support for Zionism and the state of Israel is the first prerequisite for any attempt to mobilise world Jewish opinion to favour a one-state solution. The major underlying reason for Zionist support is that many Jews believe anti-Semitism to be absolute. This belief is the heart and centre of Zionism; it dates back to the last decade of the nineteenth century and to Theodore Herzl. The argument, briefly stated, is that Jews have been in the past, and/or are being in the present and/

or will be in the future, persecuted by non-Jews in all nation-states in which they (the Jews) are a minority. Jews, therefore, so goes the argument, need a nation-state of their own in which they start out as the majority and remain hopefully the majority of the residents of the state, but certainly as the citizens who control the state.

Those who believe this argument are clearly facing a contradiction. Israel as a Zionist state has existed since the middle of May 1948. Since that time the major argument, put each year by Zionist leaders and organisations in garnering financial and political support for Israel, is that the Jews living there are in the most unsafe place for Jews in the world and need and deserve help. But the Zionist state cannot realistically at the same time be both the safest and most unsafe place for Jews.

Most Jews in the USA who regard themselves as Zionists face a contradiction in another major way as well. The great majority of these Jews have not done their *aliya* (i.e. have not left the USA to live in Israel).

Pointedly exposing this contradiction could at least motivate some Diaspora Jews, who regard themselves as Zionists, to reconsider their commitment and to begin to view a more realistic resolution to the Israeli–Palestinian conflict. Most of those Jews, moreover, understand, as do Israeli Jews, the demographic situation in the state of Israel. They know that in 2009 the number of Palestinians in Israel behind the Green Line and the occupied territories was almost equal to the number of Jews. They also know that, because of the difference between Palestinian and Israeli Jewish birth rates, Palestinians will outnumber Jews within a few years.

It is well known that increasing numbers of Jews in Israel, the USA and elsewhere have in recent years adversely criticised Israeli oppression of Palestinians and the Jewish settlements in territories occupied since 1967. Some of those Jews have also rejected the idea of a Zionist state, but most consider themselves liberal Zionists of one kind or another and support by essence the existence of a Jewish exclusivist state of Israel, perhaps bordered by a Palestinian state. These liberal Zionists at best are inclined to accept the two-state advocacy. For them one democratic, secular state, guaranteeing in law and public policy equal rights for Jews as well as non-Jews, would put Jews of that state in jeopardy and would, even in a federation or confederation set-up, seriously threaten and in time probably destroy what they consider to be the Jewishness they desire.

The situation in Gaza in late 2008 and early 2009, highlighted by Hamas rocket launchings and the Israeli incursions, generated more antagonism on both sides and made the one-state advocacy even more difficult. The calls from some Israeli Jews for 'transfer' of Palestinians out of Israel increased. The move to the Right in Israel was documented when Benjamin Netanyahu and his Likud-led coalition took control of the government after the mid-February elections. Part of this government was Avigdor Lieberman, who as head of the right-wing party Yisrael Beiteinu and as foreign minister infamously called for an introduction of an oath of loyalty to Israel as a Jewish state, something which is expanded on in the other chapters within this book. Prime Minister Netanyahu has opposed a realistic two-state solution and even more vehemently rejected one democratic secular state for Israel–Palestine as a replacement for the Zionist state.

Given all the above, it is unrealistic to be optimistic about mobilising world Jewish opinion in the foreseeable future in favour of a democratic one-state solution. Those who are committed to their vision as the necessary and only viable long-term solution should, moreover, not be misled into believing, as some people do, that in a short time most Jews will be forced against their will and desire to accept a one-state solution. Israel is presently and will probably remain for some time one of the most powerful nations in the world militarily, and the USA will most likely continue to support Israel militarily, politically and economically. Arab military confrontation with Israel will, if attempted, result in the deaths and casualties of too many people, and will not achieve a desired one-state solution.

Although difficult, changing Jewish world public opinion by peaceful means is not impossible. Some changes have already occurred, according to polls taken after Israel's excursion into Gaza in late December 2008 and January 2009. In her excellent book, *The One State Solution*, Virginia Tilley observed:

> In every country that has attempted modern nation building, change in the national ideology has always been launched by a few inspirational voices who periodically *reimagined* the national community and gave it new direction. Such a process of national reconstruction can begin in Israel–Palestine. The land needs and deserves a nobler mission: real democracy, through a bridging of peoples and their histories. It has been done elsewhere against staggering odds, and it can be done here.[5]

The best way to move sizeable world Jewish public opinion to favour a one-state solution is to emphasise historic humanitarianism, moral and ethical principles. This emphasis will probably not influence the Jewish religious extremists who sincerely believe that the present state of Israel, including most or all of the territory occupied after the June 1967 War and perhaps more land as well, belongs exclusively to Jews because of an eternal deed, given by God to the Jews. The majority of Jews in this world, however, almost certainly do not so believe. Many Jews could conceivably be influenced by reference to the tradition of Jewish humanitarianism and tolerance, especially in its modern formulations.

These modern formulations date back to Moses Mendelssohn and the Jewish Enlightenment in the eighteenth century. Ahad Ha'am, whose real name was the famous moralist Asher Ginsburg, noted as early as 1891 that the Zionist settlers in Palestine were inclined to despotism and treated Arabs with hostility and cruelty, depriving them of their rights. He warned the political orientation of Zionism was responsible and would, if continued, morally corrupt the Jewish people. Ahad Ha'am, who advocated a Jewish cultural revival in Palestine, had by 1913 totally rejected political Zionism and its emphasis upon Jewish exclusivity.

He and other critics like him distinguished between the moral values of Judaism and ethnocentric Zionism. What these early Jewish critics of Zionism specified could be used today to provide some background and context for the one-state proposal. The Holocaust, that horrific happening during which over 6 million Jews were killed by the Nazis in Europe, overwhelmed the criticism of Zionism and influenced a large majority of world Jewry, as well as great majorities of non-Jews especially in the West, to back the demand for the creation of a Jewish, exclusivist state in historical Palestine. Even so, some distinguished, outstanding Jews in the 1940s, including Hannah Arendt, Albert Einstein, Martin Buber and Judah Magnes, remained severe critics of Zionism and an exclusivist Jewish state; they argued for one state in which Jews, Arabs and others would live together with equal rights guaranteed by law. Einstein, Buber and Magnes believed that a binational state of joint sovereignty with 'complete equality of rights between the two partners' should be established. Such a state in historic Palestine, declared Einstein, would be predicated upon the love of their homeland that the two people share. In other words, one democratic secular state should be the desired goal. Both Arab and Jewish history and identity would be respected and protected.

To reiterate, the number of Jews since 1948 who have opposed both Zionism and the concept and reality of Israel's being an exclusivist Jewish state of one size or another is small. Most Jews who have criticised adversely various aspects of the oppression by Israel of Palestinians have nevertheless continued to support the idea of a Jewish state at least within the pre-June 1967 border. Avraham Burg, the speaker of the Israeli Knesset between 1999 and 2003, a former paratrooper and a religiously observant Jew, is an exception. Although not yet an advocate of one state for Israel–Palestine, Burg has rejected Zionism and its emphasis upon the absolute nature of anti-Semitism; he has become a clear, outspoken opponent of the continuing Zionist nature of the Jewish state. While Burg argues for a democratic Jewish state within the pre-June 1967 borders, he does not adequately attempt to present a logical explanation of this apparent inconsistency. Nevertheless, his many other well-stated arguments could be utilised to lay the basis for the one-state proposal to many Jews in Israel and elsewhere who are unhappy with many oppressive policies and the developing nature of the Zionist state. Avraham Burg and his views need to be emphasised in the struggle to influence world Jewry.

As a distinguished Israeli politico for many years, Burg believes in and advocates peace with the Palestinians and other Arabs. In 2004 he left his active role as a politician and became a fierce, vocal critic of Zionism; he favoured replacing the existent Jewish state with what he termed a Jewish state of all citizens. Since 2004, in writings, interviews and speeches, Burg has consistently and severely criticised the kind of oppressive state Israel has become. In his book, *The Holocaust Is Over, We Must Rise From its Ashes*, Burg writes that Israel should not be a Jewish state and that the law of return, which grants citizenship to any bona-fide Jew in the world, should be altered. Burg urges Jews in Israel and throughout the world to stop utilising the Holocaust as a major defensive theme for Jews, and as a justifying rationale for Israel's Zionist existence and oppressive actions. He points out that Israel, as opposed to being a safe haven for Jews, is, because of its policies and actions, the most unsafe place in the world for Jews to live. Burg considers Israel to be a bully that understands only the language of force. For him the essence of the Zionist character of Israel is the mistaken belief that the great majority of non-Jews hate Jews. Because of this, he alleges, Israeli Jews live in a constant state of emergency. Too few Israeli Jews, according to Burg, adhere to the positive, universal values that constitute the heart of Judaism.

Burg is harsh and precise in criticising the exclusivist nature of Israeli Jewish society and of those Jews who maintain it. Burg labels this exclusivist position 'racist' and calls its advocates 'racists'. He analyses its origin and historical development:

> From the first days of our patriarchs, two trends rose in Jewish history: exclusivity and inclusiveness. The exclusivists separated themselves from the world and detested the gentiles' being and inputs; the inclusivists were open to adopt positive spirits and ideas from other cultures. These trends began a long time ago, when Judaism was conceived. Throughout Jewish history our forefathers never succeeded in erasing the significance of the gentiles in our lives.[6]

Burg identifies some major Jewish sages and leaders throughout history who were exclusivists and stressed the negative aspects of non-Jews. These exclusivists advocated that Jews needed as much as possible to segregate themselves in the world. The morning prayer for Jews illustrates some of the motivation for this self-segregation: 'Blessed are you, O God, King of the universe, for not having made me a Gentile.'[7]

At the end of the Sabbath is another prayer, cited by Burg that emphasises segregation: 'Blessed... [are those] who differentiate between Holiness and everyday matters, between light and darkness, between Israel and the nations.'[8]

Burg's interpretation is: 'This is a distinct separation of one group, of everyday affairs, darkness, and nations of the world, from the group of holiness, light and the people of Israel. These kinds of distinctions are made in numerous sources.'[9] He suggests that 'oppressed Jews who experienced ruin and persecutions, found refuge in dreams of grandeur'.[10]

In declaring this exclusivist view as 'racist', as previously noted, Burg argues that it affects both secular and religious Jews in Israel and is opposed to the humanistic, universal values in Judaism:

> The entire Torah in one verse, Hillel the Elder told us, is not doing to others what we hated done to us when we were the others. In Israel today there are horrible layers of racism that are not essentially different from the racism that exterminated many of our ancestors. This racism is sanctimonious and slick, so we do not always notice how dangerous it is. It is also cunning and marketable; sometimes we are mistaken to think it is pure patriotism. It isn't. The conversion of everything into holiness, without leaving room for self-criticism, combined with the sanctity of nationhood and the hostile environment we try daily to withstand, turns the monopolists of the Israeli religious spirit to de facto and de jure 'racists'. It is imperative to declare a war of value with them, and to present a practical alternative of faith to the distortion they call 'Judaism' and which they present as our authentic faith.[11]

Burg urges Jews in Israel and elsewhere to build a new and healthy Israel:

> Israel must understand that after the Shoah (Holocaust), genetic Judaism has to end. We have to connect to the Judaism that shares a common fate and values with others. There will be among us descendants of Abraham and Sarah, but we will all be the children of Adam and Eve. Unlike many rabbis among us... who believed that a non-genetic Jew is not equal to us, we will adapt the medieval scholar Maimonides' astoundingly modern views and bold positions. This is what he wrote to Ovadea the proselyte, his contemporary: 'There is no difference at all between us and you in any matter... and do not underestimate your origins. If we are descended from Abraham, Isaac and Jacob, you are descended from the Creator of the World. Victory Day over Nazi Germany will also be the day of victory of the shared identity over the decisive religious law.'[12]

Burg directs his message to secular as well as to religious Jews. His analysis and advocacy can and should be combined in a unified message with the positions of other distinguished, outstanding Jewish thinkers and activists who have already advocated a one-state solution. Although not the only method to employ, this approach has a decent chance to influence a significant portion of world Jewry, including, crucially, those within Israel.

Notes

1. 'Israeli opinion regarding peace with the Palestinians', Jewish Virtual Library 2008. Available at www.jewishvirtuallibrary.org/jsource/Society_&_Culture/ispopal_2008.html.

2. Ibid.

3. Akiva Eldar, 'Haaretz poll: 64 per cent of Israelis back two-state solution', *Ha'aretz*, 17 June 2009.

4. 'Attitudes of American Jews', Jewish Virtual Library. Available at www.jewish-virtuallibrary.org/jsource/US-Israel/ajcsurvey.html#Israel.

5. Virginia Tilley, *The One State Solution* (Ann Arbor: University of Michigan, 2005), p. 234.

6. Avraham Burg, *The Holocaust Is Over, We Must Rise From its Ashes* (New York: Palgrave Macmillan, 2008), p. 184. The book was published first in Hebrew in Israel in 2007 and thereafter published in English translation in the USA in 2008.

7. Ibid., p. 185.

8. Ibid., p. 155.

9. Ibid.

10. Loc. cit.

11. Ibid., p. 198.

12. Ibid., p. 234.

CHAPTER 16

Palestinians in Israel and Binationalism: Escape from the Impasse

As'ad Ghanem

Introduction

The last decade of the twentieth century and early years of the current century have witnessed a shift in the search of Palestinians in Israel for solutions to their status: this search has shifted from a concentration on the Israeli internal domain to the wider Palestinian sphere, including those outside Israel and the West Bank (i.e. the refugees and the broader Diaspora). The period of this shift divides into two stages. The first stage lasted through the mid-1990s and was a continuation of the years that followed the cancellation of Israeli military rule over its Palestinian population and its 1967 occupation of the West Bank and Gaza Strip. In this stage, Israel allowed for the introduction of some measures of democratisation and liberalisation into the life of the Palestinians in Israel.

Until the mid-1990s, there was a growing belief among the Palestinians in Israel for the need to capitalise on their Israeli citizenship in search for solutions to their problems and defining a future for themselves. It expressed itself in several communal initiatives that included, among others: declaring the Equality Day in June 1987; rallying against Israeli policies aimed at suppressing the first Palestinian Intifada and providing material support to the Palestinians under occupation; and using their Israeli citizenship to engage in the political process and assume the status of a 'preventive block' to facilitate the achievement of peace agreements. Moreover, they engaged in calls to make Israel a 'state for all its citizens', which was proposed by the Israeli left as a solution to the Jewish state impasse.

Many of the Palestinian political movements that used to boycott Israeli politics in the past changed course. These movements included the Islamic Movement and Abna' al-Balad (Children of the Country). They became active political actors. A legal discourse also developed through civil society organisations that invoked citizenship to claim individual and group rights. Also, the Democratic National Alliance Party came up with the idea of having citizenship define the future status of the Palestinians in Israel. Together, these developments led to high rates of Palestinian voter turnout in the elections.

The second stage started with the Israeli right wing assuming office in 1996. Soon thereafter, it became clear that earlier hopes for complete citizenship (i.e. becoming Israelis), accepting the state of Israel and establishing an Israeli 'nation of citizens', were ill-founded. They were unacceptable to both the Jewish public and official Israel. The events that followed saw a sharp upsurge in feelings of racism and hostility among Jewish Israelis against the Palestinians in Israel and an increase in the number of official initiatives aimed at harassing Palestinian citizens, as in the case of basic laws and the draft constitution (legislating the Jewish character of the state as being the most important component in defining its nature), the practices of discrimination, deportation and land confiscation (particularly in the Negev area), the culmination of all of that in the killing of 13 Palestinian citizens during the demonstrations of September and October 2000, as well as other hostile measures taken later on by the state against its Palestinian citizens.

By then, a process of doubt and re-evaluation began to evolve among Palestinians regarding the nature of Israel and the chances of concretising collective and individual aspirations through the Israeli citizenship. They began to consider seriously how to move from their current course to an alternative one given the expiry of the Oslo period and the total impasse in implementing international resolutions for solving the Palestinian issue. The Islamic movement developed the idea of the 'independent community'; the call for boycotting the Israeli Knesset elections obtained stronger support and waging a struggle for the achievement of their rights outside the confines of parliament gained in popularity. A discourse was initiated and think-tanks were established to advocate ways for: getting out of the condition of reliance they were living in; demanding equality in a shared homeland and not through the Jewish state; focusing, more than ever, on the impact of the 1948 founding of Israel on the situation of the Palestinians in Israel; realising their status is interconnected to the larger Palestinian problem; and viewing their resistance as a common with that of other indigenous groups' struggle against colonialism and post-colonialism. Such perceptions hardly existed before.

The Palestinians in Israel and the Solution of the Palestinian Problem

The Declaration of Principles (DoP) signed by Israel and the PLO signalled the start of a track that was supposed to lead to solving the so-called 'Palestinian issue'. Missing in this track was the fate of the Palestinian citizens of Israel and their political status.[1] On the one hand, the PLO did not discuss or seek to negotiate this issue with the Israelis. On the other hand, Israeli authorities considered the issue an internal affair which they would not negotiate with any outsider. Consequently, a relatively odd situation was created. While efforts were being exerted to reach a comprehensive solution for the outstanding issues between Israel and the Palestinians, the future and the problems of the Palestinian minority in Israel were completely ignored.

The relationship between the PLO and the Palestinians in Israel has been problematic. There exists a gap between the latter's self-awareness as Palestinians and their affiliation to the Palestinian people under the PLO leadership. Although the PLO is considered by Palestinians, including the Palestinians in Israel, to be the sole legitimate representative of the Palestinian people, neither the PLO nor the Palestinians in Israel ever claimed that the PLO represents the Palestinians in Israel. Thus, the formula concerning Palestinian representation was not applied: (a) the PLO is the sole legitimate representative of the Palestinian people; (b) the Palestinians in Israel are an integral part of the Palestinian people; and (c) thus the PLO represents the Palestinians in Israel. After Israel embarked on the course of public negotiations with the PLO, the issue of relations between the Palestinians in Israel and the Palestinian national movement surfaced as an issue that is far more complicated than expected.

Despite the fact that the status of the Palestinians in Israel is part of the Palestinian issue, the peace process between Israel and the PLO totally ignored this subject. By overlooking the issue, the PLO persisted in pursuing an exclusion approach it had adopted long ago when dealing with the Palestinians in Israel, manifested in the low-profile interaction between the two sides. The Palestinians in Israel were not partners in establishing national and political institutions for the Palestinians, which were established in the Diaspora in the 1960s. Additionally, the national Palestinian movement did not consider the problems of the Palestinians in Israel a major item on the national agenda. As for Israel, all matters relating to the Palestinians in Israel were viewed as an internal Israeli affair. By neglecting the Palestinians in Israel in its negotiations with Israel, the PLO indirectly encouraged Israel to maintain its position. Even the Palestinians in Israel, too, did not apply any pressure on the PLO to shift its course, perhaps out of fear that such a thorny issue might undermine the whole peace process and harm their relations with the state. This posture did not prevent the PLO leadership, before and after Oslo, from attempting to utilise the Palestinian citizens of Israel in the service of its diplomatic ends. This started when the PLO sought mutual Israeli–PLO recognition, especially after the 1991 Madrid Conference, when the PLO asked to be a partner in negotiations with

Israel. At the time, it lobbied the Palestinians in Israel to cast their votes in support of leftist Zionist parties.[2]

The exclusion of the Palestinians in Israel by the Palestinian national movement has spread from the pragmatic upper-echelon political leadership level to the cultural level that defines the Palestinian collective identity and future aspirations. The post-1967 Palestinian political discourse that developed in the wake of Fateh's assumption of the leadership of the national movement, with its emphasis on resistance to occupation, liberation and building a future for all, devolved after Oslo to refer to the Palestinians in the West Bank and Gaza Strip and, to a lesser degree, the Palestinians in the Diaspora. Meanwhile, it totally excluded the Palestinians in Israel. Thus the term 'the occupied territory', which in Palestinian eyes would refer to historical Palestine, has actually come to mean those areas of Palestine occupied in 1967. Palestinians in Israel were excluded from the negotiations, informal discussions and conferences conducted or held to consider the Palestinian future, and were offered nothing more than empty slogans and worthless words of comfort.

This general attitude has not been restricted to the ranks of the PLO and the Palestinian Authority. It is shared by most of the opponents and critics of the Oslo Agreement and the peace process. They also take it as a given to consider the occupation as only including what was occupied in 1967. Only rarely is marginal attention given to the Palestinians in Israel and to their concerns. Yet all of them, almost without any exception, adopt the political stand that considers the Palestinians in Israel an internal Israeli issue. Within this milieu, a tendency has developed and has taken root in Palestinian awareness and perceptions to consider the occupation a consequence of the June 1967 War rather than a result of the 1948 Nakba.[3]

The Palestinians in Israel and the Future

The 1967 War resulted in socio-political and economic changes for the Palestinians in Israel. Their levels of national awareness were heightened and led them to organise. The early 1970s witnessed the development of a new educated sector and a larger middle class, followed by the establishment on a national level of structures to organise the Palestinian community in Israel such as the Committee for the Arab Local Authorities' Mayors of 1974, the Arab University Students' Union of 1974, the Arab Secondary School Students' Union of 1975 and the Arab Land Defense Committee of 1975. These organisations constituted new starting points for reorganising and building the Palestinian community in Israel.[4]

After the 1967 War, the Palestinians in Israel adopted a new communal ideology that connected their civil and national platforms. In general, their stand on the solution of the national Palestinian issue became close to the one proposed by the principal factions in the Palestinian national movement such as Fateh. On the civil front, they adopted the dynamic slogan 'equality and partnership' as their rallying cry. The two were seen as interconnected. Solving the national issue would improve their civil status, as their status is affected by them being an integral part of the Palestinian people.[5] This development in their ideology made it clear that their ability to resolve the issue of their citizenship in Israel was not only contingent on their struggle in Israel, but was also related to solving the Palestinian issue at large.

The signing of the Oslo agreement in September 1993 between the PLO and the state of Israel, and their mutual recognition, was the third most important event influencing Palestinians in Israel, at different levels – that is, their relations with the state, the political discourse and political activism. The timing of the Oslo agreement coincided with changes in the international field that affected them, especially the hurried pace of globalisation with its accompanying economic, political and socio-cultural changes. Emphasis in their political discourse moved from discussions of the relationship between their civil status and their national identity to consideration of the relationship between their civil status and the character and identity of the Israeli state.

Following the failure of the peace process and downfall of Oslo, the future of the Palestinian issue became paramount. Although negotiations between Israel and the PLO to end the occupation of the West Bank and Gaza and establish a Palestinian state were maintained, it soon became clear that Israel's negotiating aim had shifted from a desire for conflict resolution to conflict management in a way that served its narrow interests.[6] Palestinian, Israeli and international voices started to be heard more often calling for reconsidering the feasibility of dividing historical Palestine, and demanding a joint and binational Israeli/Palestinian political entity be established. Although the Palestinian voices engaged in this call acknowledged, in general, the Palestinians in Israel, their proposals did not sufficiently appreciate the important role they can play in this venture and the effect it will have on their lives. Today, they seem to be the most active among the Palestinians in mounting an ideological renaissance, through the 'Future Vision' project.

Binationalism as a Collective Agenda for the Palestinians in Israel

The future of the Palestinians in Israel is dependent on their ability to capitalise on international developments, their engagement with other Palestinians, and their interaction with the Jewish majority and the state. Equally, if not more important, will be their ability to deal with their situation and progress from the stage of dependency and reaction to developments that they live in into a proactive stage which would see them upholding an inspiring vision. If successful, they will be at the centre of developments. This change requires them to prepare for their future at several levels; the most important of which is the preparation of a collective national programme that reflects their needs. The following section demonstrates that the Palestinians in Israel, given their special situation as a minority living in the Jewish state, endorse the idea of binationalism.

By the end of 2006, the National Committee for the Heads of the Arab Local Authorities, which has more than 80 per cent membership in the Higher Follow-up Committee – the leading body among the Palestinians in Israel – took a serious step by publishing 'The Future Vision for the Palestinian Arabs in Israel'. In doing so, the committee formulated a collective vision for the future of the Palestinians in Israel and offered it for discussion. The prelude of the document says:

> In order to collect various versions in the self-definition of our entity, our relation with the rest of the Palestinians and our relation with the State and to connect them to create a firm integral homogeneous vision, we, the Arab Palestinians in Israel, should have a clear self-definition that includes all the political, cultural, economic, educational and social aspects.[7]

Israeli officials, scholars, journalists and academics were almost all totally and strongly opposed to the document, although the demands made were not so dissimilar from those made by indigenous minorities in other places.[8] The document had special political and media significance, being the first collective declaration of demands by Palestinians in Israel that challenged the socio-political system in Israel. It was also a document authored by noted Palestinian scholars and activists representing the full political spectrum of Palestinians in Israel, and had the support of Shawqi Khateeb, Head of the Follow-up Committee. Additionally, the document assumed special significance following its adoption by the National Committee for the Heads of the Arab Local Authorities in its January 2007 annual meeting in the Dead Sea area as its official programme. Public opinion polls of Palestinians in Israel indicated the sweeping majority supported the demands listed in the document. One such poll conducted in June and July 2008 revealed that the Palestinian public in Israel supported the position of their leadership that the demands contained in the Future Vision document be declared the core collective political aspirations of the Palestinians in Israel.[9]

The Future Vision contained several basic principles. It was viewed as a measure that would improve the structure and performance of communal organisations. Most of the interviewees in the June/July 2008 public poll agreed

Table 16.1 To what extent do you agree or disagree with each of the following statements?

	Agree	Tend to agree	Tend not to agree	Don't agree
There is a need to improve the structure and approach of the performance of the Higher Follow-up Committee.	54.3	31.1	7.7	6.9
Like the Arabs have, Jews have rights in this country.	35.7	25.5	17.1	21.6
Israel has the right to exist, within the Green Line borders, as an independent state where Jews and Arabs live.	36	27.9	16.5	19.6
Israel is a colonial (settlement) phenomenon that was illegally established on an Arab land.	54.5	23.4	12.9	9.1

The 'Green Line' refers to the ceasefire line between Arab forces and Jewish forces following the war in 1948.

(54.3 per cent) or tended to agree (31.1 per cent) with the saying that 'there is a need to improve the performance structure and approach of the Follow-up Committee'. The majority supported the idea expressed in the document that Israel was a colonial phenomenon on the one hand, and that Israeli Jews had the right to 'self-determination' on the other hand. These were considered inherent rights based on the political existence of the Jews during the twentieth century and the development of an acquired identity that qualify them to determine their fate in a binational entity, along with the indigenous people.[10] Table 16.1 shows these trends.

Poll results indicated overwhelming public support to both the political and the social demands in the Future Vision document. The level of support reached more than 90 per cent (see Table 16.2). Interviewees were asked also if these demands should be made immediately or if they could be postponed until the time was fit. Most expressed the opinion that the leadership needed to work on meeting the demands immediately. This indicates the public possesses an activist will and was not just displaying an ideological or intellectual exercise.

Judging by the above, the 'Future Vision' fits as the collective official programme of the Palestinians in Israel. Presently, it constitutes the basis for an ongoing internal discourse within the Palestinian community.[11]

Palestinians in Israel and the Binational Future

The distress of the Palestinian citizens of Israel is epitomised in the fact that they are, at one and the same time, partial Israelis and partial Palestinians; that

Table 16.2 A list of different demands included in the Future Vision. Each interviewee was asked to state, for each demand, if they agreed or disagreed with each demand and the possibility to implement it.

	Agree and work should immediately to implement this demand	Agree, but this is a demand that can be partially implemented right now	Agree, but this is a demand that can't be implemented right now	Don't agree
Israel should stop being a Jewish state and become a state for two peoples.	57.9	21.3	16.3	4.5
Arabic language should be in use just as Hebrew.	71.4	19.1	8.3	1.2
Arab citizens should run their cultural, religious and education affairs by themselves.	62.9	20.7	9.7	6.7
The law should ensure the right of the Arabs to suitable representation in all the state institutions.	69.3	21.5	7.5	1.6
The law should ensure the right of the Arabs to have their proportional share of the state budget.	68.0	22.5	8.3	1.2
The state of Israel should give the Arabs a suitable representation in its symbols, its flag and national anthem.	48.5	19.7	21.5	10.3
The state of Israel must take the consent of the Arab leadership when legislating or making any rules related to them.	54.6	25.2	13.8	6.5
The right of the Palestinians to return to inside Israel should be ensured.	41.3	17.1	32.9	8.7
The state of Israel acknowledges its responsibility over the 'Nakba' (Catastrophe) that befell the Palestinians during the 1948 war.	53.9	15.3	24.9	5.9
The state of Israel should compensate the Arab citizens for the land that was confiscated from them.	62.8	19.2	14.4	3.6
The state of Israel must recognise the Arab citizens as Palestinians and ensure their right to establish relations with the Palestinian people and the Arab nation.	50.1	25.3	19.0	5.7
The state should cancel the special status given to non-Israeli Jewish organisations such as the Jewish Agency and the Jewish National Fund.	40.3	19.4	29.4	10.9

is, both their Israeli and Palestinian identities are incomplete. In the present circumstances, neither their Israeli identity nor their Palestinian identity can be full and comprehensive. This, in a nutshell, is the problem of the collective identity of the Palestinian citizens of Israel.[12]

On the one hand, the Palestinians in Israel are officially citizens of the state. But their Israeli identity does not exist in the core of their collective identity, as a sense of psychological belonging and emotional sympathy. Israel was established with a Jewish-Zionist character to be the state of the Jewish people; its objectives, symbols and policy are built on that foundation and on denying the existence of a Palestinian national minority within its borders. Until 1948, the Palestinians in what became Israel were developing as part of Palestinian society and the Palestinian national movement. The involuntary parting of ways engendered by the outcome of 1948 left the Palestinians in Israel to develop in isolation, unable to draw directly on the vital streams of the Arab world and Palestinian national movement. The ongoing hostilities and security situation exacerbated this isolation. Even today there are still no signs of change in this domain. The Palestinian component of the identity of the Palestinians in Israel cannot be complete when the Palestinian national movement is establishing the Palestinian homeland somewhere else.

The Palestinians' quandary is not a contradiction between the two full identities – the Israeli and the Palestinian, but the incompleteness, in different ways, of each of these identities. This constitutes the most important evidence that the model of 'normal development' is fundamentally flawed with regard to the Palestinians in Israel. The appropriate model is what the literature refers to as the 'crisis development approach',[13] according to which the Palestinian community in Israel faces a crisis on two levels – the immediate and the strategic – which is likely to expand in the future. In the stream situation, the Palestinian community disposes of only limited options with regard to its relations with the state and with the Palestinian people, and cannot evolve normally.

Toward Normalisation of the Situation of the Palestinians in Israel

The author's deep conviction is that territorial separation between the Jews and the Palestinians in Israel/Palestine, or at least between Israel and the West Bank and the Gaza Strip, is impossible, due to the mixed areas and populations in all areas, including Jerusalem, the West Bank and the Galilee. A liberal state that is based on a joint people, on one *demos*, is also unfeasible, due to the national and ethnic attachment internally within the two communities (Israeli Jews and Palestinians). The only option left for normalising relations between the Jews and the Palestinians is the establishment of a binational state in the entire territory of historic Palestine, based on collective accords that bind the two peoples in a single political system with a joint and equal citizenship.

In a binational, Israeli–Palestinian state, the Israeli/Palestinian ethnic/national schism would remain a key structural feature of the political system, which would be based on the four principles of consociationalism:[14] a broad coalition between the political representatives of the Jews and the Palestinians; mutual veto power regarding fundamental and substantive issues; proportional distribution of social goods, including political and public institutions; and a significant degree of internal autonomy for each group in the management of its own affairs.

In practice, the initial conditions for the establishment of such a system already exist, though some basic changes are needed. Despite the Oslo process, the Palestinians in the West Bank and Gaza Strip still live under Israeli control, whether direct or indirect. Under certain conditions – chiefly an inflexible Israeli rejection of the establishment of an egalitarian Palestinian state and the annexation of broad stretches of the West Bank and Gaza Strip to Israel – most of the Palestinians in these areas would, for various reasons,[15] give up on the idea of the establishment of a Palestinian state. The Palestinian Authority would become no more than a way-station on the road to the establishment of a binational system. Its citizens would form a joint front with the Palestinians of Israel, constituting a single collective vis-à-vis the Jews; in the binational reality that would ensue, they would demand the conversion of the state, practically and formally, into a state that expresses both collectives. While most Israeli Jews reject a binational system and do not want to surrender their hegemony, they would have to deal with a variety of factors, including the Palestinians' demand for personal and group equality in a shared system.

In a situation similar to that of South Africa before the regime change in the late 1980s, conditions are likely to ripen, in a time-frame that depends on developments, in which the Jews and their leadership will be forced for a number of reasons to recognise the Palestinians as equal partners. They will have to hold discussions with their representatives and reach an agreement on power-sharing and control of resources. Separate and joint governmental institutions will be set up, including parliaments, cabinets and judicial systems. Each national group will be recognised as autonomous with regard to its own affairs, while common matters will be worked out in joint forums where the two groups have equal representation.

The Palestinians of Israel and the Binational System

A binational regime is a democracy based on group arrangements that give the groups equal status, in addition to the equality extended to all citizens by virtue of their equal citizenship in the shared state.

On the level of the individual, in a binational Israeli–Palestinian state, the Palestinians of Israel will have equality by virtue of their being citizens equal to all other citizens. The special status that the Israeli system gives to Jews, because of the ethnic, Jewish-Zionist regime, will be altered. In a binational polity, the state will have to grant equality to all citizens and avoid any special status for some, which would constitute a perpetual and serious threat to the stability of the system. The individual affairs of Palestinian citizens, including the Palestinians of the West Bank and Gaza Strip, will be dealt with by the state that grants equality in its relations with all citizens, Jews and Palestinians alike. This will allow the Palestinians in Israel to realise the civic dimensions of their identity in full.

On the group level, the Palestinians of Israel will be part of the Palestinian collective, of which the lion's share lives in the West Bank and the Gaza Strip. Collective matters such as leadership, representation, education, culture and the like will be managed by the group (i.e. Jewish or Palestinian), each of which has institutional and cultural autonomy. This will extend even to the territorial dimension, permitting each group to manage its own spatial planning and development. The collective life of the Palestinians in Israel will evolve as part of the overall Palestinian collective. A possible first step in this direction would be to subordinate the Palestinian citizens of Israel, living where they do today, to the 'Palestinian collective system', just as the Jews who live in the West Bank and the Gaza Strip are subject to the 'Jewish collective system'.

The fulfilment of the civic and national affiliation of the Palestinians in Israel in a binational state would permit them to escape the impasse that besets them and open before them channels for future development that do not exist today. Only the development of such channels will make it possible for the Palestinian citizens of Israel to escape their distress, as marginal Palestinians.

Notes

1. As'ad Ghanem, 'The Palestinians in Israel part of the problem not the solution: the issue of their status during peace time', *State, Government and International Relations*, Nos 41–2, 1996, pp. 132–56. In Hebrew.

2. N. Rouhana and A. Ghanem, 'The crises of minorities in ethnic states: the case of Palestinian citizens in Israel', *International Journal of Middle East Studies*, Vol. 30, No. 3, 1998, pp. 321–46.

3. Leila Farsakh (ed.), 'Commemorating the Naksa, evoking the Nakba', Special Volume of *The MIT Journal of Middle East Studies*, Vol. 8 (Spring 2008); Saree Makdisi, *Palestine Inside Out – An Everyday Occupation* (New York and London: WW Norton, 2008).

4. As'ad Ghanem, *The Palestinian Arab Minority in Israel: A Political Study* (Albany: University of New York, 2001).

5. Ibid.

6. See As'ad Ghanem, 'Israel and the "danger of demography"', in Jamil Hilal (ed.), *Where Now for Palestine?* (London: Zed books, 2006), pp. 98–116.

7. www.adalah.org/newsletter/eng/dec06/tasawor-mostaqbali.pdf.

8. As'ad Ghanem and Mohanad Mostafa, 'The Future Vision as a collective program for the Palestinians in Israel', in Sarah Ozacky-Lazar and Mustafa Kabha (eds), *Between Vision and Reality: The Documents of the Future Visions for the Arabs in Israel; 2006–2007* (Jerusalem: The Civic Reconciliation Forum, 2008). In Hebrew.

9. The field study was conducted by Dr As'ad Ghanem and Dr Nuhad Ali from Haifa University, on a sample of 500 people who were interviewed at their homes by specifically trained surveyors (with a 4 per cent error margin).

10. Many critics of the Vision allege that it negates the right of the Jews to self-determination. The author believes this to be an intentional or unintentional misunderstanding of the meaning of self-determination and contrary to the relevant political literature. The latter considers self-determination a relative issue that has to do with the existence of one or more national groups. If the national group is a civil one defined by citizenship, as in the case of France and the USA, then it has the right to self-determination. If the national affiliation is an ethnic one, as in the case of Canada, Belgium, Iraq and Switzerland, then the right to self-determination is related to ensuring the same right for all groups. Otherwise, ensuring that right for only one group would allow for a system of 'tyranny of the majority', as was the case in the USA before ensuring equality of African-Americans.

11. Ghanem and Mustafa (2008), op. cit.

12. N. Rouhana, *Identities in Conflict: Palestinian Citizens in an Ethnic Jewish State* (New Haven: Yale University Press, 1997).

13. As'ad Ghanem (1996), op. cit.; N. Rouhana and A. Ghanem, op. cit.

14. A political system based on the power-sharing principal in divided societies. See Arend Lijphart, *Democracy in Plural Societies* (New Haven CT: Yale University Press, 1977), and Arend Lijphart, *Democracies: Patterns of Majoritarian and Consensus Government in Twenty-One Countries* (New Haven: Yale University Press, 1984).

15. As'ad Ghanem, 'A bi-national, Palestinian–Israeli state in all the land of Palestine/Eretz Yisrael and the status of the Arabs in Israel within this frame', in Sara Ozacky-Lazar, As'ad Ghanem and Ilan Pappé (eds), *Theoretical Options for the Future of the Arabs in Israel* (Givaat Haviva: The Institute for Peace Research, 1999), pp. 271–303. In Hebrew; As'ad Ghanem and Sara Ozacky-Lazar, 'Towards an alternative Israeli–Palestinian discourse', *Palestine-Israel Journal*, Vol. 3, Nos 3–4, 1996, pp. 106–18.

CHAPTER 17

Reversing Defeat Through Non-violent Power

Nadia Hijab

When the Palestine Liberation Organisation (PLO) decided to embark on the two-state political platform in 1974, this constituted tacit recognition of the reality of the state of Israel in Palestine within the Green Line. The PLO's shift was also effectively an admission of defeat for the previous PLO programme that called for a secular, democratic state throughout all of Palestine.

Today, advocates of the one-state solution argue that the two-state solution is no longer possible due to the realities Israel has created on the ground in the West Bank and Gaza. In other words, the political programme launched by the PLO in 1974 has effectively been defeated. The growing one-state movement is, thus, the third time Palestinian communities are reacting to Israel's defeat of Palestinian attempts to obtain their human rights. It is against this background that this chapter attempts to address three questions:

1. Why has the two-state political programme not been achieved?
2. What sources of non-violent power could secure Palestinian human rights?
3. What is the single most important strategy of which no Palestinian political programme should ever lose sight?

Why Has the Two-State Political Programme Not Been Achieved?

The PLO's original secular democratic state programme only lasted a few years, whereas the two-state solution has been attempted for 35 long years, which prompts the question why it has not – or not yet – succeeded. A common answer is that Israel has never recognised the Palestinian right to self-determination, among other rights, and that Israel, in contrast to any Palestinian authority

structure, has been strong enough to impose its agenda. An equally important reason, however, is that the Palestinian leadership has not known how to
exploit, nurture and sustain sources of power to advance Palestinian rights and
counter Israeli strengths, particularly after 1991. During the 1970s and 1980s,
partly as a result of the adoption of the two-state political programme, the PLO
and the Palestinian people developed an impressive array of sources of power
against overwhelming odds. For example, an important source of power was
the staunch support of the non-aligned movement – at one point more countries
recognised the PLO than did the state of Israel. Moreover, the PLO had a fairly
effective cadre of diplomats. But while Israel exploited the Oslo Accords to
establish diplomatic and business ties with Third World and Arab countries,
the PLO allowed its source of power to dissipate.

Another source of power was latent in the fact that the international NGO solidarity movement had reached impressive proportions by the 1980s. Hundreds of
NGO representatives filled the UN Palais des Nations for the annual conference
on Palestine, representing a powerful movement of support. After the Madrid
Conference and the signing of the first Oslo Accord in 1993, the Palestinian leadership made no attempt to sustain these networks or to use the breakthrough in
PLO relations with the USA to reach out to new constituencies in the West, to
educate and engage them. Worse still, little investment was made to sustain Arab
solidarity with the Palestinians – especially that of Arab peoples.

An even more serious problem is that, after Oslo, the PLO also sought to
control the popular organisations and committees which sustained the first
Intifada, and which had taken root over several years. The first Intifada was
one of the best and most effective means of power the Palestinian people have
ever had. Its predominantly non-violent nature exposed not only the brutality
of the Israeli occupation regime but also the justice of the Palestinian cause, and
it galvanised international support. After the Palestinian Authority (PA) was
established, that grass-roots power was dissipated in favour of centralisation
and armed groups in what has been a huge loss to the Palestinians.

Perhaps the most serious loss of potential power has been the way that the
PLO and the PA have fragmented the Palestinian body politic. With Oslo, the
PLO effectively ceased to represent Palestinian exiles and refugees. As for the
Palestinian citizens of Israel, they had gradually begun to develop their own
political programme after the two-state solution took hold, a process that intensified after 1993. The PLO itself has been allowed to fade away to be replaced
by the PA, which represents about one-third of the Palestinian people in small
segments of Palestine. In contrast to the PLO, Israel – the much stronger power –
has continued throughout to work 24 hours a day, seven days a week to nurture
all of its sources of power, not just military but also diplomatic, political, and
community and media outreach.

The Palestinian people and not just the PLO must also bear responsibility for the failure of the two-state solution. Few Palestinian intellectuals or popular movements have really challenged the PLO on any of its political positions, or spoken out clearly and forcefully against the path its leadership was taking, and few do so today. Many Palestinians – but not all, as will be discussed below – have stood by and watched their sources of power evaporate. In the meantime, a non-representative Palestinian leadership has entrenched itself on fragments of Palestinian land, and it appears to believe that the Palestinians have no source of power other than the political favour of the US government.

In brief, a two-state political programme has not been achieved largely because the Palestinian leadership has neither understood nor used sources of power effectively. If it had done so, and if the Palestinian people had held the PLO and its leadership more accountable, there might have been a sovereign Palestinian state today. Luckily, many Palestinians believe that other sources of power are available to them and they are organising to develop these different and viable sources of power.

What Sources of Non-violent Power Could Secure Palestinian Human Rights?

Before a discussion of sources of non-violent power directed towards Palestinian human rights, it is important to address why the focus is on non-violent power and how Palestinian rights are defined. This chapter focuses on means of non-violent power because, while armed resistance is legal under international law so long as it does not involve indiscriminate attacks on civilians, armed resistance in the case of Palestine is the least effective source of power available to the Palestinian people.

It is true that PLO guerrilla actions in the past and the present actions of armed movements like Hamas, Islamic Jihad and Al-Aqsa Martyrs Brigade make it difficult to ignore the Palestinians as the international community might prefer to do. However, the cost of this strategy is too great, and the benefit too small: the use of armed force pits Palestinians against Israel in the arena where it is strongest and the Palestinians are weakest. It also suggests an appearance of two equal sides to the conflict with equal claims, rather than an oppressor and an oppressed. Because the Palestinians are weak, their resort to armed force often violates international law, making it easy for Israel to demonise them. Furthermore, as noted earlier, the non-violent first Intifada, backed by an international movement of solidarity and an internationally acceptable political programme, positioned Palestinians to take advantage of an opening in international relations under the first Bush administration. This has so far marked the acme of Palestinian power.

This chapter seeks to examine sources of power in terms of what will be necessary to achieve Palestinian human rights rather than in terms of whether a one-state or a two-state outcome is best. It should be noted here that this author believes that either outcome could potentially lead to the achievement of Palestinian human rights:

- **A two-state outcome:** If there is a fully sovereign, independent Palestinian state in the West Bank, Gaza and East Jerusalem, together with recognition of the Palestinian right of return and a just implementation of this right, and if the state of Palestine is one that provides equality to all of its citizens – whether women or men, Christian, Muslim or Jew (but not Jewish settlers imposing their presence by force of arms and illegal settlement building) – and if this state of Palestine co-exists alongside a state of Israel that provides equality to all its citizens, then this outcome would fulfil Palestinian human rights.
- **A one-state outcome:** Similarly, if there is a single state of Israel/Palestine that provides equality to all of its citizens that recognises and justly implements the Palestinian right of return, then such an outcome would also fulfil Palestinian human rights.

Either outcome – one or two states – would require Palestinians to generate an enormous amount of power to achieve its realisation, and either outcome should produce a state (or states) in which all citizens are equal[1] and in which human rights are fully upheld, including the Palestinian right of return. As it happens, most of the same sources of power are needed for either outcome and many of the same challenges would likely confront either outcome.

Before proceeding, it is important to define the set of rights to which Palestinians are entitled. The question which arises, in the absence of a representative national leadership, is who is empowered to define what constitutes Palestinian human rights based on the standards embodied in international law? The answer is that the Palestinian people are empowered to do so, and they have done so. In July 2005, over 170 Palestinian coalitions, unions, associations, groups and organisations – representing tens of thousands of Palestinians in Israel, under occupation and in exile – issued a Call for Boycott, Divestment and Sanctions (BDS) until Palestinian human rights are achieved. They identified a set of four key interrelated goals to achieve Palestinian human rights, which are:

1. the inalienable right of self-determination;
2. an end to occupation and colonisation of all Arab lands and dismantling the Wall;

3. recognition of the fundamental rights of the Arab-Palestinian citizens of Israel to full equality; and
4. respect, protection and promotion of the rights of Palestinian refugees to return to their homes and properties as stipulated in UN Resolution 194.[2]

The Call for BDS is perhaps the most significant document the Palestinian people have produced since the national movement emerged in the 1960s, for several reasons:

*   It establishes a very clear set of goals that cover the aspirations of the entire Palestinian people, whether they are living under occupation, in exile or in Israel: goals that are grounded in international law and human rights.
*   It provides a strategy to achieve these goals – boycott, divestment and sanctions – a major source of non-violent resistance available to the Palestinian people.
*   It is broadly representative of the entire Palestinian people and – because it is endorsed by so many coalitions, unions and associations from across the political spectrum throughout the occupied territories, in Israel and in exile – it truly constitutes the Palestinian people speaking with one voice.
*   It focuses on the achievement of Palestinian human rights, beginning with the right to self-determination. It does *not* take a position as to whether self-determination should be expressed in a single unitary state or in two states, and thus enables participation by the broadest possible number of Palestinians as well as the widest solidarity movement for Palestinian rights in the struggle for self-determination.
*   It recognises that Israel, as a member state of the UN and the international community, must uphold international law. Indeed, the Call goes on to say: 'We also invite conscientious Israelis to support this Call, for the sake of justice and genuine peace.'

This *clear set of goals constitutes the first and most important source of power* for the Palestinian people and their supporters. Having such a set of explicit goals is especially important, given that there is much confusion about the aims of the Palestinian struggle among both Palestinians and their supporters. The debate around outcomes – one state or two states – has obscured the need for, and the existence of, clear goals around which Palestinians and their supporters can rally, irrespective of the final outcome.

If the supporters of Palestinian human rights are not clear about the goals of the Palestinian struggle – freedom, equality, return and self-determination – then they will not know how long to struggle for this cause. Worse, they may demobilise if, for example, the USA imposes a two-state solution that offers the minimum of sovereignty, independence and human rights which shelves the right of return, and leaves the Palestinian citizens of Israel facing inequality within a 'Jewish state'.

A second important source of power is *national unity around a vision of struggle*. National unity is about much more than unity between the Hamas and Fateh movements. National unity means that the Palestinian people, whether they live in exile, under occupation or in Israel, should think of themselves *as a people* and plan for the Palestinian future in a way that addresses the rights of the *entire* people. This is happening gradually, and as noted above, the 2005 Call for BDS by Palestinian civil society addresses the rights of all sectors of the Palestinian people. In Israel, many civil society organisations among the Palestinian citizens of Israel are aware not only that they are part of the Palestinian people, but also of their responsibility towards the future of this people as a whole. They work simultaneously for their equal rights as citizens of Israel as well as for the future of the Palestinian people.

Another development worth noting is that the right of return movement is much stronger now than it was around the time of the Oslo Accords. In 1993, this movement would have been too weak to challenge late Palestinian leader Yasser Arafat in the event that Israel had been serious about reaching a two-state solution with minimal refugee rights. However, in recent years, Palestinian civil society organisations dealing with the right of return have begun encouraging Palestinian individuals not only to dream about the possibility of return, but also to find ways to implement their individual right of return. Right of return demonstrations have brought out tens of thousands of people within the occupied territories and in Israel, in a phenomenon that has been noted by the PA. Some of those marching in these demonstrations are Israeli Jews and, indeed, one of the signs of hope for the future is the growing number of Israeli Jews who believe in equal rights between Jews and Arabs in Israel.

Thus, a clear set of well-defined goals and the vision of a unified struggle by the whole Palestinian people are two sources of power available to the Palestinians. There are other sources of power available to Palestinians: economic, cultural, moral, legal and political.

Economic power is currently one of the most effective means of non-violent power that the Palestinian people have at their disposal. Something which had been untapped in previous decades, it is now at the heart of an international solidarity movement for BDS that is fast-growing – particularly since the Israeli attacks on Gaza of December 2008 and January 2009. There are many examples of the types of actions that are taking place in the areas of boycott and divestment which can be undertaken by individuals as well as by groups. There is less to report on sanctions, which require action by states, as few states have yet to show any desire to impose sanctions on Israel, although a shift in popular discourse and action could lead to a shift in state actions.

Examples of boycotts include direct action by individuals to target European supermarkets carrying goods produced in the illegal Israeli settlements in the occupied Palestinian territories. There are also remarkably successful efforts to target companies that are providing products and services to Israel's illegal occupation, such as Veolia, which has lost actual and potential contracts estimated at some US$7.5 billion, and Motorola, which sold its bomb fuses department after Human Rights Watch teams provided evidence of their illegal use in attacks on civilian targets in Gaza.[3]

Some of the boycott efforts above are closely linked to divestment efforts, which have grown again in recent years on university campuses and in churches. Churches such as the Presbyterian and the United Methodists, as well as the Quakers, are looking into divestment from companies whose work supports the occupation. Students for Justice in Palestine at Hampshire College were recently successful in a drive for the university to divest from a mutual fund that includes six companies that support Israel's occupation. Even when they are unsuccessful, boycott and divestment efforts still provide a good opportunity to educate communities directly and through the media about Israel's policies towards the Palestinians.

Many of the participants involved in the boycott and divestment movement are Jews in Europe, America, Israel and elsewhere. In the USA, for example, the national group Jewish Voice for Peace has been a leader in the effort to stop sales of Caterpillar bulldozers to Israel. In Israel, the Coalition of Women for Peace has developed a website – whoprofits.org – that lists over 200 companies directly involved in the occupation, including both US and Israeli corporations. The involvement of Jews is not only an important expression of solidarity that greatly contributes to future peace among countries and communities; it also makes it much harder for Israel to describe the BDS movement as anti-Semitic. Many Jews are also involved in the academic and cultural boycott of figures that work in Israeli academic and cultural institutions that support the Israeli occupation.[4] This campaign is also picking up very effectively around the world, especially in Europe, and the beginning stages of an academic boycott have reached the USA.

It is important to note that part of the reason that boycott and divestment are successful is because they do not question Israel's existence *as a state* but rather challenge its *occupation*, where Israel engages in the most egregious and visible violations of international law. The vast majority of countries and peoples in the West will not accept a solution in which Israel's existence is not guaranteed. However, they do respond positively to positions based on human rights and international law, including an end to occupation, equal rights and the right of return. Many groups also understand the importance of using the focus on Israel's occupation as a point of departure in education about all violations of Palestinian rights, including their dispossession and their right of return, as well as the unequal treatment of the Palestinian citizens of Israel. This is the strategy of, for example, the US Campaign to End the Israeli Occupation, a diverse national coalition of over 360 member groups.

The academic boycott is a key element of the *moral power* and *cultural power* that are becoming increasingly effective sources of power for the Palestinian people. In their education and outreach efforts and in academic and media work, more and more advocates of Palestinian human rights are focusing on what they perceive to be the root cause of the conflict: Zionism, and the attempt to create an ethnic exclusivist state in historic Palestine. It is important to remember that 1948 was not only the year of the creation of the state of Israel; it was also the year that the UN adopted the Universal Declaration of Human Rights, which articulated standards of human dignity that have been codified in international laws. In 1975, the UN passed a resolution equating Zionism with racism; this was revoked in 1991 after considerable pressure was brought to bear by the USA at the behest of Israel. One could argue that it was defeated because not enough education had been done at a popular level about the nature of Zionism. That education is being conducted today, and this is a major challenge to Israel's legitimacy in its attempt to maintain the Jewish characteristics of the state and privileging Jews over non-Jews.

This dimension of the moral argument is being furthered by the increasingly common use of the word 'apartheid': for example, in the title of a book by former president Jimmy Carter; and in campaigns by the US Campaign to End the Israeli Occupation, which in 2008 organised an 11-city US speaking tour by Diana Buttu and Eddie Makue, the General Secretary of the South African Council of Churches. The moral argument also stands to work over time by removing the underpinnings of the concept that it is possible to be both Jewish and democratic. This does not mean that the state of Israel will disappear. However, it does place considerable pressure on the state of Israel and/or any future state in historic Palestine to become states for all their citizens where everyone enjoys equal rights.

Telling the Palestinian story is one of the most effective sources of power, and cultural power is blossoming among Palestinians as well as human rights advocates engaged in this issue. Palestinian creativity in film, theatre, art and other mediums is now reaching the world in a way it never has before through exhibitions, film festivals and mainstream movie houses as well as other venues. To give just two examples: Hani Abu-Asad's *Paradise Now* was nominated for an Oscar and won a Golden Globe among other awards; and the award-winning director Annemarie Jacir's *Salt of this Sea* has been screened worldwide. Groups also hold annual Palestine film festivals in US cities like Chicago, Houston and Boston.

The Palestinian story has also gripped internationally renowned artists. For example, a few years after she was killed in March 2003 by an Israeli bulldozer as she non-violently protested the demolition of a Palestinian home, Rachel Corrie's journals were transformed into a play by British actor Alan Rickman and journalist Katherine Vine. The play won awards in Britain and played to full houses. In the USA, a controversy erupted that initially prevented the play from being performed, which resulted in excellent media and education opportunities – and, in any case, the play was eventually performed. In addition, in 2009, renowned British playwright Caryl Churchill produced a powerful short play, *Seven Jewish Children*, after the Israeli assault on Gaza, which attracted widespread attention and discussion.

As for *legal power* and *political power*, a good deal of work is being done in both these arenas, but these are among the toughest arenas in which to achieve results because they directly challenge the dominant power system, and because the Palestinians are increasingly without a leadership that is willing and able to function at these levels. Before the further weakening of the Palestinian body politic, there was a very important legal development in the form of the Advisory Opinion of the International Court of Justice, which affirmed the ways in which international law applies to this conflict. It also reaffirmed the existence of a Palestinian people with the right to self-determination. Some use is being made of the Advisory Opinion in education and outreach work, but unfortunately it has not been employed effectively by those who claim leadership over the Palestinians.

Legal challenges are being heard in court against Israelis believed to have committed war crimes. For example, in 2009 the Spanish National Court (the *Audiencia Nacional*, which claims jurisdiction over international crimes which come under the competence of Spanish courts) decided to hear a case against Israel. This case claimed that the Israelis should be charged with war crimes for dropping a one-ton bomb in a 2002 targeted assassination against a Hamas leader, which also resulted in the killing of 14 civilians. In the wake of the December–January assault on Gaza, there are said to be over 150 legal claims against Israel. Although such challenges are very time-consuming and require significant amounts of capital, the possibility of being tried for war crimes has precluded travel by several Israeli military and political leaders. There are also the beginnings of challenges and claims against countries that could have been complicit in the crimes committed in Gaza, either because they have an obligation under the Geneva conventions to hold countries accountable for war crimes or because, as in the cases of the USA or the UK, their weapons were used in Israel's assaults.

Lastly, political power is the toughest arena. Some political actions have taken advantage of US lip service to a peace process. For example, the Right to Enter campaign in the West Bank organised public and media protests against Israeli moves to begin cancelling residence and visitor visas, and managed to get some 30,000 residencies approved.[5] But they have not been able to obtain a clear policy from Israel, and now that the media attention has died down, Israel has resumed its typical course of action. Unfortunately, the emergence of a counterpart to the Right to Enter Movement that might push the issue in the USA has yet to prove possible, even if this happens to be one of the most promising avenues open to keeping Palestinians on the land. Palestinian Americans and other Americans can petition their Congressional representatives, work with Arab-American organisations and petition the State Department on this issue in order to achieve some individual and (possibly) some group successes. Still, in light of Israel's relentless strategy of expropriating land and excluding the people, forcing Israel to approve visas and residency permits was a noteworthy victory. Palestinians and their supporters ought to take advantage of the American administration's declared interest in a two-state settlement to push for measures that will freeze and reverse colonisation and enable Palestinians to stay on their land, while continuing to struggle for a rights-based solution.

There is also movement on the political front in terms of educational outreach to and lobbying of parliaments in Europe and the US Congress about Palestinian rights. This is contributing to an important change in discourse together with other elements, such as the growing number of American Jews who are challenging the American Israel Public Affairs Committee (AIPAC) approach to the Israeli–Palestinian conflict because they believe it is bad for Israel, as well as American Jews who are working for rights-based solutions. Over time, this may alter discourse in the US Congress.

One of the biggest challenges facing Palestinians on the political front is how to hold the PLO and the PA accountable for their actions and their lack of representation. It is not sufficient to work around the PA. It must be directly challenged and held accountable in order to prevent the imposition of a solution on Palestinians that will end legal claims and demobilise the solidarity movement. Unfortunately, this non-representative leadership now has a powerful military force that has been trained and armed by the Americans – a force that understands, in the words of its US trainer General Keith Dayton, that its prime role is to maintain internal security and not to challenge Israel. Indeed, during Israel's December/January assault on Gaza, this force effectively clamped down on protests in the West Bank. There is a need to find creative ways to challenge the lack of representation and reinforce the Palestinian national movement.

What is the Single Most Important Strategy of Which no Palestinian Political Programme Should Ever Lose Sight?

Although there are clear goals and growing sources of power, more attention must be paid to ways to counter directly what is understood to be the core of Israel's political programme. In spite of some minor dissenting voices, the overwhelming direction of Israel's political programme has been simple and relentless from the earliest days of Zionism: securing a land for Jewish settlement. After Israel was established in 1948, it has worked to achieve this aim through a strategy of taking the land and excluding the people, first by expulsion from Israel itself and then within Israel, as well as within the West Bank and Gaza.

Taking the Land

The tactics that Israel uses to divest Palestinians of their land are similar, whether the Palestinians are citizens of Israel or living under occupation in the West Bank and East Jerusalem. They include: home demolitions on grounds of illegal construction (homes are often built 'illegally' because permits are denied); acquisition of land for state or military purposes; allowing houses to become dilapidated and then declaring them unsafe after which they are taken over by the state; construction of Jewish-only communities, etc.

Excluding the People

While mass expulsions and population shifts of the kind that happened in 1947–8 and 1967 are no longer possible, Israel's drive to empty the land of the Palestinian people is still there. A variety of ways are used, many of which are similarly applied to the Palestinian citizens of Israel, to the Palestinians in the occupied territories, and to Palestinian refugees and exiles. They include: rejection of the right of return; cancellation of ID cards and residence permits; cancellation of visitors' visas; and death and disability from incursions, attacks, targeted assassinations, inability to access medical care and, most recently, hunger.

Against this background the core strategy of the Palestinian people – whatever the political programme adopted – must be to keep as much of the land as possible and to keep as many Palestinians on the land as possible: to keep the Palestinian people on the land of Palestine. Otherwise, all political programmes are pointless since the sources of power described above, while important over the long term, do not sustain the Palestinian people on their land. One of the few effective actions in this regard has been that of the Right to Enter group.

In this context, it is important to draw attention to Israeli escalation on one of its 'fronts' against the Palestinians. Most recently attempts have been made to further exclude the Palestinian citizens of Israel. They have always been regarded as second-class citizens, but now not only is there talk of transfer and loyalty oaths but there also are police actions. In March 2009, for example, the Israeli High Court decided to allow 100 far-right Zionist activists, flanked by 2,500 security forces in riot gear, to march in the Israeli Arab town of Umm al-Fahm (which is known for its Palestinian nationalism) in an alarming echo of Sharon's visit to Al-Aqsa Mosque. After Sharon's visit, it may be recalled, Israeli police fired on unarmed Palestinian protestors for days in what ignited the second Intifada, setting the stage for Sharon's election and the war of the cities to break the backbone of Palestinian resistance.

As Palestinians and their supporters strengthen and develop their strategies towards a solution to the conflict, a spotlight ought to be kept on Israeli policies towards the Palestinians – both within Israel and within the West Bank and the Gaza Strip.

Notes

1. The phrase 'all citizens are equal' or 'a state of all its citizens' is a more effective term than secular, which is often misunderstood in the region to mean atheist.

2. The Call's full title is 'Palestinian Civil Society Calls for Boycott, Divestment and Sanctions against Israel Until it Complies with International Law and Universal Principles of Human Rights', 9 July 2005. For the full text and list of signatories, go to www.bdsmovement.net/?q=node/52.

3. See the website for the global BDS movement at www.bdsmovement.net/?q=node/126, as well as the websites of the Palestine Solidarity Campaign in the UK, the US Campaign to End the Israeli Occupation in the USA and Australians for Palestine, among many others.

4. See www.pacbi.org.

5. For more information, see www.righttoenter.ps.

CHAPTER 18

Building Movements for the One-State Solution in Palestine and the Arab World

Leila Farsakh

Introduction

It is a great challenge for Palestinians to try to think about building move-ments for the one-state solution in Palestine and the Arab world after Israel's war of 2008–9 on Gaza, which resulted in the death of 1,419 Palestinians and the destruction of thousands of Palestinian homes and the social infrastructure in Gaza at a total estimated cost of US$1.9 billion.[1] In the circumstances, to ask the victims to reconcile with people they regard as their victimisers may be over-optimistic, even if many agree that the two-state solution is dead and there is a need to think of alternatives to the present impasse. The Palestinian people seem in no mood to talk to, let alone live with, the Israelis. The Arab street expresses outrage, as the demonstrations that followed the war testified. The Israelis are also not keen on reaching out to the Palestinians, as revealed in the Israeli elections of 2009 and Prime Minister Netanyahu's formation of a government with the right-wing party Yisrael Beiteinu, led by Avigdor Lieberman, who wants Palestinian citizens of Israel to be forced to give an oath of allegiance to a Jewish state. However, the inability to start a movement for the one-state idea in Palestine risks deepening the despair. More dangerously perhaps, inaction risks marginalising the Palestinian cause and turning it into a humanitarian problem, rather than the essentially political issue it is. And as significantly, inaction does not provide Israelis or Jews with any secure future, even if in the short run Israel can afford to be uncompromising.

The challenges to creating a one-state movement in Palestine and the Arab world are many but in my view they fundamentally hinge on three main issues. First is the necessity of rethinking the separate, two-state paradigm as the framework for the Palestinian struggle for self-determination and the solution to the Israeli–Palestinian conflict. It requires explaining how a movement based on the achievement of equal political rights within the whole of historic Palestine can meet Palestinian national and political rights, and at what cost. Second, building a one-state movement entails identifying the kind of leadership and grass-roots activism that can mobilise support for this idea among the various Palestinian constituencies and in various political forums. This in turn requires a redefinition of the processes by which these two central bodies communicate with each other, with themselves and with the outside world. The third and perhaps the most difficult challenge for the one-state movement is how to address the question of Jewish-Israeli political and civil rights within a single state in Palestine. It is the case that many in Israel, at both the levels of the political elite and civil society, may well view the one-state solution as unrealistic at best and malevolent at worst. Given the very real fears that many Israelis have of a number of security, political and cultural threats to their position within the Middle East should a single state be created (such as anti-Semitism, religious attachment to Jerusalem, being swamped by neighbouring Arab culture and the rise of Islamism), the Jewish-Israeli community will have to be engaged with extensively in order to address both the question of their rights within a single state and to convince them that this is the only just and equitable solution to the current conflict. This is all the more challenging and complicated given the recent attempts by several prominent figures among the Israeli right to hijack the one-state agenda. They called on the Jewish state to give the Palestinians in the West Bank civil political rights but no national rights. They are opposed to the two-state solution and to the creation of a separate Palestinian state, and call instead for the establishment of one Jewish-dominated state in all of historic Palestine.[2]

From Statehood to Equal Rights

The first major step towards building a Palestinian and Arab movement for the one-state solution lies in resituating the Palestinian struggle for self-determination within a rights paradigm. It requires that the Palestinian political movement and its leadership shift the political struggle from one geared towards establishing an independent Palestinian state to one focused on achieving equal political rights for all the citizens of the state. Getting rid of the Palestinian state paradigm as the aim and the strategy of the Palestinian struggle for self-determination is not an easy task, since all Palestinian political parties today continue to adhere to it. This is the case for Fateh and the PLO at large, the parties to the left (PFLP, DFLP, People's Party) as much as Hamas.[3]

The creation of a Palestinian state has been since 1974 (if not before, as some argue)[4] the framework for defining Palestinian self-determination. Although the PLO, the main Palestinian political representative, originally defined its aim in 1964 as the liberation of all of Palestine, and in 1971 in terms of the creation of a secular democratic state inclusive of Christians, Jews and Muslims, it de facto abandoned such an idea for various political reasons.[5] Diplomatically, there was no response to such a vision, since Israel was not interested in it.[6] Moreover, the international community has, ever since 1947, envisaged partition, rather than a single united state, as the solution to the Israeli–Palestinian conflict. UNGA Resolution 181, voted by a two-thirds majority of the UN General Assembly on 29 November 1947, proposed the creation of an Arab and a Jewish state in Palestine as the only means for resolving the Arab–Zionist struggle over the land. UNSC Resolution 242 in 1967, which became the basis for all Arab–Israeli peace negotiations ever since, stipulated the acceptance of the Jewish state by its Arab neighbours in exchange for land and peace. Regionally, the PLO under Yasser Arafat was determined to assert the independence of Palestinian decision-making from Arab countries' interferences and their manipulation of the Palestinian cause for their own national and political aims. Domestically, some argue, Fateh – who took the lead in talking about the one-state idea – was not genuinely interested in it.[7] Rather, it was concerned with establishing its power among the Palestinian political movements and putting the PLO on the international map as the sole legitimate representative of the Palestinian people. It wanted to ensure that the PLO alone had the sovereign right to negotiate on their behalf. In 1974, at the 12th Palestinian National Congress, the PLO officially adopted as its aim not simply liberation or return, but also 'setting up a patriotic, independent fighting people regime in every part of liberated part of Palestine' – a 'national authority' that will carry on the liberation process and establish a 'democratic Palestinian state'.[8]

The idea of the Palestinian state fulfilled four core functions for the Palestinian political struggle. First, it became the vehicle for asserting Palestinian self-determination. It made the Palestinian problem not a refugee problem in need of a humanitarian solution as UNSC Resolution 242 suggested, but rather a political struggle for national liberation.[9]

Second, the idea of a Palestinian state, however vague its boundaries, provided the framework for organising and channelling Palestinian resistance. Since 1968, the PLO leadership worked on setting up the institutions of the Palestinian state before territorialising it.[10] The PLO, with its various political institutions, electoral structure and economic services, acted as a state in exile. The fighters in Lebanon and Jordan in the 1960s and 1970s, as much as the Palestinian resistance in the West Bank and Gaza, found in the PLO their political expression as well as their protector, and in the dream of the Palestinian state, however loosely defined, their political aim and the meaning of their struggle.

Third, the independent Palestinian state became the means for fulfilling Palestinian rights, including the right of return, political rights of citizenship long denied in the West Bank and the Gaza Strip (WBGS) as well as in the Arab world, and economic rights of growth and development. While it could have compromised on Palestinian territorial rights and would have been unable to provide full justice to the Nakba (catastrophe) and Naksah (setback), the concept of a Palestinian state on the part of Palestine ensured Palestinian sovereignty. This sovereignty was crucial since it provided the *means* for ingathering all the refugees – even if on only some part of historic Palestine – to be independent of Arab countries' manipulation and to live in dignity, if not with full justice.

Fourth, the concept of the Palestinian state became the price for the Palestinian historic compromise with Israel. It was the only currency it could use in an international system that upholds the right of nations to self-determination and declares that the only solution to the Arab–Israeli conflict is partition. In 1988 the PLO announced its official acceptance of UN Resolutions 242 and 181, thereby officially accepting the principle of land for peace and the two-state solution as the only solution to the Arab–Israeli conflict. It also issued its Declaration of Independence, indicating thereby its aim to territorialise the state it had de facto built in exile over the previous 20 years, and to live in peace with Israel.

The Oslo Peace Process and the creation of the Palestinian Authority provided what was seen as the first concrete step towards the fulfilment of this struggle for national independence. However, judging by where the Palestinians find themselves today, it also stopped at it. Both the Palestinian leadership and population are presently at a loss after 15 years of failed peace negotiations and the fragmentation of the Palestinian project at the political, social and territorial levels. The Oslo years allowed the establishment of Palestinian autonomy with limited and truncated territorial jurisdiction, controlling less than 22 per cent of the territory of historic Palestine. It created a Palestinian Authority with functional jurisdiction over 93 per cent of the Palestinian people in the West Bank and Gaza, and territorial jurisdiction of less than 21 per cent of the West Bank and 75 per cent of the Gaza Strip. This Authority proved to be more concerned with security than with accountability, with policing rather than with citizens' rights. Since the Al-Aqsa Intifada, Palestinians saw further expansion of Israeli settlements and the doubling of the Jewish settler population to over 484,000 Israelis in the West Bank and East Jerusalem, the construction of the 703 km separation barrier, the imposition of 506–640 checkpoints and deepening of Palestinian territorial and political 'bantustanisation', effectively destroying any possibility for a viable Palestinian state to emerge.[11]

Yet while the dream of Palestinian sovereign independence evaporates, it is far from evident that the one-state idea, which was first proposed in the 1920s by Brit Shalom, and reinterpreted by the PLO in 1971 under the slogan of One

Democratic State in all of Palestine, can galvanise a mass movement today.[12] For it to become the vehicle for Palestinian political struggle, the one-state idea needs to fulfil the four key functions that the idea of the Palestinian state performed for the struggle so far. In a sense, it has never been so well placed to do so, given that the two-state solution has been tried and so far failed. It remains to be seen whether the one-state idea can become a coherent political project, not just an ideal, and thus offer concrete legal and political strategies that address questions of political rights, political expediency and mass mobilisation.

The One-State Solution

The case for the one-state option, as put forward by its proponents, is based on moral and practical considerations as much on legal and political arguments. From a practical political point of view, the Oslo process has shown the limits, if not the impossibility, of Palestinian territorial and political sovereignty. The Israeli redeployment from Gaza and the stagnation of Israeli–Palestinian negotiations have further confirmed the impossibility of any truncated concept of sovereignty, since Israel, under Benjamin Netanyahu as much as Olmert, is reticent to implement the internationally endorsed Road Map calling for the creation of a Palestinian state. The result of 18 years of negotiations has made the one-state solution the default outcome of the failure of the two-state option.

From a moral point of view, the one-state idea is argued to be 'superior' to the two-state option since it allows for the reinvigoration of the concept of popular sovereignty, the one tied to the right of the original inhabitants of the land. It is also better placed to fulfil Palestinian rights, both political and civil, than the two-state solution. It acknowledges and protects the 'right of return', as mandated by UNGA Resolution 194, allowing all Palestinian refugees and their descendants to return to their land.[13] It also brings the Palestinians who are inside Israel into the political equation from which Oslo excluded them. According to Omar Barghouti, the one-state solution provides relative justice, as it enables victims to live with their victimisers on an equal basis, despite any injustices of the past which bedevil them.[14]

Yet the real challenge lies in how to transfer the one-state idea from an intellectual plane into a realistic political project that has currency among the inhabitants of the land as much as internationally. This is a major political hurdle as the international community, ever since the Quartet's Road Map in 2003, declared the Palestinian state not only a right, but also the *only* solution to the conflict. Most Palestinians inside the occupied territories as much as outside remain attached to the Palestinian national goal of achieving independence for which they fought for over 40 years and whose recognition was earned after much blood, sweat and tears. The Palestinian state remains the only currency for discussing the conflict, however devalued it has become.

Advocates of the one-state solution counter the accusation that the position they advocate is utopian by drawing on concrete legal proposals that provide a political platform for the one-state idea. A number of lawyers have been trying to rehabilitate the numerous legal documents that advocate the one-state solution, as well as define its constitutional structure or shape.[15] In this regard, the United Nations Special Committee on Palestine (UNSCOP) Minority Report in 1947 is particularly significant, since it provided an internationally supported alternative to the partition plan. The UN General Assembly also voted on this plan in November 1947, giving it 50 per cent of the members' votes. The Minority Report called for the creation of a federated state with full citizenship for Jews and Arabs living in Palestine. It proposed the creation of two chambers, one based on proportional representation and the second based on equal ethnic representation, thereby protecting individual and communal rights of Jews and Arabs. The PLO Charter of 1971 also specifically stated that its programme calls for the creation of a secular democratic state in which Jews, Christians and Muslims live together in equality. While this model lacked much detail then, it seemed to suggest that individual rights have priority. It assumed that this state is going to be of Arab, if not Palestinian, nationality, but one which Jews, though not the Zionists, are part of.

Here, though, comes the second major hurdle for the one-state idea becoming a political project: the question of the state identity, its nationality and how it will protect national and individual rights of those living inside it. The major hurdle for the one-state project is to address and overcome the unwillingness of the people living in Israel/Palestine today to participate in a single polity. Palestinians at the official and the grass-roots levels have expressed doubts about the feasibility of the one-state option because of the vehemence of the Israeli opposition to it.[16] Israelis, at both the state and the civil society level, argue that the one-state negates their Jewish identity and their need to have their own state that would protect them from anti-Semitism. They consider the one-state idea a means to eliminate the Israeli polity and culture that developed in historic Palestine over the past 60 years, rather than a way for the Palestinians to live with it.[17] Meanwhile, many Palestinians struggled to achieve independence and/or return, not to live with Israelis in the same polity. Many Palestinians look at the one-state idea in opportunistic terms, arguing that it is the inevitable outcome of their resistance and demographic expansion that will make Israelis effectively a minority in historic Palestine. By 2015, Palestinians are expected to be the majority living within Israel/Palestine, between the Mediterranean Sea and the Jordan River.[18] Few have considered the moral, legal and cultural implications of living with the Israelis on an equal basis or are even interested in these questions.

Building a one-state movement in Palestine and the Arab world requires a serious reconsideration and debate over the concept of statehood, citizenship and identity. The experiences of the Arab states, as well as of the Palestinian Authority with its limited autonomy, have clearly shown that statehood per se is not a guarantee for political rights. What needs to be developed and fought for is the notion of equal citizen rights and the institutional means to protect these rights, under no matter what state. This is not easy since the nature of the state shapes the nature of political rights that people acquire in it. The Arab Spring of 2011 has shown how the Arab street is precisely caught in these questions, eager to make the state become accountable to its citizens, rather than hide behind a veneer of nationalist patriotism.

So far, Palestinian proponents of the one-state oscillate between two versions for such a state. While most adherents to the one-state solution agree that the one-state would end the notion of a single Zionist state, not all agree, or demand, that it ends the Israeli cultural identity. Proponents of the secular democratic state argue that the state will protect the individual rights of all those who live under it, whether they are Jews, Christians or Muslims. They do not negate peoples' cultural and group identity, but leave it to private initiatives, rather than to state institutions, to find the means to express and protect the Israeli and Palestinian cultures. They do not, however, accord enough attention to the implications of demographic realities on the political rights of different communities living in it – in other words, to the risk that one group, by its sheer demographic size or expansion, can compromise the individual and group rights of the minority group. Proponents of the binational state, on the other hand, seek to be sensitive to these ethnic concerns by calling for a state that allows both Israeli and Palestinian cultural and political institutions to maintain their autonomy in a single political entity. They envisage the one-state along the Belgian or Swiss models, a federated or confederated state that protects individual and group rights.

Palestinian Party Politics and the One-State Idea

The problem for the one-state project today, however, does not simply hinge on finding the constitutional and legal means to protect national rights while guaranteeing citizen rights. While this is important, the major stumbling block remains how to turn the one-state project into a vehicle for framing and organising the Palestinian struggle. This is a function of the willingness of the present political leadership to endorse it, as much as the ability of grass-roots activists for the one-state to convince the population and the leadership of its necessity.

The present Palestinian political leadership is not immune to the one-state debate. However, it has not as yet adopted it as a plan around which to mobilise the Palestinian population and campaign for it internationally. A number of senior Fateh figures, such as Ahmad Qurei and Nabeel Shaath, have used the one-state idea as a threat in the face of Israel's intransigence to withdraw from the occupied territories.[19] However, no one has taken it up as a serious political programme. Palestinian parties of the left, such as the People's Party (the ex-communist party), the Popular Front for the Liberation of Palestine or the Palestinian Initiative (Al-Mubadara) under Mustafa Barghouti, have been mainly active in explaining why and how Israel has killed the two-state solution, rather than defining what the one-state is, let alone campaigning for it. They have also focused on the importance of enhancing civic participation in framing the struggle and defending citizens' rights.[20]

Hamas, on the other hand, has long declared that its aim is the return of the land and dismantling the Zionist state.[21] Since the 2006 Mecca Reconciliation Agreement, it accepted the idea of a Palestinian state within the borders of 1967 with full sovereignty. Khaled Mishal, the head of Hamas' political bureau, maintained that Hamas does not accord much attention presently to the shape and nature of this state (i.e. whether it will be Islamic or not), so long as it entails the end of the occupation.[22] Its acknowledgement of Israel, and of the Jewish people and culture in it, is thus implicit. It reiterated this position during its reconciliation with Fatah in April 2011. Hamas' main priority now is not the one-state solution; rather, it is asserting itself as the main Palestinian political party of resistance. According to Ghassan Khatib, it is Hamas, not the one-state movement, which will dominate Palestinian politics and change its direction for the coming years.[23]

Fateh finds itself presently at a very difficult juncture, as its legitimacy weakens in contrast to Hamas, especially after the Gaza War.[24] During the sixth Fateh national convention, held in Bethlehem in August 2009, the delegates were concerned with the direction the party should take vis-à-vis the Oslo negotiation process, the question of armed resistance and relation to Hamas, not with the one-state option. The generational struggle within the party between the old guards and the young cadres for more effective presentation was partly resolved with the latter being more represented in the main Fateh organ,[25] but it is still too early to say how far they are redirecting the party away from the struggle for a Palestinian state.

What has been noted is that the young Fateh cadres in the West Bank at least have started an internal debate on whether or not to adopt the one-state solution as a political project.[26] While many were in favour of it and asserted how Fateh has been at the lead of the one-state idea, no one has yet articulated it as a project or even as a discussable political idea. Both young and old cadres cannot yet envisage a political struggle for citizenship and equal rights before first obtaining their own Palestinian state.

The PLO and Palestinian Activism for the One-State Solution

According to Karma Nabulsi, the first step towards giving the one-state project centre stage in Palestinian politics starts by reunifying the fragmented Palestinian bodies politic. It necessitates reviving the PLO as well as restituting the concept of popular sovereignty as its modus operandi. It can only happen by recentralisation of the right of return as the core of the Palestinian struggle and by reaffirming the role of the refugees in defining and leading the Palestinian cause, as they did in the 1970s and 1980s.[27]

The reform of the PLO has long been on the political agenda, particularly ever since its raison d'être was put into question with the creation of the PA in 1994. The failure of Arafat and the different Palestinian parties to maintain the autonomy of the PLO led to its demise as a central political forum for the Palestinians. Yet most political parties remain attached to it since it is the only entity which represents all Palestinians inside and outside the occupied territories. Moreover, the PLO and not the PA was the Palestinian party to the Oslo negotiations or any future agreement. However, most attempts so far to revive the PLO have focused on how to include Hamas in it. While many Palestinian figures have expressed the need to revive the PLO institutionally and politically, there has been little serious consideration by any of the present parties, including Hamas, of how to bring a more effective representation and voice to the refugees as much as to the Palestinians inside Israel. It is still unclear how the PLO can take up the mantle of the one-state solution before it first reactivates itself as the forum for Palestinian politics. This seems to depend increasingly on the ability of the various Palestinian constituencies to push their political leadership towards adopting the one-state project as their political platform and strategy.

Refugees

Refugees represent that most supportive constituency for the one-state movement. The most vocal among them are the refugees of Lebanon and Jordan and, to a lesser extent, those of the West Bank and Gaza. These groups tend to be politically organised by the main Palestinian political parties and thus adhere to the parties' political agenda. Most of their actual campaigning for the one-state idea is in Lebanon and is a function of their demand for the implementation of the right of return.[28] It is an activism that is grass roots-based and concerned with opening spaces for popular representation. It seeks to bypass rigid political parties and focuses on refugees as citizens. A number of initiatives have taken place in Lebanon, by voluntary organisations and political activists seeking to link refugees together by overcoming geographical obstacles.[29] It remains to be seen how much their voices will impact the political leadership. Refugees are far from being a unified constituency under a single leadership.

Palestinians Inside Israel

The most important Palestinian constituency framing the Palestinian struggle today in terms of equal political rights, and not statehood per se, is not inside the camps or in the West Bank and the Gaza Strip, but inside Israel and increasingly in the Diaspora. Azmi Bishara's former campaign within Israel calling for a state for all of its citizens played an important role in changing the terms of the Palestinian struggle to one of rights, rather than simply national self-determination. It has helped mobilise youth to work on a one-state campaign, mostly in the West. Yet although the Palestinians inside Israel are the best placed to lead the one-state movement, it is not clear how far they are ready or willing to do so, given how violent Israel has been towards any sign of solidarity between Palestinians inside and outside the Green Line, as last seen with the October 2000 shooting of Israeli Palestinians by the Israeli police force or the 2008 legal case against Azmi Bishara. The attacks on Bishara and Tajamu', which led the former into exile, have left many Palestinians inside Israel without leadership. However, there are various signs that several groups are working seriously on the campaign for political rights, even if they are careful how they frame it and avoid any clear political organising. This can be seen in the work of Adala, Mada Al-Carmel and the Haifa Statement, among others.[30]

The Diaspora

Palestinians living in the West, activists, students and academics have been the most vocal for the one-state solution. Edward Said is probably the most remembered among Diaspora Palestinians for advocating the one-state in the 1990s. Many have since developed the debate further and reached out to larger audiences all over the globe. The most important grass-roots organisational work for the one-state has been among students and activists in the UK and Canada, and increasingly in continental Europe, followed by the USA. Following the example of South Africa's anti-apartheid movement, these activists have relied on three important strategies that are central to any successful one-state movement. First, they emphasise what they see as the 'apartheid' nature of Israeli rule in order to show how the one-state solution is the only way out of the present state of dispossession and inequality. Second, their work is based on collaborative initiatives that include Jews and Israelis, Arabs and Palestinians. They thus show the centrality of reaching out to the other side, the Israeli as much as the Arab and Westerner, and the feasibility of such outreach once you are out of the occupied territories. Third, they rely on a civil disobedience campaign. The students' sit-ins in numerous British and some American universities during Israel's latest war on Gaza recentralised the Palestinian cause internationally. The 'Israel Apartheid Week' campaign that started at the University of Toronto in 2004 is now a major international event that includes over 40 universities, in over 20 countries in North America, Europe and the West Bank. The Boycott, Divestment and Sanctions (BDS) campaign that they adopted, with its three aims of right of return, end of the occupation and end of discrimination inside Israel, refocuses the struggle on political rights rather than on statehood per se. It also provides an example of the symbiotic link between those inside and outside Palestine.

The Occupied Territories

Various sporadic forums within the West Bank and Gaza are starting to talk about the one-state option as an inevitable and necessary option for the Palestinian political struggle today.[31] The few polls conducted on this question in the occupied territories find that over 40 per cent of the Palestinians today are in favour of the one-state solution, defined vaguely as entailing Jews, Christians and Muslims living together.[32] The nationality and constitution of this state still remain vague, for most Palestinian activism inside the West Bank and Gaza remains focused on combating the occupation, not on defining its end result. What is new in this activism is its increasing reliance on civil grass-roots action, rather than militarism, one that emphasises the apartheid nature of Israeli rule. This can be seen in the Campaign to End Israel's Apartheid Wall, the weekly demonstrations against the barrier in Ni'lin and Bil'en, and in the West Bank and the Gaza Strip's Call for Boycott, Divestment and Sanctions (BDS) campaign. This was endorsed by over 170 civil society organisations in Gaza and the West Bank, including women's organisations, students and grass-roots political activists. Although BDS does not take a position on the one-state, this campaign has become an effective organising tool for refocusing the Palestinian cause worldwide on the issue of Palestinians' rights rather than statehood per se. It has succeeded in calling attention to Israel's violation of Palestinian rights and framing this violation in an 'apartheid' framework of analysis, as well as getting numerous international companies to close down their projects in Israel. Their work, as much as of those supporting activists in the Diaspora, is important insofar as they are seeking to reframe the conflict internationally as one of 'colonialism' and 'apartheid', not one of two competing (if unequal) national movements wanting their separate states as the official narratives seek to portray it, since the reality they are faced with on the ground shows an Israel continuously encroaching on Palestinian land and dominating its people. However, unlike the South African anti-apartheid experience, the Palestinian BDS movement does not attempt to work on enlightening Israelis or converting them. So far it is not interested in engaging Israelis, for its proponents maintain that only successful international sanctions will make Israelis face up to the iniquities which Zionist aspirations have produced and eventually join hands with the Palestinians for the sake of justice and equality for all.[33]

Addressing the Jewish Identity and History: Meeting the People Where They Are

Building the one-state movement in the Arab and Palestinian world will require a society-wide discussion on the meaning of citizenship and equal rights, irrespective of the quest for territorial sovereignty. It requires addressing the issue of identity and what it means to be Palestinian and Israeli in a new state. It inevitably needs to address, rather than negate, the continuous presence of the question of Jewishness and its links to the idea of Israel. Therein lies one of its major challenges. Most of the Palestinian debate on the one-state, while inclusive of the Jews, avoids engaging with the complexity of Jewish identity and history. It clearly repudiates Zionism, but it seeks to incorporate the Jewish people of Israel. There is little discussion though of what to do with the Israeli culture that has developed over the past 60 years, with the Jews who care about their language and their culture, and want to remain in Palestine as Hebrew speakers, not necessarily as Palestinians, let alone Arabs. The binationalists argue that these people have a place in the one-state so long as they accept the democratic game. The secular democrats are either silent or expect the Jews to become de facto Palestinians. There is little discussion of what the identity of this new state will be, implicitly implying that it is either going to be Arab Palestinian or at best left open.

Meanwhile, within the Arab world, the distinction between Zionists and Jews needs to be made more often. While numerous Arab governments and business communities have established ties with the Jewish state for purely opportunistic reasons, the average person in the Arab world is averse to all such contacts that betray the Palestinian cause. While TV channels such as Al-Jazeera are keen on presenting images of anti-Israel Jews, as during the last war on Gaza, there is no debate within Arab society as to the complexity of Israeli identity. As the Islamic parties' constituency expands in the Arab world and people increasingly define their identity in religious rather than national terms, one wonders if the one-state movement will have any resonance in the Palestinian and Arab street.

In this author's view, two debates need to take place among the Palestinians and within the Arab world for the one-state movement to gain momentum. The first is an open discussion on identity and a free open space to rehabilitate the concept of the Arab Jew. Such rehabilitation can enable the average Arab and Palestinian to see the Jewish people as part of the Arab heritage, not a Western alien product, and thus somebody to live with, not to negate or expel. This requires a rediscovery of the role that Jewish people have played in Arab culture in critical rather than dismissive or romantic terms. There is an urgent need to learn and diffuse knowledge about the role of Arab Jews in the national independence movement in the twentieth century and in their opposition to Zionism in Palestine, as well as in Iraq, Morocco, Algeria or Egypt.[34] This rediscovery should not be restricted to the political domain, but should also cover other fields such as the arts, literature, sciences, etc. It is important to understand the Israeli culture, with all its worries of anti-Semitism, prejudices and fear of the Arab, and to discuss means to address them. It should not, of course, be forgotten that Israelis, Zionists and Jews will also need to be convinced of the need for a solution that promotes the individual and group rights of all its citizens in a single, unitary, secular state. The problems which this endeavour will undoubtedly face in convincing those sectors of Israeli society and the political elite which are vehemently opposed to such a solution are beyond the remit of this chapter, focused as it is on the Arab and Palestinian political imagination, but they are nevertheless essential to note. It is equally important to re-examine the role of Arab societies and governments in ostracising long-established Jewish communities in countries such as Iraq or Yemen after the establishment of Israel. Founding alliances with increasingly vocal (though mainly academic) Israelis of Arab descent that are not shy to challenge their state and re-engage with their Arab heritage can only help the movement both within the Arab world as much as with Israelis (e.g. Ella Shohat, Yehuda Shenhaf, Yossi Yona, Tali Hatuka). Building alliances with Israelis, Mizrahi and Ashkenazi, who are critical of Zionism and advocate the one-state, is a necessity.

The second debate that needs to take place relates to multiculturalism in the Arab world: namely, how to reinvigorate the present Arab identity with the cosmopolitan character that it once had. What is being proposed here is not 'seeds of peace' and humus and falafel gatherings with Israelis or Americans, but rather a serious discussion over citizenship and identity that goes beyond religion and nationalism. The Arab Spring in 2011 focused precisely on these concerns, on how to establish a state of rights. The major challenge is how to rehabilitate a truly humanist identity. The starting point of the debate has to be an agreement by both sides that there is no place for an apartheid-type ideology which favours either side in a debate on the one-state. However, the debate cannot be confined to wanting to protect or dismantle an Israeli culture or a primordial Islamic or Arab identity, which historically has always been porous. Rehabilitating the cosmopolitan nature of Arab – and, indeed, Middle Eastern – identity is as necessary to move forward as is fostering channels for effective political participation and protection of equal citizenship rights. It is all the more necessary in the global world we are living in today.

Conclusion

The one-state movement is still a young movement, but one that is growing. The greatest challenge facing it is how to translate its increasing popularity in the Diaspora into a clear political project for those inside Israel/Palestine. Its success also hinges on its ability to find the key political party that would adopt it, and on the ability of the PLO to revive itself and readopt the one-state programme.

The debate is taking place and its circle is widening. It is important to enhance and spread it. More dialogue needs to be established between the grass roots and political leadership. More transparency and accountability is needed within the Palestinian political establishment. In this respect, there is much to learn from the South African anti-apartheid struggle, in terms of discourse as much as strategy. The South African struggle emphasised equal political rights, when the white government and many blacks were pushing for separate development and Bantustans that would be declared 'sovereign states'. It also emphasised working across the board and for a state for all of its citizens. Above all, it also showed that reconciliation and working together with people whom you regard as your previous oppressors does not entail loving your partner. It necessitates respecting the equal rights of the other. Overcoming the experience of Israeli occupation and colonisation is going to be hard. Hard work and time will only tell how far the one-state movement will mobilise and politically succeed, given the serious Israeli, regional and international challenges it faces.

Notes

1. WAFA, 'Financial cost of Israel's offensive on Gaza approaches $1.9 billion', 13 March 2009. Available at www.imemc.org/article/59308.

2. Noam Sheizaf, 'The Endgame', *Ha'aretz*, 15 July 2010.

3. See interview with Khalid Mish'al in Rabbani, Mouin, 'The making of a Palestinian Islamist leader: an interview with Khalid Mish'al', *Journal of Palestine Studies*, 37(3), Spring 2008, pp. 59–73.

4. Mustapha Hussein, 'The demise of the two-state solution', *Journal of Palestine Studies*, 76, Fall 2008, pp. 31–42. In Arabic.

5. Gresh, Alain, 'The PLO and the Naksa: the search for a Palestinian state', *Electronic Journal of Middle Eastern Studies*, 8, Spring 2008, pp. 81–93.

6. See Avi Shlaim, *The Iron Wall: Israel and the Arab World* (New York and London: WW Norton & Company, 2001); and Ilan Pappé, 'The birth, demise, and future of one Palestine complete', *Electronic Journal of Middle Eastern Studies*, 8, Spring 2008, pp. 151–64.

7. Hussein, op. cit., pp. 35–8.

8. See Palestinian National Council Resolutions, June 1974, in Walter Laqueur and Barry Rubin, *The Israel-Arab Reader: A Documentary History of the Middle East Conflict* (London: Penguin Press, 2008).

9. UNSC Resolution 242 does not mention the word Palestinian and only calls for a 'just solution to the refugee problem' (read UNSC Resolution 242, available at www.domino.un.org).

10. Yazid Sayigh, *Armed Struggle and the Search for State: The Palestinian National Movement, 1949–1993* (Oxford: Oxford University Press, 1997).

11. Data from OCHA, The Closure Update, November 2008. Available at www.ochaopt.org/documents/ocha_opt_closure_update_2008_09_english.pdf.

12. Leila Farsakh, 'Time for a bi-national state?', *Monde Diplomatique*, March 2007.

13. According to official estimates, there are today 6.8 million Palestinian refugees whose families fled or were expelled from their homes in 1948, of which 4.3 million are registered with the UN Relief and Works Agency (UNRWA) for Palestine Refugees. See Badil, *Survey of Palestinian Refugees and Internally Displaced Persons 2004–2005* (Bethlehem: Badil, 2006). Available at www.badil.org/Refugees/facts&figures.htm.

14. Omar Barghouti, 'The secular democratic state is the only possible and ideal solution', *Journal of Palestine Studies*, 76, Fall 2008, pp. 1–25. In Arabic.

15. See George Bisharat, 'Maximizing rights: the state solution to the Palestinian–Israeli conflict', *Global Jurist*, 8(2), 2008; as well as George Bisharat, 'Between utopianism and realism: evaluating obstacles to the one two states solution'; and Michael Lynk, 'Partition, federalism and the future of Israel/Palestine', paper presented at Israel/Palestine: Mapping Models of Statehood and Paths to Peace, York University, Toronto, 22–24 June 2010.

16. Findings based on a series of interviews conducted with official and grass-roots organisations in the West Bank, March–July 2008.

17. See Benny Morris for an extended review of Israeli opposition to the one-state idea and why it is of great danger to Israelis and what he defined to be its Jewish Western identity. Benny Morris, *One State Two States, Resolving the Israel/Palestine Conflict* (New Haven: Yale University Press, 2009).

18. Palestinians inside Israel are growing at 2.8 per cent per annum and in the WBGS at 4 per cent. The Jewish Israeli population is growing at less than 2 per cent per annum. Ali Abunimah, *One Country: A Bold Proposal to End the Israeli–Palestinian Impasse* (New York: Metropolitan Press, 2006).

19. See *New York Times*, 9 March 2009; and *Al Hayat Al Jadida*, 10 July 2006 and 2 September 2005 (in Arabic).

20. See Al-Mubadara's statement where it calls for increased participation by Palestinian citizens in the process of nation-building: 'We wish to give them the opportunity to participate in the just struggle for the realisation of an independent, viable, democratic and prosperous state which guarantees security, justice, equality before the law, and a dignified existence for its citizens'. Available at www.almubadara.org/new_web/index_eng.htm.

21. Khalid Hroub, *Hamas: Political Thought and Practice* (Washington, DC: Institute of Palestine Studies, 2000).

22. Rabbani, op. cit., p. 61.

23. Ghassan Khatib, 'A present crisis or the end of a historical role', *Journal of Palestine Studies*, Fall 2008 (Arabic), pp. 43–51.

24. See International Crisis Group, Update Policy Briefing, September 2008, March 2009.

25. George Giacaman, 'Fateh and the two-states solution', *Journal of Palestine Studies*, Summer 2009, pp. 21–6. In Arabic.

26. Based on fieldwork data collected during a Fateh internal meeting of cadres, July 2008.

27. Karma Nabulsi, 'Popular sovereignty and justice', paper presented at the conference entitled One-State for Palestine/Israel: A Country for all its Citizens?, University of Massachusetts-Boston, Boston, 28–29 March 2009.

28. See, for example, the newly created body in Lebanon entitled The League for the Defense of Palestinian Foundations (Al Thawabet al Falastinia).

29. See also Karma Nabulsi, *Palestinians Register: Laying Foundations and Setting Directions* (Oxford: Refugees Studies Center, 2006).

30. See, for example, www.adalah.org/eng and www.madaresearch.org/archive/haifaenglish.pdf.

31. Fieldwork data. See also Ali Jarbawi, 'In order for the Palestinian crisis not to be an inevitable fate', *Journal of Palestine Studies*, 76, Fall 2008, pp. 7–27. In Arabic; Maher Al-Masri, *Al Ayam*, Ramallah, 15 May 2008. See also the publication of Regaining the Initiative in Fall 2007, a project sponsored by the Palestine Strategic Study Group over 12 months, and which included various political parties and civil society representatives from inside and outside the occupied territories; it was so far the closest para-official statement calling on the leadership to consider seriously, though not yet adopt, the one-state as an alternative option to the failure of the two-state solution.

32. Center for Development Studies, Survey on Final Status Issues, March 2007.

33. See PACBI and BDS campaign website at www.pacbi.org and www.bdsmovement.net. Read, among others, Nancy Murray, 'Dynamics of resistance: the apartheid analogy', *EJMES*, Spring 2008.

34. See Adam Shatz, 'Leaving paradise', *London Review of Books*, 6 November 2008, pp. 23–5.

CHAPTER 19

Awakening the American Conscience about Israel/Palestine

Joel Kovel

Introduction

The fierce Israeli assault on Gaza early in late 2008 and early 2009 did more than lay waste to much of Palestinian society. It also gave rise to an outrage that fractured the attachment to Israel by many in the Western world. Of special significance was a fraying of the bond between the Jewish populations of two countries. For the first time a serious rift appeared between Israeli Jews, who largely supported the war, and those of its patron state, the United States of America. In the USA, despite the efforts of the Israel lobby and the non-committal stance of the government, significant sectors of civil society began to dissent. Portions of the public, Jews included and younger Jews especially, began openly to wonder why, in a time of great economic hardship, their country was squandering so many resources on a state whose behaviour it seemed so difficult to control, even in the face of a worldwide outcry. A number of Jews did more than wonder. They protested and took direct action, occupying Israeli consulates, specifically in Los Angeles, San Francisco and Boston (while their Canadian fellows did the same in Toronto and Montreal). Others occupied university facilities, as at NYU, or began divestment proceedings at other colleges, like Hampshire in Amherst, Massachusetts. Relative to what was happening abroad these were modest efforts, dwarfed, for example, by the 30 university occupations in the UK, or the refusal of Durban, South Africa, dockworkers to offload an Israeli freighter. Nor can there be any doubt that only a tiny fraction of American Jews took direct action. However, the full measure of events like these does not lie in numbers, but in the meaning of these changes in the light of the whole historical manifold signified by the role of Zionism in the identity and fate of modern Jews.

It does seem as though a kind of sleeping giant has awakened, and a process of 'conscientisation' has begun in what has until now been the indispensable bulwark of Zionism outside Israel. As with all such processes, there have been antecedents. For some time critics of Israel and its abuses have felt a kind of sea-change. Where once meetings would be threatened by hecklers to the point of requiring police protection,[1] now one sometimes oddly misses the sting of sharp contestation as audiences politely listen and, often as not, applaud criticism of Israel. It is plain that people feel less threatened these days by hearing ideas that challenge Zionist precepts. They seem even emboldened, as though the criticism corresponds to thoughts of their own that they may have been afraid to recognise in themselves until stirred by an outside speaker. The frenzy these days that might be described as a 'Zionist thought police', trying to suppress any criticism of the Jewish state, is perhaps more a sign of weakness and doubt rather than the confidence of a truly hegemonic power. All of this calls attention to the matter of a collective conscience, how it may go to sleep, and how it can awaken.

The Emancipatory Legend

For Hegel, the dialectic of master and bondsman was central to human existence. And, indeed, a good deal of history is organised along the axis defined by the proclivity of certain groups to dominate others and the resistance by the dominated to their bondage. However problematic to define and ambiguous in practice, the drive toward freedom is ubiquitous in human existence. The panorama of freedom struggles is breathtaking, and despite the efforts of the materialists to find other, more objective layers of motivation to account for historical processes, the idea of 'freedom' still gives shape to mass movements. That which we call 'identity', the mooring of the self in history, is permeated by the narratives through which a person gives their life an essential kind of meaning and connection to the life of that larger body known as 'a people'.

In the Western tradition the main thread of these narratives leads to the Old Testament, especially the Book of Exodus, which recounts the liberation of the Israelites from their bondage in Egypt. This has most famously in modern times animated the Zionist project in Palestine. However, many English settlers in North America were similarly guided, as were the Boer-trekkers in South Africa. The common narrative ground is essential to explain the historical links between these processes.[2]

There is no contradiction between the facts that material interests motivate historical struggle, on the one hand, and that struggle requires guiding narratives to organise collective activity, on the other. We do not find it strange that a man climbing a mountain needs a well-fed stomach and strong limbs, as well as a clear understanding of the terrain and the will-power and ideals to reach its peak. The realm of historical struggle is similarly constituted, with recurrent narrative themes that organise the intellectual and spiritual faculties into a collective will.

We call such narratives 'emancipatory legends' to signify first that the narrative is of liberation from bondage, and also that these are 'legendary'. As used here, the term occupies a shadowy ground between history and myth. It is ambiguous, but no more so than human existence itself. The legend is a narrative realisation of the past, thrown forward for its present purpose. Its shape is to be organised by the desires of the collective rather than the dispassion of the historian. It is capable of entering into the multiple identities of actors in a collective process, joining them into a force greater than the sum of their individual powers. We regard myth here as a legend so rendered as to lose coherent relation to an actual past. Thus legends can be transmuted into myth, when all that remains of the original reality is an invocation by demagogues; finally, it can even turn into its opposite, when the erstwhile subaltern group loses its way, becomes a dominator and uses legends for propaganda purposes. Thus did the Puritans of the North American settlements transform an emancipatory identification with the wandering Jew[3] into the justification for an all-conquering US mission to propagate an 'American Idea', a mythic representation that present-day hard Zionists freely exploit. Likewise, the Promised Land enters the notion of Manifest Destiny, which had been prepared by the enlightened Deist Thomas Jefferson in his claims of US suzerainty over the Western hemisphere. In cases of settler-colonial societies, relations with the savages endlessly return as variations of what the French (who were on the whole less affected than the Anglo-Protestant imperialists by the Exodus story) would call *la mission civilisatrice*; most recently the world has groaned under their application by the Christian Zionist and neoconservative George W. Bush regime in America's sacred mission to bring 'democracy' to nations burdened by savage darkness, by force if necessary.

The function of conscience has a complex relation to the emancipatory legend. Conscience is necessarily open to the possibility of emancipation. But it must also resist its inversion into a facilitator of domination and, linked with this, its perversion by mythmaking. Conscience requires a higher mode of synthesis: it accepts the necessity of emancipatory legends in the striving for freedom, but under condition that these be submitted also to the requirement of universality. That is, just as the moral law requires treating other persons as ends in themselves and not as instruments of the individual will, so does conscience require the constructing of an order grounded in justice, with the universal entitlement of all human beings to the powers of being human. Conscience is the submission of egoism, whether individually exploitative or collectively chauvinistic, to the universal principle of lawfulness.

We may now consider how these potentials have played out in the recent history of the Jews in relation to Zionism.

The Question of the Jews

Western civilisation has long had a 'Jewish question' thanks to deep contradictions in its reigning Christianity that have forced Jews to accept the supersession of their religion by one of its offspring, and to pay various penalties besides, ranging from severe Judaeophobic persecution to shades of alienation.[4] This is perhaps the most abstract way of putting the matter, but it leaves unsaid a vast range of particular fates stemming from the fact that Jews do not exist in general but in specific communities in times and places undergoing uneven development. Thus there is no general predicament faced by Western Jews beyond that of existing on the margins.

The modern era, framed for Jews by the fitful acquisition of rights of citizenship in Europe in the wake of the Enlightenment, French Revolution and Napoleonic era, and today by the rise of the state of Israel, has greatly perturbed this state of affairs. The chief reason for this has been the emergence of capitalism as the dominant world system. We recognise modernity to be the cultural reflex of capitalism; it is the impression upon society made by the relentless and expansive force of capital accumulation, driving all before it, destroying the pre-capitalist community, and subsuming the world into the circuits of money and profit.[5] All identities, all collective arrangements come under threat, as well as all histories and traditions.

For Jews this has posed a whole new set of opportunities stemming from their fluid positioning in the capitalist order, and another set of extraordinary dangers deriving from the growing instability of society. One of the fates in traditional society had been for Jews to play a leading role, imposed by medieval powers, in the emerging money economy, as usurers. A backlash of this was to generate a whole new circuit of Judaeophobia, as Jewish middlemen came to bear the blame for the destructive effects of the money economy; but the same nexus set a substantial fraction of Jews on the path of modern success. Yuri Slezkine has called them 'Mercurians', fluid and adaptive couriers along the paths set down by capitalist modernity.[6]

In 1843, Karl Marx, baptised scion of generations of rabbis, recognised that the 'Jewish question' was a metaphor for the larger question of overcoming the deadly materialism imposed by capital, as embedded in the fabric of modernity. Marx tended to essentialise the Jewish relationship to money/power and has been chastised for his own anti-Semitism.[7] But Marx defined only one – albeit the most world-transformative – of the Jewish reactions to modernity. A dense and often contradictory web of existential options became available to Jews in modern times. We may schematically draw these as a fourfold set:

1. Affirmation of piety, representing a defensive resistance to modernity in order to anchor identity and social cohesion.
2. Affirmation of modernity and capitalism, most prominently displayed through migration to centres of capitalist power; this was especially so for the USA, where by the early twentieth century by far the most successful community of Jews in history had gathered.
3. The anti-capitalism epitomised by Marx drew great numbers of Jews, eternally marginalised, into various forms of rebellion in the search for justice. This has had a profound effect on virtually every 'progressive' movement within the Western world over the last century, including Soviet communism.
4. Zionism, or Jewish nationalism. This required settler-colonialism, and also that the object of the settlement, Palestine, be invested with mythological qualities given the fact that the actual Jews who became Zionist were preponderantly a people whose relation to Palestine was originally imaginary and could only become real through conquest.

All these existential positions have come to define sub-identities within Jewish society, and they have all been at one time or another combined with the others inasmuch as human beings only rarely let contradictions stop them from doing things. Thus some ultra-Orthodox Jews are in full retreat from the world, while others are immersed in business and/or capable of being either passionately pro- or anti-Zionist.[8] Similarly, Zionism had a notably left-wing orientation, through the founding of the Jewish state, and for some time thereafter, until the ruling Labour–Histadrut coalition fell in 1977.[9]

As a movement promising social transformation, Zionism requires an emancipatory legend in order to organise its supporters. And, indeed, one seemed readily at hand in the Old Testament story of the Israelites, Yahweh's chosen people, enslaved by the Pharaoh and freed from Egypt through the agency of the Prophet Moses. The power of this legend was such that no other setting held forth at one time or another as a potential homeland – Argentina, Madagascar, Uganda, etc. – had the slightest traction for the bulk of Zionist Jews.

Unfortunately, the traction held by the Biblical legend was doubly spurious, as there was neither ancestral connection of the vast majority of European Jews to Palestine nor any archaeological evidence that the Exodus narrative itself was more than myth.[10] The preconditions of whether an emancipatory legend can actually become conscientious and serve the goal of emancipation must at least include some grounding in reality. With this being absent, the acquisition of Palestine could only be by illegitimate force. As a nationalist project without a real plot of ground for their national 'home', Zionists had to focus on a land held by others, and, moreover, had to find an imperial patron for the job both before and after the conquest of Palestine. Further, the sine qua non of the project demanded a state as the instrument of Zionist conquest of what was to become Eretz Yisrael (the home of the Jews).

The result is an implacable setting of the Zionist self against not just the indigenous Palestinians who had to be displaced, but indeed against all the subalterns of the world, each and every man and woman who become an enemy in theory and practice alike. Like other settler-colonial regimes, most notably apartheid South Africa – but also the USA itself[11] – Israel is deeply sunk in an objectively reactionary stance, and also, it would be scarce necessary to mention were not the whole 'official' imperial world so set against the revelation, a profound racism. Israel, therefore, can never transcend a right-wing identity, where this signifies a role in the service of domination and exploitation of others.

Non-Zionist Jewish leftism had its own problems but none of these burdens. As Marx and Engels signified with their conclusion to the *Manifesto* – 'WORKING MEN OF ALL COUNTRIES UNITE!' – the legendary nucleus of modern emancipatory practice has been the universalisation of the Old Testament narrative. As such, the emancipatory legend is no longer subsumed exclusively to the fate of the Jews. It is not hostile to that fate, but insists on subsuming it into the common humanity shared by Jews with the rest of the world. Indeed, the core legend of the entire modern leftist tradition is nourished by Old Testament sources, less those of the Torah (its first five books) than by the grandeur of the prophetic tradition (chiefly Isaiah). It is this authentically Jewish root that nourishes the specifically Jewish contribution to the left, and shapes the third of our four options.

Differences in attitude toward anti-Semitism provided a fateful corollary to these variants of emancipatory legend. Zionism, fixated on a separate Jewish emancipation, demands Jewish unification against a hostile world, and has therefore depended on anti-Semitism even as it preached against it. There is no universality accessible to Zionism, essentially no answer to the 'Jewish question'. To the Zionist, Jewishness would be dissolved in such a world as was envisioned by Marx and embraced as such by the radical left, who have followed Marx (who himself followed Spinoza in the opening of Judaism to the universal). It follows also that these main divisions of the Jewish transformational movement would differ sharply in their practical attitude toward anti-Semitism – the universalist left committed to building a world without anti-Semitism; meanwhile, Zionists rail against anti-Semitism while advocating a continued exclusivity and using the idea of a supposed inevitability of anti-Semitism to recruit more to their cause.

Zionists, we might say, are virtuosos of *splitting*. The universalist left, existentially committed to a vision of a world in which anti-Semitism and all forms of racism are definitively overcome, retains the hope of what might be called a *differentiated* Jewish identity, one that is both retained while remaining fundamentally connected to the rest of humanity.

Thus what seems at first glance a convergence between the Zionist and non-Zionist left is actually a profound antagonism. This flared up frequently towards the end of the Second World War, especially in struggles between Zionists and the Polish Bund, a labour-based organisation with a Jewish identity obstinately differentiated in its allegiance to class-based politics. The war more or less destroyed the Bund, which had taken up arms against the Nazis, while the Zionists, tied to the goal of the Jewish separatism and therefore ready to opportunistically make deals with power, survived to build their Jewish state.[12]

In what might seem to be the ultimate paradox, the Holocaust, or *Shoah*, proved decisive for Israel's triumph. In the wake of the war, an unprecedented groundswell of support for the Jewish homeland, and, critically, for a Jewish state to secure it, sprang from every corner of Western society, including the left. To read Sartre's *Anti-Semite and Jew* – a work unthinkable in light of the present reality of Israel[13] – is to appreciate the massive, guilt-driven reaction from even the most progressive and radical thinkers. This swept up great powers, USSR and USA alike, each of which rushed to recognise the fledgling Jewish state.

Guilt over the *Shoah* may have been necessary for the success of Zionism, but was not the only factor by any means. Indeed, it was ancillary to what was crucial: the decision made by the USA to include Israel in its arsenal during the confrontation with the Soviet Union, a setting both for the triumph of Zionism and the collapse – or else the *eclipse* – of the left in general.

Eclipse

The rise of Zionism is the heir to, as well as a condition of, the decline of the left in contemporary society, certainly with respect to the Jewish society of the USA. No one who holds out hope for humanity as the self-determining subject of freedom can rest with the notion of Jewish emancipation at the expense of the Palestinian people. Indeed, to the degree one casts their lot with the universality of human rights, so must any triumph of a Jewish state be seen as radically false and contradictory to the notion of Jewish emancipation as well. Israel's strength and its appearance of moral authenticity have kept the American conscience subdued.

The great Red Scare of mid-twentieth-century America had powerful material roots – the need to reverse the rise of labour stemming from the New Deal, the need to control and, where possible, reverse the anti-colonialist currents of the post-war era, the need to keep Communist movements from prevailing in

Europe, the mutually profitable arms race and terror game with the USSR, and so forth. All of this was subsumed into its overarching signifier of the Communist, or Soviet, menace.[14] But in the immediate exercise of its repressive agenda it also had to confront and make use of the fact that Jews had come to play a powerful role in the particular social movements through which these agents were born, whether in labour, Hollywood or academia. In doing so, the forces of the political right took a page from the workbook of Adolf Hitler, and linked the signifier of the Communist with that of the Jew. 'Judaeo-Bolshevism', the Nazis called it, and the Hoover/McCarthy/House Un-American Activities Committee axis used the association with gusto. More was at stake than the suppression of actual Jews in various left-leaning organisations. The invocation of Judaeophobia, backed by the repressive power of the American state apparatus, served to strengthen that power just as the Spanish Inquisition served to solidify the imperial power of Spain. And the terror campaign – no other word describes it better – played a tremendous role in crushing the left-transformational option available to Jews.

To appreciate the ferocity of this campaign one needs only read transcriptions from HUAC's inquisition into the film industry – or realise that at least seven of the Hollywood Ten were Jewish.[15] Its full magnitude, however, was revealed in the sensational atomic spy case of Julius and Ethel Rosenberg, which transfixed the country between 1950 and 1953, when the two Judaeo-Bolsheviks were unjustly executed.[16] This was strictly a Show-Trial in the Stalinist sense of the term, in which every significant person, from the defendants to the attorneys for prosecution as well as defence, along with the witnesses and judge, were of Jewish extraction. As one who lived through this as a child, I can attest to the deep panic the Rosenberg case set forth among the eminently left-wing Jewish population of New York City, the world capital of Jewish culture.

Anti-communist repression was only one factor in the eclipse of the Jewish left. The awfulness of Stalin's regime, sharply revealed after 1956, proved equally effective. So, too, did various sociological influences, including the shallowness of American anti-Semitism, which allowed Jews rapid access to worldly success and assimilation. Of equivalent importance were the effects of suburbanisation, with its homogenisation of political difference and the subsumption to consumerism and the mall culture. Here we find the legacy of the second, and most powerful, existential option for modern Jewry: their Westward trek to affirm capitalist modernity. The fusion of this with Zionism has proven to be the dominant bloc of contemporary American Jews.

An embryonic Zionist lobby was in place before 1948, which gained influence over President Truman very early in his administration and played a decisive role in his support for the new Jewish state. One of its units, the American Zionist Council, came under the sway of the public relations wizard Isaiah 'Si' Kenan, in 1951, and was shaped by him into the juggernaut that became AIPAC in 1953 (though it was not actually to assume that name until 1959).[17] Thus the apparatus that has guided the growth of Zionist power in the USA took form as the Rosenberg case was destroying the foundations of Jewish leftism.

It was some time before this would mature into what James Petras has called the 'Zionist Power Configuration'.[18] In fact, it took the shock waves that convulsed the Jewish community during the Six Day War of 1967 to galvanise support for Israel in the USA. This became immediately associated with the omnipotent signifier of the Holocaust. And in 1973, when the actual vulnerability of Israel became exposed in the Yom Kippur War, the configuration solidified into the massive complex that has since lashed Jewish identity to the fortunes of the Jewish state under the signs of persecution and revenge.

Peter Novick, who has written the definitive study of this process, demonstrates that a major cause of the transformation of American Jewry into Israel's bastion was a kind of spiritual crisis bordering on despair. This stemmed, paradoxically, from the sumptuous fortunes of American Jews. Success had propelled Jews into positions of power throughout American society, and prepared the material base of their rightward shift into allegiance with Zionism. But the spiritual cost that led to this was great. As Novick comments:

> The survival to which Jewish leaders increasingly turned their attention did not mean the physical survival of Jews in a hostile environment. Rather it was the *absence* of hostility to Jews that was threatening. Individually American Jews were prospering; collectively they were being killed with kindness. In the words of one Jewish leader, 'the melting pot has succeeded beyond our wildest fears'. A decline in Jewish commitment and sense of Jewish identity, particularly among the young – dramatically reflected in soaring rates of intermarriage – threatened demographic catastrophe for American Jews... The threat of assimilation was frequently described as a 'quiet', 'silent', 'bloodless', or 'spiritual' Holocaust. Norman Lamm, president of (Modern Orthodox) Yeshiva University: 'With a diminishing birth rate, an intermarriage rate exceeding 40 per cent, Jewish illiteracy gaining ascendance daily -- who says that the Holocaust is over?... The monster has assumed a different and more benign form... but its evil goal remains unchanged: a *Judenrein* world.'[19]

(Italics in original.)

The better Jews did, the worse became their spiritual condition, nourished over centuries under the harsh conditions of Christendom's exclusion. This led to a kind of unnatural selection. The universalising threads of the faith tradition were tossed into history's dustbin, while the most chauvinistic and vengeful elements of Judaic being survived to become a monstrous kind of Bad Faith that rationalised and exonerated what Israel was doing in its name. Influenced by the power of the Holocaust narrative, right-wing American Jewry perceived their spiritual desolation as actual genocide, sought power as a refuge, and rushed to defend the Jewish state and help forge it into one of America's closest allies. This attitude spread from civil society to state and culminated in the emergence of the neoconservatives, locking the upper echelons of Jewry into the national security apparatus.

I do not quite agree with Novick that the 'political movement called neo-conservatism [sic] was almost exclusively a Jewish affair'.[20] A Jewish affair it most definitely has been, albeit of the Zionist stripe. However, as Zionism is also a Christian affair, we need to add that the neocons also represented the confluence of Jewish Zionism with its Christian cousin. Their entry into the higher echelons of the State Department, the National Security Council, the Pentagon and, under Cheney, the Vice-President's command bunker has amounted to what one might call a 'zionification' of the US security apparatus. Blowing back on to Israel, this has been realised in the horrors of the Second Intifada, the Invasion of Iraq, the incursions into Lebanon and Gaza, and, with these, the gathering collapse of the Zionist world view.

Awakening

Space does not permit the detailing of these processes. We should try to grasp the sweep and dialectical rapidity of the changes they entail, however, and draw some provisional conclusions. For just as the defeat of the Jewish left helped increase the Zionist right wing, so does Zionism's loss of legitimacy signify an opening for the revival of the Jewish left: its passage out of eclipse. Who today can remember the emancipatory hopes once kindled by the Zionist movement and its success? Many now see the emancipatory hopes to have been fraudulent, due to the 'ethnic' separatist element inherent to Zionism. This 'fraud' has only been exposed to the common view now that history has removed the layers of justification. There has been no better example of the adage about the corruptions inherent to power than the moral degeneration of the Zionist project, slipping now (some might say) toward borderline fascism.

All this is also instructive. The 'fraud' perpetuated by Zionism can be seen as a hijacking of an emancipatory legend that, whatever its mythic origins, has proven itself a precious part of the legacy of humanity. Ashkenazi Jews had a perfect right to partake of that, but no exclusive franchise. No group has a monopoly on this archetypal legend of escape from bondage. But there is one people that qualifies more than any other today for the laurel of being the prospective subject of emancipation from a 'Pharaonic' power in the Middle Eastern watershed of civilisation. No sane person can doubt that this role today belongs to the Palestinians themselves; certainly the most autochthonous people to be continuously descended from the original inhabitants of Old Testament terrain now become very much stateless wanderers like the original Israelites, and most definitely in a bondage equivalent to subjugation by an overbearing overlord. Some day we will appreciate better and perhaps understand the exquisite irony in this inversion of the self-chosen identity of Zionist Jews. For now we can merely marvel at how history unfolds itself in surprising ways.

The inexorable fraying of Israeli legitimacy is a lesson displayed before the world. As the idea of Israel becomes undermined by a questioning of its failing legitimacy, a hitherto hidden truth is revealed: there is an authentic emancipatory legend being enacted in the old Holy Land, one capable of grasping the collective imagination and potentially freeing the conscience of American Jews. The falling away of a corrupted emancipatory legend and the adoption of its more authentic successor is also the motion bringing the Jewish left out of eclipse.

One further condition needs to be mentioned as necessary for the realisation of this legend. The status of Palestinians as subjects of an emancipatory legend cannot be taken for granted. It depends, rather, on whether Palestinians are even perceived as a people with rights that have been violated. A main object of Zionist propaganda over the decades has been to deny this. The struggles of the Palestinians themselves to achieve the status of an actual people in the world's eye have finally borne fruit; and this, combined with the continual de-mythologising of Zionist claims, has finally created the condition for the awakening of a collective conscience on their behalf.

To the extent that a motion toward universality is resumed, so will the unity among activist forces ensue. We see this already in the Boycott, Divestment and Sanctions movement, in which it increasingly becomes the rule for Arab and Jewish activists to work side by side, as for example in the group Adalah, active in the New York metropolitan area. A vector has been created by these developments in which the calibre of an activist's contribution will no longer be measured by ethnicity, and identity itself will be determined by one's faithfulness toward the universality of human beings. A non-chauvinist world lies at the end of this road, differentiated but not split into unrecognising fractions.

What will be the endpoint for identity once conscience is awakened and a universal perspective achieved? I think it is fair to say that this question looms larger for Jews than for others: in part because of the fragment of the 'people apart' stuck in their collective consciousness; in part because of the legacy of Zionism which will have to be worked through if any resolution of Israel/Palestine is to be achieved. Certainly this will be less of a problem for the younger than the older generation of Jews. But I also think it is fair to say that no question of identity is irresolvable. No matter how terrible it may seem to give up on some shard of the past, it is really amazing how adaptable people can be, and how they can get over things once reality sets its hand over things.

Notes

1. Personal observation by the author and others, including Noam Chomsky (personal communication of March 2009).

2. Including, needless to add, the often weird relationship between Jewish and Christian Zionism. Space does not permit the extension of this argument into non-Western and especially Asian variants. Here we have the appropriation by Gandhi, who drew upon Western religious themes, especially as elaborated by his mentor Tolstoy, and combined them with native Hindu sources into the core narrative through which the national liberation of the Indians was achieved. Then there is the appropriation by Mao Zedong of the Long March, with the matrix of recurrent peasant rebellions throughout the history of China.

3. American settlers thought of themselves at times as the 13th tribe of Israel.

4. James Carroll, *Constantine's Sword* (Boston: Houghton Mifflin, 2001). Judaeophobia refers to a kind of visceral loathing of Jews; it may be thought of as the phenomenological surface of anti-Semitism.

5. This observation was first made by Marx and Engels in *The Communist Manifesto*, and is indeed its leading point, epitomised in the famous phrase describing capital's effect on tradition: 'All that is solid melts into air.'

6. Yuri Slezkine, *The Jewish Century* (Berkeley: University of California Press, 2004).

7. I treated the matter of Marx's alleged anti-Semitism in an earlier essay: Joel Kovel, 'Marx on the Jewish question', in *The Radical Spirit* (London: Free Association Books, 1988), pp. 226–50.

8. New York's B&H, one of the world's largest photographic dealers and certainly one of its most technologically advanced, is run by ultra-Orthodox Jews. Many Orthodox have made alliances with Zionism, and have been indispensable, for example, for the settling of the West Bank; while others, the 'Neturai Karta', are implacable and militant anti-Zionists.

9. Ze'ev Sternhell, *The Founding Myths of Israel* (Princeton: Princeton University Press, 1988).

10. For the Biblical evidence, see Israel Finkelstein and Neil Asher Silberman, *The Bible Unearthed* (New York: Simon and Schuster, 2001).

11. Not to mention Canada, Australia and New Zealand, all of whom virtually tripped over one another in their haste to join the USA and Israel in exiting the second Durban Conference on racism, held in Geneva, April 2009.

12. Lenni Brenner, *Zionism in the Age of Dictators* (London: Pluto, 1984).

13. Jean-Paul Sartre, *Anti-Semite and Jew* (New York: Schocken, 1948 [1965]).

14. Joel Kovel, *Red Hunting in the Promised Land* (New York: Basic Books, 1994).

15. Reynold Humphries, *Hollywood's Blacklists* (Edinburgh: University of Edinburgh Press, 2009).

16. Ethel was entirely innocent of any espionage. By way of contrast, the spy who gave away the principal secrets of the Bomb to Stalin, physicist Klaus Fuchs, was extradited to England, where he was briefly imprisoned, then exchanged for a Briton in East German hands. Fuchs died of natural causes, at liberty in the German Democratic Republic.

17. Grant F. Smith, *America's Defense Line* (Washington, DC: Institute for Research: Middle Eastern Policy, 2008), p. 91, and *passim*.

18. James Petras, *The Power of Israel in the United States* (Atlanta: Clarity Press, 2006).

19. Peter Novick, *The Holocaust in American Life* (NY: Houghton Mifflin, 1999), p. 185.

20. Ibid., p. 183.

CHAPTER 20

Building an International Movement to Promote the One-State Solution

Ghada Karmi

The idea of setting up an international movement to promote the one-state solution would seem at first sight an attractive initiative and a logical next step in the ongoing debate and growing activity that support this solution. However, one must be under no illusion as to the feasibility of such a task. There are considerable obstacles in the face of an enterprise of this sort, not least among them the question of who could organise the movement. There are no official or unofficial bodies on the Palestinian or Israeli side that have come out in open support for the one-state solution. At best, it has been various small, selected groups of individuals here and there who share a common belief in this solution. It is likely that it will be some such group, probably comprising a dispersed collection of Palestinians, Arabs, Jews, some of them Israelis, and others who share the same view, which will take up the task. This is no simple matter, for, in the absence of an official body emanating from the PLO and/or Israel, such a group will not represent the Palestinian or Israeli people, and will have no official position, at least at the outset.

There is no organisation to refer to in starting such a campaign or any similar grouping to join. Furthermore, the one-state solution is at odds with the current formal political position of both Israel and the PLO (such as it is), not to speak of the Palestinian Authority. Hamas is likewise on record as having accepted the two-state solution, at least for now. The official position of the international community is also one of support for the two-state solution, strengthened in 2009 by its adoption by the new US administration, and also by the Israeli prime minister.

This is not just a matter of political postures but of practical importance. It is clear that no international movement can ultimately succeed unless it follows the position that the concerned parties have stated they want – and articulated through a credible leadership. There is currently no Palestinian party or group that espouses the one-state solution, and certainly no Israeli one.

The Anti-apartheid Movement

The point is well illustrated by the example of the anti-apartheid movement (AAM).[1] It is probably the best available model for setting up a global one-state movement. The AAM's success lay in its basic structure: a black African leadership (the African National Congress), with a clear message and an agreed political programme, and a global network that was consequently built to support it.[2] The ANC always led both the internal and the global struggle against apartheid; indeed, it would not have been possible for such a movement to develop in the absence of an ANC or similar African organisation. Nor could it have happened without a political message that had mass appeal.

That message was articulated in the famous 'Freedom Charter' adopted by the ANC in 1953 and then passed by the 'Congress of the People' meeting two years later.[3] This meeting endorsed a document detailing the people's demands for how they saw their future. In this, they looked towards the goal of a demo-cratic South Africa 'for all its citizens'. Their slogans were attractive and readily comprehensible: 'equal rights for all' and 'one man, one vote'. The South Africa they envisioned was a country that would never be partitioned, but would remain whole and belong to all who lived in it. This new society could not be created by modifying the existing order or by assimilating into it, rejected as it was by the majority of the people.

This message had compelling resonance for the West and electrified the imagi-nation of Western liberal opinion. The ANC's vision of an inclusive, pluralist society in the making, instead of the stultified, racist world of apartheid, was an inspiration to thousands – as was the ANC's vision of a society in which the whites would fit in as equal citizens without discrimination or recrimination over their past oppression of black South Africans. The ANC made clear that it was the apartheid *state* and all who defended it that was the target of their strug-gle, not the Afrikaners who lived there. On the contrary, it offered a welcome to those who abandoned apartheid.

This was truly a master stroke, for it focused hostility on what was mani-festly an unjust and indefensible state structure, and yet provided a space for its people. By removing the distinction between white settler and black native, it paved the way for the concept of equal citizenship. The question of what would happen to the whites in a black-dominated state was thus addressed to allay anxieties inside and outside the country. The Western supporters of the anti-apartheid movement could thus be reassured that they were not supporting an incipient bloodbath of revenge and reverse oppression. The success of the anti-apartheid movement in helping to topple the South African regime can be ascribed in no small measure to the success of this coherent and appealing vision.

It is truly ironic that so many of the activists who worked with the ANC to overcome apartheid were themselves Jews who supported Zionism, and yet saw no parallels with Israeli apartheid. In fact, the anti-apartheid movement owes its inception to the communist party of South Africa, which was a white, mainly Jewish organisation. Their members in exile in London, again predominantly Jewish, were instrumental in laying the foundations of the movement in 1959. They worked by engaging political parties, trades unions, the churches and other centres of power in Britain, always remaining in scrupulous contact with the ANC and responsive to its political demands at all times.[4] There is no doubt they were helped by the political context of the time. The heated debate about racism in Britain and the growing civil rights movement in the USA were powerful in changing public perceptions. A one-state campaign, hoping to be even half as successful as the AAM, would need similar organisational backing.

The Palestinian Situation

How does any of this correspond to the Palestinian situation? What possibility is there of establishing a similar global movement to support a solution to the Israeli–Palestinian conflict? As matters stand, the outlook is bleak. There is no unified Palestinian consensus on the one-state solution. With the increasing shift in the international position towards the two-state solution, the official Palestinian position towards this solution has also strengthened. But in reality, Palestinian opinion about a solution is divided, depending on which Palestinian group is involved. And since no one has carried out a comprehensive survey of what solution these Palestinian groupings want, we can only make approximate judgements.

On this basis, it can be said that most people living under Israeli occupation do not look to a shared future with their occupiers; they would opt for an independent state in which to exercise their right of self-determination, to recover from the occupation and recoup their sense of identity.[5] Although in the last few years, as the logistical impossibility of the two-state solution becomes more evident, a growing number from the occupied territories have begun to support the one-state alternative, they see this as a last resort, something to threaten Israel with – as if to say, 'if you don't make a Palestinian state possible, you'll have us living with you in one state'. Knowing what anathema this would be to the Israeli state and its people, those who make this threat do so in the hope of 'frightening' Israel into cooperation. For example, Ahmad Qurei, the PA's Deputy Prime Minister at the time, announced in January 2004 that if the two-state solution proved impossible to achieve, then the Palestinians would aim for one state. A 2004 Palestinian Center for Policy and Survey Research survey of the West Bank and Gaza showed a 27 per cent support for one state.

The one-state idea has greatest appeal for Palestinians in the Diaspora and, even then, among a minority composed mainly of intellectuals. It is here that a number of prominent scholars and activists have written about the advantages of the one-state idea. Many more have joined these ranks in the last five years, and there is a widening and positive debate in print and on the internet about the one-state solution.[6] As for the Palestinian citizens of Israel, a majority would opt for a situation of equal rights within the current state, although a number of them have recently become supporters of the unitary state. That leaves the 4.5 million camp-dwelling refugees, who have generally been left out of the decision-making process, and whose views have rarely been sought in any systematic or comprehensive manner. However, they have traditionally and publicly adhered to their right of return to their original homes. This, by inference, must mean a return to what would be one state, although it is never articulated as such. In a rare example of a refugee study about this question, Khalil Shikaki carried out a survey among a sample of refugees in the West Bank and Gaza. Regarding Jordan and Lebanon and the right of return in 2003, Shikaki found that only 13 per cent said they would return.[7] But his question was phrased within the context of a return to Israel, not to a unitary Israel/Palestine. If it had been so phrased, the result might have been quite different.

Even if we had better data, there is still the question of a leadership capable of adopting and articulating a unified position. The body that was best able to take this role was the PLO. Through the Palestinian National Council (PNC), it was the most representative structure that the Palestinians ever produced, even though it never surveyed popular Palestinian opinion and had no reliable data on what the refugees wanted. However, with reform, it could still be the best forum for a unified and representative position. Today's reality, however, militates against such a possibility. The PLO ceased to function in its traditional capacity gradually after 1994, the date when Arafat and the Palestinian leadership went back to the Palestinian territories and abandoned the Diaspora.

Over the years since then, the PLO steadily declined, and is now virtually defunct. Attempts have been made to revive it in the last few years, but so far without success.[8] In its absence there is no Palestinian leadership. The Palestinian Authority was never a substitute for the PLO, despite the device which enabled Arafat to be both the head of the PLO and of the PA. His successor, Mahmoud Abbas, cannot be said to represent Palestinian opinion on any scale, and the split with Hamas in Gaza has worsened the fragmentation of the leadership. A Fateh conference took place in August 2009 in an attempt to revive the party's fortunes, but also to strengthen the position of Mahmoud Abbas and increase his popularity. It is not clear what effect this will have on his ability to represent wider Palestinian opinion.

Even when the situation was different, the PLO adopted a position quite unlike that of the ANC. Having been opposed to the partition of Palestine from the start, it reversed its policy, and in 1988 accepted a solution that would divide the country. And, having rejected the Zionist invasion of Palestine, as defined in its 1968 Charter, it went on to legitimise it by recognising Israel also in 1988. And by accepting a fifth of the original homeland on which to form a Palestinian state, the PLO in effect 'gave' the major share to the settlers. At one time, the PLO, like the ANC, had worked out a formula for solving the problem of the Zionist settler presence in the homeland. Israeli Jews would be accommodated within the 'democratic non-sectarian state of Palestine', which offered its citizens (whether Jews, Muslims or Christians) equality before the law.

This has distinct echoes of the inclusive state envisioned for South Africa by the ANC. But this noble plan, first proposed in 1969, was never followed through, and after 1974 it virtually dropped out of the Palestinian debate. From 1977 onwards, the idea of two states began to take hold, and the attempt to find a solution for the Jewish settler presence in Palestine became one of enclosing them in their own space, rather than living with them. The result has been that the 1988 recognition of Israel's usurpation of 78 per cent of Palestine and the subsequent commitment to the two-state solution it spearheaded have made the struggle for alternative solutions much harder.

Obstacles in the Way of an International Movement

The parallel with South Africa is not exact.[9] While valuable lessons can be learned from the anti-apartheid movement, there are crucial differences that make the Palestinian struggle infinitely more difficult. By its insistence on demographic separation, Israel had already defined the parameters of the conflict. It was not, as in South Africa, just a question of separation in function and social status, wherein South African blacks were assigned specific roles and restricted freedoms in the same space, but one of exclusion altogether. The aim of Zionism is to create a Jewish majority in Israel, which has involved the deployment of aggressive techniques – more like the takeover by the white settlers in North America. This inevitably skewed the conflict, and still does, into settler-versus-native, and makes it difficult to envisage an inclusive solution. Furthermore, the situation in South Africa was 300 years old when the regime was finally defeated, whereas in Israel/Palestine it is only 60 years old, making Zionism still a vibrant force.

The Afrikaner regime before the fall of apartheid had important economic ties with the West, especially with Britain, but did not command the network of support and passionate devotion enjoyed by the Jewish state.[10] When the anti-apartheid movement got into full swing, the South African regime had few friends to call on and was isolated in a way that is impossible to envisage with Israel. Can one imagine, for example, an American official describing Zionism as 'repugnant' and an 'odious system', as the US Assistant Secretary for African Affairs, Chester Crocker, did, speaking of apartheid in 1985?[11] Or find a third of US companies investing in Israel demanding a code of equality between Jew and Arab as a condition, as happened with US companies investing in South Africa in 1984?[12]

Israel's supporters are not only extensive and widespread, they are also influential. Their power has been demonstrated repeatedly whenever they have come to Israel's aid over any hostile word or deed levelled against it. This is especially true in the USA, where the political process has frequently been suborned to Israel's advantage. In addition, there is the emotional and psychological empathy that the Jewish state commands among a majority of Jews and non-Jewish Zionist sympathisers, and which is even harder to fight against. It can be anticipated that a movement aiming to dismantle the Israeli state will arouse an enormous backlash and mobilise thousands of Israel's supporters to fight against it. Put bluntly, the Afrikaners had no Holocaust to gain them the world's sympathy, something whose memory still animates much of Western thinking and sentiment.[13]

Add to this the negative view of Arabs and Palestinians in the West. The longstanding, historical antipathy towards Arabs has in recent years been aggravated by the events of 9/11. Many Arabs are now seen as Muslims and therefore potential terrorists. Whereas Palestinians have gained wider acceptance as a victimised people, particularly after the Israeli war on Gaza at the end of 2008, Palestinian Islamist groups like Hamas have a poor image. They have been officially designated as terrorist organisations and associated with suicide bombings, something which now elicits a universal reaction of horror. The idea of supporting a movement that includes such people will not be attractive.

More serious than all of this is the lack of a unified Palestinian position on the one-state solution. Consequently, non-Palestinian potential supporters of this option would be entitled to question the utility of advocating a solution that differs from the official Palestinian view, such as it is, and represents only a minority opinion among Palestinians. In addition, there is the Israeli side of the question. Since any such solution must involve Israeli Jews, it would be important to ascertain who among this constituency will agree with the one-state idea. On present evidence, only a tiny number of Israeli Jews have advocated it. The Palestinians, like the ANC, could have established a strategy for reaching out towards Israelis to share their vision, but, apart from the short period after 1969, in recent times they have not done so. There are no overt plans for accommodating Israeli Jews in the new Palestine, and no inclusive vision of equal rights within the state.

On the contrary, all the emphasis is on separating the two peoples into two spaces, mirroring the Zionist concept of exclusion, and an overt dismissal of the one-state solution by many Palestinians – as an attempt to throw away years of consensus building on the two-state solution, to which the international community is now signed up, and as a direct challenge to Palestinian nationalism. The idea of a Palestinian state holds considerable appeal for many Palestinians, and after the Oslo years, when quasi-institutions of state were set up by foreign governments and NGOs, giving up on the vision this offered is unpalatable. It can be expected that such people will undermine any one-state movement that is set up.

What to Do?

This chapter has outlined the obstacles and difficulties in the way of a one-state global movement. Nevertheless, the attempt to promote the one-state solution in this way should not be abandoned. Given the barren thinking on how to resolve the Israeli–Palestinian conflict evident among world leaders and decision makers, and the dangerous stalemate in the Middle East, it is right to offer alternative ways of thinking. In addition, as the futility of pursuing the two-state option becomes ever clearer, it is necessary to have a discourse about the alternative in place. At the very least, there should be a riposte to people like Tony Blair and other envoys to the Middle East, who, despite the evidence in front of them, persist in talking about two states.

This is an opportune moment. In the wake of the siege of Gaza, world public opinion seems to have changed towards Israel in a way that has not been seen before. The Boycott, Divestment and Sanctions (BDS) movement, which had been gaining strength since 2004, has developed with astonishing speed and range as a result of this, and there is an unprecedented interest in holding Israel to account. While this development does not automatically link to the one-state solution, it does allow for new thinking. In such an atmosphere, where Israel is being subjected to close scrutiny, everything is open to question. A global one-state movement can capitalise on this moment and exploit the opportunity provided by the BDS network to direct it towards adopting the one-state solution as its end point. This will be helped by the notable growth in discussion on the one-state option in the last five years, and which is accelerating, due at least in part to the growing disillusionment with the two-state solution.

With this background in mind, there are two ways of proceeding.

The first is to start at the Palestinian end and concentrate on building a consensus on the one-state solution among Palestinians (and Israelis). On the Palestinian side, this will involve helping Palestinians to elaborate a unified position which can take the lead of the global movement, or at least conform with the aims of such a movement. Such an effort must address the role of the PLO and the question of reviving it, since it already exists, and can be built upon. Palestinian supporters of the one-state option should investigate ways of doing this and of encouraging links with like-minded Israelis. At the same time, a parallel effort should be mounted on the Israeli side, initiated and led by Israeli and Jewish supporters of the one-state solution. Even if the Israeli effort has limited success, in view of the anticipated and formidable popular Israeli opposition to it, it should not detract from the work on the Palestinian side. At this stage, it is more important to achieve a unified Palestinian stand, since it is the Palestinians who are the principal victims.

The second is to concentrate instead on creating an international consensus, irrespective of whether there is a unified Palestinian position. The current group of one-state advocates, which includes a number of prominent names, would organise themselves as a formal body to coordinate the creation of a worldwide network of supporters and keep the issue in the public eye. The object of the campaign would be to raise awareness of the one-state alternative, to promote the debate among all levels of society – the media, politicians and academics – and to reach decision makers.

An example of this activity is the draft UN General Assembly resolution that I and several colleagues drew up in 2007.[14] This advocates the creation of a unitary state in Israel–Palestine on the basis of Israel's repeated breaches of international law, and its structure as a discriminatory, exclusivist state to the detriment of the indigenous people. If this resolution were to be put before the General Assembly (and this is not impossible if a member state is persuaded to propose it), it would promote a discussion of the one-state solution at the very highest level, and help push the debate forward. In this context, the current climate of opinion regarding Israel is an opportunity for the launching of such an initiative.

Conclusion

The possibility of setting up an effective global movement to promote the one-state solution on the lines of the anti-apartheid movement is remote in the present situation. Palestinian opinion is disunited and lacks a coherent leadership strategy. Even without that, the obstacles to such a movement are immense.

This does not mean, however, that nothing should be done. The best way would be for a formal one-state movement to be set up, composed of individuals who support this solution, and this movement should work to promote discussion of the issue on a global basis. It will not have the force of the anti-apartheid movement, due to inherent weaknesses in the Palestinian formal position and other factors. But insofar as it will present alternative solutions for the Israeli–Palestinian conflict, and may become something to be built on for the future, it is a worthwhile effort.

Notes

1. E. S. Reddy, *The Struggle for Liberation in South Africa and International Solidarity* (New Delhi: Sterling Publications, 1992); 'AAM and UN: partners in the international campaign against apartheid', paper given at The Anti-Apartheid Movement, a 40-year Perspective, conference, South Africa House, London, 25–26 June 1999; Audie Klotz, *Norms in International Relations: The Struggle Against Apartheid* (Ithaca: Cornell University Press, 1995).

2. Mokagheti Motlhabi, *The Theory and Practice of Black Resistance to Apartheid* (Johannesburg: Skotaville Publishers, 1984); Morgan Norval, *Inside the ANC: the Evolution of a Terrorist Organisation* (Washington, DC: Selous Foundation Press, 1987).

3. Raymond Suttner and Jeremy Cronin (eds), *50 years of the Freedom Charter. Hidden Histories Series, University of South Africa* (Pretoria: Unisa Press, 2006); David Mermetstein (ed.), *The Anti-apartheid Reader: The Struggle Against White Racist Rule in South Africa* (New York: Grove Press, 1987), p. 208.

4. Wikipedia.org/anti-apartheid movement; http://en.wikipedia.org/wiki/Anti-apartheid_movement.

5. Muhammad Baraka, 'Between the one-state and two-state solution independence is not a luxury, it is a necessity', *Al Majdal*, Badil Resource Centre for Palestinian Residency and Refugee Rights, Winter 2005, pp. 20–4.

6. See for example, Mazin Qumsiyeh, *Sharing the Land of Canaan: Human Rights and the Israeli–Palestinian Struggle* (London: Pluto Press, 2004); Ali Abunimah, *One Country: a Bold Proposal to End the Israeli–Palestinian Impasse* (New York: Metropolitan Books, 2006); Ghada Karmi, *Married to Another Man: Israel's Dilemma in Palestine* (London: Pluto Books, 2007), Chapters 6 and 7.

7. Palestinian Centre for Policy and Survey Research, poll, January–June 2003.

8. In May 2007, a group of about 30 Palestinians from the occupied territories and the Diaspora met in Beirut under the chairmanship of the late Shafiq al-Hout, to start a process of revival of the PLO. Regional committees were formed, but so far this initiative has come to nothing.

9. Virginia Tilley uses the South African model for comparison several times in her *The One-State Solution* (Ann Arbor: University of Michigan Press, 2005), pp. 135–7.

10. 'Economic sanctions', paper given at The Anti-Apartheid Movement, a 40-year Perspective, South Africa House, London, 25–26 June 1999; George Shepherd (ed.), *Effective Sanctions on South Africa* (New York: Praeger, 1991).

11. Mermetstein, op. cit., pp. 346–50.

12. Ibid., pp. 383–419.

13. Uri Avnery, the veteran Israeli who campaigned for a two-state solution, sums up these issues well in his 'A binational state? God forbid', *Journal of Palestine Studies*, 28(4), 1999, pp. 55–60.

14. The full text of this resolution is appended at the end.

Appendix

DRAFT UN RESOLUTION

Israel/Palestine and the Establishment of a Unified Secular Democratic State

The General Assembly,

Guided by the principles of the Charter of the United Nations,

Considering that the territory now claimed or occupied by the state of Israel was formerly the Mandatory territory of Palestine, with a population of Arabs and Jews who shared the rights of habitation and of self-determination, and that the establishment of the state of Israel in 1948 and the occupation of further territories in 1967 and 1973 were accomplished against the wishes of the Palestinians,

Recognising also that the state of Israel as currently constituted is a *de jure* racially defined state in which Jewish citizens enjoy preferential treatment over non-Jewish ones;

Recalling its resolutions GA194 (1948) on the repatriation of the Palestinian refugees displaced in the hostilities of 1948–9, and GA273 (III) 1949, admitting Israel as a member of the United Nations on Israel's willingness to carry out the obligations of the UN Charter and 'to honour them from the day of its acceptance', including Resolutions 181 and 194,

Recalling also relevant Security Council resolutions on the illegality of settlement building and the status of Jerusalem, the illegality of the construction of a wall in the Occupied Palestinian Territory.

Aware that Israeli settlement activities involve, inter alia, the transfer of nationals of the occupying Power into the occupied territories, the confiscation of land, the exploitation of natural resources and other illegal actions against the Palestinian civilian population,

Reaffirming the applicability of the Geneva Convention relative to the Protection of Civilian Persons in Time of War, of 12 August 1949, to the Occupied Palestinian Territory, including East Jerusalem,

Reiterating its opposition to settlement activities in the Occupied Palestinian Territory, including East Jerusalem, and to any activities involving the confiscation of land, the disruption of the livelihood of protected persons and the de facto annexation of land,

Recalling the need to end all acts of violence between the parties,

Gravely concerned about the dangerous situation resulting from actions taken by the illegal armed Israeli settlers in the occupied territory,

Noting Israel's non-compliance with repeated attempts to arrive at a negotiated settlement to the conflict, including, UNSC Resolutions 242 (1967) and 338 (1973), the Oslo Accords (1993), and the Road Map (2002);

Taking note of the relevant reports of the Secretary-General, and of the recent report of the Special Rapporteur of the Human Rights Council on the situation of human rights in the Palestinian territories occupied by Israel since 1967,

Recognising that Israel has on a number of occasions claimed and sought to acquire the whole territory of Mandate Palestine;

Recognising also that the Palestinians have sought and have a right to continue to live in, or to return to, cities, towns, villages and communities that they and their families have inhabited for generations in accordance with international law;

Recognising also that Israeli citizens, aided by the government of Israel, have illegally built communities and settlements which, in spite of the illegality, they wish to continue to inhabit:

Calls upon representatives of Israel and Palestine to agree on behalf of their peoples to share the land between the Mediterranean and the river Jordan, currently divided between Israel, the West Bank and Gaza, by setting up a state which is democratic and secular, in which the rights of all people living within its borders to freedom of worship, security from violence and equality under the law are enshrined in a new constitution, to replace the separate forms of government instrument that apply currently in Israel, the West Bank and Gaza.

Calls upon the new state to ensure that per capita expenditure on public services, education, transport, health and local authorities is applied impartially to all citizens, regardless of creed;

Requires the new state of Israel/Palestine (or whatever name its constitution shall finally determine) to abide by the provisions of the United Nations Charter;

Offers the offices of the United Nations to all parties to the dispute to host an interim constitutional conference to draw up heads of agreement covering a new parliamentary structure, legislative and executive structures, foreign relations and citizenship redefinitions for the new state;

Requires all parties to participate in a Border Dismantling and Redefining Committee, with the following brief:

To schedule the removal of the illegal wall currently constructed on Palestinian land,

To ensure free passage on all public roads in the new state to all citizens,

To remove all security fences and armed guards from every housing estate or community, other than privately owned estates, to allow free access for all citizens of the new state;

To enact new land laws that apply equally and fairly to all citizens of the new state;

To ensure the equitable sharing of resources, including water;

To respect the special status of Jerusalem in regard to its unique importance for the three main religions by instituting an appropriate administration for the holy places;

Demands that the new state abide by Strategic Arms Limitation Treaties, banning the holding or development of nuclear weapons;

Calls upon the world community to support the efforts of all parties to establish the new state, with economic assistance and expert advice;

Emphasises the strong will of the world community to put every effort into the one-state solution of this intractable problem;

Recognises the recent efforts made by regional and international parties to resolve the conflict through the creation of two states;

Recommends the adoption of this measure or any other agreed arrangement, including federation and binationalism, provided these are adopted as interim stages in the attainment of the one-state solution, and provided they do not hinder this end result;

Requests the Secretary-General to report to the General Assembly at its sixty-fourth session on the implementation of the present resolution.

Select Bibliography

I. Books

Abdul-Hadi, Mahdi (ed.), *Palestinian-Israeli Impasse: Exploring Alternative Solutions to the Palestinian–Israeli Conflict* (Jerusalem: PASSIA (Palestinian Academic Society for the Study of International Affairs), 2005).

Abu-Lughod, Ibrahim (ed.), *The Transformation of Palestine* (Evanston: Northwestern University Press, 1971).

Abunimah, Ali, *One Country: A Bold Proposal to End the Israeli–Palestinian Impasse* (New York: Metropolitan Books, 2006).

Abu-Sitta, Salman, *The Atlas of Palestine 1948* (London: Palestine Land Society, 2005).

Aruri, Naseer, *The Obstruction of Peace, the US, Israel and the Palestinians* (Monroe, Maine: Common Courage Press, 1995).

Aruri, Naseer, *Dishonest Broker, The US Role in Israel and Palestine* (Boston: South End Press, 2003).

Beinin, Joel and Stein, Rebecca L. (eds), *Oslo to Intifada* (Stanford: Stanford University Press, 2006).

Benvenisti, Meron, *Intimate Enemies, Jews and Arabs in a Shared Land* (Berkeley: University of California Press, 1995).

Benvenisti, Meron, *City of Stone: The Hidden History of Jerusalem* (Berkeley: University of California Press, 1996).

Buber, M., Magnes, J. L. and Simon, E. (eds), *Towards Union of Palestine: Essays on Zionism and Jewish-Arab Cooperation* (Westport, CT: Greenwood Press, 1948).

Burg, Avraham, *The Holocaust Is Over, We Must Rise From its Ashes* (New York: Palgrave Macmillan, 2008).

Carter, Jimmy, *Palestine: Peace Not Apartheid* (New York: Simon and Schuster, 2006).

Carter, Jimmy, *We Can Have Peace In The Holy Land: A Plan That Will Work* (New York: Simon and Schuster, 2009).

Cheshin, Amir; Hutman, Bill and Melamed, Avi, *Separate and Unequal: The Inside Story of Israeli Rule in East Jerusalem* (Cambridge, MA: Harvard University Press, 1999).

Cook, Jonathan, *Disappearing Palestine: Israel's Experiments in Human Despair* (London: Zed Books, 2008).

Dascal, Marcelo, 'Identities in flux: Arabs and Jews in Israel', in Weiss, G. and Wodak, R. (eds), *Critical Discourse Analysis: Theory and Interdisciplinarity* (Houndmills, Basingstoke, Hampshire: Palgrave Macmillan, 1993).

Elazar, Daniel, *Two Peoples – One Land: Federal Solutions for Israel, the Palestinians, and Jordan* (Lanham, MD: University Press of America, 1991).

Ellis, Marc, *Toward a Jewish Theology of Liberation: Into the 21st Century* (Waco: Baylor University Press, 2004).

Ellis, Marc, *Judaism Does Not Equal Israel* (New York: New Press, 2009).

Farsoun, Samih and Aruri, Naseer, *Palestine and the Palestinians: A Social and Political History* (second edition) (Boulder, Colorado: Westview Press, 2006).

Finkelstein, Norman, *Image and Reality of the Israel–Palestine Conflict* (London: Verso, 1995).

Fischbach, Michael R., *Records of Dispossession: Palestinian Refugee Property and the Arab-Israeli Conflict* (New York: Columbia University Press, 2003).

Flapan, Simha, *The Birth of Israel, Myths and Realities* (London: Sydney Croom Helm, 1987).

Freire, Paulo, *Pedagogy of the Oppressed* (New York: Continuum Books, 1993).

Halper, Jeff, *Obstacles to Peace: A Reframing of the Palestinian-Israeli Conflict* (third edition) (Jerusalem: Palestine Mapping Center, 2005).

Halwani, Raja and Kapitan, Tomis, *The Israeli–Palestinian Conflict: Philosophical Essays on Self-Determination, Terrorism and the One-State Solution* (London: Palgrave Macmillan, 2008).

Hammer, Julianne, *Palestinians Born in Exile* (Austin: University of Texas Press, 2005).

Hilal, Jamil (ed.), *Where Now for Palestine? The Demise of the Two States Solution* (London: Zed Books, 2007).

Hovsepian, Noubar, *Palestinian State Formation: Education and the Construction of National Identity* (Newcastle: Cambridge Scholars, 2008).

Hroub, Khalid, *Hamas: Political Thought and Practice* (Washington, DC: Institute of Palestine Studies, 2000).

Ibish, Hussein, *What's Wrong with the One-State Agenda? Why Ending the Occupation and Peace with Israel is Still the Palestinian National Goal* (Washington, DC: American Task Force on Palestine, 2009).

Karmi, Ghada and Cotran, Eugene (eds), *The Palestinian Exodus* (London: Ithaca, 1999).

Karmi, Ghada, *Married to Another Man: Israel's Dilemma in Palestine* (London: Pluto Press, 2007).

Kaufman-Lacusta, Maxine, *Refusing to be Enemies: Palestinian and Israeli Nonviolent Resistance to the Israeli Occupation* (Reading, UK: Ithaca Press, 2010).

Keating, M., Le More, A. and Lowe, R. (eds), *Aid, Diplomacy and Facts on the Ground: The Case of Palestine* (London: The Royal Institute for Strategic Studies, 2005).

Khalidi, Rashid, *Palestinian Identity, the Construction of Modern National Consciousness* (New York, NY: Columbia University Press, 1997).

Khalidi, Walid, *All That Remains: The Palestinian Villages Occupied and Depopulated by Israel in 1948* (Washington, DC: Institute for Palestine Studies, 1992).

Khan, M. H. (ed.), *State Formation in Palestine: Viability and Governance During a Social Transformation* (London: Routledge, 2004).

Kimmerling, Baruch, *Politicide, Ariel Sharon's War Against the Palestinians* (London: Verso, 2003).

Kovel, Joel, *Overcoming Zionism: Creating a Single Democratic State in Israel/Palestine* (London: Pluto Press, 2007).

Laqueur, Walter and Rubin, Barry, *The Israel-Arab Reader: A Documentary History of the Middle East Conflict* (London: Penguin Press, 2008).

Le More, Anne, *International Assistance to the Palestinians after Oslo: Political Guilt, Wasted Money* (London: Routledge, 2008).

Lustick, Ian, *For the Land and the Lord: Jewish Fundamentalism in Israel* (New York: Council on Foreign Relations, 1988).

Makdisi, Saree, *Palestine Inside Out: An Everyday Occupation* (New York: WW Norton, 2008).

Mallison, W. T. and Mallison, S. V., *The Palestine Problem in International Law and World Order* (Essex: Longman, 1986).

Masalha, Nur, *Expulsion of the Palestinians: The Concept of Transfer in Zionist Political Thought 1882–1948* (Washington, DC: Institute of Palestine Studies, 1992).

Masalha, Nur, *A Land Without a People: Israel, Transfer and the Palestinians* (London: Faber and Faber, 1997).

Masalha, Nur, *Imperial Israel and the Palestinians: The Politics of Expansion* (London: Pluto Press, 2000).

Masalha, Nur, *The Politics of Denial: Israel and the Palestinian Refugee Problem* (London: Pluto Press, 2003).

Massad, Joseph A., *The Persistence of the Palestinian Question: Essays on Zionism and the Palestinians* (London: Routledge, 2006).

Mazor, Adam, *Israel Plan 2020* (Haifa: The Technion, 1997).

Morris, Benny, *The Birth of the Palestinian Refugee Problem Revisited, 1947–1949* (Cambridge: Cambridge University Press, 2004).

Morris, Benny, *One State Two States, Resolving the Israel/Palestine Conflict* (New Haven: Yale University Press, 2009).

Nabulsi, Karma, *Palestinians Register: Laying Foundations and Setting Directions* (Oxford: Refugees Studies Center, 2006).

Nimni, Ephraim (ed.), *The Challenge of Post-Zionism: Alternatives to Israeli Fundamentalist Politics* (London: Zed Books, 2003).

Nusseibeh, Sari with David, Anthony, *Once Upon a Country: A Palestinian Life* (New York: Farrar, Straus and Giroux, 2007).

Pappé, Ilan, *The Making of the Arab-Israeli Conflict, 1947–1951* (London and New York: I.B.Tauris, 1992).

Pappé, Ilan, *A History of Modern Palestine; One Country, Two Peoples* (second edition) (Cambridge: Cambridge University Press, 2006).

Pappé, Ilan, *The Ethnic Cleansing of Palestine* (London: One World, 2007).

Peled, Miko, *The General's Son: Journey of an Israeli in Palestine* (Charlottesville, Virginia: First World Books, 2012).

Peres, Shimon, *The New Middle East* (London: Shaftesbury, 1993).

Piterberg, Gabriel, *The Returns of Zionism: Myths, Politics and Scholarship in Israel* (London: Verso, 2008).

Quandt, William B., *Peace Process: American Diplomacy and the Arab-Israeli Conflict Since 1967* (third edition) (Washington, DC and Berkeley: The Brookings Institution and University of California Press, 2005).

Quigley, John, *Palestine and Israel: A Challenge to Justice* (Durham: Durham University Press, 1990).

Quigley, John, *The Case for Palestine* (Durham: Duke University Press, 2005).

Qumsiyeh, Mazin, *Sharing the Land of Canaan: Human Rights and the Israeli–Palestinian Struggle* (London: Pluto Press, 2004).

Qurei, Ahmed, *From Oslo To Jerusalem: The Palestinian Story of the Secret Negotiations* (London: I.B.Tauris, 2006).

Rienhart, Tanya, *The Road Map to Nowhere: Israel/Palestine Since 2003* (London and New York: Verso, 2006).

Roy, Sara, *Failing Peace: Gaza and the Palestinian–Israeli Conflict* (London: Pluto Press, 2007).

Rubenberg, Cheryl A. (ed.), *Encyclopedia of the Israeli Palestinian Conflict* (Boulder & London: Lynne Rienner Publishers, 2010).

Said, Edward W., *The Question of Palestine* (New York: Vintage, 1979).

Sayigh, Yezid, *Armed Struggle and the Search for State: The Palestinian National Movement, 1949–1993* (Oxford: Oxford University Press, 1997).

Schultz, Helena Lindholm, *The Palestinian Diaspora: Formation of Identities and Politics of Homeland* (London: Routledge, 2003).

Segev, Tom, *One Palestine, Complete: Jews and Arabs under the British Mandate* (New York: Henry Holt, 2000).

Shlaim, Avi, 'The rise and fall of the Oslo peace process', in Fawcett, L. (ed.), *International Relations of the Middle East* (Oxford: Oxford University Press, 2005), pp. 241–61.

Sultany, Nimer (ed.), *Citizens without Citizenship* (Haifa: Mada-Arab Center for Applied Social Research, 2003).

Tilley, Virginia Q., *The One-State Solution: A Breakthrough for Peace in the Israeli–Palestinian Deadlock* (Ann Arbor: Michigan University Press, 2005).

Veit, Winfried (ed.), *Learning from South Africa. Lessons to the Israeli–Palestinian Case* (Herzliya, Friedrich Ebert Stiftung, 2003).

II. Journals, Documents, Monographs

Abarjel, Reuven and Lavie, Smadar, 'A year into the Lebanon2 War NGO-ing Mizrahi-Arab paradoxes, and a one state vision for Palestine/Israel', *Left Curve*, 33, 2009, pp. 29–36.

Abunimah, Ali, *President Obama and the Prospects for Israeli–Palestinian Peace: An Analysis*, Palestine Center Information Brief No. 169, Washington, DC, 17 November 2008.

Amnesty International, *Israel and the Occupied Territories: the issue of settlements must be addressed according to international law*, 8 September 2003. Available at www.amnesty.org/en/library/asset/MDE15/085/2003/en/84b15c82-d695-11ddab95-a13b602c0642/mde150852003en.html.

Avnery, Uri, 'A binational state? God forbid', *Journal of Palestine Studies*, 28(4), 1999, pp. 55–60.

Bakan, Abigail B. and Abu-Laban, Yasmeen, 'Israel/Palestine, South Africa and the "one-state solution": the case for an apartheid analysis', *Politikon*, 37(2–3), December 2010, pp. 331–51.

Baraka, Muhammad, 'Between the one-state and two-state solution independence is not a luxury, it is a necessity', *Al Majdal*, Badil Resource Centre for Palestinian Residency and Refugee Rights, Winter 2005, pp. 20–4.

Barghouti, Omar, 'The secular democratic state is the only possible and ideal solution', *Journal of Palestine Studies*, 76, Fall 2008, pp. 1–25. In Arabic.

BDS Movement, *Palestinian Civil Society Calls for Boycott, Divestment and Sanctions against Israel Until it Complies with International Law and Universal Principles of Human Rights*, 9 July 2005. For the full text and list of signatories, go to www.bdsmovement.net/?q=node/52.

Benvenisti, Meron, 'The case for shared sovereignty', *The Nation*, 18 June 2007, pp. 11–14.

Bisharat, George, 'Maximizing rights: the one state solution to the Palestinian–Israeli conflict', *Global Jurist*, 8(2), 2008, pp. 1–36.

Boston Study Group on Middle East Peace. Israel and Palestine: Two States for Two Peoples. If Not Now, When?, March 2010. Available at www.fpa.org/usr_doc/Israel_and_Palestine_Two_States_for_Two_Peoples_2010.pdf.

Brzezinski, Zbigniew; Hagel, Chuck; Hamilton, Lee H.; Hills, Carla; Kassebaum-Baker, Nancy; Pickering, Thomas R.; Scowcroft, Brent; Sorensen, Theodore C.; Volcker, Paul A. and Wolfensohn, James D., *A Last Chance for a Two-State Israel–Palestine Agreement: A Bipartisan Statement on U.S. Middle East Peacemaking* (New York: US/Middle East Project, 2009).

Declaration of Principles on Interim Self-Government Arrangements (Oslo Agreement), 13 September 1993. Available at www.unhcr.org/refworld/docid/3de5e96e4.html.

Doumani, Beshara, 'Palestine versus the Palestinians? The iron laws and ironies of a people denied', *Journal of Palestine Studies*, 36(4), Summer 2007, pp. 49–64.

Ducker, Clare Louise, *Jews, Arabs, and Arab Jews: The Politics of Identity and Reproduction in Israel*, Research Paper, Institute of Social Studies, The Hague, Netherlands, 2005.

Dugard, John, *Report of the Special Rapporteur on the Situation of Human Rights in the Palestinian Territories Occupied Since 1967*, UN Human Rights Council, 29 January 2007.

Dugard, John, 'Apartheid and occupation under international law', Hisham B. Sharabi Memorial Lecture, Washington, DC, *The Palestine Centre*, 30 March 2009.

Dumper, Mick, 'A false dichotomy? The binationalism debate and the future of divided Jerusalem', *International Affairs*, 87(3), May 2011, pp. 671–85.

Ellis, Marc, 'The mural-colored wall: on separation and the future of Jews and Palestinians in Israel/Palestine and the Diaspora', *Chicago Journal of International Law*, 5, Summer 2004, pp. 271–85.

Farsakh, Leila, 'The one-state solution and the Israeli–Palestinian conflict: Palestinian challenges and prospects', *The Middle East Journal*, 65(1), Winter 2011, pp. 55–71.

Ghanem, As'ad, 'The bi-national state solution', *Israel Studies*, 14(2), Summer 2009, pp. 120–33.

Giacaman, George, 'Fateh and the two-states solution', *Journal of Palestine Studies*, Summer 2009, pp. 21–6. In Arabic.

Halper, Jeff, 'The three Jerusalems and their role in the occupation', *Jerusalem Quarterly*, File 15, 2002.

Halper, Jeff, *One State: Preparing for a post Road-Map struggle against apartheid*. UN International Conference on Civil Society in Support of the Palestinian People, New York, 5 September 2003. Available at www.fromoccupiedpalestine.org/node/772.

Halper, Jeff, 'Paralysis over Palestine: questions of strategy', *Journal of Palestine Studies*, 34(2), January 2005, pp. 55–69.

Hermann, Tamar, 'The bi-national idea in Israel/Palestine', *Nations and Nationalism*, 11(3), 2005, pp. 381–401.

Hussein, Mustapha, 'The demise of the two-state solution', *Journal of Palestine Studies*, 76, Fall 2008, pp. 31–42. In Arabic.

International Court of Justice, *Legal Consequences of the Construction of a Wall in the Occupied Palestinian Territory*, Advisory Opinion of 9 July 2004. For text, see www.icj-cij.org/docket/files/131/1671.pdf.

Kadman, Noga, *Erased from Space and Consciousness-Depopulated Palestinian villages in the Israeli–Zionist Discourse*, Master's thesis in Peace and Development studies, Dept. of Peace and Development Research, Göteborg University, Sweden, November 2001.

Kelman, Herbert, 'A one-country / two-state solution to the Israeli–Palestinian conflict', *Middle East Policy Journal*, 18(1), 2011, pp. 27–41.

Khalidi, Walid, 'Thinking the unthinkable: a sovereign Palestinian state', *Foreign Affairs*, 56(4), July 1978, pp. 695–713.

Le More, Anne, *Bad Choices: International Aid Politics and the Israeli–Palestinian Peace Process, 1994–2004*, Doctoral thesis, Oxford University, 2006.

Li, Darryl, 'Occupation law and the one-state reality', *Jadaliyya*, 2 August 2011. www.jadaliyya.com/pages/index/2295/occupation-law-and-the-one-state-reality.

Nabulsi, Karma, 'The peace process and the Palestinians: a road map to Mars', *International Affairs*, 80(2), March 2004, pp. 221–31.

Occupation, Colonialism, Apartheid? A re-assessment of Israel's practices in the occupied Palestinian territories under international law, study coordinated by the Middle East Project of the Democracy and Governance programme, Human Sciences Research Council of South Africa, May 2009, Cape Town, South Africa.

Peled, Yoav, 'Zionist realities: debating Israel–Palestine', *New Left Review*, 38, March–April 2006.

Sayigh, Yezid, 'The Palestinian strategic impasse', *Survival*, 44(4), Winter 2002–3, pp. 7–21.

Stuttgart Declaration issued by the Palestine Solidarity Conference, titled 'Separated in the past – together in the future' of 26–28 November 2010, in Stuttgart, Germany. Available at http://kupola.de/petition/Stuttgart_Declaration_EN_final.pdf.

Sussman, Gary, 'Is the two-state solution dead?', *Current History*, 103(669), January 2004, pp. 37–43.

Sussman, Gary, 'The challenge to the two-state solution', *Middle East Report*, 231, Summer 2004, pp. 8–15.

Talhami, Ghada, 'The one state solution: an alternative vision for Israeli–Palestinian peace', *Journal of Palestine Studies*, XL(2), Winter 2011, pp. 62–76.

Tamari, Salim, 'The dubious lure of binationalism', *Journal of Palestine Studies*, 30(1), October 2000.

The Boston Declaration on the One State, issued by the conference on the one state held in Boston, USA, 28–29 March 2009. For the text and names of signatories, see www.tari.org/images/BostonDeclarationEnglishText.pdf.

The Future Vision of the Palestinian Arabs in Israel, the National Committee for the Heads of the Arab Local Authorities in Israel, Nazareth, Israel, 2006. Available at http://reut-institute.org/data/uploads/PDFVer/ENG.pdf.

The Haifa Declaration, a collective vision that Palestinian citizens in Israel articulate about themselves. Mada al-Carmel – Arab Center for Applied Social Research. 15 May 2007, Haifa, Israel. Available at www.mada-research.org/UserFiles/file/haifaen-glish.pdf.

The One State Declaration, statement issued by participants in the July 2007 Madrid meeting on a one-state solution and the November 2007 London Conference. For the text, check the *Electronic Intifada*, 9 July 2007. Available at at http://electronicinti-fada.net/v2/article9134.shtml.

The Palestine Strategy Study Group, *Regaining the initiative: Palestinian strategic options to end Israeli occupation*, 27 August 2008, Ramallah: The Palestine Strategy Study Group. Available at www.palestinestrategygroup.ps.

Tilley, Virginia, *Has Palestine Passed the Tipping Point? Sovereignty and Settler Colonialism in South Africa and Israel–Palestine*, paper delivered at the Centre for Humanities Research and Department of History of the University of the Western Cape in South Africa on 17 February 2009, and distributed in North America by Academics for Justice on the same date.

UN Office for the Coordination of Humanitarian Affairs, *The humanitarian impact of the West Bank barrier on Palestinian communities: East Jerusalem*, June 2007.

United Nations, Human Rights Council, Twelfth session, Agenda item 7: *Human Rights in Palestine and Other Occupied Arab Territories*, Report of the United Nations Fact-Finding Mission on the Gaza Conflict (Goldstone Report), Geneva, 29 September 2009.

Usher, Graham, 'Bantustanisation or bi-nationalism? An interview with Azmi Bishara', *Race & Class*, 37(2), October 1995, pp. 43–9.

III. Newspapers, Magazines, Websites

Abufarha, Nasser, 'Proposal for an alternative configuration in Palestine–Israel', published online by Alternative Palestinian Agenda. Available at www.ap-agenda.org/initiative.htm.

Abunimah, Ali, 'Israeli Jews and the one-state solution', *Electronic Intifada*, 10 November 2009. Available at http://electronicintifada.net/v2/article10883.shtml.

Abu-Odeh, Lama, 'The case for binationalism: why one state – liberal and constitutionalist – may be the key to peace in the Middle East', *Boston Review*, December 2001/ January 2002, pp. 4–7. Available at http://bostonreview.net/BR26.6/abu-odeh.html.

Amayreh, Khaled, 'Embracing the one-state solution', *Al-Ahram Weekly On-Line*, 889, 20–26 March 2008. Available at http://weekly.ahram.org.eg/2008/889/re61.htm.

Assadi, Mohammed, 'Palestinian state may have to be abandoned – Saeb Erekat', *Reuters*, 4 November 2009. www.reuters.com/article/2009/11/04/idUSL4593611.

Avnery, Uri, 'The binational state: the wolf shall dwell with the lamb', *Counterpunch*, 15 July 2003.

B'tselem, *Land Grab: Israel's Settlement Policy in the West Bank*, 2007. Available at www.btselem.org/English/Publications/Summaries/200205_Land_Grab.asp.

Badil, *Survey of Palestinian Refugees and Internally Displaced Persons 2004–2005*, Bethlehem: Badil, 2006. Available at www.badil.org/Refugees/facts&figures.htm.

Barghouti, Omar, 'Our South Africa moment has arrived', *The Palestine Chronicle*, 18 March 2009. Available at http://palestinechronicle.com/view_article_details. php?id=14921.

Benvenisti, Meron, 'The binationalism vogue', *Ha'aretz*, 30 April 2009. Available at www.haaretz.com/print-edition/opinion/the-binationalism-vogue-1.275085.

Benvenisti, Meron, 'Which kind of binational state?', *Ha'aretz*, 20 November 2003.

Benvenisti, Meron, 'How Israel became a bi-national state', *Ha'aretz*, 23 January 2010. In Hebrew.

Benvenisti, Meron, 'United we stand', *Ha'aretz*, 29 January 2010. Available at www. haaretz.com/hasen/spages/1145896.html.

Bishara, Azmi, 'Separation spells racism', *Al-Ahram*, 697, 1–7 July 2004. Available at Document4http://weekly.ahram.org.eg/print/2004/697/op2.htm.

Bisharat, George, 'Israel and Palestine: a true one-state solution', *Washington Post*, 3 September 2010. Available at www.washingtonpost.com/wp-dyn/content/article/ 2010/09/02/AR2010090204665.html.

Bisharat, George, 'A one-state solution for Israel and Palestine', *Huffington Post*, 10 April 2012.

Bresheeth, Haim, 'Two states, too little, too late', *Al-Ahram Weekly*, 681, 11–17 March 2004.

Burston, Bradley, 'One state – one vote: rethinking an Israeli spring', *Ha'aretz*, 27 March 2012. Available at www.haaretz.com/blogs/a-special-place-in-hell/one-state-one-vote-rethinking-an-israeli-spring-1.421087.

Buttu, Diana, 'A united, democratic nation with equal rights for all', *Boston Globe*, 29 February 2012. Available at http://articles.boston.com/2012-02-29/opinion/ 31106871_1_palestinian-territories-equal-rights-gaza-strip.

Carter, Jimmy, 'Don't give up on Mideast peace', *New York Times*, 12 April 2012.

Cook, Jonathan, 'One-state debate explodes myth about Zionist left', *Mondoweiss*, 20 July 2010. Available at http://tinyurl.com/2uf2s5w.

Cordesman, Anthony, *The Gaza War: A Strategic Analysis*, Final Review Draft, 2 February 2009, Centre for Strategic and International Studies. Available at http://csis. org/files/media/csis/pubs/090202_gaza_war.pdf.

Farsakh, Leila, 'Time for a bi-national state?', *Monde Diplomatique*, March 2007.

Farsakh, Leila, 'Islands of voices', *Lux Magazine*, University of Massachusetts-Boston, April 2009.

For One Democratic Secular State in Israel Palestine, An Online One State Bibliography in English, Internet Activist Organisation. Available at http://oss.internetactivist.org/ index.html.

Gresh, Alain, 'The PLO and the Naksa: the search for a Palestinian state', *Electronic Journal of Middle Eastern Studies*, 8, Spring 2008, pp. 81–93.

Gresh, Alain, 'Problematic partition of Palestine: a history of conflict between opposing ideals', *Monde Diplomatique*, English edition, October 2010. Available at http://mondediplo.com/2010/10/03binationalism.

Gresh, Alain, 'Problematic partition of Palestine: one state, two dreams', *Monde Diplomatique*, English edition, October 2010. Available at http://mondediplo.com/2010/10/02palestine.

Halwani, Raja, 'Palestinian options: the one-state solution', *Palestine Report*, 31 March 2004.

Hanania, Ray, 'One-state solution a pipedream', ynetnews, 19 November 2006. Available at www.ynetnews.com/articles/0,7340,L-3329865,00.html.

Hasan, Rumy, 'Just one state', *Al-Ahram Weekly Online*, 20–26 December 2007.

Hass, Amira, 'Separating Jerusalem from the West Bank', *Ha'aretz*, 26 January 2005.

Hijab, Nadia, 'Olmert's nightmare: the growing belief in a one-state solution', *Counterpunch*, 8 April 2009.

Hirschberg, Peter, 'One-state awakening', *Ha'aretz*, 10 December 2004.

Israel / Palestine and the One State Solution, a conference held 3–4 March 2012, at the Forum at the Harvard Kennedy School. Available at www.onestateconference.org/program.html.

Jewish Virtual Library, a Division of the American-Israeli Cooperative Enterprise, *Attitudes of American Jews*, 2008. Available at www.jewishvirtuallibrary.org/jsource/US-Israel/ajcsurvey.html#Israel.

Joffe-Walt, Benjamin, 'Palestinians increasingly back 1-state', *Jerusalem Post*, 22 March 2010. Available at www.jpost.com/LandedPages/PrintArticle.aspx?id=171559.

Judt, Tony, 'Israel: the alternative', *New York Review of Books*, 50(16), 23 October 2003. Available at www.nybooks.com/articles/archives/2003/oct/23/israel-the-alternative.

Kaplan, Morton A., 'Why plans for a two-state solution in the Middle East have failed', *Professors World Peace Academy*, 27 October 2007. Available at www.pwpa.org/2007/10/why-plans-for-a-two-state-solution-in-the-middle-east-have-failed/#more-3.

Karmi, Ghada, 'The legacy of Resolution 194 – the UN resolution that time forgot', *Counterpunch*, 9 December 2008. Available at www.counterpunch.org/karmi12092008.html.

Karmi, Ghada, 'Palestinians need a one-state solution', *The Guardian*, September 20, 2012. Available at http://gu.com/p/3ahnh/em.

Kershner, Isabel, 'Support for 2-state plan erodes', *New York Times*, 3 September 2008.

Lazare, David, 'The one-state solution', *The Nation*, 3 November 2003. Available at www.thenation.com/article/one-state-solution.

Lerman, Antony, 'Israel–Palestine is already a de facto single state', *Guardian*, 29 April 2009. Available at www.guardian.co.uk/commentisfree/2009/apr/29/israel-palestine-one-state-solution.

Levine, Andrew, 'Israel and the two-state solution: the bully is a coward', *Counterpunch*, 10–12 June 2011. Available online at www.counterpunch.com/levine06102011.html.

Makdisi, Saree, 'Forget the two-state solution: Israelis and Palestinians must share the land. Equally', *Los Angeles Times*, 11 May 2008. Available at www.latimes.com/news/opinion/commentary/la-op-makdisi11-2008may11,0,2553769.story.

Makdisi, Saree, 'End of the two-state solution', *Guardian*, 28 July 2008. Available at www.guardian.co.uk/commentisfree/2008/jul/28/israelandthepalestinians.middleeast.

Makdisi, Saree, 'Netanyahu's two-state goal?', *Huffington Post*, 8 July 2009. Available at www.huffingtonpost.com/saree-makdisi/netanyahus-two-state-goal_b_227785.html.

Makdisi, Saree, 'If Not Two, Then One', *New York Times*, December 5, 2012. Available at http://nyti.ms/11DSziR.

McCarthy, Rory, 'Palestinians lose faith in two-state solution', *Guardian*, 4 September 2011.

Munayyer, Yousef, 'When will time run out for a two-state solution? The Palestinians must draw the line on settlements, or the facade of a two-state discussion will continue ad infinitum', *Guardian*, 27 April 2010. Available at www.guardian.co.uk/commentisfree/2010/apr/27/israel-palestinian-territories.

Nafaa, Hassan, 'No room for two states: the case for a single state solution for Palestine is irrefutable', *Al-Ahram Weekly*, 883, February 2008, pp. 7–13. Available at http://weekly.ahram.org.eg/2008/883/op23.htm.

Nusseibeh, Sari, 'The one-state solution', *Newsweek*, 20 September 2008. Available at www.newsweek.com/id/160030.

Olmert, Ehud, 'Peace now, or never', *New York Times*, 21 September 2011. Available at www.nytimes.com/2011/09/22/opinion/Olmert-peace-now-or-never.html?_r=1&hp.

One Democratic Secular State for all its citizens in Israel and Palestine. Available at http://onedemocracy.co.uk.

Pappé, Ilan, 'The birth, demise, and future of one Palestine complete', *Electronic Journal of Middle Eastern Studies*, 8, Spring 2008, pp. 151–64.

Pappé, Ilan, 'At the UN, the funeral of the two-state solution', *Electronic Intifada*, 12 September 2011. Available at http://electronicintifada.net/content/un-funeral-two-state-solution/10370.

Peres, Shimon, 'Israelis, Palestinians need two states', *Washington Post*, 10 February 2009. Available at www.washingtonpost.com/wp-dyn/content/article/2009/02/09/AR2009020902098.html.

Poort, David, 'The Palestine papers. The threat of a one-state solution: PA negotiators are increasingly proposing an idea that's met with derision from Israelis, sharp criticism from the US', Aljazeera.net. Available at http://english.aljazeera.net/palestinepapers/2011/01/201112612953672648.html.

Qurei, Ahmed, 'Palestinians might demand citizenship', *Jerusalem Post*, 11 August 2008.

Rubinstein, Danny, 'One state/two states: rethinking Israel and Palestine', *Dissent*, Summer 2010.

Said, Edward, 'The one-state solution', *New York Times*, 10 January 1999.

Sheizaf, Noam, 'The endgame', *Ha'aretz Magazine*, 15 July 2010.

Sheleg, Yair, 'The settlers and a binational state', *Ha'aretz*, 31 August 2003.

Shemoelof, Mati, 'A new spirit – a letter from the [Jewish] descendants of the countries of Islam', jvoices.com, 8 June 2009. Available at http://jvoices.com/author/mati.

Shlaim, Avi, 'How Israel brought Gaza to the brink of humanitarian catastrophe', *Guardian*, 7 January 2009.

Tarazi, Michael, 'Two peoples, one state', *New York Times*, 4 October 2004.

Tilley, Virginia, 'The one-state solution', *London Review of Books*, 25(21), 6 November 2003, pp. 13–16.

Tucker, Roger, 'The Israel/Palestine one-state solution sounds like a good idea, but...', *Redress Information & Analysis*, 18 June 2010. Available at www.redress.cc/palestine/rtucker20100618.

Wright, Robert, 'A one-to-two-state solution', *New York Times*, 28 September 2010. Available at http://opinionator.blogs.nytimes.com/author/robert-wright.

Yaar, Ephraim and Hermann, Tamar, 'Peace index: demographic fears favor unilateral separation', *Ha'aretz*, 5 January 2004.

Zrahiya, Zvi and Ha'aretz Service, 'Israel official: accepting Palestinians into Israel better than two states', *Ha'aretz*, 29 April 2010. Available at www.haaretz.com/news/national/israel-official-accepting-palestinians-into-israel-better-than-two-states-1.287421.

Index